G000096282

MANHATTAN MANNERS

MANHATTAN MANNERS

ARCHITECTURE AND STYLE 1850-1900

M. CHRISTINE BOYER

RIZZOLI
NEW YORK

To my parents

First published in the United States of America in 1985 by
RIZZOLI INTERNATIONAL PUBLICATIONS, INC.
597 Fifth Avenue, New York, NY 10017

Copyright © 1985 M. Christine Boyer

All rights reserved.
No part of this publication may be published in
any manner whatsoever without permission in writing
by Rizzoli International Publications, Inc.

Designed by Gilda Hannah
Set in type by Talbot Typographics Inc.
Printed and bound in the U.S.A.

Library of Congress Cataloging-in-Publication Data

Boyer, M. Christine.
    Manhattan manners.
    Bibliography: p.
    Includes index.
    1. Architecture—New York (N.Y.) 2. Architecture,
Modern—19th century—New York (N.Y.) 3. New York (N.Y.)
—Buildings, structures, etc. 4. Manhattan (New York,
N.Y.)—Buildings, structures, etc. I. Title.
NA735.N5B69 1985   720′.9747′1   85–42966
ISBN 0-8478-0650-2

CONTENTS

ACKNOWLEDGMENTS

There are many people to thank for their help in the preparation of this book, a project that evolved slowly over time. Three seminal studies, which I undertook with students in the School of Architecture and Planning at Columbia University, form the background for this later work. The first, a research monograph entitled "The Development and Boundaries of Luxury Neighborhoods in New York: 1625–1890," was coauthored by Jessica Scheer in 1980. This study led to the subsequent focus on residential districts in Manhattan during the late nineteenth century. The second study was a studio report called "Ladies Mile: The History of the Retail Shopping District of Manhattan in the Nineteenth Century," and was produced in the spring of 1981. The students involved with this project were: Marshall Brown, Jamie Gibbs, Elsa Gilbertson, Mary Sue Griesman, Diane Jung, Darcy Keen, Leah Ness, Nancy O'Neill, Michael Rebic, Gary Sauchau, Sophia Schachter, and Terry Tatum. This project report analyzed the changes in real estate and architectural development, the transformations in lot ownership, and the shifts in land uses and functions along Ladies Mile from 1859 to 1900. Elsa Gilbertson and Sophia Schachter did further research work in 1982, focusing specifically on the real estate development and commercial uses of Union Square.

I also wish to thank Kenneth Frampton for his enthusiastic response to the early manuscript. His critical comments and references have helped to sharpen the work in innumerable ways. Stephanie Salomon's skillful hand edited the final version. The maps and building plans were drawn by Constantine J. Karalis. In researching photographs, I was assisted by Wendy Shadwell and Helena Zinkham at The New-York Historical Society and Jennifer Bright at the Museum of the City of New York. Shirley Driks faithfully remained responsible for both typing and organizing the typing of various manuscript editions.

CONTROLLING MANHATTAN'S DESIGN

Unless the stranger who visits New York for the first time be an architectural expert, no matter how many large cities he may have visited elsewhere, he will scarcely escape arriving at the conclusion that never before has he seen so many magnificent warehouses, shops, hotels, and dwelling houses, or more substantial churches, with a greater variety of steeples and ritualistic projections; large plateglass windows, or broader streets, and smoother pavements; and long after he has been forced to relinquish the idea that the pavements of the ways generally are all smooth, he will remain under the impression that architecturally New York surpasses any city of modern construction. Under this delusion many strangers on their way through the capital may leave the city, may carry home a want of knowledge, of what they have seen, and will bear in their minds a doubtful remembrance regarding Stewart's great shops, the Women's Hotel, and other pseudo-marble palaces, and in after-years would be shocked to hear that the gorgeous recollections which have abided with him were, after all, inspired by shams and imitations of bad copies.—"Imitated Architecture in New York," *The Builder* 36 (May 18, 1878): 505

T ravelers in the second half of the nineteenth century visited New York not in search of architectural monuments, magnificent cathedrals, or stately mansions but to marvel at the rich, magnetic city of commerce. New York City, or its nineteenth-century equivalent—Manhattan—in the eyes of the world was the quintessential bourgeois society. As the wealth of New Yorkers increased, so did their appetites for material goods, which they extravagantly displayed in public places and indiscriminately collected in private spaces. The spectacle of commercial New York was most apparent to the visitor who strolled north along Broadway (fig. 1), where for five or six miles, shop windows were filled with luxury items from around the world, set off in gigantic facades of stone and iron. This was a littered commercial landscape: signs and posters plastered the faces of buildings, top-heavy telegraph poles punctuated the sky, and a horrific noise arose as carriages rolled across the uneven pavement (fig. 2).

Yet the architectural critic visiting commercial New York judged this theater of riches harshly, for the age offered no architecture of its own but pilfered the storehouses of history, irreverently culling every past architectural treasure for its

Fig. 1. Broadway, looking north from the foot of City Hall, 1860. An "instantaneous stereopticon view." (Courtesy of the New-York Historical Society, New York City)

own spectacular effect. But how could this babel of architectural styles express more than the materialism of the age? And how could inaccurate copies of historical forms properly educate and uplift their audiences? According to the then current critical wisdom, architecture not only expressed the spirit of the age to which it belonged but at the same time determined the values and morals of contemporary society. Thus urban architecture, these critics complained, should have a social mission, for around the cultivated elite flowed a sea of uneducated laborers. The laboring classes were denied access to painting and works of art, but a magnificent building in their midst could not be hidden; it was a collective possession in which everyone could share. Consequently, critics felt that the great public buildings of a city should provide neither a parade of eccentric forms nor be cast in molds, for the dead uniformity of machine production could neither teach nor elevate.[1]

In the United States the brutal force of money seemed to outweigh and to damage this social, moral mission of art. Without a cultivated aristocracy, with a fledgling Academy of Art, there were few established cultural values against which architectural innovators and creative designers could measure their steps. The mechanization of production techniques in fashion design, furniture construction, interior decoration, and architecture made these forms the nineteenth century's consumable arts. Energetic New Yorkers were restless. Never settling for long on one style, they engaged in a perpetual search for new household items, new palatial homes, and corresponding manners and dress. They built and tore down whole sections of the city in ever-narrowing cycles without any idea of the direction these forces were taking. Yet underneath this pageant of fashionable life, the disquietudes of a modern age were beginning to take shape.

As New York developed into a modern commercial and industrial city, real estate investment began to separate industrial areas from residential quarters, shopping districts from business centers. In consequence, a breach developed between the public realm and the private sphere: the space where money was made and goods were displayed became divorced from residential neighborhoods which retreated northward as commerce advanced. In *Mechanization Takes Command,* Sigfried Giedion described the decisive steps the nineteenth century took toward the disintegration of public and private space.[2] Architecture was treated like furniture; both were designed as self-sufficient entities divorced from their immediate surroundings. Space could not hold its own against the gigantic proportions of monumental buildings or overstuffed upholstered furniture. The same disintegration of space occurred along Manhattan's streets: mono-

Fig. 2. Intersection of Broadway, Fifth Avenue and Twenty-third Street, looking south, ca. 1888. (Courtesy of the New-York Historical Society, New York City)

Fig. 3. New York panorama from the Latting Observatory, ca. 1855. The Croton Reservoir appears in the immediate foreground along Forty-second Street. The Crystal Palace is to the right of the reservoir. Toward the southern horizon, only church spires interrupt the skyline. (Courtesy of the New-York Historical Society, New York City)

lithic structures punctuated the orthogonal grid pattern at random points along its avenues, while scraps of architecture were glued together into tight compositions across its side streets. In a similar spirit, ever more exotic furniture dominated the narrow and darkened interiors of New York town houses, while layers of carpentry, drapery, and coverings protected them from unexpected intrusions. Yet these rents and tears in the urban fabric, these silenced and suffocating residential interiors, had not always existed.

In the early decades of the nineteenth century, Manhattan presented the stroller with an image of enclosed space and explicit boundaries. Individual buildings tended to relate to one another: the street to the building walls, solids to voids, the public to the private realm. The gridiron pattern of streets offered a regulating harmony, and buildings, no matter how eclectic their style, tended to be uniform in height. A few outstanding monuments stood out against the background: church spires, city halls, and commemorative statues (fig. 3). In the later decades business and industry placed new economic demands on urban space. To move through modern New York, as Walter Benjamin wrote of nineteenth-century Paris, involved one in a series of shocks and collisions. The sense of spatial enclosure was voided, freestanding, mammoth structures such as department stores and office buildings began to float about in space, and the interdependent relationship of public structures and residential districts was broken.

Development of urban America meant simultaneously the creation of vast new building programs and their contingent types. Until the nineteenth century, with the exception of isolated monuments, no commercial architecture—and similarly, no theaters, railroad stations, capitols, post offices, or museums—had existed. So rapid had been the change in modern building forms, so complex their programs, so technical and mathematical their structural requirements that experimentation, adaptation, and diversity were the ruling concerns. No wonder eclecticism reigned, for there was no accepted manner of building that had been tested by engineers and architects and which could be applied to the railroad station as well as to the office building.

Until the end of the nineteenth century, neither the public nor the private space of Manhattan was the creation of architects or city planners. New York's orthogonal grid, an inheritance from the Commissioners' Plan of 1811, presented a pattern of undifferentiated streets open in every direction and was avidly exploited by real estate developers and building speculators. The undeveloped land above Thirty-fourth Street became a new source of revenue after the Civil War, a market where land prices carefully created different zones of the city. But land prices alone would not be sufficient to produce fashionable districts. Social conventions—the finely tuned codes of architectural styles and fashionable appearances—also dictated their boundaries. The great public space for these luxury districts where the refined consumer could promenade was the longitudinal boulevard down Fifth Avenue to Madison Square and beyond on Broadway as far as one could stroll. In this area were located the new places of mass entertainment: the department stores, the theaters and exhibition halls, the artists' and photographers' studios, and the clubs and restaurants.

As business expanded and fashion commanded, however, whole sections of the traditional city were leveled and renewed to make way for the reign of commerce. Residential districts retreated uptown, advancing with trepidation into untamed northern Manhattan. If one wandered too far, moving laterally across the grid from the spine of Fifth Avenue, one rapidly descended the social scale. To venture too far north beyond the building line brought social isolation and indifference. Within the fashionable quarter, the domestic interior became a shrine, a compensatory bourgeois realm for the needs and desires that a materialistic society seemed to eradicate. But above all, it sheltered the bourgeois family from the complex and ambivalent feelings that urban life produced. While economic and social advances were both rapid and dramatic throughout the nineteenth century, their effects were neither widespread nor evenly distributed. The well-to-do and the emergent middle class were surrounded by a sea of poverty and a cohort of new arrivals. Urban life, heroically celebrated in public spaces, was itself a new adventure. The bourgeoisie faced an unknown and uncertain future, its status unclear and its collective desires increasingly fragmented. The lushly layered and decorated domestic interiors became a soothing protection against the insecurities and anxieties of urban existence.

New York City, for some critics of the late nineteenth century, was the epitome of an architecturally confused, artistically deficient, and socially fragmented agglomeration. Its unhealthy pattern of group living destroyed the accepted American standards of the single-family home, whether by its rows of ostentatious town houses or in the frightening and impersonal appearance of its tenement house districts. Everything had to be big and grand in this city, and every structure was dedicated to the making of money. Boxlike commercial buildings covered whole city blocks and were similar in sheer size and monotony to the iron-plated warehouses on which rows of identical ornamentation were repeated over eight or ten stories. Tall office structures would before long "convert the streets into narrow gorges, as inaccessible to the light and air as they must be concentrative of the increasing noise and dirt of incessant money-spending."[3]

A seemingly universal fear of the void guaranteed that evey space in Manhattan would be broken into tightly composed fragments and every blank wall covered with ornamentation. Beyond the imposition of the grid pattern, no one had thought to regulate the spatial development of the city. Real estate speculation constantly created new building types, new neighborhoods, new land values that played to bourgeois desires for new comforts, new materials, and new fashion. New York was the commercial capital of America, where people came to exchange goods, to produce, to be entertained, to promenade. Everything and everyone seemed to be in perpetual motion, buffeted by crowded streets, thwarted by obstacles in passage, delayed by congested traffic. In nineteenth-century Manhattan no figure comparable to Haussmann in Paris arose to organize this multitude of people, goods, and vehicles into a functional whole. No one pierced through the dense urban fabric with diagonal boulevards so that commerce could flow unobstructed from end to end. Nor did any designer suggest that the anonymous structures which jostled against imposing buildings be swept away to reveal these monuments in their isolated glory. No one proposed a hierarchical system of open spaces to cleanse the city and to link peripheral parks with tree-lined boulevards and small formal squares. Nor were idiosyncratic architectural forms attacked by any designer prescribing a uniform system of regulated and aligned building facades. Individual architects and builders struggled against the rigid pattern of orthogonal streets and blocks, but no one suggested that a more unified order be imposed on its architectural form.

In the last decade of the nineteenth-century, at least for a few East Coast architects, a new hope seemed to be in the air. A.D.F. Hamlin proclaimed that a distinctly American architectural form was converging toward a unity of style: the best commercial buildings were copies of either Romanesque or early Renais-

Fig. 4. Proposed New York Civic Center to surround City Hall Park. This Beaux-Arts plan was presented to the Municipal Art Society by the Committee on Civic Centers in 1902 but was never built. (Courtesy of Avery Library, Columbia University, New York City)

sance forms.[4] No doubt, this was caused partly by the training and influence of the Ecole des Beaux-Arts on American architects, beginning with the careers of Richard Morris Hunt and Henry Hobson Richardson. The renaissance in aesthetic awareness engendered by the 1876 Philadelphia Centennial Exposition, together with the establishment of architecture as a discipline in 1868 with the founding of the Department of Architecture at the Massachusetts Institute of Technology, collectively began to educate the profession in self-restraint and to stress the formal clarity, systemic order, and ideal unity of classical design. But this *rappel à l'ordre* would prove to be a utopian compensation for the tasteless creations of egotistical architects and individualistic builders even as it led to a devaluation of architectural styles that responded to the fads and fashions of commercialization.

What was offensive about New York architecture, a critic lamented in 1878, was not the lack of art, but "the look as if art . . . had been considered overmuch; the decorator appears invariably to have been called in too early to make unsightly a construction sufficiently simple to be able to rely on its own beauty. . . ."[5] Clearly, the imposition of classical architecture at the end of the century was an authoritarian attempt by an elite body of architects to direct the experimental and resourceful forces of American architecture into educated and rational channels. Classical design as an art of abstinence speaks nostalgically of the dignity of pure forms and the fusion of art with life. It reifies the distant past, finding heroic images that establish a new aesthetic orthodoxy. With the development of the entertainment arts in the nineteenth century, however, architecture, the decorative arts, and fashion design had become the sensuously dressed-up arts of mass consumption. They had taught Americans how to become spectators of scenographic spaces and collectors of the ephemerally new. Formalistic neoclassical architecture exploited the popular appeal of scenographic spaces, and eclecticism still managed to triumph (fig. 4). But Beaux-Arts neoclassicism did place a rein on fashionable tastes: it banished the collection of bric-a-brac and memorabilia from the domestic interior and moralistically railed against the decomposition of collective space. This neoclassical revival presented a struggle against the marginalization of architects and artists within a consumer culture,[6] but it was at the same time a battle over symbols and imagery involving the right to represent modern Manhattan.

Who then would control the spatial form of late-nineteenth-century New York: the real estate investor or the cultivated architect? Should the representational principles reflect the needs for ceremonial embellishment or utilitarian functionalism? Would the reality of the capitalist market or the compositional abstractions of a modern mentality determine the new urban form? These are concerns that the discourse of architecture and building in the late nineteenth century reveal.[7]

In the dawn of the twentieth century it was apparent that it would be the formalist architect and the new city planner who would set the direction of growth for the metropolitan whole. But how did this come about? Before new technologies and materials significantly affected the art of building and disciplined architectural training, before ideal plans were formulated for urban improvements, before the regulatory concept of zoning was imposed on the urban order, how did the builder and architect organize their aesthetic control over urban development?

CHAPTER ONE
THE INHERITANCE OF THE GRID

The great advance northward in the building of New York, since 1807 has been strictly according to the street plan which a commission of its citizens then laid down for it. The objections at first hotly urged against this plan (chiefly by property holders whose lands it would divide inconveniently, whose lawns and gardens it would destroy and whose houses it would leave in awkward positions), have long since been generally forgotten, and so far as streets have been opened and houses built upon them, the system has apparently met all popular requirements. Habits and customs accommodated to it have become fixed upon the people of the city.—Frederick Law Olmsted and James R. Cross, ''Preliminary Report of the Landscape Architect and the Civil and Topological Engineer, upon the Laying Out of the Twenty-third and Twenty-fourth Wards,'' 1876, in Albert Fein, ed., *Landscape into Cityscape* (New York: Van Nostrand Reinhold Company, 1967): 350

Manhattan's rectangular grid of streets was imposed in 1811 by city commissioners on the empty terrain that lay north of Fourteenth Street and extended as far as 155th Street. Since that time, it has remained the fundamental visual impression we have of the city and the formative structure that every architect and builder must acknowledge. Prior to real estate development, the grid rigidly mapped the wilds of Manhattan onto a rational Cartesian plane. Extending logically in all directions, arbitrarily terminating at the island's shores, this grid denied the priorities of natural topography as its vertical and horizontal lines were raised above land depressions and leveled beneath the crests of hills. This modular repetitive structure, subdivided into equivalent patterns of blocks and lots, became the infrastructure for real estate speculation. It was also the public sphere of Manhattan, to be embellished with ceremonial squares, parks, and architecture. Yet no matter how many alternative plans were proposed, the grid remained impervious to picturesque improvement and defiant against architectural correction.

We sometimes hear it said that the American people are different from Europeans; that they are a home-loving race; whereas the Europeans, especially
the French, have no homes, have no word for "home" in their language,
and are forever gadding about: whereas the Americans do not care for
pleasures that are only to be had in public; hence, for them no need of
squares, "piazzas," "places," public gardens, parks, etc.—"Central Park,"
Scribner's Monthly 6 (1873):525

In the early decades of its history, Manhattan seemed naturally to bestow on
its populace those public spaces so strikingly absent in the later metropolis. Even
as late as 1825, the city was so sparsely settled and gardens so numerous that
parks or squares for pleasant walks and promenades could be found in almost
every district of lower Manhattan, and delightful drives through open countryside abounded in its upper reaches. But the growth of Manhattan by the 1850s
erased all traces of a semirural character. After this period a Manhattan street or
avenue was seldom interrupted by an ornamental square, park, or garden, affecting the picturesqueness of the entire city. But how did this lack of embellishment
become so determinant?

The first plan for developing the land north of Fourteenth Street was
proposed to the city council by Joseph Mangin in 1800. As the newly appointed
city surveyor and architect for City Hall, Mangin based his plans on the previous
work of Casimir Goerck. His improvement scheme girdled the entire island with
a series of blocks and open quays. Since the interior of the island was so varied in
topography, he proposed street grids with different orientations: where commerce developed, there should be small blocks with streets close together, and
where residential districts occurred, the blocks should be more open and spacious. At all the awkward intersections of streets Mangin planned parks, so that
the entire city would be laid out from the point of view of enhancing health, recreation, and architecture.[1]

Nothing became of Mangin's plan, and in 1807 the state legislature
appointed three commissioners, Gouverneur Morris, Simeon De Witt, and John
Rutherford, to lay out the streets, avenues, and public squares in the upper part
of Manhattan. Because the commissioners expected land traffic to be focused on
the waterfront, two and one half times as many east-west streets were planned as
north-south arteries, and of these avenues, which were 100 feet wide and
separated by blocks of uneven widths, only one was planned as an unbroken
line. In this rectangular grid one diagonal street was allowed to remain—present-
day Broadway. Most of the surveying work for this plan was done by John
Randel, Jr., between 1811 and 1820.[2] The task of acquiring land, compensating
property owners, and opening streets was a very slow process. Beginning in
1811, about 100 special cases were dealt with per year, and nearly $4 million was
granted in annual compensation. Although streets were usually opened from
river to river, there was no fixed schedule, and grading and improving could lag
far beind. Thus the plan reached as far north as Thirty-fifth Street in 1839, and
Ninety-fourth Street in 1874. Avenues were usually opened a section at a time; for
example, Fifth Avenue stretched as far north as Thirteenth Street in 1819, to
Twenty-fourth Street in 1830, to Ninetieth Street in 1838, and arrived in Harlem in
1868.[3]

Although the commissioners did consider stars, ovals, residential squares,
and circles, they rejected these forms and decided on the universally neutral rec-

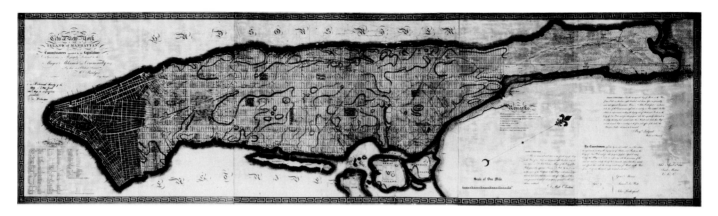

Fig. 5. Commissioners' Map of 1811, showing planned public parks. (Courtesy of the New-York Historical Society, New York City)

tangular grid since a "city is to be composed principally for the habitations of men, and that straight-sided and right-angled houses are the most cheap to build, and the most convenient to live in."[4]

> If the city of New York were destined to stand on the side of a small Stream such as the Seine or the Thames a great number of ample Places might be needful. But those large arms of the Sea which embrace Manhattan Island render its situation in Regard of Health and Pleasure as well as to the Convenience of Commerce peculiarly felicitous. When therefore from the same causes the price of Land is so uncommonly great it seemed proper to admit the principles of Economy to greater influence than might under circumstances of a different kind have consisted with the dictates of Prudence and the sense of Duty.[5]

Although this city plan would from then on be dedicated to the cause of commerce and real estate development, it did seem proper at first to set aside at least 450 acres for parks (fig. 5). A space large enough for a city reservoir and possibly an observatory was reserved on an elevated bluff. A space known as the Parade, lying below Twenty-third Street and extending west from Third Avenue to Sixth Avenue, was allocated for military drills. Another large open space, the Market Place, was set aside between Seventh and Tenth streets, running from First Avenue to the East River. The awkward leftover trapezoid formed by the junction of the Bowery and present-day Broadway was designated as Union Place because ". . . the Union of so many large Roads demands space for the Security and convenience and the morsels into which it would be cut by continuing across it the several Streets and Avenues would be of little use or value."[6] Union Place would be renamed Union Square in 1832. In addition, the 1807 Commissioners' Plan scattered five other squares—Manhattan Square, Harlem Square, Harlem Marsh, Bloomingdale Square, and Hamilton Square—across the fields of Manhattan. Few of these survived the onslaught of commerce as the nineteenth century progressed. In 1832 the Common Council, the governing body of the city, nevertheless felt apologetic and uneasy about taking private property for public purposes, stressing "the advantages that would necessarily accrue to them from having such squares in various parts of the city for purposes of military and civic parades and festivities and what is perhaps most important to serve as ventilators to a densely populated city."[7] In the mid-1840s, however, the city began to sell off much of the public land in the northern part of the island, claiming that all open spaces should be placed in private hands and on the tax rolls.

By 1840 the *New York Mirror* complained that the Common Council had "destroyed nearly all the green shaded nooks which the commissioners who laid out the city designed as public squares."[8] Indeed, the city never acquired the land called the Parade, and, beginning in 1812, continuously passed legislation to reduce its planned size. Eventually, in 1829 a new act abolished the idea of this public square, although near its site in 1837 the city did acquire land for present-day Madison Square. The Market Place fared no better. By 1824 this space was no longer reserved for public use, and streets and avenues were continued through it. Union Place was treated more kindly: by 1830 it had been appropriated for public purpose and opened as a park the following year. The Common Council "on the petition of owners of property in the vicinity, resolved to have Union Place enlarged to its present space . . . an irregular parallelogram, something after the plan of the Rue de la Paix and the Place Vendôme in Paris . . ."[9]

Manhattan Square, located between Seventy-seventh and Eighty-first streets, from Central Park West to Columbus Avenue, was officially acquired by the city between 1832 and 1850. Annexed to Central Park in 1864, it was selected as the site for the American Museum of Natural History in 1871 (see fig. 240). The museum's founder, Albert S. Bickmore, remembered that:

> Within the boundaries of our area the prospect was most desolate and forbidding. There was a high hill at the northeast corner . . . and in the northwest corner another hill of solid rock arose much higher than the elevated railroad station . . . in the southern and central part of the square, just where the first section of our building was to be erected, was a third hill, whose crest rose as high as the ceiling of our present Hall of Birds. As I sat on top of this rock, the surrounding view was dreary and my only companions were scores of goats.[10]

Observatory Place, located between Eighty-ninth and Ninety-fourth streets and running from Park Avenue to Fifth Avenue, a site of twenty-six acres, never was acquired by the city, and in 1865 the Common Council ordered that streets be laid down across its width and that its plan be henceforth abolished. No action was ever taken by the city to acquire Bloomingdale Square, which was supposed to have been situated between Eighth and Ninth avenues, extending from Fifty-third to Fifty-seventh street, and in 1857 streets were also extended across this site. Hamilton Square, lying between Third and Fifth avenues and running from Sixty-sixth to Sixty-eighth Street, was an exception. The city was forced to reconvey its lots, originally divided up for private development in 1807, and return the purchase money to the original owners. Hamilton Square stood until 1868, when the city, having offered some of the square's eastern parts to such institutions as Hahnemann Hospital, the New York Foundling Hospital, and Mount Sinai Hospital, usurped the rest of the public grounds[11] (fig. 6).

RESIDENTIAL SQUARES AND PLEASURE PARKS

Where the city was slow to provide public open spaces, some developers planned residential squares following the example of the great estates of

Fig. 6. Detail from the Robinson Insurance Map of 1885, showing hospitals located near the former Hamilton Square, Sixty-sixth to Sixty-eighth Street, Fifth to Third Avenue. (Courtesy of the New York Public Library, New York City)

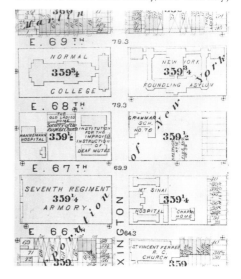

Fig. 7. Saint John's Chapel, east side of Saint John's Park (Hudson Square). The chapel, built to the designs of John and Isaac McComb in 1807, became the fulcrum of a fashionable nineteenth-century residential area that existed from 1807 to 1867 and was known as the court end of town. It was demolished in 1919. (Courtesy of the New-York Historical Society, New York City)

Fig. 8. Hudson River Railroad Terminal, designed by John B. Snook. Erected on the site of Saint John's Park in 1867, the terminal was decorated with Ernst Plassman's metal bas-relief statue of Commodore Vanderbilt flanked by allegorical depictions of marine and railroad scenes. It was demolished in 1936. (Courtesy of the New-York Historical Society, New York City)

London's West End; other entrepreneurs offered pleasure gardens—outdoor pastoral retreats operated as businesses and opened to the public at a fee for purposes of promenading and acquiring refreshment and entertainment. By the mid-nineteenth century neither of these approaches was sufficient to relieve the monotony of the rectangular grid or to provide adequate space for healthful and recreational purposes, and in any case most of them had given way to the crush of development.

The earliest residential square, Saint John's Park, began to take form in 1802 when the vestry of Trinity Church decided to build Saint John's Chapel on its farmlands, which extended as far north as Christopher Street (fig. 7). The chapel, located on the east side of Saint John's Park, also called Hudson Square—a site defined by present-day Hudson, Varick, Laight, and Beach streets—was completed in 1807 from plans by John and Isaac McComb. It soon attracted fashionable residents, among them William E. Burton, John Ericsson, Silas Holmes, and James K. Paulding, who filled in the boggy land and developed the square with elegant town houses. An ornamental park planted with a specimen of almost every American tree was restricted to the private use and maintenance of residents fronting the park. In spite of its elegant and unique setting, the park began to feel the pressure of commercial development as the city grew northward: between 1827 and 1867 land in the immediately surrounding blocks was purchased by several New York banks. Reflecting this commercial pressure, as early as 1856 the vestry sold both the park frontage and the park itself to the U.S. government. Residents fled, although no redevelopment action took place until 1867 when the church resold the park to the Hudson River Railroad Company. On this site Cornelius Vanderbilt erected a freight depot designed by John B. Snook (fig. 8). In desolate isolation, the chapel stood until 1919 and the depot until 1936 when the entrance ramps to the Holland Tunnel completely erased the memory of Saint John's Park.[12]

Two other residential squares—Tompkins Square and Stuyvesant Square—fared little better. Following the example of Saint John's Park, Tompkins Square was planned in 1815 and developed a few years later with elegant town houses. Located between Avenues A and B, and East Seventh and East Tenth streets, the square was far from the spine of luxury development along Broadway and only two blocks away from tanneries, warehouses, and shanties along the East River. By 1850 the stench from the tanneries and the lack of proximity to other wealthy areas brought about the demise of this square as a desirable address. A few blocks to the north Peter Stuyvesant designed a private park, Stuyvesant Square, in 1836, along Second Avenue between East Fifteenth and East Seventeenth streets (fig. 9). He too constructed luxury housing—along Second Avenue from East Seventh to East Seventeenth Street—but even this more extensive development was unable to stabilize the area as an exclusive enclave. By the 1840s the more fashionable residences had located along Fifth Avenue above Washington Square and in the vicinity of Union and Madison squares, leaving Stuyvesant Square in the backwater.

"Come what will, our open squares will remain forever imperishable," declared Samuel Ruggles in 1831 when he planned the only successful private residential square, Gramercy Park, located between Third and Fourth avenues, from Nineteenth to Twenty-first Street. Ruggles set aside forty-two lots for a residential square and sixty-two surrounding lots for residential development. Although he did not develop the land himself, he did determine its residential quality through deeds and covenants. The park was deeded to the sixty-two future lot owners,

Fig. 9. Detail from the Jalt and Hoy Map of 1879, showing Stuyvesant Square. (Courtesy of the New York Public Library, New York City)

who were required to surround it with an iron fence with stone coping and ornamental gates and to lay out the square grounds with walks, plants, and shrubbery. With additional covenants he ensured that no livery stable, slaughterhouse, smoke shop, forge or furnace, brewery, public museum, circus, or any kind of polluting nuisance would ever violate the residential sanctity of Gramercy Park. Houses were required to be set back from the street by forty feet, to be constructed in brick or stone, and to be at least three stories high. By the mid-1850s, most of the sixty-two lots had been developed with well-designed residences, although some of the houses were used for educational and charitable purposes, such as Miss Henrietta B. Haines' School for Girls (10 Gramercy Park South) or the Evangeline Residence for Young Women (18 Gramercy Park South), and some of the vacant lots had been developed for houses of worship, such as the Friends Meeting House and the Calvary Church. But none of these buildings impinged on the residential quality of the square. In the 1880s three lots were assembled for a large apartment building, but even this early cooperative apartment maintained the quality of the residential district.[13]

Fig. 10. Locations of Manhattan's nineteenth-century pleasure gardens. (Redrawn from Garrett, "A History of Pleasure Gardens in New York City: 1700–1865")

The few residential squares scattered about Manhattan, however, hardly provided the city with enough social and pastoral retreats. Thus some entrepreneurial spirits found, especially in the first quarter of the nineteenth century, that pleasure gardens could be a lucrative alternative to public and private parks (fig. 10). The most famous of all New York pleasure gardens was Niblo's, which opened in 1822 at the northeast corner of Broadway and Prince Street. Located on the outskirts of town, Niblo's attracted famous neighbors even in its early days: James Fenimore Cooper leased the next-door building; John Jacob Astor had a house across from the garden; and even in the rear of the garden the mansions of the Episcopal bishop Hobart, the Catholic bishop Dubois, and former U.S. president James Monroe could be found.[14] As an outdoor pastoral retreat, Niblo's disappeared in 1859 when it was incorporated into Van Rensselaer's Metropolitan Hotel.

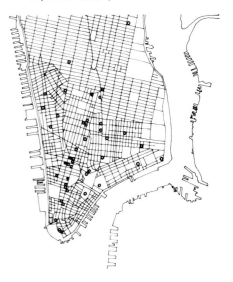

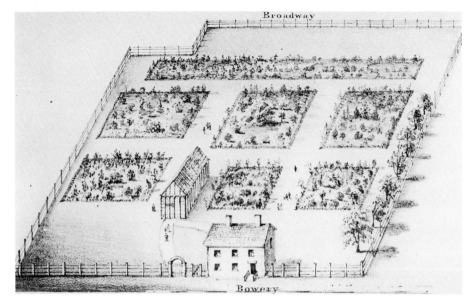

Fig. 11. Vauxhall Garden, 1803 lithograph. This pleasure garden opened in 1806 on land owned by John Jacob Astor, between the Bowery and Broadway, Fourth to Eighth Street. In 1826 Astor created Lafayette Place, which bisected the garden. Vauxhall Garden was demolished in 1855. (Courtesy of the New-York Historical Society, New York City)

Fig. 12. La Grange Terrace, or Colonnade Row, ca. 1862–72. Built to designs attributed to Seth Greer, this row of houses was erected on the west side of Lafayette Street in 1833. The buildings are extant. (Courtesy of the New-York Historical Society, New York City)

Another famous pleasure retreat was Vauxhall Garden, on the Bowery, at Astor Place and East Fourth Street (fig. 11). Run by a Mr. Delacroix and then a Mr. Madden on a lease from J. J. Astor originating in 1805, this garden had a quixotic history. Taking his cue from the example of other residential enclaves, Astor believed in 1826 that he too could create an aristocratic quarter by opening an imposing 100-foot-wide street, Lafayette Place, right through the middle of Vauxhall Garden and developing the western land. Astor erected a mansion along Lafayette Place, the Astor Library, and a row of houses called La Grange Terrace, or Colonnade Row (fig. 12). But even these elegant gestures could not withstand the course of fashion. The area of luxury town houses on Bond and Bleecker streets gave way to trade in the mid-1840s; and the garden declined into a favored place for rowdy Bowery types and then was demolished, while La Grange Terrace became a hotel in 1844.

The Trinity Church farmlands on the west side of the island provided ample room for shaded retreats. Not surprisingly, it had a history of several famous pleasure gardens. Richmond Hill Garden, on the southeast corner of Varick and Charleton streets, was the most noteworthy. Once the home of Aaron Burr, Richmond Hill was soon leased from Trinity Church by J. J. Astor after Burr was tried for treason. Successive managers of the mansion on the property, originally called Mortier House, tried from 1822 to 1848 to lure citizens to the outskirts of town by presenting circuses, operas, dramas, and melodramas, but all efforts failed. In 1848, when the lease expired, the property reverted to Trinity Church, the house was demolished, and the land quickly lotted for sale.[15]

An open pleasure garden, known as the Palace Garden, lay on the north side of Fourteenth Street, 100 feet west of Sixth Avenue. It opened in 1858, but the city encroached on its space in 1865 when the Twenty-second Armory was erected and when the Théâtre Français took one third of its grounds. Suffering several changes of name and management during the 1860s, the Palace Garden too had vanished by 1867. For a brief decade or two on the edge of the fastest growing fashionable residential area, a maze garden known as Mount Croton

Gardens could be found. Opposite the Croton Reservoir, on the east side of Fifth Avenue between Thirty-ninth and Fortieth streets, this garden disappeared in 1859 when its block was lotted and sold[16] (see fig. 3). The largest pleasure garden of mid-nineteenth century Manhattan, Bellevue Gardens, opened in 1856 on eleven acres of land just west of the East River between Seventy-ninth and Eighty-first streets. Two miles above the closest residential development and five miles from the center of town, this garden could be reached by taking a five-cent horsecar drive along Second or Third Avenue and thus became a popular spot for picnics, shooting parties, and family outings.[17]

For many reasons pleasure gardens went out of fashion in the second half of the nineteenth century. The increasing value of land made it far too expensive to retain undeveloped, albeit commercial, gardens in the center of town, and popular taste in entertainment shifted to organized spectator sports. In addition, steam railroads and ferry boats now made the countryside in Staten Island, Astoria, and Coney Island easily accessible for inexpensive day outings. Finally, the acquisition of 17,000 building lots for Central Park in 1857 sounded the death knell of these pleasure spots.

MITIGATING THE GRID

Nineteenth-century Manhattan was run by men dedicated to its commercial development who appropriated as much open parkland as possible. In 1833 the Common Council approved a resolution to erect commercial buildings in City Hall Park (set aside as City Common ca. 1700), although sufficient public opposition brought a rescinding vote. In 1854 the council decided again to sell all the public land below and a good deal above Seventy-second Street, although a mayor's veto rejected this effort as well. Even a large public park on the periphery of the city was feared for the depressing impact it might have on real estate values.

Andrew Jackson Downing asked in 1848, "Is New York really not rich enough, or is there absolutely not land enough in America to give our citizens public parks of more than ten acres?"[18] After much discussion over the merits of a large public park, Mayor A. C. Kingsland finally proposed in 1851 that a 160-acre site known as Jones' Woods be claimed as this new public park (from Sixty-sixth to Seventy-fifth Street, Third Avenue to the East River). But Jones' Woods was owned by the Schermerhorn family who objected that "a park is not of sufficient public necessity to justify its being taken by the state in opposition to the wishes of the owner and by the violent exercise of eminent domain."[19] Nevertheless, the Common Council applied to Albany for legislation to turn this pleasure garden into a new public park although Jones' Woods was far from a restful retreat suitable for picturesque landscaping in the 1850s (fig. 13). A *Harper's Weekly* account noted that in Jones' Woods the business of pleasure prevailed, where hundreds of straggling wanderers could be seen "toiling earnestly to experience amusement." Evidently, Jones' Woods was lined with avenues flanked by booths and stalls, and tents were spread throughout offering shooting galleries, gymnastic apparatus, bowling alleys, billiard halls, and numerous places for cheap refreshment.[20]

Opposition to turning Jones' Woods into a park broke out in the press. The *Journal of Commerce* attacked the plan, noting that the high cost of acquisition would fall to the taxpayer and claiming that New York already owned sufficient parkland and in addition was surrounded by both cool waters and green, open

Fig. 13. The Great International Caledonian Games at Jones' Woods, 1867. A picturesque woodland along the East River, Jones' Woods was used as a private pleasure garden during the 1850s and 1860s. (Courtesy of the New-York Historical Society, New York City)

countryside, which made any provision for more public space completely unnecessary.[21] Others felt that Jones' Woods was too small for riding horses and driving carriages and that a large central park would distribute the benefits and costs more equitably. The *New York Times,* however, claimed that one large central park was not necessary, that it would be inaccessible to most of the laboring classes who needed its benefits most, and that it would in addition decrease the total supply of land and therefore drive up the level of rents in lower Manhattan. If land for public parks must be reserved, the *Times* suggested, then give the city eight parks of 100 acres each and "disperse them over the island that the air, the trees, the flowers, may be brought within the reach of all. This certainly would be less aristocratic, but more democratic and far more conducive to public health."[22]

Public interest was keen, and legislation was enacted for the acquisition of both Jones' Woods and land for Central Park. Sustained opposition held out against Jones' Woods, but in 1853 the city was given the final authority to acquire enough land for Central Park. Although the area to be reclaimed was well above the developed portions of Manhattan, with much of its land already used for commercial purposes, graded with streets, or generally of poor quality and of little scenic potential, it was to be salvaged and artfully rearranged as Central Park (fig. 14). By 1856 over 17,000 building lots between Fifth and Eighth avenues, from Fifty-ninth to 106th Street, were purchased by the city at a cost of over $5

million. The extension to 110th Street was acquired by 1863 (fig. 15). Consequently, the city plan of Manhattan included a vast open space, a void in the very heart of its monotonous gridiron plan, but it was questionable whether it would provide the meeting place for architecture and nature that seemed impossible in the sections of lower Manhattan dedicated to commerce.

Real estate investors had preached the value and necessity of parks as magnets attracting luxury development for over fifty years. When they began their real estate careers in the early 1800s, however, Fourteenth Street was the north-

Fig. 14. View into Central Park, looking south from the Arsenal, Fifth Avenue and Sixty-fourth Street, 1858. (Courtesy of the New-York Historical Society, New York City)

Fig. 15. Plans for Central Park, 1858 and 1868, from a pamphlet by Calvert Vaux and Frederick Law Olmsted. (Courtesy of the New-York Historical Society, New York City)

FIRST STUDY OF DESIGN FOR THE CENTRAL PARK.
From a Wood-cut made in 1858.

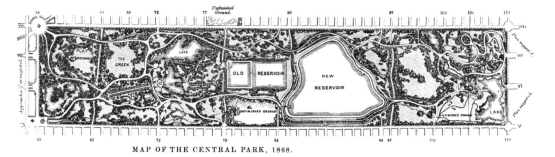

MAP OF THE CENTRAL PARK, 1868.

ern limit of urban growth and the building line was near Houston Street. Land north of Fourteenth Street was sold by the acre and treated as farmland or for country estates. Thus these men promoted the idea of urban parks in order to take some of the vast quantities of undeveloped Manhattan land out of the real estate market, creating a false scarcity of residential sites. In the late nineteenth century, however, the realtors changed their traditional perspective, arguing, like the commissioners of the 1811 plan, that New York was a great seaport and that its land should be developed without the obstacle of urban parks. It could never become a garden city, and a system of parks and open residential spaces, which might be appropriate for a retiring inland town abounding in cheap and accessible land, should be avoided in Manhattan. Two and a half square miles of Central Park were now seen as an impediment to uptown development. Land on both sides of the park would remain unimproved and inexpensive until fashionable neighborhoods emerged to their east and west.[23]

The wealthy, it was now recorded, did not like to reside near an unbroken tract of land. A new avenue running parallel to Fifth Avenue, the eastern border of the park, would provide Fifth Avenue homes with opposite neighbors whose backyards and gardens would border the park. The parks that previously had been the centers for fashionable life such as Saint John's Park or Gramercy Park all offered the benefit of opposite and visible neighbors. The wealthy were gregarious and social beings who sought residential locations for "exhibitory display and counterdisplay, acts which permeated the whole fabric of fashionable social life."[24] The real estate community had wrongly assumed, since the beginnings of Central Park, that around this center would congregate "the fastidious and representative wealth of the city."[25] From the late 1860s to the economic panic of 1873, a time when the city experienced unparalleled economic prosperity and growth, speculators bought up most of the 1,100 lots surrounding Central Park. Hoping for fashionable buyers, they held these lots off the market and were caught by the panic of 1873. Dismayed by this economic downturn, the real estate community was now convinced that the establishment of Central Park had been a "topographical blunder for the Park had conferred on fashionable Fifth Avenue nothing compared with what it had taken away."[26]

There were those who agitated, on the other hand, for even more park space, believing that the ideal park should be a pastoral preserve as well as the fresh air lungs of the city. Considerable interest arose in setting aside the belt of "picturesque precipia" on the west side of Manhattan from Seventy-second to 130th Street for ornamental purposes. As early as 1865, William R. Martin had written a pamphlet suggesting what is today known as Riverside Park. A topographical map was developed and shown to the Central Park Commissions, who in 1866 began to survey the West End plateau (the Upper West Side) and prepare their own report. An avenue 100 feet wide was proposed for the top of the bluff midway between Eleventh and Twelfth avenues. The sloping land to the river was to be reserved for a park. It took five years to acquire this park from resisting land owners, and it was not until 1875 that Frederick Law Olmsted was asked by the park commissioners to file his own map and plan for the improvement of Riverside Park and Drive[27] (see fig. 38). Soon afterward, bids for carrying out the plan were accepted, the job going to Nicholas Decker who began the work of improvement in 1877. But two years later, the Park Department refused to accept what they termed an incomplete job. In defense Decker closed the park to the public, obstructed its entrances with large derricks, boarded up each intersecting road, and even employed watchmen. As late as 1880, Decker and the Park Department remained at an impasse until one May night when indignant property owners forced the park's opening, and in the morning carriages began to roll along the forbidden land.[28] Olmsted had also prepared preliminary plans in 1873 for Morningside Park on a strip of steep hillside to the northwest of Central Park. It would not be completed until 1886.

By the 1880s, as residential development still failed to move north above Fifty-ninth Street on the western side of Manhattan, it seemed to real estate developers that Central Park's location in the center of Manhattan presented another topographical blunder that inhibited the architectural enhancement of its bordering avenues. Now it was believed that its southern boundary should have been located at Seventy-second Street and its northern extremity at 125th Street. The city needed a larger district for the expansion of luxury mansions on the south side of the park; consequently fashionable residences were beginning to appear above Fifty-ninth Street to the east of the park. The west side, however, remained cut off from this fashionable growth, isolated by the oblique corner of Broadway and its awkward joint at Fifty-ninth Street.[29] The difference between the east and west sides of the park were obvious by 1885. The east side was adorned with four residential avenues—Fifth, Madison, Fourth, and Lexington—while the west side, with the exception of Eighth Avenue, which was still largely undeveloped, contained three business streets developing along Ninth and Tenth avenues and Broadway. Eleventh Avenue and Riverside Drive were the only appropriate areas left for fashionable development.

No avenue in Manhattan could surpass Riverside Drive in healthfulness, as a park frontage with a fine elevation, and in its broad and commanding river view, and it was still believed that this excellent location would eventually be adorned with splendid mansions.[30] Martha Lamb described the land reserved for Riverside Park in these years as a charming "suburb," with its sequestered dells, its bluffs and views, ranging along three miles of waterfront. But it was only in 1888 that plans for the eventual beautification of Riverside Drive and the extensive surveying required to implement these plans finally were finished after years of delay. Walks would be laid out, cozy arbors constructed, and in time, trees, shrubs, and flowers would be planted.[31] But in 1888 Riverside Park still remained treeless, exposing the drive to the summer sun and the winter wind, the cause, or so it was believed, for the arrested development of what should have been an elegant quarter. Inaccessible to anyone without a carriage, it needed transverse roads connecting it to the elevated railway stations and Central Park before it could overcome its forced isolation.[32]

In 1889 it was proposed to New Yorkers that Riverside Park, Morningside Park, and the northern portions of Central Park become the site of the 1892 World's Fair. This proposal seemed likely to succeed as New York was the only city that did not appeal to Congress for financial assistance to carry out its plan.[33] In addition two plots were chosen for the projected exposition buildings: one between 110th and 113th streets, from Fifth Avenue to Manhattan Avenue, and the other between 108th and 116th streets, from Manhattan Avenue to the Hudson River. Even Frederick Law Olmsted did not object to using some of Central Park for the fair, proposing that the reservoir be floored over and the site used for some of the main buildings, thus enabling the "natural beauties" of the park to remain unimpaired.[34] The legal questions surrounding the acquisition of these lands beyond Central Park for a public fair, however, seemed insurmountable since the taking of private land to be used primarily for recreation and amusement, while it might aid the development of trade and commerce, was not recognized as serving a public purpose.[35]

As it became more apparent that the two plots suggested could not be obtained by the city, even more pressure was brought to bear on the use of Central Park as the site of the exposition. Why, asked the *Real Estate Record and Builders' Guide,* should not the poor and the moderately well-off sacrifice a few trees and a little open space for the sake of making the fair a success and possibly gaining a permanent exhibition hall? If it could be shown that the park could be used without serious injury to its landscaping and that only adjacent land had to be condemned, then surely this was the common sense solution to the whole matter.[36] Thus, new legislation was presented to Albany that would empower the city to take less extensive land—land that would eventually be used for additional public park space but that should be allocated for a short time to the exposition. The land to be taken was now the restricted area lying immediately north of Central Park, and a stretch of Bloomingdale Heights, which would be used to connect Riverside Park with Morningside Park.[37]

If the 1892 World's Fair was to celebrate "the material addition Columbus made to the real estate and breathing space of civilization"[38] by discovering America in 1492, what more appropriate site could be found than the very heart of Manhattan? Other cities felt differently and competed for the fair, believing that garish and corrupt New York was not a typical American city and could never adequately represent the material and financial resources of the nation. It was up to the U.S. Congress to select a winner, and in March 1890 the *Real Estate Record* reported that the World's Fair would be held in Chicago. Of New York's defeat, the *Real Estate Record* admonished that New York must recognize that it now had rivals who disputed its claim as the chief city of the country. It might be true that New York's commerce was larger than any other city and that it was the financial center of the country, but was it the preeminent center of the intelligence and culture of the nation? Not yet fifty years old, the city of Chicago, which pledged up to $10 million to subsidize the fair, was able to take the coveted prize away from New York. This was a great blow to the city and to the real estate interests especially. For, it was argued, a large amount of capital from other states and foreign countries had been invested annually in New York property because the city was regarded as *the* great city of America, the city where real estate values were the most certain and stable.[39]

The desire of New Yorkers for the fair, the *Real Estate Record* continued, had more to do with a pardonable weakness and vanity to parade themselves in holiday attire than with any bona fide expectation that the exhibition would create a "boom" in this self-reliant town. New York, the *Real Estate Record* believed, was wholly deficient in every characteristic that distinguished a great metropolis. Its municipal works and public conveniences would disgrace a second-rate city. Architecturally, except for office structures, its work was thought to be inferior, tasteless, and vulgar and its government inefficient and extravagant. It would be desirable if the $15 million already allocated for the World's Fair could be spent to make the city a worthy site for the greatest capital of the country.[40] There would be, however, more plans for improvement than actual implementation.

METROPOLITAN INTENTIONS

City Hall Park would also become the subject of architectural improvement. In the early 1890s architects complained that it was too small to provide an oasis in the midst of downtown development and that it took up space needed for the important municipal and commercial buildings. Several architects suggested in 1891 that the old city hall be removed to one of the uptown parks, and that in its place a new municipal building and other city buildings be designed around a

Fig. 16. City Hall and City Hall Park, as they would appear cleared of all intruding structures. The proposed Municipal Building on Chambers Street was eventually built according to designs by McKim, Mead and White in 1905. (Courtesy of Avery Library, Columbia University, New York City)

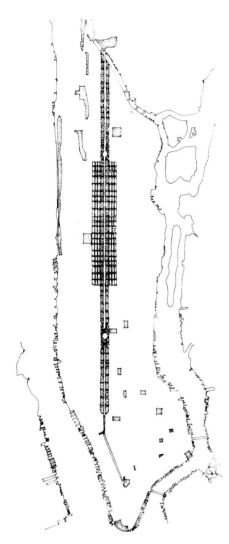

Fig. 17. Ernest Flagg's proposed parkway to replace Central Park, 1904. The Beaux-Arts boulevard would have connected City Hall Park with Bleecker Street, where it then would have turned northward and continued to the Harlem River. All land above Christopher Street between Sixth and Seventh avenues was to be cleared of buildings. (Redrawn from *Scribner's Monthly* 3, August 1904: 256)

central court or plaza accessible from the surrounding streets through broad-arched passageways. The center of this interesting pile of architecture might have a commemorative structure or campanile, making it vaguely reminiscent of the piazza of Saint Mark's in Venice. Only architect Henry Janeway Hardenbergh objected to such intrusive uses of City Hall Park, believing that City Hall was one of New York's few monuments and that it should be preserved for all time on the site it graced (fig. 16). Instead, he proposed that all the other buildings, which in his view defaced the park, be removed, allowing City Hall to be the central and only building on the park. New Yorkers, he said, should be ashamed of their restless urge that destroyed everything which was instructive from the city's past.[41]

As late as 1904, architects continued to grapple with the problems of Central Park. Ernest Flagg complained that a vast rectangular block of naturalistically planned open space was inappropriate for a large modern city and that this attempt to imitate the effects of nature should never have been made. Instead, he suggested, a broad open strip of land along each waterfront, and another through the center of Manhattan, might mitigate the huge gridiron lock that had held the city captive since 1811. Central Park, Flagg claimed, aggravated the worst features of the rectangular gridiron plan by failing to provide a central artery. It had outlived its purpose; in its picturesque treatment it was essentially a suburban pleasure ground, its lakes, groves, and meadows intended to offer a view of rural landscape. Flagg felt that the tall buildings which surrounded the park intruded upon this rural scene and disrupted its illusions, making this ornamental space a barrier between adjacent parts of the city. Instead of a naturalistic park, Flagg preferred a formal order: open grounds that formed a beautiful foil for the buildings and buildings that in turn ornamented these grounds. According to Flagg, the

> . . . purpose of such pleasure grounds should be to open up and enliven the appearance of the city, to bring sunlight, air, and verdure into the heart of the town; to afford agreeable promenades and drives; and by a judicious choice of location to distribute these benefits within reach of the greatest possible number of people.[42]

Thus, he believed, New York should sell its parkland and with the funds purchase all the lands between Sixth and Seventh avenues, from Christopher Street to the Harlem River, providing the city with a parkway strip 1,000 feet wide and more than 10 miles long. On this land a thoroughfare worthy of the metropolis of the new world could be constructed (fig. 17).

Even Frederick Law Olmsted had wondered earlier why the commissioners had adopted the gridiron plan of 1811. This plan required that no building lot should be more than 100 feet in depth and the clerk or mechanic of modest means must be provided with the same amount of land as the wealthy. Olmsted suggested that probably a mason's sieve lay near the commissioners' map of the ground to be laid out, and when placed upon the map one of the commissioners had asked, "What do you want better than this?"

> If a proposed cathedral, a military depot, great manufacturing enterprise, house of religious seclusion or seat of learning needs a space of ground more than sixty-six yards in extent from north to south, the system forbids that it shall be built in New York.

On the other hand, it equally forbids a museum, library, theatre exchange, post office or hotel, unless of great breadth to be lighted or to open upon streets from opposite sides.

There are numerous structures, both public and private, in London and Paris, and most other large towns in Europe, which could not be built in New York, for want of a site of suitable extent and proportions.

The few tolerable sites for noble buildings north of Grace Church and within the built part of the city remain, because Broadway, laid out curvilinearly, in free adaptation to natural circumstances, had already become too important a thoroughfare to be obliterated from the system.[43]

Even Broadway was a disappointment to architects. By 1898 J. F. Harder complained that what should have become our most magnificent and impressive street had forever lost its opportunity to be so. Once planned for two-story buildings, its width would never adequately provide for twelve-, sixteen-, or even twenty-story modern structures. Broadway had become so choked with surface transit that it had been rendered all but useless as a major commercial thoroughfare. Harder found it remarkable that the men who had laid down the gridiron pattern of Manhattan had completely omitted a diagonal system of primary avenues. The only way to improve the plan of Manhattan, he believed, was to extend Union Square to the north, south, and east, thus creating a monumental site for a new city hall, an official mayor's residence, and other architectural structures, and by carving out six diagonal boulevards that would converge on this magnificent new square[44] (fig. 18).

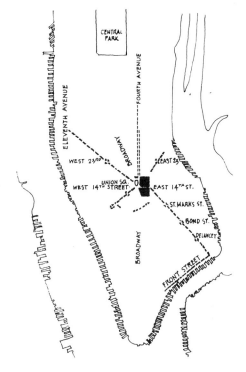

Fig. 18. J. F. Harder's improvement plan for New York, 1898. This Beaux-Arts scheme proposed a system of diagonal boulevards converging at Union Square. (Redrawn from *Municipal Affairs* 2, 1898: 30)

There was, however, little hope for the redemption of New York's street plan through such Haussmann-type schemes. The most that could be accommodated was a larger house on the standard 25-by-100-foot city lot. Above Fourteenth Street each rectangular block contained at least forty to sixty lots of identical dimensions. The rigid uniformity of this system meant the complete absence of any system of alleys, courtyards, or other means of access to the rear of any structure. Since the rear yard with no access was useless, the average New York house tended to extend its depth to sixty and even seventy feet. "This New York system says to the architect, the builder, the physician, the sanitarian, the philanthropist: 'expand yourselves. Let us see what you can do.' "[45]

Because of the drawbacks of the deep lot there were many suggestions throughout the nineteenth century for its improvement. One proposal in 1878 ventured the hope that real estate owners consider the advantage of running short streets from north to south through their blocks, supplying the ends of these new streets with gates. Such courtlike streets could be well lighted and orderly and yet have shallow lots along their sides adequate for moderately expensive houses. But instead, a twenty-five-foot wide and seventy-foot deep tenement, housing at least four families per floor, was a common New York occurrence. Because its brownstone front faced a wide street, this structure often made a good public appearance. But inadequate ventilation and crowded and darkened rooms were hidden behind this generous facade.[46]

In the areas of Manhattan below Fourteenth Street that had escaped the control of those "unconscious vandals," as Montgomery Schuyler referred to the commissioners who invented the deep lot of the 1811 city plan, the average

Fig. 19. Marble Row (1867–1929), erected on the east side of Fifth Avenue between Fifty-seventh and Fifty-eighth streets according to the designs of Robert Mook. The English concept of terrace housing, combining several town houses within a unified monumental facade, was an unusual addition to the New York streetscape, which was more commonly developed with rows of identical high-stooped brownstone houses. (Courtesy of the Museum of the City of New York, New York City)

block depth was seldom more than 150 feet.[47] With this smaller depth, the owner of modest means could command more frontage, and the wealthy builder could buy the through lot and place his stables at the rear of the house without great expense. A forty-foot-deep house retained almost half its lot for light and air, and became common for the small town houses built below Fourteenth Street in the early nineteenth century. By the 1850s, Schuyler explained, the high price of land above Fourteenth Street had narrowed the width of most row houses, and it was not an uncommon practice to find four houses crowded onto three lots, each nineteen feet wide, or reduced to having fifteen-foot fronts when five houses were squeezed onto three city lots. Even Calvert Vaux had commented in 1857 that it was not unusual to find two houses built on a twenty-five-foot-wide lot, forcing the residents to live on a ladder, so to speak, in houses with long, narrow rooms and dark, crowded stairways.[48] Gradually, genteel, spacious row houses were obliterated.

The system of fixed lot lines in the Manhattan grid was responsible not only for overcrowding both houses on lots and people in tenements, but it also forbade a more picturesque cityscape and led to the creation of monotonous long rows of identical brownstone houses. If the architect and builder could be rid of these standard lot lines, Calvert Vaux felt, they could produce an architecture of grandeur. For example, Richard Morris Hunt, in his Stuyvesant Apartment House on Eighteenth Street and Third Avenue (see fig. 183), created a unified thirty-six-foot facade for his "newfangled" apartment house rather than two ordinary eighteen-foot town houses.[49] Henry J. Hardenbergh claimed that the uniformity in street architecture was really the fault of the individual owners rather than of architectural form. Where one owner prevailed and a whole block could be de-

Fig. 20. Colford Jones Row, designed by Detlef Lienau and built in 1869 for Rebecca Jones. This refined row, located two blocks south of Marble Row on the east side of Fifth Avenue between Fifty-fifth and Fifty-sixth streets, integrated eight monumental houses within its scheme. The northern half of the row was razed in 1911, the southern half in 1925. (Courtesy of the Museum of the City of New York, New York City)

signed by one architect, such as Fifth Avenue between Fifty-fifth and Fifty-sixth streets by Detlef Lienau, the best blocks in New York could be found [50] (figs. 19, 20; see fig. 168).

When the commissioners laid out the city above Fourteenth Street, they provided for a few longitudinal avenues and many transverse streets, partly because of a provincial notion that the business center would always lie below City Hall and that the city beyond would be devoted to suburban residences, kitchen gardens, and farms. They never considered the heavy north-south traffic that was the apparent norm by the 1890s. As a legacy, there were only a few vertical avenues and New York was left with long transverse blocks that it had yet to deal with architecturally or urbanistically. New Yorkers clung to their stereotypical block and lot development. Yet the blocks between Fifth and Sixth avenues were 920 feet long and 200 feet wide. If ordinary 20-foot houses were constructed on one of these blocks, it would present a solid perimeter of at least 92 houses. There were, however, many other ways of dividing these blocks with additional avenues and alleys so that four square blocks of 200 by 200 feet could result, providing more corner lots, facilitating commercial traffic, and breaking up the long monotonous rows of houses.

The principle of the arcade store, prominent in London, Berlin, Paris, Leipzig, and Dresden, could have been used to divide the long New York City block. A proposal illustrated in the *Real Estate Record* would have had an arcade running from street to street, opened at both entrances during business hours, and closed by grilles at night. The arcade itself would extend through every story to the roof, where a glazed arch would form its shelter; a main staircase would be constructed in the center; a gallery would surround it at every floor, and every store fronting on the arcade would thus be open for the display of wares and for announcements[51] (fig. 21).

Anyone who wandered through the city streets of New York in the late nineteenth century could not fail to note that many splendid opportunities to erect buildings which would have been an ornament to the city and exceedingly profitable to their owners had been lost long ago. Now architects sought to rearrange the grid pattern of streets through Beaux-Arts expressions. New York, they felt, required open plazas for civic enhancement. Where a number of streets crossed one another, sufficient ground should be cleared so that new monumental structures could grace the opening. For example, the *Real Estate Record* criticized Cooper Union — the junction of Fourth, Third, and Second avenues and Broadway, close to Eighth and Ninth streets and Lafayette Place — should have been the site for a great place of amusement with churches, public halls, and palatial stores calculated to attract heavy retail traffic. The intersection of Broadway, Sixth Avenue, and Thirty-fourth Street should have been another natural headquarters for business and amusement as well as the location for a new opera house and department stores.[52]

New York, these Beaux-Arts critics complained, needed a magnificent boulevard for promenading. When the commissioners divided the city by Fifth Avenue, however, they did not foresee that certain districts would become centers of luxury where presentation and display were necessary accompaniments. Yet Fifth Avenue had been the street on which the fashionable had settled since the 1830s, and should have been planned as a grand boulevard for parading, two or three times its original width.[53] On the other hand, these critics noted, Beaux-Arts compositions

Fig. 21. Elevation and plan for a proposed arcade store designed by Monty Cutler but never built. (Elevation courtesy of Avery Library, Columbia University, New York City; plan redrawn from the *Real Estate Record and Builders' Guide*, Dec. 2, 1893: 682)

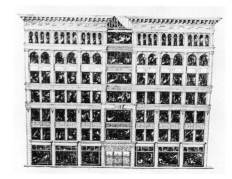

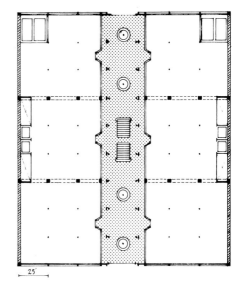

Fig. 22. The Fuller (Flatiron) Building, erected by Burnham and Company in 1902 at the intersection of Twenty-third Street, at Fifth Avenue and Broadway. Rising more than twice as high as any of its neighbors, the arrowheaded structure shocked New Yorkers at the turn of the century. (Courtesy of the New-York Historical Society, New York City)

required frontal perspectives, an expression that the rigid rectangular frame all but forbade. Montgomery Schuyler suggested that rounding the acute corners of Broadway might yield picturesque treatments of entrances and stopping the streets perpendicular to stately structures as had been done for Bryant Park and East Forty-first Street, and for the Metropolitan Museum and East Eighty-second Street, might relieve the monotonous grid and provide frontal vantage points.[54] Others believed that any scheme for street improvement that could put onto the market a large number of open-sided plots, affording the Beaux-Arts architect an opportunity to formally arrange a composition without the restrictions of the grid, would quickly create the lacking architectural enhancement of the streets of Manhattan.[55] This seemed a realistic alternative as large plots of land were increasingly necessary for real estate development: tall office buildings began to require corner lots of 15,000 or 20,000 square feet or plots that fronted on streets along three or four of their sides. Thus a tall structure such as the Fuller (Flatiron) Building had an advantage over other tall buildings, by advertising itself on its dramatic site and thus commanding high rents (fig. 22).

With these ideas in mind and in spite of past experience, Beaux-Arts designers tried once again to overcome the limitations of the grid. The Municipal Art Society proposed in 1904 several diagonal boulevards to open up vistas and offer new opportunities for ornamental architecture: one from Cooper Union stretching southeast for three-quarters of a mile to the Williamsburg Bridge; another extending from the bridge southwest to Canal and Chrystie streets where the new Manhattan Bridge would terminate; and a third extending Christopher Street in a northwesterly direction to Union Square and Seventeenth Street.[56]

The city's rectangular layout and plan would prevail, nevertheless, giving form to its architectural order and guiding its future development. No matter how the improver might try, the logic of the city's straight-angled streets was the generative force behind its development; the principle of order that became the city's special history. Nineteenth-century Manhattan would develop into specialized districts, not planned or ordered in themselves, and so fragilely constructed that they would change and disappear over time. In the 1860s to the 1890s a Victorian amusement district, Ladies Mile, arose in the vicinity of Broadway and Fourteenth Street, while luxury residential areas began to expropriate the undeveloped lands above Fifty-ninth Street. But this arrangement was far from permanent, and by the early twentieth century Forty-second Street had become the focus for entertainment and business, while the fashionable elite had reached the suburbs beyond; superblock development eventually would isolate different parts of the city, and superimposed highways would restructure the whole. New York's rectangular fabric of isolated blocks and individualized lots was the price it paid for being a gridded city. Commercial New York expressed in its form its material and utilitarian being, which was inherently controlled by economic factors and speculative real estate practices.

CHAPTER TWO
AN ECONOMIC BASE FOR MANHATTAN ARCHITECTURE

. . . if we are to obtain a correct conception of the status of city architecture in America, (it) is that current American architecture is not a matter of art, but of business. A building must pay or there will be no investor ready with his money to meet its cost. This is at once the curse and glory of American architecture.

City architecture in America is not understood or appreciated because the conditions under which it is built are not comprehended or fully allowed for. The designing of a building in a modern city is not, as every architect knows, the making of a pleasing facade, but the adjustment of a multitude of conditions and circumstances which he cannot alter in the least, and which, often enough, prevent the obtaining of an even approximately satisfactory result.

Architecture like every rational art, business, profession, trade, and industry has reason at its basis. . . . One general type of structure serves as a model for commercial building because experience has shown that particular type to be the best suited for that purpose . . . each have their own general types, derived from the uses to which the building has been put. Architecture, therefore, rests on a rational basis, and the more thoroughly studied, the more completely the building fills these conditions, the more successful it is and the more admirable it becomes as a building, as a piece of construction, and a work of architecture.—Barr Ferree, "Economic Conditions of Architecture in America," *Proceedings of the 27th Annual Convention of the American Institute of Architects* (Chicago: 1893):231, 229, 240

Barr Ferree's remarks about the priorities of reason meant that the nineteenth-century urban architect had to learn to classify all the elements making up architectural production: the economic base, technical and regulatory restrictions, the control exerted by the city plan, and the block and lot morphology. But the most important of these components would be the pattern of real estate investment. Speculation in land can be called the nineteenth century's most popular gamble; huge sums of money were invested in the development of western farmlands and in the building of large cities. The expansion of transportation systems throughout the nineteenth century brought vast new fields of land within reach of the market, determining the structure and development of the urban pattern, for suddenly it produced a city without boundaries. Real estate values or prices became the important controls, reflecting changes in the trends in consumption and producing investments with maximum returns. These values, not architectural forms, caused different zones of the city to emerge: a business center here, new recreational or shopping centers there. Architecture, now confined to sites that were uniform and interchangeable, no longer determined—as it had in the eighteenth century—the shape of the American city.

If architecture were to become a rational science in the twentieth century, it would need to incorporate all the speculator's knowledge that had been used to control the production of space in the nineteenth century. This would be a considerable compromise for, as Montgomery Schuyler wrote in 1883:

> People talk as if the middle part of Fifth Avenue, the brown-stone high-stoop house with its bloated detail, which displaced the prim precision of the older work, had been done by educated architects. . . . But the bulk of the building which gave its architectural character to New York and to the country continued to be done by mechanics, who continued, so far as they could, to supply the demand of the market, who gradually lost the training their predecessors had enjoyed, and who lost all sense of the necessity for that training in the new demand that their work should be above all things, "American." As the slang of today puts it, they were exhorted, as the architects are still sometime exhorted, to "talk United States." They might have answered that there was no such language, and that a few bits of slang did not constitute a poetical vocabulary.[1]

Just when architectural discourse was turned back on itself, when it began to remove its historicist wrappings to search for the influences that lay beneath its artistic form, this was exactly the moment when it became critically aware of its own dilemma. The aesthetic dialogue, which had previously focused on visual imagery, would now have to be brought into line with the economic and political practices that had formed the American city. For all their wariness of the speculative builder, architects by the 1890s began to question and review the empirical knowledge that builders and speculators had accrued.

No better record of these real estate practices in Manhattan exists than in the pages of the *Real Estate Record and Builders' Guide*. Beginning as a modest weekly, the *Real Estate Record* listed only conveyances and mortgage transactions when it first appeared in 1868. But as the importance of real estate investments increased, and as the awareness grew that they were affected simultaneously by political questions, stock fluctuations, currency rates, and the general state of other markets, the *Real Estate Record* grew from a limited trade review to a broad-ranging business journal.[2] In August 1891 the *Real Estate Record* expanded in a new direction and began to publish a separate journal, the *Architectural Record*. Commending the *Real Estate Record and Builders' Guide* for this departure, the architectural community responded that such a scholarly review would finally offer the public a much needed forum for commentary on and criticism of American architecture. Within the realm of real estate itself, by the end of the nineteenth-century new lines were being drawn with which to classify and discipline the practice of architecture.

This movement was reflected in a *Real Estate Record* article of February 1891 in which a critic complained that a great deal of discussion of American architecture had taken place although no one had taken the care to define what was meant by the term or where one could find examples of this phenomenon. Certainly not even the most fervent critic would go so far as claim that American architecture was responsible for all the building in New York, but questions arose as to the boundaries of the term and who should be allowed to fix them. The domain of architecture was a major new concern for the *Real Estate Record.*

> The truth is . . . "American Architecture" plays a very small part in the building of our great cities, and this we all overlook. Take New York as an example. Look at all the upper parts of the city—the great West Side and East Side, wherein hundreds of millions of dollars have been spent in brick and mortar. Is "American Architecture" chargeable with those weary acres of cheapness (in its worse sense), tawdryness and vulgarity? West 72nd Street is one of the most "expensive" streets in the city. Yet let anyone pass along it from end to end and then say it may be taken as fairly representative of the average ability of American architecture! Can American architecture, using the term in quite a wide sense, produce nothing better?[3]

In a further effort to distinguish between architecture and building, a bill to license architects was introduced into the New York State legislature in 1891. A licensing procedure, it was thought, would necessarily raise the standards of architecture and save the public from exposure to the works of young men who, without any training yet through the support of wealthy friends and relatives, became full-fledged architects. On the other hand, others argued that no country in the world required the licensing of architects and the United States was far too new and the demands for builders and architects too great for any such law. The United States was seen as being too democratic to resort to these aristocratic means; a licensing system would affect the poorer aspiring architect more heavily by requiring that, instead of working for wages, young men who wished to pass the licensing examination attend classes at Columbia College or the Massachusetts Institute of Technology. The state, it was held, should have nothing to do with the regulation of aesthetic matters: moreover, good building laws and the careful inspection of faulty construction were regarded as the only safeguards necessary to control the building of cities. Even though the bill of 1891 would fail to become law, forces were gathering across the country, determined to reformulate the division between architecture and building and to discipline the practice of architecture.[4] A review of Manhattan's real estate strategies and construction is necessary to uncover the roots of this dialogue.

THE REAL ESTATE CYCLE

The decades after the Civil War were times of massive economic expansion— quick speculative gains, and easy losses, that brought with them a tastelessly commercial boom-and-bust building cycle. In New York this cycle displayed its own periods of speculation, depression, and development that left many speculators perplexed. Some made windfall profits, others experienced bankruptcy. It was argued that the introduction of "greenback" paper currency into the American monetary system in 1861 had much to do with the rise and fall of real estate values. Land suddenly appeared to be a solid investment in an economy otherwise based on an intangible currency.[5]

Yet the rise of real estate values was not a linear process, even for stable investors, experiencing lags and spurts as adjustments were made continuously between population demand and building supply, labor activities and construction processes, and financing methods and investment responses. Many of the reasons for the uneven development lay outside the real estate market, for example, the greenback issue, the California gold rush, or the various railroad wars. But a myriad of internal reasons existed that also created these extraordinary vicissitudes, such as decisions of where to invest in land, what type of structure to build, and whether to rent or buy. All these reasons were loosely held together by a climate of opinion, the optimistic expectation that profit could be made in the present location, at the present time, or through the perception of new client needs and the subsequent creation of speculative demand.[6]

The motivators of real estate activity were the wealthy and middle-class clients who in the nineteenth-century had the ability to choose the location they wanted to live in as well as the taste for new fashions in comfort, luxury, and materials. Working-class housing, although a lucrative investment, was banished to less fashionable areas of the city where its supply responded directly to demographic pressure. But the making of luxury residential areas was based on pure speculation: the creation of new value that in turn commanded higher prices. Since speculative profits were made from the rapid exchange of land at inflated value, rather than from the sale of constructed buildings, this increase in value depended on the imaginary projection of new luxury areas of the city. Again it was the well-to-do bourgeoisie who could afford to pay inflated land prices and sustain this speculation. In Manhattan, after the Civil War, the real estate community focused special attention on the area then called the fashionable district, between Thirty-fourth and Fifty-ninth streets adjacent to Fifth Avenue, and speculated about the creation of new luxury neighborhoods north of Fifty-ninth Street, to the east and west of Central Park.

The real estate community in the nineteenth century continually hoped to rationalize its market and thus overcome its bust-and-boom cycle. This was echoed especially by the founding editor of the *Real Estate Record*, David Goodman Croly, who was an ardent advocator and student of the positivist movement.[7] It is not surprising to find that the *Real Estate Record* focused on property values in the fashionable district of Manhattan where the most costly structures were built, commanding the highest real estate prices, and where vacant lots were more expensive than they had ever been.[8] Real estate in the fashionable district set the pitch for land transactions across the entire city. If the dynamics of luxury investment could be understood, the *Real Estate Record* reasoned, rational order would surround real estate investment elsewhere. Thus developers began to question how this luxury area exercised control over capital investment and why this area survived, even benefited, from economic depression and crisis. A new debate occurred in the years between 1865 and the 1890s over what constituted luxury real estate: what was the basis for the economic strength displayed in the old luxury area between Thirty-fourth and Fifty-ninth streets; what was the stabilizing value of the new entertainment district between Fourteenth and Twenty-thirty streets; and what were the procedures by which to project the development of new luxury areas.

SPECULATIVE INVESTMENT: 1865–1873:

When the Civil War ended in 1865, Forty-second Street was the northern limit of Manhattan's building activity. Below Eighty-sixth Street, 25,261 vacant lots remained; beyond lay a jumble of ungraded and unimproved streets. The great

[Fig. 23]

BUILDING PLANS FILED IN MANHATTAN: 1868–1897	
Dates	Number of plans filed
1868–1872	11,223
1873–1877	6,916
1878–1882	11,248
1883–1887	17,287
1888–1893	15,992
1894–1897	13,095

West Side was a bleak and barren wasteland; its street lines and grades and the tentatively drawn boundaries of Morningside and Riverside parks were filed only in March 1868. Although the Civil War period was devoid of building activity, it was a time when New York City's expanding population continually demanded new residential areas. Thus when peace arrived, money flowed into real estate development. Low land values, reasonable labor costs, and modest prices in materials, coupled with a real demand for new commercial and residential buildings, created a land and building boom that lasted from 1865 to 1873.

Capitalists, newly enriched by their war investments, began to turn their pocketbooks inside out for new places of residence and business, pushing many of the vacant areas of Manhattan into development. Unfortunately, unlimited expense and costly improvements were the unquestioned corollaries of such land speculation. The *Real Estate Record* complained that New York had entered a period of excessive elaboration and pretentiousness in its architectural taste, where fraud and disgrace adorned its streets in ungainly examples. So much pressure had built up for new buildings of every type, that inexperienced architects and builders with questionable strategies were scarcely capable of adopting dignified and well-tried solutions. A review of building plans filed in Manhattan between 1868 and 1873 (fig. 23) gives some indication as to how much improvisation and haste must have prevailed.[9]

As a legacy of this speculative period, so-called bonanza buildings were produced, none of which could return an investment of more than 1 or 2 percent. These unsound business ventures only served to aggravate the problem of inflation. Among the costly buildings that the *Real Estate Record* criticized were the Gilsey House (fig. 24), Edwin Booth's Theatre (fig. 25), Alexander Stewart's ostentatious palace (fig. 26), and the Gothic mansion of Frederick W. Stevens (see fig. 33). All of these elaborate structures were located near the new entertainment district of Ladies Mile (running from Fourteenth Street to Twenty-third Street, and extending from Broadway to Sixth Avenue) or in the fashionable quarter. The *Real Estate Record* complained that none of them had been constructed with sufficient consideration for prudence, efficiency, and the economically stressful times. The editors noted that Edwin Booth had been bankrupted by his theater, having forsaken the site plans of his wiser predecessors. Imprudent designs, the *Real Estate Record* argued, only added pressure to the speculative balloon. And yet entertainment speculation was in principle profitable enough, since successful theaters acquired lots on which only the main entrance had to be located on the expensive thoroughfare, placing the theater itself in the rear on less costly property and reserving the street for commercial enterprises[10] (fig. 27).

Fig. 24. *Upper left.* An 1880 view of the Gilsey House, on the northeast corner of Broadway and Twenty-ninth Street. One of the "bonanza buildings" constructed during the years of speculation after the Civil War, the Gilsey House, designed by S. D. Hatch in 1869 and still existing, was the earliest iron-clad hotel in New York City. (Courtesy of the New-York Historical Society, New York City)

Fig. 25. *Lower left.* Booth's Theatre, on the southeast corner of Sixth Avenue and Twenty-third Street. This Second Empire theater, designed by Renwick and Sands in 1868, was an ensemble building with stores along the Sixth Avenue facade. By 1883, the structure had become a dry-goods store and was demolished by the 1890s. (Courtesy of the Museum of the City of New York, New York City)

Fig. 26. *Upper right.* A. T. Stewart's mansion, ca. 1900. The marble palace on the northwest corner of Thirty-fourth Street and Fifth Avenue was a tribute to the innovative architectural taste of a department store millionaire. Built between 1864 and 1869 by John Kellum, it would be replaced by McKim, Mead and White's Knickerbocker Trust Building in 1902. (Courtesy of the New York Public Library, New York City)

The hand of Tammany had indelibly written the map of New York. By dictating the location of public improvements, Tammany Hall controlled the laying out of boulevards and the levying of new assessments. Moreover, by restricting or promoting public works it favored some builders over others. Nor were these so-called public benefactors reluctant to speculate in land themselves. The highest market price was not too little to pay under their conviction that investment value would double or triple within a few months. All of these actions simply fed the speculative process.[11]

The promise of an adequate rapid transit system was another cause for inflated property values: vacant lots far removed from the center of town were inviting investments when compared to the higher cost and value of land below Fifty-ninth Street, especially if the installation of rapid transit was imminent. As elsewhere, the residential growth of Manhattan depended on the expansion of a rapid transit system. The era of the omnibus enabled the city to stretch as far as Fourteenth Street and perhaps to Twenty-third Street, but it was not until the horsecar era, which began in 1852, that the city reached its northern end of Fifty-ninth Street where it stalled, anticipating further developments in the transit system. Daily promises in the press of public improvements in transportation gave investors no reason to doubt that upper Manhattan would soon be as close to City Hall as Forty-second Street. This speculation, however, was entirely confined to the trading of vacant lots above Fifty-ninth Street. Even as late as 1868 the West Side remained an abandoned wilderness of rock outcroppings and dilapidated shanties, country farms and a few wayside inns (fig. 28). On the East Side, however, by changing trains twice, a traveler could reach as far north as Eighty-sixth Street by the Third Avenue line, so that by the same year Third Avenue was already lined with stores and houses, a development that began to spill over to Second Avenue as well. Yet with the exception of a small settlement at Yorkville, the rest of the East Side also lay undeveloped and barren.[12]

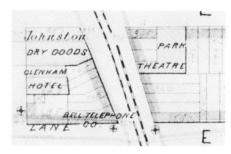

Fig. 27. Park Theatre. (Detail from the Bromley Insurance Map of 1879.) Located on the east side of Broadway between Twenty-first and Twenty-second streets, this theater was built in 1874 according to an economical plan that concealed its Broadway front behind a row of commercial structures. The auditorium was reached through a narrow passageway. Never prosperous during the mid- to late 1870s, the theater was not rebuilt when it burned to the ground in 1882. It became the future site for Brooks Brothers clothing store. (Courtesy of the New York Public Library, New York City)

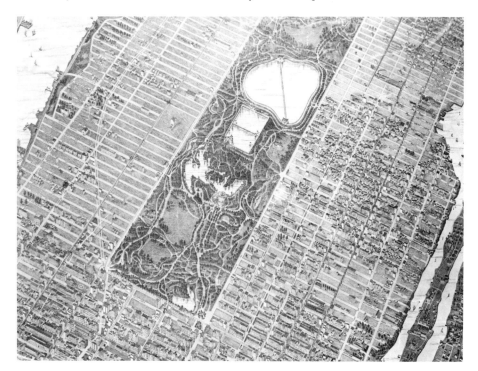

Fig. 28. Jalt and Hoy isonometric map of New York City in 1879, showing the comparative development of the east and west sides of Central Park. (Courtesy of the New-York Public Library, New York City)

While downtown speculation was slower, in the mid-1860s an important change occurred as retail business began to invade the future Ladies Mile district. The commercial ''avant-garde'' had already entered the area in which A. T. Stewart was just completing his cast-iron palace at Broadway and Tenth Street and where Arnold Constable and Company had begun to build their elaborate store at the corner of Broadway and Nineteenth Street. Around the same time, Lake and McCreery had purchased the corner of Eleventh Street and Broadway opposite Grace Church for their new dry goods mart. In 1867 the iron-clad Tiffany building would be erected along Broadway at Union Square. By the end of the 1860s, Lord and Taylor's new store could be seen rising at the corner of Broadway and Twentieth Street, and Stewart's hotel at Park Avenue and Thirty-fourth Street was added to the list.[13]

With this onslaught of commerce, residential areas began to retreat farther uptown. While clinging to their strongholds on the east and northeast sides of Union and Madison squares and to certain places along Fourteenth Street, fashionable residences were now locating between Thirty-ninth and Fiftieth streets off Fifth Avenue. Changes were rapid in this fashionable neighborhood, with the churches leading the way. In spite of the fact that Grand Central Depot was under construction, in the 1870s Madison Avenue became a street of churches: St. Bartholomew's Episcopal Church was being built at the southwest corner of Forty-fourth Street, the Church of the Disciples at Forty-fifth Street, the Collegiate Reformed Episcopal Church at Forty-Eighth Street, the Presbyterian Church at Fifty-third Street, and the Reformed Episcopal Church at Fifty-fifth Street[14] (figs. 29, 30).

Fig. 29. Church of the Disciples, southeast corner of Madison Avenue and Forty-fifth Street, ca. 1875. The Moorish-style church was dedicated in 1873. To its right, one of the pavilions of Grand Central Depot can be seen. (Courtesy of the New-York Historical Society, New York City)

Still another cause of inflated property values after the Civil War was said to be the standard eight-hour working day, which increased the cost of every development. In New York these high labor costs affected the cost of street improvements, swelling the property owner's tax and assessment bill. Naturally such expenses, in their turn, were passed on in the price for vacant lots.[15]

The final cause of inflated values could be found in the mode of building itself. Three basic classes of builders existed in New York; legitimate builders who worked under contract, never taking risks except to agree to produce a given amount of work for a stated price; architect-builders (firms such as Duggin and Crossman), who combined both the talents of the architect and the builder and who went into business during the boom years of the 1860s; and finally, the speculative builders who took great risks in their building adventures, paying for all the land costs, materials, labor, and financing expenses out of their own pockets and hoping to recoup their investment on the sale of the building. The great majority of Manhattan side streets had been produced by speculative builders, often shady characters whose profits were made on fraudulent gains and inferior craftsmanship.[16]

Only a few corporations, estates, and wealthy individuals considered building for investment purposes. Yet few speculative builders could acquire land and construct and market their building schemes without financial aid. Consequently, the building loan became common, but it too encouraged land speculation. Under normal conditions the building loan was simply an equitable agreement based on good faith between the capitalist and the master builder who both cooperated for mutual profit. But in the speculative years of the early 1870s, fraudulent practices characterized many building loan transactions. Under these conditions the capitalist was known to have purchased lots that he subsequently sold to the builder at a fixed profit rate of 25 percent, 50 percent, and at times an outrageous 100 percent, agreeing at this point to advance the money for the cost of at least half the improvements, his loans being secured by mortgages on the property involved. When the builder's money supply was depleted and his ability to borrow needed amounts failed, the capitalist foreclosed his mortgage, not only ruining the builder but leaving subcontractors and material suppliers unpaid as well. Easy times and a rising market based on the fictitious and inflated value of land bred this iniquitous scheme and caused sudden and ruinous collapses in real estate values. So wary had the public become of such schemes in the 1870s, that when the capitalist foreclosed he often found that he was the only bidder for the property put up for sale and in the end he too suffered financial distress.[17]

ECONOMIC DEPRESSION: 1873–1879

The year 1873 ushered in a period of depression. By 1874 a process of liquidation began in real estate, lasting three years. The inflated balloon of land speculation above Fifty-ninth Street burst, and thousands of property owners suffered losses as a result of foreclosures. It was estimated that fully half the speculators who had been active in the earlier period were destroyed by the depression of the 1870s. It was found as well, that after the period of inflated prices, vacant lot owners suffered the most. North of Fifty-ninth Street, property was seen as totally useless and few investors were found willing to make needed improvements.[18]

Not until 1879 did the clouds begin to clear over the prostrate real estate market. In earlier economic panics, real estate had been affected primarily be-

Fig. 30. An 1876 view of the Reformed Episcopal Church, built on the northeast corner of Madison Avenue and Fifty-fifth Street. At the time this photograph was taken, the architect-builders Duggin and Crossman were erecting modern residences on the vacant lots in front of the church on Madison Avenue between Fifty-fifth and Fifty-sixth streets. It is likely that the row of houses under construction to the right on the south side of Fifty-fifth Street was also their work. (Courtesy of the Museum of the City of New York, New York City)

[Fig. 31]

BUILDINGS ERECTED IN MANHATTAN: 1868–1880

Year	Total Buildings Erected	First-Class Residences	Apartment Buildings	Other
1868	2,014	853	0	1,161
1869	2,348	840	1	1,507
1870	2,351	822	0	1,529
1871	2,782	1,049	0	1,733
1872	1,728	499	1	1,228
1873	1,311	206	0	1,105
1874	1,388	234	0	1,154
1875	1,406	382	112	912
1876	1,379	439	115	825
1877	1,432	421	157	854
1878	1,672	525	99	1,048
1879	2,065	764	253	1,048
1880	2,252	900	516	836

Data compiled from the *Real Estate Record and Builders' Guide* 27 (April 2, 1881): 299.

cause the supply of buildings was greater than the demand to buy. But now real estate was stung by a shrinkage in land values and massive foreclosures among building developers.[19] During the years that followed the crash of 1873, no real evidence existed that an excess of good housing had surpassed its demand. As figure 31 illustrates, there was no fear of overbuilding in Manhattan; new structures had not kept pace with the growth of needs in the mid-1870s.

Other factors were influencing the Manhattan real estate market. A few properties, such as the individually inherited estates of Astor, Goelet, Beekman, Rhinelander, Stuyvesant, Cutting, Lenox, Hoffman, Jones, Spingler, and a score of smaller and less reknowned names, were unaffected by market fluctuations. The same was true for corporations such as Trinity Church, the Sailors' Snug Harbor, New York Hospital, Columbia College, and the City Corporation itself, whose owners bought but rarely sold. Excluding these landowners, the major purchasers in Manhattan were the capitalist investors and the average house buyers. The former were self-made merchants or manufacturers, including known names such as Hammersley, Livingston, Verplanch-Hoffman, Eno, Sage, Kemp, Keep, Bonner, and Vanderpoel. These capitalists were conservative investors who wanted to own land without a mortgage debt and who were not swayed by the much publicized speculation. When these investors withdrew from the market, as they did in the years between 1870 and 1876, the *Real Estate Record* declared that it showed the degree to which the real estate market had become distorted.[20]

The mainstay of the market, however, was the thrifty and public-spirited house buyer. Although he may never have thought of speculating in land, he counted his dollars, measured his buying power, and entertained the dream of one day owning his own home. It was this middle-class buyer who was being driven out of Manhattan by the speculation of the 1860s, leaving the city to the millionaire and the pauper.[21] During the entire depression there were no buyers for medium-priced houses, those costing less than $50,000. Only the return to stable land and building prices would keep the prudent middle-class buyers in Manhattan. In order to hold onto the average citizen, as early as 1876 the Superintendent of Buildings proposed a new fire line to divide the city into a district composed of brick and brownstone houses and another district of cheaper, roomier frame structures.[22] As a result, a new suburban district above Eighty-sixth Street was planned, consisting of neat wooden cottages and tasteful frame villas. But all of this projected development would have to wait for a stronger economy. During the panic of 1873 to 1876, an interest in house buying could be found only in the fashionable quarter where first-class houses brought from $50,000 to $100,000. By 1876 over 200 costly houses were being erected in this area, a stock judged sufficient to cover the housing demand for four or five years to come.[23]

The depression deflated prices. It was estimated that a house costing $50,000 to build in 1873 could be built in 1876 for as little as $35,000.[24] The period of inflation was passing, lowering the prices of materials and labor and enabling real estate prices to reflect reduced, more stable construction costs. It was hoped that a new building cycle would begin. Nevertheless, even as late as the winter of 1878, the real estate market remained sluggish. The only notable large investments were David McAlpin's purchase of the Sweeney block on Broadway between Thirty-third and Thirty-fourth streets for retail use, and Edward Clark's purchase of two large tracts on the West Side (30 lots on Central Park West between Seventy-second and Seventy-third streets, and 29 lots off Columbus Avenue on Seventy-third Street) for an undisclosed purpose. The fashionable builders Duggin and Crossman were also erecting modestly priced houses along the entire frontage of Madison Avenue between Fifty-fifth and Fifty-sixth streets.[25]

After five years of stagnation, the wealthy capitalists who had withdrawn from the market in the early 1870s finally wanted to erect fashionable homes of their own. Consequently, they began in the late 1870s to assemble large parcels of land for their elaborate residences.[26] At a more modest scale, an inventory of more than 400 vacant lots in the fashionable district revealed in 1878 that at least 300 of these were potentially for sale: 95 lots stood on Fifth Avenue between Forty-third and Fifty-ninth streets, 66 lots on Madison Avenue, and 244 lots on the side streets.[27]

Fig. 32. Fifth Avenue and Fifty-fourth Street looking west, ca. 1865. Saint Luke's Hospital is on the right and William Rockefeller's mansion is on the left. (Courtesy of the Museum of the City of New York, New York City)

Fig. 33. Frederick W. Stevens residence. (From *Frank Leslie's Illustrated Newspaper* 209, November 27, 1880.) The earliest mansion to be built in the future fashionable district, the Stevens house was designed in the style of a modified French chateau on the southwest corner of Fifth Avenue and Fifty-seventh Street in the late 1870s. The houses that were demolished for this newer residence were reconstructed stone by stone on a new site one block east. (Courtesy of the New-York Historical Society, New York City)

The mansions of William Rockefeller, J. A. Bostwick, and Frederick W. Stevens (figs. 32, 33) along Fifth Avenue began to be completed during the late 1870s. Simultaneously, in the blocks of the fifties between Fifth and Madison avenues, architect-builders were actively constructing, and new construction began, very slowly at first, to push northeast above Fifty-ninth Street.[28] During the same period investors were also beginning to rebuild lower Manhattan, and new commercial structures were built near Union Square, such as the Jefferson Market Police Court, the Domestic Sewing Machine Building, and Chickering Hall. In addition, by the mid-1870s, apartment houses had become an important new outlet for capital investment. Some of the most prominent early apartment buildings were located near Ladies Mile and the fashionable quarter, including the Knickerbocker on the southwest corner of Fifth Avenue and Fourteenth Street, the Osborne on Fifth Avenue and Fifty-fourth Street, and the Bradley Apartment House on Fifty-ninth Street between Fifth and Sixth avenues.[29]

DEVELOPMENT: 1879–1893

Once the real estate market gained stability, investment turned in earnest to the development of the fashionable Ladies Mile, where Arnold Constable, A. T. Stewart, and Lake and McCreery started to build additional warehouses for their businesses. This area was proclaimed to control the entire retail trade of New York, in which the leading jewelry, dry goods and fancy goods stores were concentrated.[30] By 1881 it was clear that the pace of house building had fallen far behind the growth of the city's population: massive construction of row houses plus apartments and tenements would have to fill this need. New York also required at least ten new hotels; most of the existing first-class hotels were located far downtown and were always full to capacity. With rapid transit about to become a reality, the region near and above Fifty-ninth Street seemed well suited for this urgently needed development.

The 1880s were years of active development. While the United States was affected by the assassination of President Garfield, crop shortages, the California gold rush, and the railways wars—all of which sent economic tremors throughout the country—New York real estate investment remained immune.[31] With cheap money and reduced costs for materials and labor, brisk building activity began in the mid-1880s, producing the boom of the late 1880s. In fact, discouraged by failures in railway construction and manufacturing, capitalists pushed more and more money into real estate. In 1893 the *Real Estate Record* proclaimed that New York real estate was more stable than stocks or bonds.[32]

The entire period between 1879 and 1893 was affected by the extension of the elevated railroads (figs. 34, 35). Begun as an experiment in 1867, a single car ran between the Battery and Cortlandt Street along Greenwich Avenue. This system was extended piecemeal, until in 1870 it reached Thirty-first Street and Ninth Avenue. Experimentation and further extensions continued throughout the 1870s, and in 1879 the Ninth Avenue El was extended as far north as 155th Street. By 1878 on the East Side the Third Avenue El went as far as 129th Street, and by 1880 the Second Avenue El reached there as well. The upper reaches of Manhattan thus became accessible to the lower parts of the island, strengthening the overall cycle of real estate development.[33]

The *Real Estate Record* had first mentioned in 1877 the relocation of the fashionable quarter above Fifty-ninth Street to Eighty-sixth Street on the east side of Central Park.[34] Until this time it was still believed that although costly investments were occurring on the East Side, they would ultimately move west, surrounding the southern borders of Central Park, and then distribute themselves equally on either side of the park.[35] Instead, the Upper East Side above Fifty-ninth Street became the new fashionable district, producing in the 1890s a millionaires' row along Fifth Avenue. On the west side of the park, however, the pace of development was slower and less secure. Although Edward Clark had begun in 1879 to build the Dakota apartment house and a row of elegant town houses near Central Park and West Seventy-third Street, most of the development on the West

Fig. 34. *Below left.* Third Avenue elevated railway, 1878. Looking north from the Ninth Street station. (Courtesy of the New-York Historical Society, New York City)

Fig. 35. *Below right.* Elevated railway structure being erected on Ninth (now Columbus) Avenue in 1878. Looking east from West Ninety-seventh Street toward Central Park. (Courtesy of the New-York Historical Society, New York City)

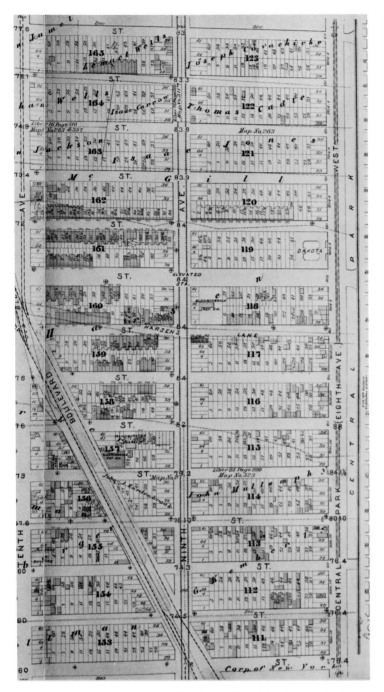

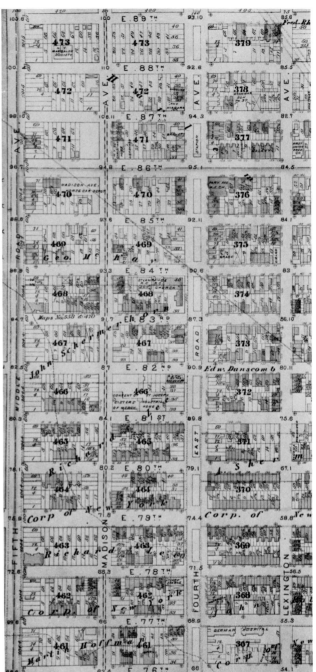

Fig. 36. Robinson Insurance Map of 1885. The Upper West Side. At the time of this street plan, the Dakota apartment house on Seventy-second Street and its companion row houses on Seventy-third Street were the most significant signs of development on the sparsely settled blocks between Eighth and Ninth avenues. The western blocks between Seventy-first and Seventy-third streets, Ninth to Tenth avenues, close to the elevated railway stop at Seventy-second Street, also show some development. (Courtesy of the New York Public Library, New York City)

Fig. 37. Robinson Insurance Map of 1885. The Upper East Side. More developed than the Upper West Side, the Upper East Side boasted rows of town houses located to the east and west of Madison Avenue from Seventy-sixth to Eighty-eighth Street. East of Fourth (Park) Avenue, institutions such as the Normal College, the Seventh Regiment Armory, the New York Foundling Hospital, and Mount Sinai Hospital clustered on land formerly occupied by Hamilton Square. (Courtesy of the New York Public Library, New York City)

Side was sporadic, combining modest row houses with tenements and apartment houses. Even though the West Side was just as well served as the East Side by rapid transit, it lay virtually abandoned (figs. 36, 37). In 1880 the price of land on the West Side was lower than land on the East Side; many of the streets were unpaved, ungraded, and without flagging or sidewalks, and portions of most side streets between Fifty-ninth and 125th streets were not even legally opened. Nevertheless, Clark's important work was followed by others. John D. Crimmins shifted his attention from the new fashionable quarter on the East Side to erect a series of flats in 1879 near Ninth Avenue and Sixty-third Street, and H. H. Cammann focused his activity on tenement construction near Tenth Avenue and Eighty-Second Street. Other developers followed these examples, albeit slowly and sporadically.[36]

It had always been imagined among real estate circles that the great Upper West Side would be the ideal location for fashionable residences. The picturesque locations of both Riverside Drive and Eighth Avenue could not be duplicated elsewhere in Manhattan, and both streets were thought of as being reserved for millionaires' homes. The Boulevard (present-day Broadway above Fifty-ninth Street), regally planned in the 1860s, was set aside for theaters and amusement halls that would never be realized. But across the West Side plateau, clusters of development could be found at each El stop, near Seventy-second, Eighty-first, Ninety-third, 104th, and 125th streets.[37] In 1885, building on the West Side began to gather more momentum.

Phenomenal real estate activity took hold of both the upper east and upper west sides in 1886 and 1887. Trading in property continued to feed a boom stimulated by the availability of cheap money, cheaper materials, and more efficient labor.[38] Still, the most active section of the city for real estate investment lay between Fifteenth and Fifty-ninth streets in an area that the *Real Estate Record* began to refer to as the "amusement section." In this area in 1889, 302 building plans were filed for large and costly structures and another 376 were planned the following year for eight new hotels, several new club buildings, stores, and office buildings.[39]

In 1890 the market once again became restricted, preventing builders from obtaining loans and investors from making new purchases. A lull appeared in all three development districts.[40] The only important real estate transaction to occur in the early 1890s was the proposed improvement of Morningside Heights on the West Side above 110th Street. In 1889 the grounds of the Bloomingdale Asylum, owned by the Society of the City of New York Hospital, was suddenly put up for sale. In 1891 three blocks between 110th and 113th streets along Morningside Drive were sold to the Cathedral of Saint John the Divine, and in 1892 Saint Luke's Hospital acquired the blocks just north of the cathedral's lands. Within a few years, in 1894, Columbia University would acquire the site located between 116th and 120th streets from the Boulevard to Amsterdam Avenue[41] (fig. 38).

These developments would be institutional improvements and spatial compositions that would have their real effect in the twentieth century. By 1893, however, it was apparent throughout real estate circles that new fields must be opened for the builder and the speculator before the boom years of 1886 to 1890 could be repeated. The shrewdest speculators began to retire to the areas below Fifty-ninth Street. Labor troubles in the early 1890s and the tightening of credit had injurious effects on the building market. On the West Side as well, accessible

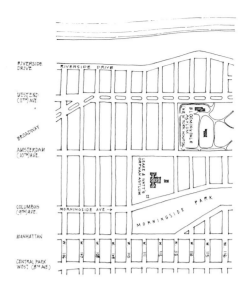

Fig. 38. Morningside Heights. (Redrawn from the Robinson Insurance Map of 1885; courtesy of the New York Public Library, New York City)

yet undeveloped property was held off the market at speculatively high prices.[42]

As public transit only expanded in the latter part of the nineteenth century, New York became an urban site whose boundaries were not reached until the 1890s. Vast new fields for real estate development were opened, and the street plan and the efficiency of travel determined the structure of this nineteenth-century city. New York became a city of parts: a downtown center of business, an amusement and shopping district, and luxury residential areas. In these semiautonomous zones, the bourgeoisie reshaped the city in its own image, expressing the temperament of the economy and market values.

Development of nineteenth-century Manhattan was accomplished with a minimum of public intervention. In 1811 the commissioners' grid plan established the fundamental structure to the land market by rigorously dividing the territory above Fourteenth Street into uniform blocks and lots. Nineteenth-century Manhattan produced no city planner capable of or willing to manage and compose the urban totality. Unlike Haussmann's Paris, Manhattan had no quasipublic credit organization to risk financing construction or an expanded law of expropriation to facilitate the acquisition of land and its subsequent development. Instead, the dynamics of the real estate market and the regulatory framework of the 25- by 100-foot lot turned parcels of land into transferable goods and facilitated the autonomy of individual developers. New Yorkers were in a hurry to exploit the abundance of land above Fourteenth Street, which improvements in transportation increasingly made accessible. Development was an unquestioned value, and nineteenth-century New Yorkers consequently placed few restrictions on the individual developer. Private property was an instrument of growth, and regulatory laws and controls were utilized only to secure a market in which many might venture.[43] This held true until the late 1890s, when the architectural profession began to dream of asserting rational control over such idiosyncratic development.

CHAPTER THREE

LADIES MILE:
THE RISE OF A VICTORIAN
AMUSEMENT DISTRICT

The sweetest thing in life, And no one dare say nay,
On a Saturday afternoon, Is walking down Broadway.
My sisters, thro' the Park And at Long Branch wish to stay,
But I prefer to walk down the festive, gay Broadway.
Last Wednesday afternoon, My cousin Will did say,
Nellie, come along with me, I'll take you down Broadway.
To the theatre comique, To see, Captain Jinks so gay,
Then we'll dine at Delmonico's 'Fore returning down Broadway.

CHORUS:
Walking down Broadway. The festive gay Broadway.
The O.K. thing on Saturday; is walking down Broadway.

Sheet Music, "Walking Down Broadway," lyrics written by W.H. Lingard, arranged by
C.E. Pratt (1868)

In the second half of the nineteenth century, Ladies Mile, the area near Broadway from Fourteenth Street to Twenty-third Street, was the spatial center that distilled the sentiments of New York's cultural and political life (fig. 39). It was a place to go to, to be seen, to promenade, to be entertained, to eat, to converse and—even to protest—and then to retreat from uptown to a quiet, private realm. This procedural space juxtaposed the centers for hotels, theaters, artists' galleries, private clubs, and political assemblies in complex relationship to the city's major focus of entertainment: consuming. Celebrations, gatherings, and public places stimulated the purposes of fashion by which classes were separated, moral codes were preached, and needs were developed in step with the escalating supplies of commodities. The simultaneous juxtaposition of so many special districts was an essential element supporting the fragile network of Ladies Mile.

Fig. 39. Detail of Ladies Mile, Broadway, Four-teenth to Twenty-third Street, from the Jalt and Hoy Map of 1879. (Courtesy of the New York Public Library, New York City)

RESIDENTIAL DISPLACEMENT

No one planned the emergence of this amusement district; it simply appeared in the interstices of the fashionable residential district surrounding Union Square, at first without being recognized, then with minor shifts in appearance until a battle was waged to clear the field of residential holdouts so that commerce could dominate. The rituals of power that commerce commanded required continuous change in fashions, in architectural forms, in spatial location—every item for sale, every notion of style, every concept of desire was kept in constant motion. This became the modern nineteenth-century drama; the double play of exchange between a menacing objective world to be acquired and consumed and a retreating, purely subjective, and compensatory private existence.

The fashionable residence withdrew. By the mid-1840s luxury trade had upseated the fine old town houses along Bleecker and Bond streets, and those along Broadway below Astor Place. Colonnade Row, which united a row of town houses under a giant colonnade of Greek Corinthian columns, was transformed into a hotel in 1844 (see fig. 12), and even fashionable Greenwich Street on the West Side lost its residential status when its elegant town houses were turned into boarding houses or were replaced by warehouses and stores. The location for fashionable districts shifted northward to Union Square and still farther north to Madison Square in the 1850s. Union Square, only a frontier of the city in 1835, was called one decade later the court end of town.[1]

Fashionable families tended to move from one luxury residential neighborhood to another, continuing northward, to avoid the onslaught of commerce. Amos Eno, the future developer of the Fifth Avenue Hotel, was no exception, and his changes of address trace fashion's footsteps. Eno's daughter, Mary Jane Eno Pinchot, born in 1837, remembered living in a house near Battery Park. In 1841 the family moved up to Fourth Street close to Washington Square. But this location was too far from Eno's retail establishment at 14 Broadway, and so the family moved to the Leeman Reid House at 13 Greenwich Street. Mary Eno Pinchot described this house.

It was then [in the mid-1840s] the finest building in the City, and it was considered quite a wonder, and, as I recall, was certainly the finest one I have ever lived in. Mr. Reid . . . had sent to Italy for all the marble used in the house; the baseboards and door casings all were made of the finest Italian marble, and the marble fireplaces in the drawing room were the most beautiful I have ever seen in this country, and I might say I have seen but few that are equal to them. The doors were all of solid mahogany. The gas fixtures were the finest that had ever been brought to this country up to that time, the house had a beautiful, although a not very large garden and as the Croton water was not introduced into it, it depended for its supply of water upon three beautiful white marble cisterns in the garden, which caught the rain water . . . [But] the neighborhood changed rapidly and most of our friends . . . the Grahams, Townsends, deForests, Berghs, Kips, Kerries, LeRoys, Wilmerdings, Whitneys, and others of the old New York families . . . moved away. We remained here until we were surrounded by immigrant boarding houses, and then went uptown to live [in 1853].[2]

Broadway was the only serviceable transportation thoroughfare running north and south. Below Bleecker Street it was completely dedicated to commerce. In 1857, 598 licensed hacks, 4,500 carts, and 190 express wagons plowed down its streets every day.[3] The crush of traffic, along with the ensuing cursing, fighting, abusive horse drivers, clubbing by police, and delays caused by accidents, caused lower Broadway to be considered a nuisance, which expelled the fashionable elite farther northward. Philip Hone reported in his diary in 1850 that:

> The mania for converting Broadway into a street of shops is greater than ever. There is scarcely a block in the whole extent of this fine street of which some part is not in a state of transmutation. Three or four good brick houses on the corner of Broadway and Spring Street have been leveled, I know not for what purpose, shops no doubt. The houses, fine costly edifices, opposite to me, are to make way for a grand concert establishment.[4]

In an 1853 *Putnam's Monthly* it was noted:

> Aristocracy, startled and disgusted with the near approach of plebeian trade which already threatened to lay its insolvent hand upon her mantle, and to come tramping into her silken parlors with its heavy boots and rough attire, fled by dignified degrees up Broadway, lingered for a time in Greenwich-Street, Park Place and Barclay-Street, until at length finding the enemy still persistent, she took a great leap into the wilderness above Bleecker-Street [in the 1830s]. Alas, for the poor lady, every day drives her higher and higher; Twenty-eighth street is now familiar with her presence, and she is already casting her longing eyes still further.[5]

By the late 1840s Union Square was completely residential (fig. 40), surrounded by simple row houses broken here by a church, there by a small hotel.[6] In addition to the three- or four-story small city houses fronting the square, several large town houses and a number of freestanding mansions that occupied more than two city lots appeared. But there never arose the great blocks of apartment houses or the elaborate rows of terrace housing that graced so many streets of European cities. Union Square's history as a residential enclave was brief, for already by 1860 the dramatic march of commerce had begun (figs. 41–45).

Nor was commerce shy about dispersing itself among residential buildings above Seventeenth Street. Up the spine of Broadway, for example, the only mansion of substance was the Peter Goelet residence on the northeast corner of Nineteenth Street (fig. 47). A little farther north, the DePeyster House, built around 1845, stood on the northeast corner of Twenty-first Street and Broadway.[7] In the early 1850s the rest of Broadway, between Seventeenth and Twenty-second streets, was filled with modest houses two or three stories high, most of which had stores in their basement or first floors[8] (see fig. 145).

Fifth Avenue claimed more elegance. In the United States, *Putnam's Monthly* editorialized in 1854, the true development of national taste could be found in private mansions rather than in public buildings, for "here every man is a monarch in his own right, and . . . palaces are built by the people for their own enjoyment and not for the comforts of a prince."[9] Long after commerce had pealed its bell, Fifth Avenue would remain a stronghold for palatial residences. Another writer in the 1850s noted that "Fifth Avenue was the street of aristocracy; the street of blood, the street, as my friend very emphatically said, 'where beauty is displayed, admired, and selected . . .'"[10]

Fig. 40. Residences on Union Square, 1849. (Drawn from information in I.N. Phelps Stokes, *The Iconography of Manhattan*, vol. 3, 1849: 702–705)

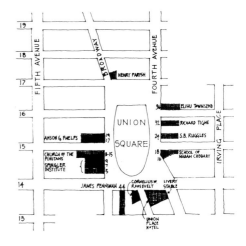

Fig. 41. Union Square, west side, looking north from Fourteenth Street. The circular fountain dating from 1842 celebrated the arrival of Croton water in Manhattan. The Church of the Puritans (1846–1869) by James Renwick was flanked along the west side of the square by town houses owned and developed by the Spingler-Van Buren estate. The Anson Phelps mansion, designed by John B. Snook and Joseph Trench in 1844, stood opposite the church. The blocks to the north above Sixteenth Street were put up for sale as early as 1835 and developed over the next decade into rows of town houses. (Courtesy of the New-York Historical Society, New York City)

Fig. 42. Spingler House, Union Square, ca. 1890. A fashionable hotel in the 1870s, adjacent to the Church of the Puritans on Union Square West, the Spingler House would be replaced by a commercial structure in 1896. The edge of the cast-iron Tiffany building, which replaced the Church of the Puritans in 1869, can be seen to the right. (Courtesy of the New-York Historical Society, New York City)

Fig. 43. Everett House, Union Square. In 1853 the Everett House, a hotel that catered to a literary and theatrical clientele, helped to establish the cultural character of Union Square. Located on the northwest corner of Fourth Avenue and Seventeenth Street, it housed up to 250 guests and in 1882 was the first hotel in the city to install electric lighting. (Courtesy of the New-York Historical Society, New York City)

Fig. 44. Northeast corner of Broadway and Seventeenth Street, 1985. Many commercial successors to the Parish Mansion, including the new Union Place Hotel, would continue to take over this corner until 1893 when lots were merged and the extant six-story commercial structure designed by Detlef Lienau was erected.

Fig. 45. Number 32 Union Square Place, ca. 1903. One of the bow-fronted houses erected by Samuel B. Ruggles in the 1830s, number 32 was the last private residence to remain on the square, and was demolished only in 1904 after the death of its first owner, Richard Tighe, in 1896. Talbot Hamlin, in *Greek Revival Architecture in America*, proclaimed that these houses resembled, in scale, basic form, and detail, Alexander Parris's Boston town houses more than they did the typical New York houses of the 1830s. (Courtesy of the Museum of the City of New York, New York City)

Fig. 46. Union Square, south side, 1849. An elegant row of eight bow-fronted houses east of Union Square between Fifteenth and Sixteenth streets was erected by Samuel B. Ruggles in the late 1830s. On the southeast corner of Fifteenth Street stood Madame Chegary's School for Girls, which would become a second-class hotel in the mid-1860s. South of the square, between Fourth Avenue and Broadway, a small merchant's house and a livery stable stood next to the taller Union Place Hotel. Courtlandt Palmer was an active developer of the row of town houses between Broadway and Union Place on Fourteenth Street. The southwest corner house was built for Cornelius V. Roosevelt and one of the row houses to its right was the James Penniman House. (Courtesy of the Museum of the City of New York, New York City)

Fig. 47. Peter Goelet's mansion, northeast corner of Broadway and Nineteenth Street. The four-story structure became famous as a veritable *rus in urbe*. Goelet kept his garden stocked with animals, including peacocks, long after this part of Broadway had become commercial. Constructed some time before 1853, it stood on this site until 1897 when it was replaced by a still existing eight-story warehouse designed by John B. Snook. (Courtesy of the Museum of the City of New York, New York City)

Elegant town houses already adorned the north side of Washington Square in the 1830s and reached up to Murray Hill in the 1840s. Far above this area, on Fifth Avenue and Thirty-seventh Street, a Gothic Revival house, the surburban Waddell villa, stood enclosed in a salubrious garden, reminding the visitor of the rural conditions of most of northern Manhattan (fig. 48). It would be gone by the 1850s. Residences attracted churches in close succession. Two churches were built below Fourteenth Street: the Episcopal Church of the Ascension at the northwest corner of Tenth Street and Fifth Avenue in 1841, and the First Presbyterian Church on the northwest corner of Eleventh Street and Fifth Avenue in 1846. By 1849 the Palladian residence designed for Richard K. Haight stood on the southeast corner of Fifteenth Street, and Colonel Herman Thorne's freestanding brownstone mansion appeared at 22 West Sixteenth Street, a few feet from Fifth Avenue. Perhaps the earliest mansard roof in New York was introduced around 1850 in the Hart M. Schiff House on the southwest corner of Tenth Street and Fifth Avenue. Architectural historians have pointed out that this so-called French chateau with its squat mansard roof, designed by Detlef Lienau, created a sensation in New York and mansard roofs quickly became a dominant architectural feature.[11]

Two restrained mansions were built in the 1850s on the east side of Fifth Avenue between Thirty-third and Thirty-fourth streets[12] (fig. 49). William B. Astor II built his plain four-story brownstone in 1856 on the northern corner; and opposite a garden to the south, John J. Astor III erected a three-story brick house with brownstone trim and mansard roof in 1859 (fig. 50). If this was too much restraint for the tastes of aristocratic New Yorkers, for a brief decade between 1854 and 1864 relief could be found on the northeast corner of Thirty-fourth Street and Fifth Avenue where the sarsaparilla king, Samuel B. Townsend, constructed one of the ugliest brownstone mansions in New York.

Standing like a ruin amid the increasingly urban fabric, Fifth Avenue from Washington Square to Twenty-Second Street would continue to be a sanctuary for wealthy families such as the Belmonts, Lenoxes, Talbots, Taylors, and Minturns, all firmly settled in their spacious homes until an anomalous condition arose in the mid-1870s. One by one, these stately old mansions were slowly renovated as stores (fig. 51). The *Real Estate Record* complained, however, that none of these converted residences could compete favorably with the modern department stores already established along Ladies Mile. Conservative tastes had kept these families wedded to lower Fifth Avenue, and conservative business practices regrettably influenced their decisions to avoid the more economical route by tearing down the old structures and rebuilding anew.[13]

On the other side of Ladies Mile, along Fourth Avenue up to Madison

Fig. 48. Exterior view and plans of the Waddell villa. The house, located on the northwest corner of Fifth Avenue and Thirty-seventh Street and designed by Alexander Jackson Davis, stood from 1844 to 1857. (Courtesy of the Museum of the City of New York, New York City)

Fig. 49. William B. Astor II's house, Thirty-fourth Street and Fifth Avenue. Built in 1856, this simple brick house with modest brownstone trim had a few windows looking out onto the adjoining garden. Across Thirty-fourth Street, the corner of the Stewart mansion is visible. (Courtesy of the Museum of the City of New York, New York City)

Fig. 50. West side of Fifth Avenue, 1885. Looking south from Thirty-fourth to Twenty-ninth Street on the occasion of the funeral parade of Ulysses S. Grant. The mansard roof and shrouded windows belong to John J. Astor III's house, separated by the garden from William B. Astor's house. South of the William B. Astor mansion are blocks of identical brownstone row houses terminated by the Fifth Avenue Dutch Reformed Church. Both Astor houses were demolished in the early 1890s and replaced by the Astoria Hotel. (Courtesy of the New-York Historical Society, New York City)

Square, residential buildings were mixed in with commercial ones. Elegant free-standing mansions faced both sides of Fourth Avenue between Eighteenth and Nineteenth streets in the 1840s, but these areas were soon invaded by commerce when the Clarendon Residential Hotel opened its doors in 1846 on the southeast corner of Eighteenth Street (fig. 52). And Madison Square, finally cleared of squatters, somewhat improved, and opened officially for promenading in 1844, would become a magnet for aristocratic New Yorkers. Aside from official announcements, however, the square's improvements consisted of a few dirt paths leading to the surrounding streets and avenues, and the erection of a simple wooden fence around its perimeter.[14] The Madison Square Presbyterian Church was the first indication that residential buildings would follow when it was constructed in 1853 at Twenty-fourth Street and Madison Avenue[15] (fig. 53). By the late 1850s the homes of New York's first families could be found on all the adjacent side streets between Fourth and Sixth avenues.

To the west of the square, between Twenty-third and Twenty-fourth streets, Amos Richard Eno's legendary Fifth Avenue Hotel, the design of which is attributed to Griffith Thomas and Son, was constructed between 1856 and 1858. In order to keep a watchful eye on the construction of his hotel, Eno moved his family to a house at 26 East Twenty-third Street, overlooking Madison Square Park, in 1856. His daughter Mary Eno Pinchot recalled:

> I had, of course, a very gay winter [sometime between 1856 and 1864], and as in those days, society was very much less formal than it afterwards became, we young people could do very much as we liked. It was then the custom to make visits in the evenings, and our home was the resort for many young men, so that frequently out of season we used to send for our neighborhood girl friends and impromptu dances often took place. . . . We had many delightful families living on our square and nearby, and we were very social. . . . Our friends and neighbors were the Corlies, Odells, Barlows, Schermerhorns, Leupps, Townsends, Lanes, Appletons, Colgates,

Fig. 51. Fifth Avenue, west side between Twenty-sixth and Twenty-seventh streets, ca. 1881. Two ornately trimmed brownstone houses in the process of being transformed into commercial establishments. Mrs. Schuyler Van Rensselaer remembered that "No one much younger than I can realize what a wail went up in New York when the first shop window was cut on [Fifth Avenue in 1870] . . . if I am not mistaken, at the south-east corner of 17th Street. . . . I, too, put ashes on my head, and believed that what Mr. Wegg would have called the 'decline and fall of New York' had certainly set in." (Courtesy of the New-York Historical Society, New York City)

Fig. 52. East side of Fourth Avenue at Eighteenth Street, ca. 1906. In the right foreground is the Clarendon Residential Hotel of 1846, an early intrusion in an area of freestanding mansions. Opposite, on the northeast corner of Eighteenth Street, is the Florence Apartment House of 1878, designed to accommodate families that preferred the traditional style of housekeeping, young marrieds who wanted minimum household responsibilities, and bachelors. Next to the Florence stands the twelve-story Parker Building, which replaced two freestanding mansions. (Courtesy of the New-York Historical Society, New York City)

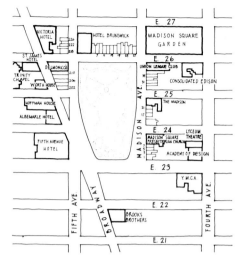

Fig. 53. Madison Square, ca. 1879. The first residence, 37 Madison Square East, was built by the metalwork industrialist, James Stokes, in 1856. His neighbors soon included the New York state senator William Laimberr, who lived at number 19, the Bellevue Hospital gynecologist Dr. Edmund Peaslee, at number 25, and a fine row of brownstone residences to the north and south. Notable residents on the north side of the square included the Iselin family, Mrs. Morgan, a collector of bric-a-brac, and the bankers William and John O'Brien. (Courtesy of the New York Public Library, New York City)

Chases, Cuttings, Fields and others. . . . On warm nights it was the custom to sit upon the balconies of our homes, to walk up and down the side walk in front, and our balcony was the great resort for the young men of the neighborhood. The City at that time did not extend much further than Murray Hill, and in my horseback rides, which I frequently took, attended by a coachman behind, and in which I was joined by my friends, we used to go to Central Park across lots in the upper part of the city.[16]

Eno's Fifth Avenue Hotel (figs. 54–56), located so far above the crowded areas of Manhattan and invading the exclusive preserve of luxury town houses, was called Eno's Folly. Its savvy manager, Paran Stevens, who leased the hotel until its demolition in 1908, quickly reversed this slanderous joke by initiating a late supper, a fourth meal, to lure patrons to this remote spot. Other luxuries such as a fireplace in every bedroom, many private bathrooms, and lavishly decorated public rooms helped make this hotel, which housed 800 guests, an instant success. Four hundred servants attended the clientele and fifty coaches and carriages stood ready to ferry guests about the city. Outstanding among all the novelties was the introduction of an Otis passenger elevator. One observer noted: ''You need not weary yourself with climbing; the lift, like the streetcar, is always on the move, always going up , except when it is coming down, which is the time you want to go up.''[17]

Amazingly, The Fifth Avenue Hotel failed to take advantage of its magnificent site; its portico set at the point where Broadway crossed Fifth Avenue was a restrained statement, and its facade was commanding only because of its monu-

Fig. 54. Fifth Avenue Hotel, at the intersection of Fifth Avenue, Broadway, and Twenty-third Street, ca. 1891. The six-story, white marble-faced hotel, built by Amos Eno in 1856, was a ''palace for the people.'' Its Corinthian-style portico, facing Madison Square, was flanked by luxury stores such as Knox's (milliners), Maillard's Confectionaries, and Eno's own Second National Bank. Costing approximately $2 million to build, it occupied eighteen city lots. (Courtesy of the New-York Historical Society, New York City)

Fig. 55. Dining Room, Fifth Avenue Hotel. (From *Harper's Weekly* 3, October 1, 1859: 632.) The imposing interior (84 by 64 feet) was furnished by William Washburn of Boston in the popular French fashion. By using round tables and minimizing the standing space for waiters, the dining room could seat 300. Junius Browne commented in 1869 that "ill-breeding never appears so ill as when it is heavily gilded; and the well-fed guests of the Fifth Avenue [Hotel] are often amused, and then disgusted, with the pretentious commonality they cannot escape." (Courtesy of the New-York Historical Society, New York City)

Fig. 56. Ladies Drawing Room, Fifth Avenue Hotel. (From *Harper's Weekly* 3, October 1, 1859: 663.) The drawing rooms were filled with gilt wood, rich crimson or green curtains, and fancy patterned carpets. *Harper's* noted that a person with dirty boots in one evening could ruin a carpet worth $50,000, and with a muddy coat destroy a light-blue couch or easy chair costing as much. Junius Browne remarked that while talk on the first floor was dominated by the closing rate of gold and the next bulletin from Wall Street, the second-floor parlors were where the opposite sex held sway. (Courtesy of the New-York Historical Society, New York City)

Fig. 57. Madison Square Garden, the former New York and Harlem Railroad and Passenger Depot at Fourth Avenue, Twenty-sixth to Twenty-seventh streets. Until the Grand Central Terminal opened in 1871, travelers from the north arrived at this depot, demolished in 1889. (Courtesy of the Museum of the City of New York, New York City)

Fig. 58. Madison Square Garden viewed from Madison Square Park, at Twenty-sixth Street and Fourth Avenue, ca. 1893. The second Garden, attributed to Stanford White, contained a concert hall, an amphitheater, a theater, a roof garden, a restaurant, and a row of shops. Its central tower rose 300 feet above the sidewalk and dominated the panorama from Madison Square. It was demolished in 1925. (Courtesy of the New-York Historical Society, New York City)

mental size. Broadway, the only diagonal thoroughfare to traverse Manhattan, was at this location particularly spectacular, obliquely joining the residential enclave of Union Square with that of Madison Square. Yet, this so-called Renaissance marble palazzo was little more than an ornamented box that referred more to the rectangularity of the gridiron street plan than to its imposing site.[18] Nevertheless, within a few years after its opening, it was "an undisputed fact that the hotel's register contained the names of more celebrities than those of any other hotel in this or any other country."[19]

The architectural historian John Summerson has claimed that the railroad created the grand hotels of Victorian London, and indeed the railroad was instrumental in developing the vicinity of Ladies Mile as a hotel center.[20] But railroad depots would fare no better than luxury hotels since no elaborate structure, such as the Greek Revival portico of Euston Station in London, designed by Philip Hardwick, ever distinguished Ladies Mile. Americans were more utilitarian. The Madison Square depot was simply a transfer point for those arriving in the city or traveling northward into the outreaches of Manhattan, Harlem, and beyond. The Common Council had empowered the New York and Harlem Railroad Company in 1831 to run horsecars from the Astor House, opposite City Hall Park, up the Bowery to Fourth Avenue and on to Twenty-sixth Street, where a huge, albeit plain, passenger depot, freight shed, and stables were erected on the block between Fourth and Madison avenues (fig. 57). From this point horses pulled large cars to the openings of the railroad tunnel between Thirty-third and Forty-second streets on Fourth Avenue, where steam locomotives took over, transporting goods and passengers to Harlem. When Grand Central Station, designed by John B. Snook, opened in 1871, the Twenty-sixth Street depot was abandoned. P. T. Barnum leased the structure and rebuilt the sheds to house the immense Roman Hippodrome. In 1875 the site became Gilmore's Garden, and later it became the home of the great revivalist Mr. Moody and the bandmaster Mr. Sankey. In 1879 the Vanderbilt family reasserted control over the property and opened the first Madison Square Garden where boxing matches, athletic tournaments, and even masked balls were held. In time this Garden would be replaced by a second magnificent structure, designed by Stanford White in 1889[21] (fig. 58).

DEVELOPMENT OF A HOTEL DISTRICT

One of the most important reasons for the success of Ladies Mile was the early development of the area as a first-class hotel district (fig. 59). Union Square achieved preeminence as a center for hotels in the early 1850s. Opposite Grace Church at Broadway and Eleventh Street stood the Saint Denis Hotel. Designed by James Renwick, it offered a refined and homelike atmosphere in its well-appointed reading and colonial dining rooms. Alexander Graham Bell first publicly demonstrated his new invention, the telephone, from this hotel, speaking with his assistant in Brooklyn, two miles away.[22] The Clarendon, the most distinguished hotel, just north of the square, promised its patrons Croton water and huge bathtubs in every suite (see fig. 52). Right around the corner on Irving Place and Sixteenth Street could be found the Westminster Hotel, and more than one hotel named Union Square or Union Place bordered the square (fig. 60).

Several hotels that were established along Ladies Mile during the 1850s con-

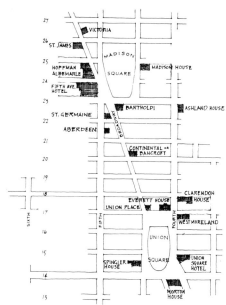

Fig. 59. Hotels on Ladies Mile.

Fig. 60. Union Square Hotel, Union Place and Fifteenth Street, ca. 1890. Several hotels fronting Union Square adopted the name Union Place, including the Union Place Hotel on the south side of Fourteenth Street, known as the Morton House in the 1880s, and the second Union Place Hotel, which for a time could be found in the old Parish mansion on the northeast corner of Broadway and Seventeenth Street. (Courtesy of the New York Public Library, New York City)

Fig. 61. Broadway, east side, looking north from Twentieth Street, ca. 1909. The Bancroft House Hotel (ca. 1858–1912), owned by the interior designer Gustave Herter, was located on the northeast corner of Twenty-first Street. The four-story brick building, which combined five lots on the block to the north, also dates from the 1850s, and housed many different commercial enterprises until it was demolished in 1916. The block beyond above Twenty-first Street shows the corner of the still-existing three-story DePeyster Home, built about 1845, and on the southeast corner of Twenty-second Street, the five-story Brooks Brothers store (1884–1937) stood, covered with advertising. Designed by Charles Haight, the store occupied the site in which the old Park Theatre had once stood before it burned down in 1882. (Courtesy of the New-York Historical Society, New York City)

Fig. 62. The Hotel Bartholdi, on the southeast corner of Broadway and Twenty-third Street, seen from the Fifth Avenue Hotel, ca. 1885. In the 1880s the busy intersection pictured accommodated thirty-three omnibus lines and five streetcar lines, as well as many carriages and wagons. (Courtesy of the New-York Historical Society, New York City)

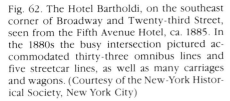

tinued to offer first- and second-class accommodations throughout the latter half of the nineteenth century. At the southwest corner of Broadway and East Twenty-first Street, the Madison Square Hotel, built in the late 1850s, was later known as the Aberdeen Hotel and was not demolished until 1924 (see fig. 98). Opposite the Madison Square Hotel, on the east side of Broadway, a four-story brick structure, the Bancroft House Hotel (fig. 61), was also flourishing in 1859, as was the Hotel Saint Germain on the north side of East Twenty-second Street, between Fifth Avenue and Broadway. The only latecomer to Ladies Mile was the seven-story Hotel Bartholdi, which graced the corner of Twenty-third Street on the east side of Broadway sometime by the late 1870s (fig. 62).

With the presence of the railroad depot and the Fifth Avenue Hotel, Madison Square soon attracted other hotels and retail establishments. The Albemarle (fig. 63), a refined hotel, replaced a stone yard on the corner of Twenty-fourth Street and Broadway in 1860, and in 1864, in spite of the austerity imposed by the Civil War, the white marble Hoffman House, accommodating nearly 400 guests, opened its doors on the adjacent property at the corner of Twenty-fifth Street (fig. 64). For years election results were posted in the triangle between Fifth Avenue and Broadway, which lay opposite these two hotels. An 1866 guide to New York[23] noted that these hotels were "central locations for all Eastern and Northern railroads, and form a most eligible and convenient stopping-place for travelers."

The Fifth Avenue Hotel, the Hoffman House, and the Albermarle, all opposite Madison Square, had been joined in the 1870s by the Hotel Brunswick, which stood on Fifth Avenue between Twenty-sixth and Twenty-seventh streets. Known for its superior cuisine, this hotel soon became associated with the "coaching set," the members of the popular Coaching Club who every spring and fall paraded from the hotel up to Central Park and on to Harlem before returning to the Brunswick for a festive dinner of fowl and various game accompanied with rare vintage wines.[24] The overblown, iron-clad Gilsey House, at

Twenty-ninth Street and Broadway, opened in 1870 and had a "very wealthy, and extremely particular clientele, especially army and navy officers, congressmen, coal operators and mine operators, and railroad magnates"[25] (see fig. 24).

The modern American hotel, which is claimed to have been an original architectural contribution of nineteenth-century America, far from offering an aesthetic embellishment to the streets of New York, was really a labor-saving contrivance—a monster structure, many stories in height, covering numerous city lots, and containing hundreds of rooms. Mrs. H. B. Plunkett, writing in 1873, declared that the American hotel "is a massive pile of marble, and brick, and iron, with a handsome architectural front, and so vermiculated at stated and well chosen intervals, with water-pipes and steam-pipes, gas-pipes, speaking-tubes and nerve-like bell-wires, that, viewed as a whole, it is like a living organism. It certainly constitutes a marvelous mechanical monument. . ." [to a host of industrial inventors.][26] Emphasizing efficiency, these buildings were adapted to the requirements of the moment. Although their interiors may have offered oases of luxury in the midst of chaotic American city streets, during the latter half of the nine-

Fig. 63. Broadway, west side, between Twenty-fourth and Twenty-fifth streets, ca. 1887. The Albemarle Hotel erected in 1860, can be seen on the left, and the Hoffman House, designed by John B. Snook in 1864, stands on its right. Moses King's 1893 *Handbook of New York* noted that the Albemarle was a quiet and exclusive place, with many permanent residents and foreigners of distinction. (Courtesy of the New-York Historical Society, New York City)

Fig. 64. Hoffman House, interior. (From an advertisement for Hoffman House Cigars.) The hotel was noted for its banquet hall, its excellent cuisine, and Bouguereau's notorious painting, *Nymphs and Satyrs*, which hung in the bar. (Courtesy of the Bella C. Landauer Collection, New-York Historical Society, New York City)

teenth century, hotel entrepreneurs placed a higher value on comfort, convenience, and interior luxury than on architectural appearance.

Indeed, many a European critic of American architecture in the 1870s and 1880s noted that it was perhaps America's proficiency in the mechanical arts that had stifled its artistic progress. *The Builder* in 1885 quoted the criticism of an English visitor to New York, noting that:

> An American has a great deal to do, and is always in too great a hurry to do it, ever to submit to the long, patient study and discipline requisite to master any one style of architecture permanently. Still less is he likely to submit to that amount of self-negation which is indispensable if a man would attempt to be original. Why should he try to proportion every part

harmoniously, or to apply each ornament appropriately? Why submit to all this drudgery when Classic pillars and Gothic pinnacles stuck on ad libitum get over all difficulties and satisfy himself and his employees? The perfection of art, in an American's eyes, would be attained by the invention of a self-acting machine, which should produce plans of cities and designs of Gothic churches or Classic municipal buildings at so much per square foot super., and so save trouble and thought.[27]

Perhaps the architect John Kellum typifies this go-ahead American architecture. A critic wrote in 1879 that Kellum never "for a moment regarded his latter-day vocation as other than a trade by which to make money—particularly where large iron constructions were concerned—out of wealthy people who fancied themselves architectural amateurs, and found comfort in playing the role of art-patron to one whose mental and educational equipments, being inferior to their own, prevented any jar to their amour propre."[28]

In 1869 it was announced that A. T. Stewart, the department store king, would dedicate more than $6 million for the creation of two working-class hotels. Far over on the west side of Fourth Avenue between Thirty-second and Thirty-third streets, opposite the Fourth Avenue Passenger Railroad Depot, Stewart had already begun excavation for the first hotel for workingwomen. Designed by John Kellum, the architect of many of Stewart's lavish developments, this iron-clad Women's Hotel was a baroque addition to the rectangular hotel boxes of earlier years. An interior courtyard, 94 by 116 feet, was to contain an elegant fountain full of goldfish. The kitchens and laundries were located in the back of the structure, with dining rooms, lecture and concert halls, reading rooms, and libraries above. Two kinds of sleeping rooms were proposed: rooms that measured 16 by 18 feet to be shared by two sisters or two friends, and smaller rooms, 8 by 9 feet for single women. *Appleton's Journal* proclaimed that Mr. Stewart's so-called club for mutual economy would foster individuality and independence for more than 1,500 workingwomen, at a fixed cost of $2.00 per day.[29]

Hit by the depression of 1873, this structure was left standing vacant throughout the 1870s. Stewart died in 1876, before his project could advance, but thousands of workingwomen and many members of the growing feminist movement continued to express great interest in building the hotel, and Stewart's executor, Henry Hilton, announced plans that the project would be completed. Opening on April 2, 1878, the hotel charged extremely high rates ($6.00 per week for minimum room and board) and imposed strict rules (no visitors were allowed in any of the rooms, no extra furniture or decorations were allowed, and all guests were required to patronize the hotel's laundry). Custom-made black walnut furniture in the Eastlake mode (too massive for the small bedrooms) and more than $300,000 worth of paintings and sculpture from Stewart's personal collection made it apparent at the outset that this hotel was not planned as a home for working-class women. Indeed, the philanthropic adventure lasted only fifty-three days. On May 23, Hilton announced that the charity had failed and that the hotel would be remodeled and reopened in June. The renamed Park Avenue Hotel opened as planned and remained for four decades one of the most popular hotels in New York (fig. 65).

Hilton claimed that the Women's Hotel never had had more than fifty guests at any one time, that the daily loss was somewhere near $500, and that "a hotel

Fig. 65. Park Avenue Hotel, east side of Park Avenue, between Thirty-second and Thirty-third streets, ca. 1895. John Kellum displayed his ironmonger's skill in his 1869 design of this hotel. Six stories tall, its highly ornamented mechanical-looking, iron-clad facade culminated in a mansard roof and was further embellished by a giant two-story portico. Twenty-four plate-glass-fronted stores lined the sidewalk on the first floor. It was noted in 1878 that ''the thousand and more lighted windows gave the hotel the appearance from a little distance of a vulgar fairy palace.'' (Courtesy of the New York Public Library, New York City)

Fig. 66. Buckingham Hotel, designed by William Field in 1876 and located on the east side of Fifth Avenue and Fiftieth Street, ca. 1877. Built while Saint Patrick's Cathedral was still under construction, the seven-story hotel took up one small Fifth Avenue lot but extended south through to Forty-ninth Street. (Courtesy of the New-York Historical Society, New York City)

Fig. 67. Windsor Hotel, ca. 1886. In the midst of rows of brownstone town houses, the Windsor Hotel fronted the east side of Fifth Avenue between Forty-sixth and Forty-seventh streets. It was ridiculed in the early 1880s for having located so far above the fashionable hotel district near Ladies Mile. Shortly after it opened, the powerful financier Jay Gould moved into a town house on the northeast corner of Forty-seventh Street opposite the Windsor and began to entertain his Wall Street friends at the hotel. Built in 1880 by an unknown architect, it was destroyed by fire in 1901. (Courtesy of the New-York Historical Society, New York City)

on an extensive scale for women is an impossibility. Women want to associate with the other sex and the restrictions imposed upon them in this house were so severe that many who would gladly have taken advantage of its benefits declined for that reason.''[30] A storm of protest arose from newspapers and militant feminists. A few days before the Park Avenue Hotel opened, a meeting was organized at Cooper Institute at which the feminists declared that at no time had the hotel been opened for working-class women; the women employed by Stewart's stores could not even afford the high prices of the rooms. Pledges were signed not to purchase as much as a spool of thread from A. T. Stewart and Company for a period of five years. The boycott was successful: thousands of patrons shifted their accounts to other stores, and Stewart's shrinking retail trade forced the liquidation of the firm four years later. The Tenth Street structure stood vacant for several years until it was purchased by Wanamaker Brothers in the 1890s. (It burned down in 1956.) The downtown store (of which the building is extant), opposite City Hall, was converted into offices in the 1880s, and rented to the municipal government.

While most of the new hotel construction from the 1840s to the 1870s was occurring in close proximity to Ladies Mile, new events were pushing the hotel district northward. As early as the 1870s, some hotels had already made a pioneering effort to move into the frontier regions of the city. The Buckingham Hotel, designed by architect William Field and primarily a residential hotel, led the way when it opened its doors in 1876 on the east side of Fifth Avenue and Fiftieth Street (fig. 66). Several moderately rated hotels, moreover, took advantage of the new Grand Central Terminal, which had opened on Forty-second Street in 1871. The Grand Union Hotel stood opposite the terminal, and one block away at Forty-second Street and Fifth Avenue, the Bristol Hotel attracted new visitors to the city. Farther west, the Rossmore and Saint Cloud hotels adorned the intersection of Broadway and Forty-second Street. When the deluxe Windsor Hotel was

Fig. 68. The Savoy Hotel, designed by William Hume, and the New Netherland Hotel, designed by Ralph S. Townsend, Fifth Avenue and Fifty-ninth Street, ca. 1893. These new hotels opened in 1892, announcing the decline of Ladies Mile as the fashionable hotel district. Moses King's *Handbook of New York* declared in 1893 that "the great hotel district is between Twenty-third and Fifty-ninth streets, and Fourth and Seventh avenues. There are admirable hotels outside these limits, as in Union Square; in Broadway, below 14th Street; and in Fifth Avenue, between Twenty-third Street and Washington Square and elsewhere; but they are few in number and are overshadowed by their modern rivals up-town." (Courtesy of the Museum of the City of New York, New York City)

ready for occupants in 1880 (located on Fifth Avenue between Forty-sixth and Forty-seventh streets), it was the subject of much ridicule, for who could imagine the day when a location so far north would ever be really fashionable (fig. 67)? Yet it would not be long before Fifty-ninth Street would become the new focus for luxury hotels, when the Plaza (1891), the New Netherland (1892), and the Savoy (1892) hotels looked out on the prospect of Central Park in the early 1890s (fig. 68). Just as Union and Madison squares had provided the focus for luxury hotels in the 1850s, Central Park would determine the new fashionable quarter in the late 1890s, bringing with it the retail trade from lower Manhattan.[31]

THE THEATER DISTRICT

Beyond Ladies Mile, where Broadway and Fifth Avenue merged opposite Madison Square, the beginnings of a new entertainment district appeared as early as 1853 with the opening of Franconi's Hippodrome (fig. 69). Although it operated for only two seasons in a two-story structure topped by an elaborate canvas tent and sported two octagonal towers 30 feet high, nearly 10,000 spectators watched chariot and ostrich races, dancing horses, and the famous touring Course des Singes—a pony race with monkeys for jockeys. Each program concluded with a pageant called the Field of the Cloth of Gold in which more than 200 actors reenacted a tournament of knights. In 1854 Amos Eno began to construct what would become the famous Fifth Avenue Hotel, demolishing the Hippodrome. Places for mass entertainment did not disappear, however. Adjacent to the hotel, the Fifth Avenue Opera House would become the home for the popular Christy Minstrels, burlesque shows, and light comedies throughout the 1860s until it burned down in 1873.[32]

Americans seemed to prefer novelty in their entertainment, and novelty lent itself to elaborate structures. At the same time as the Hippodrome was drawing eager crowds uptown, the Crystal Palace opened for a few seasons in 1853 on the site of present-day Bryant Park (see fig. 3). The competition among architects

Fig. 69. Franconi's Hippodrome, 1853, northeast corner of Broadway and Twenty-third Street, opposite Madison Square. With turreted abutments and a green-and-white striped tent, this fanciful hippodrome became the site for steeplechases, stag hunts, "Olympic games," and aerial flights. (Courtesy of the Theatre Collection, the Museum of the City of New York, New York City)

to design the first large-scale cast-iron and glass construction in New York was keen. Sir Joseph Paxton sent plans that proved unsuitable for the site; Andrew Jackson Downing, Leopold Eidlitz, James Bogardus, and Mr. Adams all offered other remarkable schemes, but the association of private speculators that sponsored the development selected the plans of the entrepreneurs Carstensen and Gildermeister[33] (figs. 70, 71). The Crystal Palace opened with the Exhibition of the Industry of All Nations. Never a profitable venture, until it burned down in 1858 it offered the city a spectacular array of fairs, marching military bands, grand choruses, and balls accompanied with a massive organ.[34] Although contemporaries complained that its site was too close to the massive granite walls of the Croton Reservoir, which dwarfed and crushed the building's fine dimensions, and that it stood in the midst of shanties, the Crystal Palace was viewed as a triumph of American mechanical ingenuity.

Fairs, circuses, and burlesque shows seemed to inspire architectural fantasies not always found in legitimate theaters. At the opposite end of Ladies Mile a more cultured note was struck in 1854, heralding the grand future of a new entertainment district. The Academy of Music, designed by Alexander Saeltzer

Fig. 70. Bird's-eye view of the Crystal Palace, New York 1853. Based on a rectangular octagon and surmounted by a Greek cross, George Carstensen and Charles Gildermeister's winning design featured a 100-foot-span dome that rose 183 feet at its crown. Each corner was marked by a 76-foot-high octagonal spire. The dome was the largest and one of the few to be built in America at this time and it stirred the pride of New Yorkers. The external walls were of cast-iron framing and panel work filled with vitrified translucent glass. (Courtesy of the New-York Historical Society, New York City)

(fig. 72), and paid for by private subscription, was located close to the residences of its fashionable audience on the north side of Fourteenth Street and the east side of Irving Place. A critic of the day wrote just before its opening that:

> the new opera house was to be a veritable academy of music, an educational institution. Not only was fashionable society to have a place in which to display and disport itself, but popular taste and popular knowledge were to be cultivated. To this end, the auditorium was three times as commodious as that of the Astor Place Opera House, and the low prices which had been prevalent only at Niblo's, Burton's, and Castle Garden [places of popular entertainment] were to be the rule. . . .[35]

Grand opera, then as today, was a social event, a rendezvous for the wealthy, a place to ostentatiously display jewels, costumes, and daughters, and a way to further social ambitions. Why was it housed in such staid structures? Evolving from the settings for baroque court entertainment, the Italian plan for opera houses had been well established by the eighteenth century: a horseshoe-shaped auditorium with tiers of boxes rising vertically, one above the other, with a small gallery squeezed in at the top. In the nineteenth century this basic form was elaborated on, as the European bourgeoisie demanded opulent entertainment, elegant box structures, grand box-foyers, multiple lobbies, salons, and

Fig. 71. Interior of the Crystal Palace, ca. 1852. The interior, designed by artist Henry Greenough, burst with colors; the cast-iron members were painted buff or cream with tints of vermilion, garnet, sky-blue, orange and gold. Divided by two naves, the ground floor was further subdivided into aisles and display compartments by 190 cast-iron columns that supported the gallery above. (Courtesy of the New-York Historical Society, New York City)

Fig. 72. The first Academy of Music, looking east on Fourteenth Street toward the northeast corner of Irving Place. When it opened in 1854, the Academy seated 4,600 people and its stage was among the largest in America. Its plush interior, however, when compared to European opera houses, was as rudimentary as its exterior. It included only a small number of private boxes—a source of constant complaint. The Academy was rebuilt in 1866 and demolished in 1926. (Courtesy of the New York Public Library, New York City)

dress-circle promenades.³⁶ Americans had nothing so magnificent to offer. Still linked theatrically to England, America had no opera company, no grand civic theaters, hence no elaborate opera houses to rival its European counterparts. At a time when every European municipality of reasonable stature was building grand civic opera houses, America still clung to the formal and ordered theaters of the early nineteenth century. Perhaps this prejudice against grand playhouses stemmed from America's Puritan inheritance.

Greek Revival simplicity had set the theme for early American theaters, and its spartan nature still influenced theater design until the 1880s. America's first permanent playhouse, the Park Theatre (originally built in 1795, but redesigned several times, the last by Hugh Reinagle in 1821),³⁷ exemplified such modest designs, offering an exterior that was simple to the point of austerity (fig. 73). An early English visitor to the theater in October of 1821 remarked that:

Fig. 73. Park Theatre, Park Row north of Ann Street, ca. 1821. One of the several architects to redesign the staid theater, Hugh Reinagle covered its facade with an oil cement material he invented to imitate the smooth finish of brownstone. (Courtesy of the Theatre Collection, Museum of the City of New York)

> The Park . . . I found to be about the size of Portman Square, but a shape defying any geometrical term to convey the form of it. It had been surrounded by a wooden, unpainted rough fence, but a storm . . . had prostrated the larger portion, together with some fine old button-wood trees . . . and the little grass the cows and pigs allowed to remain was checkered o'er by the short cuts to the different streets in the neighborhood. The exterior of the theatre was the most prison-like place I have ever seen appropriated to such a purpose . . . The house was excessively dark; oil, of course, was then used, in common Liverpool lamps, ten or twelve of which were placed in a large sheet-iron hoop, painted green, hanging from the ceiling, in the centre, and one, half the size, on each side of the stage. The front of the boxes was decorated, if it could be so called with on continuous American ensign . . . the seats were covered with green baize, and the back of the boxes with whitewash, and the iron columns which supported them covered with burnished gold! and looking as if they had no business there . . .³⁸

In 1845, after twenty-five years of operation, the Park Theatre again was criticized by the great Shakespearian editor Richard G. White.

> Its boxes were like pens for beasts. Across them were stretched benches consisting of a mere board covered with faded red moreen, a narrower board, shoulder high, being stretched behind to serve for a back . . . These sybaritic enclosures were kept under lock and key by a fee-expecting creature who was always half drunk except when he was wholly drunk. The pit . . . was in the Park Theatre hardly superior to that in which the Jacquerie of old stood upon the base ground (par terre) and thus gave the place its French name. The floor was dirty and broken into holes; the seats were bare, backless benches. Women were never seen in the pit, and, although the excellence of position . . . and the cheapness of admission . . . took gentlemen there, few went there who could afford to study comfort and luxury in their amusements. The place was pervaded with evil smells; and not uncommonly in the midst of a performance, rats ran out of the holes in the floor and across into the orchestra. This delectable place was approached by a long underground passage with bare whitewashed walls, dimly lighted except at a sort of booth, at which vile fluids and viler solids were sold . . .[39]

It was this combination of crude conditions and disreputable patrons that the Academy of Music was intended to uplift and educate. As early as 1833 the first National Opera House was constructed without the popular pit, and the price of tickets was raised considerably in order to eliminate the attendance of rowdy people. A sloping floor enabled the parterre to be fitted with upholstered chairs and sofas instead of benches; the floor was covered with carpets, and tiers of boxes were elegantly outfitted. Nevertheless, within three years, the Opera House was a financial failure. But New York would have its opera, and a second attempt, the Astor Place Opera House—a restrained Greek Revival building—was

Fig. 74. *Great Riot at the Astor Place Opera House, New York, on Thursday Evening, May 10, 1849.* Lithograph by N. Currier. Originally, a simple dispute arose between the English actor Mr. Macready and the American tragedian Mr. Forrest. Forrest complained that he had been ill-treated in England due to the influence of Macready who he claimed was jealous of his acting prowess. Forrest convinced his followers in New York to demonstrate against Macready's performance there. Macready backed down and said that he would never appear on the stage again in New York, but influential New Yorkers persuaded him to reappear. Unfortunately, a second demonstration turned into a bloody riot in which many people were killed. (Courtesy of the Museum of the City of New York, New York City)

designed by Isaiah Rogers in 1847. Its interior, for acoustical reasons, consisted entirely of wood paneling, with a painted canvas ceiling that served as a sounding board. Although it was successful acoustically, the structure, confined by its site and its meager proportions, as well as by a sordid reputation garnered after the Astor Place Riots, soon closed and was transformed into a library (fig. 74).[40] In a third attempt the Academy of Music was built, and while it was not quite a financial success, closing its first season more than $50,000 in debt, grand opera prevailed and the Academy remained a stabilizing force over popular culture well into the 1880s. As New York society grew in numbers, one opera house with only twenty-five private boxes, well-subscribed each season, could not provide for the expanding numbers of the nouveau riche. In 1883 a new Metropolitan Opera House was built on Broadway and Thirty-ninth Street, an indication that luxury residential neighborhoods themselves had retreated even farther uptown above Fifty-ninth Street.

New York's population by 1850 (nearly a half million) had developed a taste for theater in all forms—opera, drama, light comedy, variety shows, burlesque, and circuses. Its six legitimate theaters could not exhaust the crowds who, with greater affluence and more leisure time than ever before, attended and called for more theaters. The result was the development of the New York playhouse in the latter half of the nineteenth century. Housed in larger and sometimes more ornamented structures than in the early years of the century, with greater technical equipment, "realistic" three-dimensional scenery and historically accurate costuming, with electric lighting and hydraulic scenery lifts, American theater became more and more technically advanced, reaching its apex in 1895 with the opening of the first American theater complex, Oscar Hammerstein's Olympia theaters.[41] The story of this theater development had a twofold nature: one of managerial centralization, and the other of technical innovation.

Sometime during the 1850s the "star" system of theatrical promotion developed whereby an English actor began to tour American cities, supported in each theater by members of a stock company. Theaters soon realized, however, that they could make more money from theater-goers if they hired more stars, and the stars began to see that they could make more money by traveling than by being a member of a stock company. Theater in America began to be big business: newspapers hired drama critics; theaters were leased by more traveling shows; and as the railroad network spread across America, theater companies began to tour with more elaborate road shows, moving their scenery, costumes, and even brass bands.[42]

Entertainment took on its American peculiarities. In the 1850s Wallack's Lyceum Theatre, located at the corner of Broome Street and Broadway, presented the first showing of *Uncle Tom's Cabin*, a play that would have more performances in the nineteenth century than any other form of entertainment (fig. 75). By 1879 there were approximately fifty different "Tom shows" on the road, and at the peak of their popularity in the 1890s, more than 450 companies. Competition led to circuslike performances. When P. T. Barnum and J. A. Bailey amalgamated their circuses in 1881, they advertised two circuses for the price of one, with twice as many clowns, twice as many animals, and twice as much fun. In similar fashion the "Tom shows" paraded into town in costumes, with brass bands, gilded chariots, and horses flamboyantly advertising the presence of two Topseys or two Simon Legrees.[43] Circuslike entertainment always thrilled Ameri-

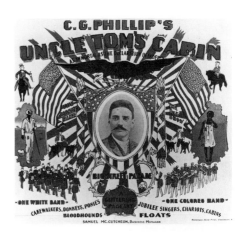

Fig. 75. Poster advertising a glittering pageant of two brass bands, floats, jubilee singers, and bloodhounds, all part of the C. G. Phillip's traveling Tom Show, which competed against hundreds of similar shows crossing America. (Courtesy of the Theatre Collection, the Museum of the City of New York, New York City)

Fig. 76. Willimantic Thread trade card. When P. T. Barnum purchased the world's largest elephant from the Royal Zoological Gardens in 1882, Londoners, including Jumbo, protested the sale. (Courtesy of the Bella C. Landauer Collection, the New-York Historical Society, New York City)

Fig. 77. *Above.* Lydia Thompson in the leading role in *Robinson Crusoe*, ca. 1877. Not only did Lydia introduce burlesque to America, she was the first woman to appear on stage scandalously wearing tights. (Courtesy of the Theatre Collection, the Museum of the City of New York, New York City)

Fig. 78. *Right.* Union Square East, showing numbers 2 through 12 from the northeast corner of Fourteenth Street, ca. 1887. Once entirely residential, by the 1880s Union Square had become a theatrical center. Francis Koehler's costume shop can be seen to the right, and F. Roemer's stood a few doors away. Several dramatic agents such as James E. Johnson, Morris Simmonds, and Charles Gardener shared the upper floors of these houses. Theatrical shoes and pianos could be purchased at number 12 (at the left). The statue of George Washington, was designed by Henry K. Brown and paid for by prominent New Yorkers such as William Astor and August Belmont. (Courtesy of the New-York Historical Society, New York City)

can crowds, perhaps nowhere better shown than when Jumbo the elephant was purchased from the London Royal Zoological Gardens in 1882, touching off an international incident as the English protested his departure (fig. 76). Arriving in New York after so much publicity, Jumbo was paraded by torchlight through a cheering throng of a half million to Madison Square Garden.

Blackface was an early form of American entertainment. Originally a one-man show, it became a group form with the Virginia Minstrels in 1843. Minstrels increased in popularity so that by the 1870s the group sometimes numbered forty, and multiple shows criss-crossed the stretches of America. Burlesque, beginning as a parody of the pretentiousness of the upper classes or the self-imposed stature of certain "stars," was great entertainment. But soon "legs" began to crowd out wit, and in 1869 New York's first burlesque show, a melange of songs, dances, jokes, and impersonations entitled "Lydia Thompson and the British Blondes" began its triumphant ten-year road show (fig. 77). Variety shows, or vaudeville, combining a series of unrelated specialty acts with an emphasis on comedy, also became another popular form of entertainment. Rough and rowdy in its early days, by the 1880s this genre was turned into a clean show, suitable for families, by Tony Pastor, the one-time singer and tambourine player for Barnum's American Museum who later established his own variety theater housed in Tammany Hall on Fourteenth Street. No swearing, drinking, smoking, foul language, or obscene entertainment, were allowed in this reformed and dignified vaudeville.[44]

As theaters in America became serious business, a small group of New York businessmen began in the 1870s to syndicate and thus control American theaters. The booking offices of these theater managers were located near Union Square, the vicinity where production companies were put together, where business deals were made on the square's park benches and in its hotel lobbies, where new stars were discovered, and popular shows were seen.[45] Within a few years,

Fig. 79. Star Theatre (formerly Wallack's Theatre), designed by Thomas R. Jackson in 1860,
on the northeast corner of Broadway and Thirteenth Street. The Star was noted for its lavish
productions that ranked among the best in the
city until the 1880s. A White Horse Café can be
seen squeezed in between the theater and the
edge of the Morton House. (Courtesy of the
Theatre Collection, the Museum of the City of
New York, New York City)

not only theaters and music halls but artists' studios, and all of the supporting
cast of scenery painters, costume makers, piano salespeople, and music printers,
congregated close to Union and Madison squares (fig. 78). The *New York World*
wrote in 1873 that Union Square housed not only Seer's theatrical printshop but
Koehler's costume shops, the publication houses for Byrne's *Dramatic News*
and Leslie's *Sporting and Dramatic Times,* Sarony's studio for stage photography, Samuel French's play-publishing house, and many theatrical bookshops.[46]

No wonder an English traveler noted in 1867 that:

> unlike the system that exists in London of scattering the theaters, the plan
> adopted in New York has been to bring them as nearly as possible together,
> so that the overflow of one house finds another theater ready at hand.
> Hence, the New York houses are nearly all situated in the Broadway, and
> have therefore a continual stream of life passing backward and forward
> before their doors. . . . With few exceptions, the American theaters are not
> distinguishable from the surrounding houses until a close proximity reveals
> the name, lights, and other outside paraphernalia of a place of amusement;
> for on either side of the spacious entrances are usually to be found shops or
> cafes, and above, the windows of a hotel or retail store.[47]

It is quite possible that Ladies Mile as a theater district began with the introduction of Irving Hall, which opened in 1860 (demolished in 1984), west of Irving Place on Fifteenth Street, as a center for balls, concerts, and lectures[48] (fig.
79). In the vicinity the following year, the world-famous new Wallack's Theatre,
designed by Thomas R. Jackson, and later renamed the Star Theatre, located on
the northeast corner of Broadway and Thirteenth Street (fig. 80). Located on this
site for twenty years, Wallack's offered lavish productions by a brilliant cast never
equaled before in New York.[49] For a few years between 1862 and 1867, a small
elite theater, the Fifth Avenue Music Hall, could be found on the southeast corner
of Twenty-third Street and Broadway. The opposite in entertainment, Nixon's Al-

Fig. 80. Theaters in the vicinity of Ladies Mile.

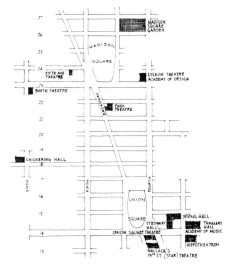

Fig. 81. The Hippotheatron, Fourteenth Street, opposite the Academy of Music. Opening in 1864, the supposedly fireproof iron construction burned down December 24, 1871. (Courtesy of the Theatre Collection, the Museum of the City of New York, New York City)

hambra circus tent stood in 1863 on Fourteenth Street, right across from the Academy of Music.[50] A curious corrugated iron structure known as the Hippotheatron, housing 1,700 people, was erected on the site of the Alhambra the next year, topped with a dome that rose 75 feet in height (fig. 81). A little farther south, a theater invaded the sanctuary of an unused church at 728 Broadway near Waverly Place, when the department store king A. T. Stewart turned it into a showplace for his protégé Lucy Fashton. Never very successful — most of Stewart's real estate ventures were failures—it burned to the ground in 1884.[51]

Between Union Square and the Academy of Music in 1866, Steinway and Sons built their main showrooms at 71–73 East Fourteenth Street, in a structure that extended through to Fifteenth Street (fig. 82). In 1868 Tammany Hall built its new political club next door to the Academy of Music (143 East Fourteenth Street), including several theaters within its walls (fig. 83). A risqué upstairs burlesque and vaudeville hall lasted only a few years, but the first-floor theater, which opened in 1868, was for a time the popular home of Bryant's Minstrels.[52]

Far over on Sixth Avenue in 1868, the most elaborate theater of all arose— Booth's Theatre on the southeast corner of Twenty-third Street and Sixth Avenue (see fig. 25). Some critics would call this theater, "the most magnificent building in the American continent" and "a great national temple" dedicated to high drama.[53] When the Winter Garden burned down in 1866, America's great Shakespearian actor, Edwin Booth, had no suitable house in which to perform. He and a series of partners constructed the large granite Booth's Theatre, designed by Renwick and Sands, in the florid but extremely popular Second Empire mode. The bloated structure stood 70 feet high to its main cornice, above which rose a mansard roof. Fronting Twenty-third Street, its main facade ran 143 feet in length and contained a 34-foot wing fronting Sixth Avenue. This wing was designed to produce rental income and thus had stores, studios, and rooms for various renters. In combining a series of different uses under the same roof, Booth's was America's first modern theater and set the standards for theater design for several decades to come. Although far less sumptuous than the European theaters, Booth's Theatre catered to the bourgeois tastes of American audiences. The theater patron entered under a main archway and crossed Italian marble flooring into a semicircular vestibule extending to the rear of the auditorium. It was so narrow and cramped, however, that an opening-night critic complained of stepping on ladies' trailing dresses. This vestibule opened on the traditional horseshoe-shaped auditorium containing the parquette and orchestra. Patrons who entered through a secondary arched entrance on Sixth Avenue, could ascend by a narrow and inelegant stairway up to the balcony complete with its own promenade, then to a second gallery, and above that, to an amphitheater. In all, the theater seated 1,700 people and had standing room for another 300.

The real importance of Booth's Theatre, however, lay in its technical innovations, for ''it is Mr. Booth's design to supersede as far as possible by scientific means, the necessity of manual labor.''[54] For the first time, the orchestra pit was sunk beneath the level of the main floor in front of the stage where it no longer

Fig. 82. Steinway and Sons, East Fourteenth Street, ca. 1902. Above the first floor showrooms, which were reserved for selling pianos. Steinway Hall, a simple auditorium, was designed for concerts and lectures. Charles Dickens charmed New Yorkers in a series of seventeen lectures in this hall during the winter of 1868. A vaudeville agent's office stood next door. (Courtesy of the Byron Collection, the Museum of the City of New York, New York City)

Fig. 83. Tammany Hall, view from the southeast on Fourteenth Street, ca. 1870. On the left of this red brick and marble structure designed in 1868 by Thomas R. Jackson, the same architect who designed the Star Theatre, the entrance to Bryant's famous minstrel shows can be seen. (Courtesy of the New-York Historical Society, New York City)

obstructed the view. Also, for the first time, the stage was flat instead of raked. Audiences thus faced a 76-foot-high proscenium from which all traces of the apron stage had been erased (fig. 84). Portions of the 55-foot-deep stage floor had elevator traps 32 feet deep so that drops could be lifted and lowered out of sight rather than rolled up and awkwardly stored.[55] Scenery storage rooms were located to the south of the stage, and above these were five stories of rooms for wardrobes, the private apartments for Booth, and nearly thirty different dressing rooms. Every space was utilized for theatrical functions: carpenter shops were located under the Twenty-third Street sidewalks, and large boiler rooms under the Sixth Avenue vaults. Yet, the practical *Real Estate Record* had labeled this theater one of New York's "bonanza buildings," which were based on faulty financial plans. The theater did indeed go bankrupt. Booth was able to retain control of the theater until 1874, but within a decade it was converted into a dry goods store and then torn down.[56]

The vicinity of Ladies Mile continued to attract additional theaters in the 1870s as the district gained in popularity. Two years after the opening of Booth's Theatre, an unsuccessful variety house, The Union Square Theatre, opened in the Morton House south of Union Square on Fourteenth Street. A simple but commodious portico and a brilliantly frescoed vestibule advertised a gallery room that could seat 1,200.[57] The only theater to actually locate along Ladies Mile was the Park Theatre, which stood at 932 Broadway, on the east side between Twenty-first and Twenty-Second streets. Much more in keeping with the *Real Estate Record*'s financial suggestions for a successful theater, the Broadway facade, 110 feet in length, was concealed by a row of commercial structures, and entry to the theater itself was gained through a narrow passageway (see fig. 27). The simple and chaste interior with an orchestra pit sadly sunk out of sight, so that music seemed to come from a hole in the stage floor, did not inspire audiences. The mid-1870s were years of economic depression, and this theater, which opened in 1874 with only moderate success, remained until 1882 when it burned to the ground and never returned to Broadway.[58]

One of the most successful concert halls in the whole district, Chickering Hall (designed by George B. Post), opened in 1875 on the northwest corner of Fifth Avenue and Eighteenth Street (fig. 85). But even this beautiful arcaded structure gave way to commerce in 1892 when it was remodeled for business use.[59] By the 1880s fashionable theaters had followed the luxury residences uptown and were relocating along Broadway near Herald Square. The last important theaters of the 1880s to locate near Ladies Mile were two structures that helped to publicize the theatrical inventions of J. Steele MacKaye. The first, the Madison Square Theatre, rebuilt on the site of the old Fifth Avenue Theatre in 1877 (designed in an Egyptian mode by architects Kimball and Wiseman), was managed by MacKaye in 1880[60] (fig. 86). In it he installed a movable stage (fig. 87). Although popularly acclaimed, MacKaye was a poor manager and was forced to resign from the Madison Square Theatre. In 1885 he reappeared at the new Lyceum Theatre (fig. 88), located next to the Academy of Music on the west side of Fourth Avenue between Twenty-third and Twenty-fourth streets. Four steam engines ran machinery for lifting scenery, removing sets from the stage or revolving the stage, lighting the theater and stage, and raising and lowering the balcony on which musicians sat. Even in this theater, MacKaye's success was as brief as it was brilliant, and he left within a few years.[61]

In 1893 MacKaye put his theatrical fantasies to the supreme test with the design of a giant theater — the Spectatorium, seating 10,000 — for the Chicago World's Fair. Although the theater was never realized, MacKaye planned a great musical and dramatic spectacle about Columbus the "World Finder" arriving in America, to be accompanied by music specially commissioned from Antonin Dvorak. Light shows, realistically simulating day, night, and even rainbows, were to flood a 150- by 70-foot stage, encircled by a sky dome diffusing light upon the stage and the audience.[62] Light was beginning to literally dawn on a new age, and as it did, Union Square ceased to be the grand theater district it had been in the decades following the Civil War. Already in the 1890s, as theaters were moving uptown, Thomas Edison, who had supervised MacKaye's lighting scheme in the Madison Square and Lyceum theaters, was now experimenting with moving pictures. In 1896 New York would witness the first such picture projection at Koster and Bial's Music Hall on the north side of Twenty-third Street just west of Sixth Avenue, marking the beginning of the era in which those theaters still remaining near Ladies Mile would become motion picture palaces.[63]

A CENTER FOR MUSIC AND ART

In obvious response to the rising theatrical district, Union Square quickly became a center for the manufacture and sale of pianos. Steinway and Sons led the way in 1853, and Myron Decker first set up his piano business, Decker Brothers, at 2 Union Square East in 1856, to be followed over the next decade by nine different piano makers (figs. 89, 90). Among the more famous was Chickering and Sons, who had warehouses at 11 East Fourteenth Street in the 1860s. Piano ware-

Fig. 84. *Above.* Watercolor of Booth's Theatre interior. The stage is set for the first act of *Romeo and Juliet*, opening night, February 1869. Scenery was normally changed by hand; new sets were run onto the stage along grooves in the floor. At Booth's Theatre, for the first time, a hydraulic machine lifted scenery from beneath the stage. (Courtesy of the Theatre Collection, the Museum of the City of New York, New York City)

Fig. 85. *Left.* Chickering Hall, northeast corner of Fifth Avenue and Eighteenth Street, ca. 1900. George B. Post designed the concert hall in 1875, but as the fashionable theater district pushed north toward Herald Square during the 1880s, it was finally renovated for office purposes in 1892. (Courtesy of the New-York Historical Society, New York City)

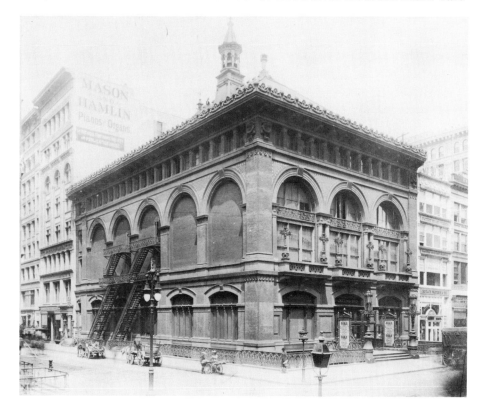

Fig. 86. Madison Square Theatre, interior (1877–1908), behind the Fifth Avenue Hotel on Twenty-fourth Street. Louis C. Tiffany and Thomas Edison first began to work together with Steele McKaye at the Madison Square Theater in 1879. Thomas Edison advised McKaye on the installation of the first electric footlights with gaslights for backups. In association with Mrs. Candace Wheeler, who was reintroducing the art of decorative needlework to America, Tiffany created the embroidered drop curtain. An unusual feature was the placement of the orchestra in a balcony at the top of the proscenium arch. (Courtesy of the New-York Historical Society, New York City)

houses and salesrooms eventually attracted music stores and music publishers. Charles Ditson and Company, publishers of music books, sheet music, and all kinds of musical merchandise, took over four floors of 867 Broadway. Music from Gustave Schirmer could be purchased at 25 Union Square West in the 1880s and 1890s, and the *Musical Courier,* founded in 1880, was published at 20 East Fourteenth Street. On the opposite side of the street in the 1890s, the Thomas Music Company sold every item imaginable, from sheet music to piano scarves.[64]

Just a little to the south of Union Square, at 839 Broadway between Thirteenth and Fourteenth streets, one of the first public art galleries in the city opened in 1853, Thomas Jefferson Bryan's Gallery of Christian Art. Amassing an eclectic collection of paintings by European masters, often of questionable authenticity, Bryan wanted to persuade the American public to open a national museum of art. First offering the collection to his hometown of Philadelphia, he found that the city fathers were reluctant to set aside public space for these "rare old pictures."[65] Thus, he opened a public art gallery on the second floor of a

Broadway house. Although admission was only 25 cents, and a descriptive catalog another 12½ cents, the gallery was never very popular and was attended mainly by art students.[66] Bryan had hoped that his gallery would raise the impoverished level of American artistic knowledge and elevate the general sense of public taste, but instead he set off a new fashion for picture buying, and a veri-

Fig. 87. *Left.* Madison Square Theatre, movable stage (From *Scientific American* 59, April 1884: 1.) To facilitate the creation of realistic scenery changes and to reduce the intermission time needed for changing sets, a backstage double-decker elevator was used, containing two platform stages. While the lower level stage was shown to the audience, the upper level was being set by stage hands. (Courtesy of the New York Public Library, New York City)

Fig. 88. *Above.* Lyceum Theatre, Fourth Avenue, between Twenty-third and Twenty-fourth streets, ca. 1896. The Lyceum was the first theater to use electricity to illuminate both the auditorium and the stage. Thomas Edison invented new "focusable lamps" for the theater and Louis C. Tiffany designed special chandeliers for Edison's incandescent lamps. (Courtesy of the Byron Collection, the Museum of the City of New York, New York City)

Fig. 89. *Below.* Piano Showrooms on Union Square, 1870, 1880, and 1890.

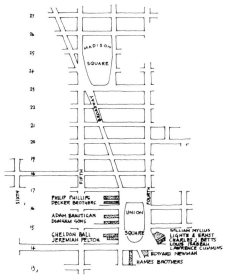

table art market took place after the Civil War. Numerous art galleries and photography studios were located all along Broadway on Ladies Mile during the 1870s and 1880s, selling good, bad, and indifferent art[67] (fig. 91).

Nineteenth-century Manhattan business directories indicate that many landscape, figure, marine, and portrait painters, photographers, and sculptors were located in the upper-floor studios of buildings that stood along Ladies Mile, especially along Union Square West, moving from year to year as economy demanded. For example, Harriet Hunter's boardinghouse (35 Union Square West, between Sixteenth and Seventeenth streets) had become by 1870 an artists' studio for painters William Magrath, Charles C. Ward, and William D. Washington and the studios of the landscape painter Alfred Orday and the portrait painters Daniel M. Carter and J. Robertson. By 1880 Gustave Schirmer, the music publisher, occupied some of this building along with a new group of portrait painters (Adam Springfield, Joseph Gaertner, Robert Koehler, Voltaire Combe, Paul Nefflen, and S. Austin), and next door at 37 Union Square West the studio of Napoleon Sarony, the famous theatrical photographer, could be found. One of the most famous art specialists of the nineteenth century, John Rogers, the creator of the small plaster-cast groupings that were prominent in so many American homes of the nineteenth century, had his studio at 23 Union Square West in the 1880s and 1890s (fig. 93). *Harper's Weekly* noted in 1879 that "the art of Rogers [was] to the last degree unconventional, and in no sense appertains to what is called high art, but it springs from a nature moved by correct impulses, beating in unison with time, and occupying the position of pioneer in the art of the future."[68]

The artists' studios of Ladies Mile, as well as its hotels and theaters, were instrumental in creating the concept of the "star" or stage celebrity in the late nine-

Fig. 90. Decker Brothers trade card. Nineteenth-century American advertising techniques were simple but effective. They included trade cards; newspaper advertisements, huge white price cards placed in windows; "gutter snipes," or notices pasted onto high curbstones; boards plastered onto the side of buildings; and "pullers-in," or boys stationed in front of the store shouting out the items for sale. The imagery of trade cards often used domestic scenery or idealized portraits of innocent American women. (Courtesy of the Bella C. Landauer Collection, the New-York Historical Society)

Fig. 91. Studio of the distinguished American painter, H. Humphrey Moore, at 11 East Fourteenth Street (From *Frank Leslie's Illustrated Newspaper*, Jan. 10, 1880: 345.) *Leslie's* described Moore's studio as resembling the interior of the Alhambra, with brilliant colors reflected from Oriental rugs hung on walls or covering the floors, Moorish saddle bags, Saracenic headpieces, and Japanese umbrellas. (Courtesy of the Museum of the City of New York, New York City)

Fig. 92. Union Square West, Sixteenth to Seventeenth Street, early 1880s. The three-story corner building on the left with the curious portico was designed by Henry R. Marshall in the 1870s and contained the studios of many artists. Remodeled in the 1880s, it would become Brentano's bookstore. Adjacent stands the Venetian-style brick and stone structure, designed by Leopold Eidlitz in 1870, that housed the Decker Brothers piano salesroom. The building to its right, attributed to D. and J. Jardine in 1880, was a store and warehouse for Schirmer sheet music. The five-story white structure was redesigned by William Schickel in 1881. Napoleon Sarony's photographic studio was located in this building, and next door to Sarony's was the Florence Sewing Machine Company. The brick and stone six-story building on the far right housed the French flats designed by James Stroud in 1881. It was demolished in 1895. (Courtesy of the Theatre Collection, the Museum of the City of New York, New York City)

teenth century. Napoleon Sarony's photographic studio became famous for its elegant portraits of actors and actresses in their theatrical costumes (fig. 94). In 1866 the cabinet photograph became popular and its enlarged size (4½ by 6½ inches) allowed Sarony to experiment with lighting, elaborately painted backdrops, and costuming. Theatrical poses became his forte, and it is said that he produced over 40,000 photographs of actors and actresses alone. A visitor to the fourth floor of Sarony's Union Square Gallery would have arrived by way of a small and jerky hydraulic elevator, passed an Egyptian mummy standing guard, and then entered the reception room, which itself contained a bizarre collection of stuffed birds, ancient armor, and a profusion of paintings. Not only did his daring signature adorn the facade of his gallery but it also embellished—in red ink—the bottom of each of his photographs, which were sold through mail-order catalogs and in the lobbies of the theaters and hotels gracing Ladies Mile[69] (see fig. 92).

Perhaps one early indication that Ladies Mile would become an art center was the opening in 1857 of the first commercial art studio: Richard Morris Hunt's studio building at 51 West Tenth Street, housing twenty-five studios and a much-needed exhibition space (fig. 95). The artists John La Farge, W. P. W. Dana, and William Beard were among the first to occupy these studios, followed in 1858 by Hunt himself who brought with him his students George B. Post, Charles D. Gambrill, and later Henry Van Brunt, William R. Ware, Edward Quincey, and Frank Furness.[70] The opposite end of Ladies Mile represented the high note of art with the 1865 construction of the white and gray marble National Academy of Design. The building, at the northwest corner of East Twenty-third Street and Fourth Avenue, housed art galleries and an art school in a Venetian-Gothic structure resembling the Doge's Palace, designed by P. B. Wight (fig. 96). With Booth's Theatre at the Sixth Avenue end and the National Academy of Design at Fourth Avenue, Twenty-third Street was for a moment the architectural apex of the amusement district.

Fig. 93. John Rogers in his Union Square studio, ca. 1865. (Courtesy of the New-York Historical Society, New York City)

Fig. 94. Napoleon Sarony, photographic study, 1866. The 1860s heralded a flamboyant period of photography with the introduction of new posing and lighting techniques that enabled more dramatic compositions. Sarony invented a posing machine that would hold a sitter's back, arms, sides, and head and as result supposedly would produce a more natural facial and body expression. This machine allowed Sarony to expose eight different poses quickly on a single plate before the plate dried. (Courtesy of the New-York Historical Society, New York City)

EATING ESTABLISHMENTS

With increased prosperity in the decade after the Civil War, and with the rise of the entertainment district near Ladies Mile, eating out became an important part of New York's social life (fig. 97). It has been estimated that by the 1870s there were more than 6,000 restaurants in the city, ranging from Delmonico's with its Continental cuisine, to the oyster houses on Fourteenth Street.[71] Along with the special menus offered by most hotels in the vicinity of Ladies Mile, numerous eating places sprang up amid the retail shops and adjacent to theaters to appease the appetites of hungry consumers. Junius Browne described eating out in New York in 1869 by claiming that on ''. . .14th Street, you pay for a single meal what would keep you for a week below Chambers Street, and gives you dyspepsia withal unless you have the stomach of an ostrich.'' But what seemed more appalling to him was that elegantly dressed women, single or married, arrived by

Fig. 95. Tenth Street studio (43–55 West Tenth Street), 1906. One of Richard Morris Hunt's earliest buildings, designed in 1857 in a vernacular French mode, the atelier contained twenty-five studios, exhibition space for artists, and offered the first American training in architecture. (Courtesy of the New-York Historical Society, New York City)

Fig. 96. The National Academy of Design, designed by P. B. Wight in 1865, northwest corner of Fourth Avenue and Twenty-third Street, ca. 1890. *Harper's Weekly* described an exhibition at the Academy in 1870, stating that it contained "fewer really bad pictures than any one we have had for years back, and gives a very fair impression of the condition of Art in America . . ." (Courtesy of the New-York Public Library, New York City)

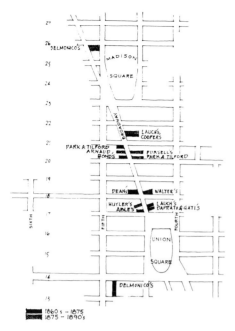

Fig. 97. Confectioners, eating houses, and food shops along Ladies Mile.

Fig. 98. Park and Tilford grocers, southwest corner of Broadway and Twenty-first Street, ca. 1877. This famous grocery store was located on the ground floor of the Madison Square Hotel throughout the history of Ladies Mile. Built before 1860, the five-story structure, capped with a mansard roof, was demolished in 1924. (Courtesy of the New-York Historical Society, New York City)

carriage with their escorts to dine on upper Broadway and Fourteenth Street. Cautiously he warned that "late suppers and rich wines, and low voices and delicious flattery are dangerous, dear madame, even if you think it not."[72]

If one wanted to shop for a sweet while promenading the length of Ladies Mile in the 1860s and 1870s, a stop at the confectionaries of Anthony Lauch, Charles Dean, or John Cooper, might satisfy one's taste. All these confectioners were gone by the 1890s although the famous Huyler's on Broadway and Seventeenth Street and Petra Arnaud's shop between Twentieth and Twenty-first streets, took their place. In addition, the well-known grocers Park and Tilford had opened their doors at least by 1860 on the southwest corner of Twenty-first Street (fig. 98). They remained on Ladies Mile into the twentieth century.[73]

In addition to confectioners and grocers, several eating houses were located along Ladies Mile. In the 1860s L. D. Able's Eating House opened its doors, followed in the 1870s by A. Daprato and N. Gati's Eating Place, William Bond's Eating House, and in the 1880s by George Walter's Eating House, and Pursell's Confectionary and Restaurant. Delmonico's Restaurant remained the unrivaled center of New York's social system throughout the economic life of Ladies Mile. A visitor to New York in 1866 described Delmonico's at 1 East Fourteenth Street, located in the old Grinnell mansion, as the "most magnificently-appointed restaurant, comprising regular saloons, private cabinets, and apartments for dinner-parties. . . ." In 1876 Delmonico's moved to the south side of Twenty-sixth Street between Eighth Avenue and Broadway where its public dining rooms surveyed Madison Square and its Gentleman's Café overlooked Broadway (fig. 99).

In the heyday of Ladies Mile a hungry shopper could choose from the following first-class restaurants according to *Putnam's Guide to New York City of 1885:*

Café Brunswick	225 Fifth Avenue
Nathan Clarke's	22 West Twenty-third Street
Coleman House	1169 Broadway
D'Orlan's	10 East Twenty-third Street
Henry Maillard's	1097 Broadway
Vienna Model Bakery	Broadway and Tenth Street

If one preferred lesser fare, all along Fourteenth Street and up and down Sixth Avenue Bohemian beer gardens, or *weinstubens,* and oyster houses had become as popular as the department stores and gift shops along Ladies Mile (fig. 100).

CLUBS AND ASSOCIATIONS

Although club life for men in America was much less influential and important than it was in London, and not the only passport to higher social circles, many such associations gathered near Ladies Mile in the late nineteenth century (fig. 101). Francis G. Fairfield, a chronicler of club life noted in 1873 that:

> though in one aspect the age is one of intense commercialism, and of general crooking of supple knee to the God Mammon, in another aspect it is the age of intense and speculative groping after the real; a groping that

Fig. 99. Delmonico's Restaurant, southwest corner of Fifth Avenue and Twenty-sixth Street, ca. 1888. The fashionable restaurant moved to this address from ten blocks farther south in 1876. (Courtesy of the New-York Historical Society, New York City)

fertilizes seminal ideas, long asleep in fallow ground, as no groping after Utopia has done before.[74]

There were at this time over 100 different men's clubs, with a total membership exceeding 50,000, three-quarters of which consisted of married men and one-quarter of bankers and businessmen. Junius Browne complained that "clubs are the late fruit of a high civilization . . . the outgrowth of leisure, luxury and cultivated unrestraint. . . . They are anti-matrimonial and anti-domestic and present the paradox of longing for society and a tendency to isolation."[75]

Late-nineteenth-century clubs and associations did indeed divide the world into men's and women's spheres. Although women too had formed many associations that appeared near Ladies Mile, men's clubs were always housed in more elegant structures with more pretentious interiors. Women, in addition, were only allowed to enter a man's club at certain prescribed times of the day, week, or year and then often were restricted to specific areas of the club. While men formed sporting, political, and business-related societies, following artistic or

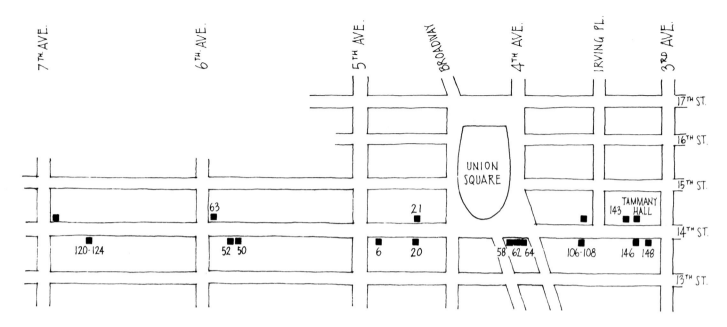

NORTH SIDE OF 14TH STREET:

143 GERMANIA THEATRE BUFFET
CORNER OF IRVING PLACE: PETER W. MAGUIRE'S
      WINE AND LUNCH ROOM
21 LAGER BEER AND LUNCH ROOM
63 BERCKMANN LAGER BEER SALOON
CORNER OF 7TH AVENUE: ALDERNEY
      ICE CREAM COMPANY

SOUTH SIDE OF 14TH STREET:

148 W. WITZ'S "RAPID TRANSIT"
      LAGER BEER SALOON
146 CAFE MORETTE
106-108 GEORGE H. HUBER'S PROSPECT GARDEN
      AND OYSTER HOUSE
64 H. FAHRENHOR'S LAGER BEER SALOON
62 J. SLATTERY'S COFFEE AND LUNCH ROOM
58 JOHN GALLAT'S OYSTERS AND LUNCH ROOM
20 BIGOT'S RESTAURANT OYSTER AND COMPANY
6 FIRST VIENNA BAKERY
50 CAROL'S AND REGAN'S LADIES' AND GENTS'
      OYSTER PARLORS AND ICE CREAM
52 PURSELL'S LADIES' RESTAURANT
120-124 WINDSOR GARDEN

Fig. 100. Fourteenth Street, showing saloons and oyster houses. (Redrawn from *Shaft's Sixth Avenue Saturday Night* 1, July 31, 1880: 2)

Fig. 101. Clubs near Ladies Mile.

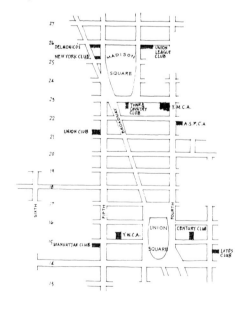

religious pursuits, women tended to establish philanthropic associations. Thus, the first women's club, formed in 1868 and called the Sorosis Club, had the specific aim "to render women helpful to each other; actively benevolent to the world; and to aid promoting useful and agreeable relations between women of literary, artistic, and scientific tastes."[76]

In 1854 the Union Club built an elaborate and monumental brownstone edifice at Fifth Avenue and Twenty-first Street (fig. 102), while the Manhattan Club took over a former residence at Fifth Avenue and Fifteenth Street and the Atheneum settled at Fifth Avenue and Sixteenth Street in 1859. The Union Club had been formed in 1836 for "gentlemen of social distinction" and represented patrician families of New York such as the Livingstons, Van Cortlandts, and Van Rensselaers. Its sole operating rule was "ease and comfort within the limits of courtesy."[77] From the nucleus of a small arts club, the Century Club expanded in 1847 to include members drawn from a list of 100 prominent New York authors, artists, and amateurs in the fields of letters and the fine arts. The club established itself in 1857 at 109 East Fifteenth Street, next door to a studio elegantly redesigned by Stanford White, another popular center for the discussion of art and literature. The club's annual Twelfth Night Celebration displayed wit and humor when gifts were exchanged: "a box of vesuvians there, to somebody rather vesuvian in temper; a bundle of cigars there, to somebody who didn't smoke; a doll elsewhere to somebody hopelessly single; and so on with a punctuation of bons-bons of wit, joke and hearty laughter."[78]

The University Club's original quarters in 1865 were at East Tenth Street, where they remained until the 1880s when the club moved into the vacated Jerome mansion on Twenty-sixth Street. Attributed to the architect Thomas R. Jackson, who had already designed Wallack's Theatre and Tammany Hall, the Jerome mansion was an imposing group of three structures: a five-story marble-fronted mansion with a mansard roof and an adjacent theater and stables. Originally intended for the American Jockey Club of which Jerome was the vice president, these buildings were instead leased by the Union League Club, becoming the club's headquarters from 1868 until 1881 (fig. 103). This club, founded in 1863 by "gentle men of prominence [provided] unwavering support to the government; to suppress the rebellion; to resist corruption and to promote reform in national, state and municipal affairs." Before moving to the Jerome mansion, the Union League Club first was located in the old Parish mansion on Seventeenth Street and Broadway, where club members supervised the organization of black troops during the Civil War.[79]

A few years later, in 1868, the cornerstone was laid for the first New York Young Men's Christian Association building at the southwest corner of Fourth Avenue and Twenty-third Street, opposite the National Academy of Design. Ren-

Fig. 102. Union Club, northwest corner of Twenty-first Street and Fifth Avenue, before 1890. At the time it was constructed, in 1854, the club building cost an extravagant $25,000. Architectural critics complained that this brownstone cube, regardless of expense, simply exaggerated the mass and detail of a three-story brownstone town house. (Courtesy of the New-York Public Library, New York City)

Fig. 103. Madison Avenue, looking south from the north corner of Twenty-sixth Street, ca. 1877–78. The Leonard W. Jerome mansion, leased by the Union League Club from 1868 until 1881, grouped three buildings under a continuous facade along Twenty-sixth Street. It became the home for the University Club in the late 1880s and the Manhattan Club in the 1890s. It was demolished circa 1974. (Courtesy of the New-York Historical Society, New York City)

Fig. 104. The first Young Men's Christian Association building in New York City, erected in 1868 on the southeast corner of Twenty-third Street and Fourth Avenue. Opposite the National Academy of Design, the Y.M.C.A., designed by Renwick and Sands, contained a tower in the center of its facade, marking the 22-foot wide entrance. The first floor was rented by eight stores; reception rooms, reading rooms, parlors, and dressing rooms, as well as a large two-story lecture room, which could accommodate 1,640 persons, occupied the second story. The third through fifth floors contained smaller lecture rooms and classrooms, a library housing over 60,000 volumes, artists' studios, and a picture gallery. (Courtesy of the New-York Historical Society, New York City)

wick and Sands won the competition for its design (fig. 104). In 1870 a new club, the Lotos Club, organized by six young journalists, all of whom were either drama, music, or art critics, rented 2 Irving Place around the corner from the Academy of Music. The club's membership grew through the reputation of the Lotos Saturday Nights, when sumptuous meals were served, accompanied by the exhibition of new artwork, musical events, and recitations. Throughout the years of Ladies Mile clubs would continue to congregate close to this theater and amusement district, inserting themselves into leftover mansions or vacated brownstones instead of erecting elaborate houses of their own. It would not be until the late 1890s, when the most prominent clubs relocated to the fashionable quarter near Fifty-ninth Street, that an era of grand club architecture finally arrived in New York.

POLITICAL PROTESTS, PARADES, AND CELEBRATIONS

City Hall Park had been the nineteenth century's center for political protests, triumphal marches, and popular celebrations.[80] From the Civil War until the Second World War, however, Union Square took over that role in response to the location of residential neighborhoods, which themselves had moved still farther uptown. Even before the Civil War, the square had become a popular gathering place. George Templeton Strong, the son-in-law of the developer Samuel Ruggles, lived at 54 Union Place in the 1850s and recorded in his diary several of these events. One night in 1859 he saw

> a grand demonstration by the exiled Polish, French, German and Italian patriots domiciled in the city in honor of the pious Orsini and his colleague who killed twelve inoffensive people hurling explosives into the crowd trying to kill Louis Napoleon. . . . The glaring torches and the great black "catafalque" made it quite imposing to look at. But the Reds were not numerically strong, hardly two thousand.[81]

The same year, Strong saw several thousand people gathering in the square, "worn sewing-women, hungry children, Celts, insolvent and solvent of every type," drawn by the expectations of a man who promised to distribute free bread and meat on Thanksgiving.[82]

In December 1859, just before the Civil War, the Great Union Meeting filled the Academy of Music on Fourteenth Street, spilling out onto the streets and the square (fig. 105). Inside, the stage and auditorium were decorated with stars and

Fig. 105. Union Square, on the occasion of a meeting to express Union sentiment during the Civil War. (From *Harper's Weekly*, April 20, 1861.) (Courtesy of the New-York Historical Society, New York City)

stripes and mottoes and inscriptions such as "The Union must and shall be preserved." Accompanied by Dodsworth's Band and a thirty-two gun salute, the rectitude and purity of Northern sentiment was defended and exalted.[83] One of the largest gatherings that may have established the importance of Union Square as a center for political protests occurred after the Confederate Army fired on Fort Sumter in 1861. Gathering first around the statue of Washington where a flag from Sumter was raised, the crowd grew until Strong estimated it had reached 250,000[84] (fig. 105). Many large meetings continued to be held in Union Square throughout the Civil War, and in March 1864 a crowd gathered near the Union League clubhouse on the northeast corner of Broadway and Seventeenth Street to watch the New York Negro Regiment receive its colors and depart for war. Another Civil War event to draw attention to Union Square was the Metropolitan Fair, for which a temporary structure was erected on the northern side of the square in April 1864. This fair, one of the Sanitary Fairs first organized in Chicago in 1863, was intended to raise money to support relief work, sanitary inspections, and hospital and nursing services offered to the Union Army by the U.S. Sanitary Commission. Richard Morris Hunt was responsible for the interior decoration of the fair's structures, and Strong claimed they were "most artistic and splendid . . . at little cost."[85]

Sometime during the Civil War it also became the custom to celebrate the Fourth of July at Union Square instead of at City Hall Park. And when Lincoln's body was brought to New York City to lie in state at City Hall on April 24, 1865,

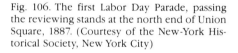

Fig. 106. The first Labor Day Parade, passing the reviewing stands at the north end of Union Square, 1887. (Courtesy of the New-York Historical Society, New York City)

the next day a great funeral procession marched from City Hall up Broadway to Fourteenth Street, across to Fifth Avenue, and northward to the Hudson River Railroad Depot. Even before the Civil War, however, Union Square had become a popular destination for marches. Dressed in red shirts and carrying torches, the men of Tammany Hall would often march at night from City Hall up Broadway, down Fourteenth Street to Fifth Avenue, up to Twenty-sixth Street, and finally south on Fourth Avenue and down the Bowery. When Tammany Hall located on East Fourteenth Street in 1869, it continued its famous demonstrations but accompanied with booming brass bands, earsplitting cannons, and dazzling fireworks.[86]

As the political and economic turmoil of the latter part of the nineteenth century gathered momentum, Union Square became the center for many labor protests. As early as 1860 striking railroad drovers assembled around the statue of Washington, and during the economic crisis of 1873 a protesting crowd demanded the city provide jobs for the unemployed. By this time the city, in recognition of the square's prominence as a place to review parades and for crowds to assemble, erected a speaker's platform at the northern end of the square and strung gas lights along its Seventeenth Street end. Growing in numbers and power, the Knights of Labor, the first of the American labor groups to call for an eight-hour working day, proposed that the first Monday in September be celebrated as Labor Day. When New York finally adopted legislation proclaiming Labor Day an official holiday in 1887, a crowd of 20,000 men and women passed by the square's reviewing stands (fig. 106). Labor troubles continued to mount through the 1890s and early 1900s, and after the Chicago Haymarket Riot of 1886, New York policemen, as well, began to use clubs against protesting crowds. In opposition, The Progressive Labor Party organized a Union Square demonstration in 1887. When the Second Socialist International called for workers across the world to lay down their tools and unite on May 1, 1889, demonstrating in favor of an eight-hour working day, Union Square quickly became the focus for annual May Day parades. The first parade in 1890 began peacefully enough when 9,000 union members marched through the square.[87] In 1891, however, divisiveness appeared among the Left. The anarchists, led by Emma Goldman and Alexander Berkman, demanded time on the speaker's podium. The Socialists refused, but Berkman prevailed by lifting Emma onto a wagon. When she began to speak, someone intentionally hitched a horse to her platform and the wagon rolled away. The next day's newspaper proclaimed that there had been ''a mysterious young woman on a truck who had waved a red flag and urged revolution, her high-pitched voice putting the horse to flight.''[88] From the late 1890s until World War II, Union Square continued to be associated with labor groups protesting against unemployment, in favor of free speech, against U.S. involvement in World War I, in reaction to the ''red scare'' of the 1920s, and against police brutality in the 1930s. As if symbolic of the decline of labor movements in America, however, the square was remodeled in 1930, marking an end to the era of political protests.

THE SHOPPING DISTRICT

If one climbed to the top of the most conspicuous structure on Union Square in 1872, the 150-foot cast-iron Domestic Sewing Machine Building (designed by Griffith Thomas) on the southwest corner of Broadway and Fourteenth Street

Fig. 107. Domestic Sewing Machine Building, 837–843 Broadway at Fourteenth Street. Following a period of restrained cast-iron facades, the 1870s and 1880s witnessed more flamboyant designs in imitation of stone structures in which the cast-iron facade was treated like a metal skin drawn over the entire structure and then molded and shaped into elaborate forms. The Domestic Building, designed by Griffith Thomas in 1872, offered colossal Corinthian columns, executed in two-dimensional relief, carved brackets, pediments, balconies, and a corner pavilion topped with a dome, to produce an eclectic landmark that dominated Union Square. (Courtesy of the New-York Historical Society, New York City)

(fig. 107), one would have seen from the dome what a Domestic Company advertisement described as:

> . . . one of the finest views in this country . . . New York city lies stretched at its feet; looking out over the Bay of New York the beholder realizes something of its greatness, its surface covered with all varieties of sailing craft and the noble steamship bringing to our shores the wealth of foreign countries, or carrying the well-known "Domestic" to the uttermost parts of the earth. Our country friends are earnestly invited when in New York to take in this magnificent view.[89]

From above, one looked down on a mosaic of buildings along the spine of Broadway where all the values of a new consumer society were concentrated and condensed: its department stores, its artists' studios, its theaters, its hotels, its cafes and restaurants, its publishing houses, its promenades, its crowds and public festivals (see fig. 39). Below lay a cultural map of New York, for New York's social classes were bracketed by the amount of ambition they held, the money they possessed, and the pleasure and amusement in which they indulged.

It was the style of one's life that determined the social rank of the nineteenth-century bourgeoisie. Money was spent to achieve a certain decorum evidenced by the clothes one wore, the house one furnished, and the food one ate. To show off one's wealth and cultural status, the home had to have at least one receiving salon furnished with a piano, paintings, crystal chandeliers, and every nook and cranny filled with cast statuary, clocks, and clutter, underlined and muffled by draperies, doilies, and cushions.[90] One of the major indications of social status—apart from this conspicuous consumption—was the waste of time, shown by a leisurely promenade, and by the possession of servants, or decorative women, who indirectly advertised one's status. Thus women, who were not significantly in the work force until after 1914, were luxuriously dressed, becoming demonstrable signs of uselessness and decoration who, while they were themselves nonfunctional, delimited male social rank and style.[91]

When a New Yorker was asked in the 1890s why he preferred to reside in the city, the *Real Estate Record* claimed he most often replied: "because of its liveliness, or to use a phrase so beloved of architects, it gives the best opportunity to see and assume 'all the modern improvements' in dress, conversation, manners, literature and thought."[92] And a *Scribner's* article of the same vintage noted that "'. . . the 'flaneur' seems at last to have made his appearance. The crowd is beginning to stroll, instead of hurrying and rushing heretofore. People look at each other, and are even conscious of being looked at. . . . Cabs have sprung up. Hansoms have really become an established institution. In a word, the out-of-doors spectacle is far more interesting than it used to be, and in natural consequence, the promenading procession of spectators is becoming so too."[93] The *Real Estate Record* continued, "When men take more leisure and come to desire a wider variety and a better quality of things, when, in short, they occupy more time in spending and less time in making money, they at once tend to increase the aggregate of production and its quality, besides enriching their own lives with a more bounteous experience and enobling it with a fine taste."[94] Thus each promenader along Ladies Mile was repeatedly taught to catalogue and consequently master the mappings of a new cultural system. "Department stores and display windows, popular newspapers and mass advertisement . . . sought to codify the world of dominant and desirable values for a population prepared by ambition but not by instruction, for the complex hierarchization of capital.''[95]

In the early days of retailing, when Catherine Street in lower Manhattan was its center, little knowledge of such instruction of buyers — of advertising techniques—existed.[96] Taking over a double store in 1833, Lord and Taylor, with no concern for the artistic display of its goods, simply filled its shelves and windows with bolts of English dry goods to be used for dresses, blankets, and linens, plainly advertising the quality and price of its merchandise by sidewalk placards. But things would soon change. By 1853, when New York City had become the great clothing emporium of the world, where half of all its commerce was devoted to the dry goods business, retailing had taken on a different appearance. As an advertising gesture, the finest retail store in the city was erected in 1846: A. T. Stewart's white Tuckahoe marble palace (which was attributed to Joseph Trench and John B. Snook) on the east side of Broadway just north of City Hall Park (fig. 108).

Reporting on the opening of this great store, the *Herald* proclaimed, ''Mr. Stewart had paid the ladies of this city a high compliment in giving them such a

Fig. 108. A. T. Stewart's dry goods store, Broadway and Chambers Street, 1851. Stewart's first store was considered his best building. The stately, refined, yet mammoth white Tuckahoe marble facade with its daring plate-glass windows started a revolution in New York's commercial architecture when it was erected in 1846. The building is extant. (Courtesy of the New-York Historical Society, New York City)

beautiful resort in which to while away their leisure hours of the morning.[97] And P. B. Wight wrote that this remarkable structure was "an important link between two styles of store architecture which have prevailed in New York. The one . . . the old stores of Broad and Beaver Streets of which the fronts seldom ever had anything more elaborate in the first story than plain square granite posts, carrying granite lintel and water table, while the fronts above this were of brick with square windows with one small moulding to each."[98] A. T. Stewart's dry goods store, on the other hand, was "a real sensation. Nothing like it in the line of store-building had been seen." The *Broadway Journal* claimed, "its design makes a nearer approach to some of the facades of the London Clubhouses than that of any other building in the city."[99]

The interior of this commercial palace created a sensation as well. Polished mahogany counters with marble shelves, a large circular hall topped by a magnificent dome, paintings, frescoes, and chandeliers, dandified floowalkers and handsome young clerks, and a Ladies Parlor with full-length Parisian mirrors on the second floor to preen in or to view the first American fashion shows, were important gestures Stewart offered in the first retail store to cater entirely to women.[100] Although, strictly speaking, not a department store, Stewart's store was divided into different specialty floors: the first was for retail customers, the basement was for carpeting and floor cloths, and the upper lofts were reserved for the wholesale departments. More than 300 salesmen and clerks, over 2,000 French windowpanes, and 400 gas burners used at night helped to create such an illusion of splendor and magnificence that Stewart's business soon produced more than $7 million per year.[101]

Philip Hone, the illustrious mayor of New York, referred to this commercial palace as architecturally a "useless piece of extravagance." But later Winston Weisman would credit it to a reaction against the staid pre-1845 Republican period of Greek Revival architecture.[102] The Greek mode, with its porticoes and symmetrical plan, failed to provide a solution for commercial architecture, while the adoption of the Italian Renaissance palazzo form offered spacious and well-lighted interiors, a plan that could be enlarged in segments and at minimal expense as commerce demanded. A relatively permeable space allowed the circulation network of the store to dominate the interior arrangement: open stairways, magnificent entryways, and a flexible floor plan filled with display cases through which customers could wander in dreamlike abandonment.

The department store of the nineteenth century was the archetypal symbol of the rising bourgeois culture.[103] Through their architectural style, the great marble and cast-iron emporiums of New York expressed the bourgeoisie's desire to legitimate the world of commerce, to turn the experience of shopping into a cultural event, and to create popular tastes with commanding displays of sumptuous items. But the rise of the department store was as much a managerial revolution as a cultural celebration; for the first time, large groups of workers, hierarchically organized, were assembled together in one work place. Women began to enter the work force in the 1850s, albeit on a limited basis, first as seamstresses and laundresses and then as shop workers. The traditional values of sovereign loyalty, thrift, self-restraint, and familial alignments were necessarily displaced in a new world that stressed conspicuous consumption, competitive advancement, the debtor and the creditor, and the fickleness of fashion. The department store, by symbolizing the new world of luxury and displacing authentic values by com-

Fig. 109. R. H. Macy's Store at 204–206 Sixth Avenue, south of Fourteenth Street, 1858. Quaker merchant Rowland Macy opened a fancy dry-goods store in 1858 in which he developed a fixed price system for every item: he sold goods at lower prices than his competitors, bought and sold only for cash rather than credit, and advertised vigorously. (Courtesy of the New-York Historical Society, New York City)

Fig. 110. Completed Gilbert elevated railroad, passenger station at Sixth Avenue and Fourteenth Street. (From *Frank Leslie's Illustrated Newspaper*, June 8, 1878: 241.) View west shows the six properties R. H. Macy added and remodeled along Fourteenth Street between 1866 and 1872. (Courtesy of the New-York Historical Society, New York City)

mercial events, brought forward what was feared in modernization: a crisis of cultural authority and the threat of spiritual and moral decadence.

The architecture of the department store epitomized the new style of consumption. Crowds were drawn into its open interior to gaze on and purchase the vast array of commodities, lured by luxurious items in newfangled iron-clad shop windows, tricked by every feat of advertisement and opulent displays. In these early years of merchandising, no marble palace could be too magnificent in size or design to adequately seduce this consumer crowd. "Commodities," Walter Benjamin has written:

> derive the same effect [charm displayed by addicts under the influence of drugs] from the crowd that surges around them and intoxicates them. The concentration of customers which makes the market, which in turn makes the commodity into a commodity, enhances its attractiveness to the average buyer. When Baudelaire speaks of "the big cities' state of religious intoxication," the commodity is probably the unnamed subject of this state. And the "holy prostitution of the soul" compared with "that which people call love is quite small, quite limited, and quite feeble," really can be nothing else than the prostitution of the commodity soul.[104]

The commercial era of Ladies Mile began in 1858 when R. H. Macy opened a store at 204 Sixth Avenue on the south side of Fourteenth Street and began to expand through the gradual acquisition of neighboring town houses (fig. 109). Six properties were added between 1866 and 1872, and eventually four more were included until the store was modernized in the early 1880s and new fronts were added[105] (fig. 110). Once again, A. T. Stewart embarked on a pioneering venture when his cast-iron palace designed by John Kellum was constructed on

Fig. 111. A. T. Stewart broadsheet advertising the fall season stocks, October 11, 1879. (Courtesy of the New-York Historical Society, New York City)

Broadway between Ninth and Tenth streets in 1862. Believed to be the largest block in the United States devoted to a single retail firm, it offered as a first view to the visitor entering this magnificent store a great rotunda 80 by 48 feet reaching up to the dome. An army of clerks and a swarm of cash boys (who ran back and forth between cashier and clerk) stood on the first floor where silks, dress-goods, men's furnishings, linens, domestics' clothing, boy's clothing, gloves, trimmings, and notions were on display. Indian shawls, wedding trousseaux, cloaks, and mantillas could be obtained on the second floor. On the third floor splendid carpets—Aubussons, Axminsters, Moquettes, and Persian rugs—were unrolled (fig. 111). A laundry room, the receiving rooms from foreign manufacturers, the distributing rooms, and 400 to 500 sewing girls were all to be found on the fourth floor. On the fifth floor a major part of the enterprise took place: a linen service that laundered and supplied hotels, steamers, and public buildings with fresh linen. Nearly 1,000 employees (800 of whom were women or girls) worked on the fourth and fifth floors alone, and another 100 superintendents, cashiers, bookkeepers, ushers, porters, clerks, and cash boys kept this great machine in operation.[106] A. T. Stewart, it was said:

regarded his employees as cogs in the complicated machinery of his establishment. . . the men are numbered and timed. There is a penalty attached to all delinquencies. It takes all a man can earn for the first month or so to pay his fines. He is fined if he exceeds the few minutes alloted to dinner. He is fined if he eats on the premises. He is fined if he sits during business hours. He is fined if he comes late or goes early. He is fined if he misdirects a bundle. He is fined if he mistakes a street or number. He is fined if he miscounts the money, or gives the wrong change.[107]

The Commercial Palazzo

Much has been written about the commercial "palazzo" of nineteenth-century Manhattan,[108] and yet when compared to the grand European emporiums of similar decades, how austere and utilitarian its architecture appears. The origins of the Parisian department stores go back to the Palais Royal. In the gardens of the Palais, which were open to the public, the Duc d'Orléans rented space where ordinary Parisians were welcome to wile away their leisure hours, to spend their money in cafés, theaters, clubs, brothels, gambling saloons, apartments, and in the first arcade of shops selling luxury goods. Such arcades, dealing in exotic curiosities, objets d'art, furniture and painting, gave rise to the fashionable Parisian department store.[109]

When Aristide Boucicault built the Bon Marché in 1868, designed by L. C. Boileau and engineered by Gustave Eiffel, the same concept remained: no expense was too great, no building too elegant if it could lure vast numbers of people to consume huge quantities of goods. And indeed, the Bon Marché was a spectacular building: its skeleton iron-frame construction with glass-covered roofing sent cascades of light down to the shopping floor; its free-hanging staircases and galleries lined with balconies enabled shoppers to experience visually the store in all its dimensions. A great exposition hall crowned with cupolas dominated the Paris skyline. Decorated with monumental and ornate gateways and a portal rising the entire height of the structure, the building beckoned the promenader with promises of unimagined delight.[110]

New Yorkers had to be content with less spectacular fare. Ten years after it originally opened in 1862, the second Stewart store, a cast-iron palace, had expanded to cover an entire city block. Yet P. B. Wight complained there was nothing about this warehouse architecture that would attract the attention of ordinary passersby except for its giant size (fig. 112).

> It bears all over it an evidence of cheapness, especially when we observe it is of iron . . . a cheapness which comes from the desire to save pattern-making. In all probability, not more than six patterns were required to cast the several thousand tons which are put in this great iron wall. There is nothing inside of this store except iron columns, all cast from one pattern and no end of plaster-corniced girders, save the great cast-iron well-hole over the glove counter with its bull's eye skylight above. This is a perfect mine of wasted iron, which, if properly used, would construct several respectable buildings. It is safe to say that this building has done more to retard architectural progress in New York than any other dozen buildings of the worst possible designs. It overawes the thoughtless by its sheer size and seizes the sympathy of the sentimental by the purity of its white paint,— when it is fresh.[111]

Stewart's first store, P. B. Wight believed, had been an innovative design (see fig. 108).

> Even the Westchester Marble was a novelty. Soon it began to be copied, but only in an indifferent way. Cast-iron had just been introduced in the first store fronts as a substitution for granite; and immediately Stewart's marble

Fig. 112. A. T. Stewart's uptown store at the corner of Broadway and Tenth Street, built to the designs of John Kellum in 1862 before its final enlargement, ca. 1869. The essence of the store's classically detailed cast-iron architecture was its standardized form and its prefabricated parts. Yet contemporaries felt the ratio of solid wall to openings was so attenuated that the dominance of voids became unpleasant to the eye. The discriminating critic reacted against this mass-produced architecture as makeshift and impermanent. The building was demolished in 1954. (Courtesy of the New-York Historical Society, New York City)

Corinthian columns were copied in that material; and to this day they are considered by the average New York architect to be the proper thing for first-class wholesale stores. Since the Devil had not yet invented galvanized-iron cornices, Stewart's cornice was copied generally in wood, and sometimes in stone or marble, while his Italian windows were imitated everywhere; but invariably the details were made coarse and clumsy. For, though the architects were for years trying to copy this building, they never produced anything half so good, and the old building stands to this day as the best example of classic or Italian store architecture in New York.[112]

Flat facades and flat-roofed cast-iron buildings, with their ready-made fronts clumsily repeating the same architectural details, no matter how many stories high or how broad the width, did not necessarily increase the artistic merit of the architecture, yet this was the American Renaissance style witnessed in the flowering of the commercial palace during the 1850s and 1860s. Henry Van Brunt eloquently lectured his fellow architects in the winter of 1859 that this was the cast-iron age and with it came the opening of immense new fields for inventive and reformative architecture and new methods for decorative construction. But architecture refused to admit cast iron, or in doing so merely enslaved it to the basest uses, denying it honor and respect. A mechanical architecture, Van Brunt believed, would follow strict unities and formal repetitions, expressing the mechanical means by which it was formed: "... the use of iron actually demands from us a mechanical treatment of it with the mould, we may fairly expect that the principle of monotony, usually so repugnant to a stone architecture, may under these more favorable circumstances be elevated to a beauty and an honor. For... monotony is as noble in iron as variety in stone."[113] Leopold Eidlitz retorted "... iron never can, and never will be, a suitable material for forming the main walls of architectural monuments. The only material for that purpose always has been, and now is, stone... a building bedizened with cast iron ornaments would give to the question, for what purpose the building is erected, would be plain to me as though it was written upon it with large cast iron letters: 'FOR SHOW MORE THAN FOR ANY OTHER PURPOSE.'"[114]

By the 1880s, visiting architects from Europe found that this go-ahead American iron architecture that merely bolted sheets of iron onto a steel frame never rose above the rawness of a railway shed, for they believed the artistic quality of a building instead must reside in the grandeur of its facade, a grandeur that must be free from deceitful tamperings and mechanical effects.[115] Certainly some of the chaotic confusion of New York streets could be attributed to the plethoric detailing of the cast-iron storefronts that lined the length of Broadway from City Hall Park to Madison Square. Iron edifices, the *Real Estate Record* quoted Ruskin in 1876 as saying, "are not architecture at all, they lack that element which gives value. It is the machine, the lathe, the mould that has been at work, not the hand of the skillfull artisan."[116] Why were owners and builders so infatuated with this treacherous and unreliable material? Not only had the Chicago and Boston fires of 1871 and 1872, respectively, shown the material to be vulnerable to the ravages of fire, but wherever such a structure burned down in New York, the iron curled up like scrolls.[117] Yet other features of cast-iron architecture captured the utilitarian spirit of the times. By becoming a science rather than an art, architecture, it was hoped, would give itself over to the use of new materials, to the development of new building types, and the creation of new structural forms. Iron architecture, some critics and architects believed, would develop an expressive form entirely its own and finally offer the nineteenth century an architecture for its time.

It is thought that James Bogardus was the first to erect a completely cast-iron facade in New York with the design of a drugstore for John Milnau in 1848.[118] This was soon followed by his own warehouse and five stores for Edgar Laing on the northwest corner of Washington and Murray streets. It took three days to erect these prefabricated structures, probably the reason why cast-iron facades became so popular. They were cheap to fabricate, quick to erect, easy to maintain, and believed to be fireproof. The popularization and advertisement of cast-iron architecture was carried out in the 1850s and 1860s by Badger's Architectural Iron Works. Badger even hired a designer, George Johnston, to develop stock items and, by interpreting an architect's specific drawings, add to the stock. Hence, any builder could draw from a catalog of standard cast-iron elements, although this did not necessarily improve on the art.[119]

Montgomery Schuyler pointed out that Richard Morris Hunt designed two experiments in iron. Hunt was generally successful in metallic detailing, but Schuyler believed:

> store fronts [were] another matter, and many architects of twenty years ago [1870s] were condemned for their sins to try their hands at store fronts. The architectural iron works used to have facades on hand of any style you wanted, or they were of no style that the judicious wanted, being only imitations of masonry. The architects when they were appealed to, made various kinds of struggles to respect the material. Among these effects none were more interesting than the two fronts erected on the east side of middle Broadway from Mr. Hunt's designs. . . . [in 1871 and 1874].[120]

> The "iron age" in commercial architecture produced nothing better than these two fronts and very few things so good. But, like the other comparative successes they indicated that the problems were not really soluble. It is a matter of congratulations upon architectural grounds that at about the time when these fronts were done, experimentaton in iron fronts should have been brought to an end by the demonstration of the fires of Chicago and Boston that fronts of unprotected iron-work were not practically trustworthy, and architects were thus released from the attempt to solve the insoluble.[121]

And the *Real Estate Record* complained in 1877:

> the introduction of these fronts must be regarded as a bold and successful attempt on the part of iron founders to magnify their office in the construction of store buildings. There may have been a time within the past fifteen years, owing to the high price of mechanical labor, and the exorbitant rates exacted by stone quarries and brick manufacturers, when the relative cost was in favor of iron-work, but this period has long passed away and become obsolete. Brick and stone now compete easily and successfully with iron. . . . It is true that architects in dealing with brick and stone are apt to over-elaborate the designs, and in this way add greatly to the expense. But this is a matter entirely under the control of the respective owners, and

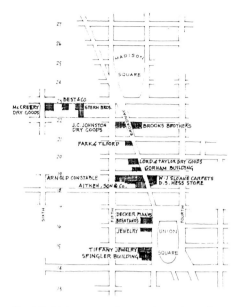

Fig. 113. Major stores along Ladies Mile: 1860s–1890s.

they have only to insist upon having strictly observed the two prime factors of successful store architecture, to wit, strength and simplicity of design, in order to secure the desired economic effect in the working of brick and stone.[122]

Along Ladies Mile, however, cast iron would prevail.

The Boundaries of Commerce

American commercial architecture adopted a functional form: beauty was found in perfect mechanical efficiency. Ladies Mile of the late 1860s through the 1880s abounded in Renaissance boxlike buildings and flat cast-iron facades (figs. 113, 114). Diagonally opposite the Stewart Store, John Kellum designed another cast-iron structure, the James McCreery store in 1868[123] (fig. 115). The real inroads of commercialization above Fourteenth Street were felt, however, when Renwick's Church of the Puritans was torn down in 1869 and replaced by yet another Kellum-designed cast-iron building, the five-story Tiffany Building, at the southwest corner of Fifteenth Street and Union Square (fig. 116). It was not long before the older downtown dry goods stores joined this march northward. Arnold Constable and Company opened a new store in 1869 in a marble-fronted five-story building (881–883 Broadway) on the west side of Broadway between Eighteenth and Nineteenth streets, designed by Griffith Thomas (fig. 117). In 1873 Thomas added a huge two-story mansard roof for extra floor space and in 1877 a cast-iron replica of the Broadway facade was designed, again by Thomas, for the new Fifth Avenue extension.[124] In the same year that Arnold Constable and Company began to build, Lord and Taylor moved into a highly ornate five-story cast-iron building, designed by James Giles, on the southwest corner of Broadway and Twentieth Street at 901 Broadway (fig. 118).

Two of the most unusual of all the cast-iron stores in the vicinity of Ladies Mile were for the Domestic Sewing Machine Company, designed by Griffith Thomas, on the southwest corner of Broadway and Fourteenth Street in 1872 (see fig. 107) and Hugh O'Neill's store, designed by Mortimer Merritt in 1875, on the west side of Sixth Avenue between Twentieth and Twenty-first streets. The architectural glory of the Domestic building was carried still further in the O'Neill store with its bulbous Byzantine domes rising above the five-story towers that rounded each corner. A center pavilion higher than its adjacent side bays was crowned by a sculpted pediment supported by a great bracketed cornice.[125]

Because the major property owners along Broadway below Fourteenth Street, A. T. Stewart among them, had opposed any form of rapid transit along this avenue, by the 1870s lower Broadway had been all but deserted by the fashionable retail trade. The sole means of transport was still the lumbering omnibus; awkward to enter and alight from, it was a particularly undesirable vehicle for ladies, exacerbated by the absence of a superintendent who could enforce decorum on the part of the unruly passengers. Although horsecar railroads ran parallel to both sides of Broadway below Fourteenth Street, they did not contribute to the welfare of the avenue, for they either crossed objectionable parts of the city or else diverged at sharp angles from Broadway, making it inaccessible to women shoppers whose patronage alone created the best shopping district.[126] Sixth Avenue, on the other hand, was the earliest thoroughfare to accept horsecars, and it soon became the favored seat for trade, with new business streets developing

[Fig. 114]

RETAIL BUSINESSES NEAR LADIES MILE: 1860s–1880s

	Date	Architect	Location
Broadway			
A. T. Stewart Store	1862	John Kellum	Broadway and Tenth Street (east side) (demolished 1954)
Tiffany Building	1869	John Kellum	Broadway and Fifteenth Street (southwest corner)
James McCreery Store	1868	John Kellum	Broadway and Eleventh Street (west side)
Aitken, Son & Company (Hoyt Building)	1868	Griffith Thomas	Broadway and Eighteenth Street (northwest corner) (moved into this structure in 1875)
Arnold Constable and Company	1868	Griffith Thomas	Broadway and Nineteenth Street (southwest corner)
Lord and Taylor	1869	James Giles	Broadway and Twentieth Street (southwest corner)
Myron Decker Pianos	1870	Leopold Eidlitz	33 Union Square West (demolished 1892)
Domestic Sewing Machine Company	1872	Griffith Thomas	Broadway and Fourteenth Street (southwest corner) (demolished)
Spingler Building	1878	Benjamin Warner	Union Square West between Fourteenth and Fifteenth streets (demolished 1896)
J. C. Johnston, Dry Goods	1879	Unknown	Moved into brownstone building on Broadway and Twenty-second Street (southwest corner), erected in the 1860s
W. & J. Sloane Store	1881	W. Wheeler Smith	Broadway and Nineteenth Street (southeast corner)
Gorham Building	1883	Edward Kendall	Broadway and Nineteenth Street (northwest corner)
D. S. Hess Store	1883	Henry Fernbach	876 Broadway between Eighteenth and Nineteenth streets (east side)
Brooks Brothers	1884	Charles Haight	Broadway and Twenty-first Street (east side, former site of Park Theatre) (demolished 1937)
Sixth Avenue			
Hugh O'Neill's Store	1875	Mortimer Merritt	Sixth Avenue between Twentieth and Twenty-first streets (west side)
B. Altman and Company	1876	D. & J. Jardine	Sixth Avenue and Nineteenth Street (southwest corner)
Simpson, Crawford and Simpson Dry Goods	1879	unknown	Sixth Avenue between Nineteenth and Twentieth streets (west side; redesigned by William H. Hume, 1900)

(continued on following page)

Ehrich Brothers Dry Goods	1889	Alfred Zucker & Co	Sixth Avenue and Twenty-third Street (southwest corner)
Siegel-Cooper and Company	1896	Delemos and Cordes	Sixth Avenue between Eighteenth and Nineteenth streets (east side)

Twenty-third Street

Stern Brothers Department Store	1878	Henry Fernbach	32–36 Twenty-third Street (south side) between Fifth and Sixth avenues (38–46 added in 1892; architect William Schickel)
LeBoutillier Brothers	1882	unknown	31 Twenty-third Street (north side) between Fifth and Sixth avenues
Best and Company	1882	unknown	60 Twenty-third Street (south side) near Sixth Avenue (remodeled 1905, architect James B. Snook and Sons)
James McCutcheon and Company	1882	Henry J. Hardenbergh	14 West Twenty-third Street (remodeled 1892; architect G. H. Billings)
James McCreery Store	1884	unknown	Twenty-third Street and Sixth Avenue (southeast corner) (former site of Booth Theatre)
Robert J. Horner's Furniture Store	1886	John B. Snook	61–65 Twenty-third Street (north side)

Fig. 115. West side of Broadway between Eleventh and Twelfth streets, ca. 1890. The still existing but altered James McCreery and Company Store, designed by John Kellum, is on the extreme left. Unlike Stewart's store, the McCreery building included broad arched windows flanked by three-quarter, round, engaged columns supporting heavy cornices that demarcated the stories. A mansard roof accented with dormers and lacy ironwork ornamented this Renaissance version of the commercial palace. (Courtesy of the New-York Historical Society, New York City)

at right angles and acting as fenders for the avenue. Within less than a year after the opening of the rapid transit line along Sixth Avenue, Fourteenth Street and Twenty-third Street from Fifth Avenue to Seventh Avenue were largely turned over to retail shops.[127] In the meantime lower Broadway, especially during the economic depression of the 1870s, was downgraded: in 1876 there were at least 200 "for let" placards on various buildings.[128] Wholesale stores were

Fig. 116. Tiffany and Company, 11–15 Union Square West, 1903. Designed by John Kellum in 1869 for the showrooms and silversmith operations of Charles Tiffany, the five-story cast-iron structure was slightly more ornamented than the Stewart store. In the Tiffany building also, the repetition of Corinthian columns and arches enabled large expanses of plate glass to allow light into the interior. Tiffany moved uptown in 1906, leaving the building to the Star Shirt Company and several other garment manufacturers. The building is extant, but entirely remodeled. (Courtesy of the Museum of the City of New York, New York City)

transformed into offices, the remaining mercantile buildings were mainly clothing stores, and many structures were temporarily occupied by auction marts, jobbing houses, and businesses selling bankrupt stocks.[129]

During the 1870s the area of Union Square and Fourteenth Street beame the important retail and wholesale district of New York, probably because it received an influx of customers from several directions—down or up Broadway, and from the two rivers. Macy's, at the corner of Fourteenth Street and Sixth Avenue, through its practice of bargain prices and reputable goods, had built up an immense retail business on its corner and in 1880 proposed to build a great arcade 150 feet along Fourteenth Street, extending back some 200 feet toward Thirteenth Street. Tiffany's and the stores on Union Square attracted vast throngs of customers, and Twenty-third Street, while still not so important, would some day profit from its close proximity to the luxurious hotels.[130] Ladies Mile by this time was virtually controlled by the retail trade: the leading jewelry, dry goods, and fancy goods establishments had all concentrated within this district where wealthy ladies as well as ordinary shoppers congregated.

The steady march of commerce up the Broadway spine as far as Madison Square was a matter of concern by the late 1870s, for it was possible to imagine that all eligible property below Thirty-fourth Street might soon be used for business purposes. Already hotels and shops were cropping up on Fifth Avenue at isolated intervals as far north as Fifty-ninth Street, and in 1877 a row of shops was projected on Sixtieth Street just off Fifth Avenue. Commercial investors, even in times of economic depression, were willing to pay exorbitant prices, and it was rumored that R. H. Macy and Company had offered nearly a half million dollars for ten lots of the Sweeney block, the east side of Broadway, between Thirty-third and Thirty-fourth streets.[131]

Many of the former mansions along Union Square were being renovated as commercial structures. On the southeast corner of Seventeenth Street and Fourth Avenue Mrs. Jacob Little started to partially reconstruct the old Westmoreland Hotel, but finally realizing that the bearing walls were not strong enough to support the new superstructure, she razed the old building and began with a completely new construction. On the corner of Sixteenth Street and Union Square, the Austin-Spicer family reconstructed its building and pushed the facade out to the building line; while this was an attractive solution, the *Real Estate Record* regretted that the family did not rebuild anew and offer the square a modern construction.[132] Holding out against the inroads of commerce, the Van Buren estate still retained many of its brownstone mansions along Fourteenth Street as well as the Spingler house on Union Square West. Finally in 1878 the Spingler house was torn down and, next door to the Tiffany Building, a five-story massive cast-iron warehouse was erected.[133]

Fig. 117. *Below left.* West side of Broadway between Eighteenth and Nineteenth streets, showing the Hoyt Building on the left and the Arnold Constable store on the right, ca. 1870s. Both buildings were designed by Griffith Thomas between 1868 and 1869. These still existing marble structures exemplify what critic Winston Weisman called the baroque phase of the commercial palace, which featured a greater number of architectural elements, sculpted moldings and ornamentation, statuary, recessed windows, pavilions, corner towers, and mansard roofs. (Courtesy of the New-York Historical Society, New York City)

Fig. 118. *Below right.* Lord and Taylor's store, 1872. Designed by James Giles in 1869, the cast-iron frontage extended 100 feet along Broadway and 125 feet on Twentieth Street. This building and its later extensions are extant. (Courtesy of the New-York Historical Society, New York City)

A stroll along the sidewalks of Fourteenth Street between Union Square and Sixth Avenue in 1879 would convince anyone of how thoroughly this area of Manhattan had been given over to shopping. In 1879 Edward Kendall was the architect of yet another new store designed on the site of the old Delmonico's, at the northeast corner of Fourteenth Street and Fifth Avenue. With a frontage of 128 feet on Fifth Avenue and 42 feet on Fourteenth Street, the building surpassed anything New Yorkers had ever seen before. A five-story brick structure, it was crowned with a mansard roof, and its outer walls were trimmed with brownstone and molded brick.[134] While the extraordinary popularity of Macy's store signaled the radical change along Fourteenth Street, no real estate investor benefited more from this change than W. Jennings Demorest, who converted at least fourteen private houses into stores, until not one unremodeled house remained on the street[135] (figs. 119, 120).

Nothing seemed to stop the advertising gimmicks of the retailers. The *Real Estate Record* proclaimed:

O'Neill, on Sixth Avenue, has tried the effect of a novelty in color in painting the outside of his store, which will probably have many imitators. Instead of the ordinary red, he has given his store a coating of yellow with black lines and brown trimmings, which is certainly very attractive and striking. . . . It is something to have any relief from the browns and stone or red brick of New York City . . . an apartment house of yellow Milwaukee brick, etc. would, we think, be a pleasing novelty and will prove attractive. It will be remembered that yellow is the color which can be seen farthest. The most distant object in nature is the yellow star with its background of dark blue. The most effective signs on the streets are gold with a background of black, and we hope that architects and designers in constructing or recommending new edifices in New York will try the effects of yellow . . .[136]

In 1878 New York's largest and most magnificent department store, Stern Brothers, opened on Twenty-third Street, and would not be outdone in grandeur until Siegel-Cooper and Company opened its doors in 1896 (fig. 121). The *Real Estate Record* announced:

The firm of Stern Bros. whose Sixth Avenue establishment has become a household word among lady shoppers generally, have just moved into their magnificent bazaar on Twenty-third street, near Fifth Avenue. Aside from the building proper, which is an ornament even to that prominent thoroughfare, the very fact of such a business being moved to the locality shows the shrewd foresight and keen observation which characterizes most of our leading retail merchants. In the immediate vicinity of the Fifth Avenue Hotel, whence daily hundreds of ladies from all parts of the country temporarily residing there go out on shopping expeditions, in the very centre of what is to-day New York's most prominent rendez-vous for all that is elegant and wealthy, the new establishment of Stern Bros. will soon prove not only a remunerative investment to the owners, but an attractive place for those thousands of purchasers who, somehow or other, have been inspired with the idea that it is no longer fashionable to go below Twenty-third Street.[137]

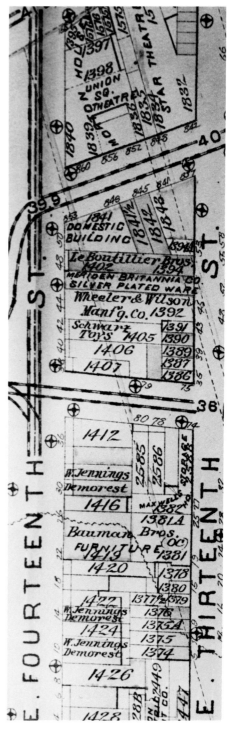

Fig. 119. Detail from Robinson's Insurance Map of 1885, showing the south side of East Fourteenth Street, between Fifth Avenue and Broadway. Demorest properties are identified as 2, 10–12, 14–16, and 30–32. (Courtesy of the New York Public Library, New York City)

Fig. 120. *Above.* Two residential structures remodeled into commercial buildings (Henry Stede, Furst, and New York Bazaar) by W. Jennings Demorest, south side of East Fourteenth Street, ca. 1880. (Courtesy of the New-York Historical Society, New York City)

Fig. 121. *Right.* Stern Brothers department store, south side of Twenty-third Street between Fifth and Sixth Avenues, 1885. The seven-story, cast-iron structure, more than 200 feet wide, was designed by Henry Fernbach in 1878. A shopper entered the ultra-modern store through large walnut doors surrounded by heavy plate-glass windows. The Otis elevator enclosures were lined with mahogany and cherry wood, while a system of electric bells facilitated communication between all departments. An elaborate main staircase located in a central rotunda made Stern Brothers one of the most luxurious stores in the city. The extant structure was remodeled by William Schickel in 1892. A photographer's studio building located to the right of the store is provided with a canvas shade against southern light, which doubled as an advertisement. (Courtesy of the New York Public Library, New York City)

Gentlemen's Walk

> From Madison to Union Square, I often stroll to take the air,
> And at the pretty girls to stare, Walking up and down.
> I sometimes catch a gentle glance, That makes my heart with rapture dance,
> When I meet a lady friend, "by chance" walking up and down.
>
> At four each day I leave my home. And up and down Broadway I roam,
> Of course I seldom walk alone, I am known so well,
> I'm known at every step I take, and Oh, such pretty bows I make
> I was born the ladies hearts to break, And to be a swell.

(Sheet Music, "From Madison to Union Square," by Joseph Skelley, copyright 1874)

Union Square to Madison Square, a staid British tourist in the latter half of the nineteenth century noted, was the most cosmopolitan district of Manhattan, with all sorts of people—shopgirls, the latest pickpockets, beautiful women, politicians, and bookmakers—all offering various forms of reputable and disreputable purchase.[138] In addition, Ladies Mile was a place of rendezvous, a gentlemen's walk where four, five, or six men could be seen lolling about on the sidewalks, spreading, or so it was feared in those days, a system of indecent morality by gazing upon the "swell girls" getting in and out of their fashionable carriages and by making daily contact with women shop attendants in every store.[139]

The shop girl was a definite threat to the traditional boundaries of social control; she was blamed for being promiscuous, seduced by faddish clothes, and

FASHIONABLE STORE.

ONE OF THE FIRST LADIES IN THE CITY. "Is it customary to allow such low people to frequent your establishment? It is so annoying to overhear such vulgar remarks, as wishing to buy a
three dollar shawl even, when they know that every cent they can earn should be expended on something to eat, and not to wear. Such people ruin themselves by imitating their betters in dress; in
fact, it has entirely disgusted me with buying this set of sable. Just observe Fido! he can never
bear the sight of those miserable creatures. Dear Fido!"

HANDSOME CLERK. "Mr. Smasher will attend to her case. Indeed, Madam, it is very disagree-
able, I assure you. We will guard against such annoyances again in the future."

Fig. 122. "Rich and Poor in a Fashionable
Store," *Harper's Weekly*, 3, 1859: 32. (Courtesy
of the New-York Historical Society, New York
City)

unashamed to promenade without an escort. She often began to work as a
cashier at the age of twelve or thirteen, and for a tenement child the opulence of
the great department stores was seen as the high road to fortune (fig. 122). She
knew the rich and imitated them where she could: her cheap shoe had its French
heel, her neck its tin dog collar. "Gilt rings, bracelets and bangles, frizzes, bangs,
and cheap trimming of every order, swallow up her earnings. The imitation is
often more attractive than the real one, the girl knows it. She aspires to a
'manicure' set, to an opera glass, to anything that will simulate the daily life
paraded before her and most passionately desired."[140]

Another side of department store luxury that touched the nerve of bourgeois sensitivity was the discovery of the woman's ailment of "kleptomania."
Most of the items taken were of little value, such as lingerie or cheap jewelry, but

[Fig. 123]

TEMPLES OF LOVE IN THE VICINITY OF LADIES MILE, 1870
(From *The Gentleman's Directory of New York City,* 1870)

(House numbers began with 0 at Fifth Avenue, 100 at Sixth Avenue, and 100 at Fourth Avenue)

126 E. 12th Street	Ida Thompson, first-class parlor house, 4 lady boarders
112 E. 12th Street	Fanny Turnball, first-class parlor house, 4 lady boarders
55 E. 12th Street	Mrs. Fulton's house of assignation, first class, 10 rooms
30 E. 12th Street	Mrs. Leslie's house of assignation
16 E. 13th Street	Laura Howard, snobbish parlor house, 6 boarders
18 E. 13th Street	Mrs. Van Beuren's parlor and assignation house
20 E. 13th Street	Ida Parker's house of assignation
24 E. 13th Street	Minnie Grace parlor house, two lady boarders
104 E. 14th Street	Irme McGreedy, a first-class parlor house, 6 boarders
63 W. 15th Street	Mrs. Hall's first-class house of assignation
42 W. 15th Street	Jane McCord, first-class parlor house, 8 boarders
36 W. 15th Street	Fanny Phippany, second-class parlor house, 6 boarders
140 W. 16th Street	Bettie White, house of assignation
53 W. 16th Street	Fanny Bell, first-class parlor house
136 E. 22d Street	Mrs. Douglass's house of assignation
138 E. 22d Street	Mrs. Thompson's house of assignation
140 E. 22d Street	Mrs. Barclay's house of assignation
152 E. 22d Street	Mrs. Wilson's house of assignation
102 W. 22d Street	Mrs. Van Ness's house of assignation
103 W. 22d Street	Mrs. Porter's house of assignation and bar
140 W. 24th Street	Mrs. Woodbury's house of assignation
103 W. 25th Street	Mrs. Prescott's house of assignation
105 W. 25th Street	Kate Wood's ''Hotel de Wood''
109 W. 25th Street	Netti Smith's second-class boardinghouse
111 W. 25th Street	Mrs. Jolly's second-class boardinghouse
113 W. 25th Street	Mrs. King's second-class boardinghouse
115 W. 25th Street	Jennie Bennett's second-class boardinghouse
114 W. 26th Street	Mrs. Moultrie's ladies' boardinghouse
116 W. 26th Street	Sarah Wilburt's first-class parlor house
119 W. 26th Street	Mrs. Conklin's ladies' boardinghouse
121 W. 26th Street	Mrs. Cutler's ladies' boardinghouse
123 W. 26th Street	Margaret Belmont's first-class parlor house
124 W. 26th Street	Mrs. Brown's boardinghouse
127 W. 26th Street	Mme. Beaumont's second-class boardinghouse
129 W. 26th Street	Mrs. Morton's first-class house
131 W. 26th Street	Sallie Richard's house of assignation
131 W. 26th Street	Mrs. Sanchez's first-class house
143 W. 26th Street	Ida Langdon's house of assignation
145 W. 26th Street	Mrs. Bath's house for transient ladies

the losses mounted and so stores were vigorously policed. ''The female shoplifter,'' it was said, ''has that touch of nature left in her which makes a dry-goods store, variety store, or jewelry establishment, a most delightful spot to exercise her cunning."[141] The general exposure of the increasing throngs of customers to the goods on the counter, and the constant distraction of the surveillants, made shoplifting an easy trade but it startled bourgeois morality.[142]

The middle class in the late nineteenth century, desiring a civilized home life, began to flee the city for the peaceful shores of New Jersey, Long Island, or even Westchester County, leaving the wealthy and the aspiring to deal with the collection of bedouins, ruffians, and political jugglers. New York's morals and manners thus drifted from bad to worse and a corrupt municipal government only shared in the spread of vice. Covert crime increased, and houses of assignation grew in numbers and began to introduce prostitution into circles and places where it had never been known. Many frequenters of these houses of assignation, one account of the nether side of New York claimed in 1872, were married women driven by their insane desire for costumed display to add to their scanty incomes. Other young girls were led astray by faulty education and some by sheer necessity, but the chief dangers to the city were not the streetwalkers or residents of brothels but "on the contrary those women who are unsuspected prostitutes [who] occupy and defile the holiest position of domestic life, and there is no limit to the evil which their crimes produce."[143]

Broadway near Ladies Mile in the 1870s and 1880s was a haunt of many streetwalkers (fig. 123). After dark, from 7 to 11 o'clock, many well-dressed and comely females around fifteen to twenty-five years old were to be found promenading its length. These "nymphes des paves" or "cruisers" were generally small, good-looking, well educated, and had furnished rooms nearby to receive their gentlemen visitors.[144] Or one could select a "temple of love" from the *Gentleman's Directory.* Yet moralists warned, "It is always dangerous for the most virtuous to come in contact with pollution. Neither would we advise you to read minute accounts of this degradation. You will incur fearful risks in pursuing the story of demoralization. But you ought to know, you can not but know, that these places of wretchedness exist hard by."[145]

Items for Sale

A search of city directories between 1860 and 1900 yields a plausible explanation of why the area became known as Ladies Mile. Although the district between Union and Madison squares was still a fashionable residential area in 1860, six fancy dry goods stores had already invaded Broadway between Eighteenth and Nineteenth streets (fig. 124). By the 1870s the trend toward women's shopping needs had clearly emerged: eleven dressmakers, eleven milliners, and six hairdressers were on the scene. Luxury items such as pianos, jewelry, and furniture could also be purchased (fig. 125). In keeping with the 1860s trend toward retail, by the end of this decade the large department stores such as Arnold Constable and Lord and Taylor had made their appearance, accompanied by the well-known grocery store of Park and Tilford. During the economic depression of the 1870s, two more retail stores located in the vicinity of Ladies Mile, Aitken Sons and J. C. Johnston and Company (see fig. 113).

Lockwood's Illustrated Guide of 1872 claimed that the sightseer on Broadway passed many fine buildings where all sorts of fancy goods were sold and where "... handsome women standing at every show-window make the street-scene even more fascinating than the glowing colors shining behind the plate-glass."[146] Clearly, the intoxicating commodity drew a continuous stream of richly

[Fig. 124]

STORES AND SERVICES ON BROADWAY, FOURTEENTH TO TWENTY-THIRD STREET

	1860	1870	1880	1890	1900
SHOPS OR SERVICES RELATED TO DRESS					
Dressmaker	0	11	2	0	0
Dry goods	2	2	4	4	3
Fancy goods	6	4	3	3	1
Gentlemen's furnishings	0	3	5	2	3
Hairdresser	1	6	3	0	2
Laces and embroideries	1	4	1	0	0
Ladies dress trimmings	0	1	6	2	1
Milliner	0	11	9	7	0
Tailor	3	5	13	10	3
STORES WITH OTHER LUXURY GOODS					
Bookseller	3	4	7	1	1
China, glass	3	1	4	1	1
Confectioner	5	4	7	1	1
Florist	2	7	8	2	2
Furniture	0	6	3	6	1
Music	1	2	4	5	6
Pianoforte	0	4	5	3	4
Picture dealer	0	1	2	3	1
Silversmith	0	0	3	5	18
Watches and jewelry	1	5	5	4	8
OTHER					
Architect	1	4	5	5	17
Carpets, wholesale	0	0	0	0	23
Chiropodist	0	1	4	6	5
Druggist	5	4	2	1	1
Hotels	4	2	3	4	2
Jewelry manufacturing	0	1	11	8	15
Painter (genre)	0	3	3	0	0
Painter (landscape)	0	4	7	0	2
Painter (portrait)	0	5	16	2	5
Photographer	0	4	9	2	4
Physician	2	6	3	1	1
Schools	4	4	0	0	0

Data compiled from city directories by Sophia Schachter in "Ladies Mile: The History of the Retail Shopping District of Manhattan in the Nineteenth Century," 1981.

dressed women into Tiffany's to explore the "... grand museum of the most exquisite articles in jewels, gold and silver work, bronzes, statuary, bric-a-brac, and all the costly forms of ornament with which wealth delights to surround itself."[147] In 1869 Tiffany introduced the first flatware pattern, followed in the next few years by eight other styles. By 1880 its famous "chrysanthemum" pattern reflected the increasing influence of Japanese design, and in 1870 it intro-

Fig. 125. The Diamond Room at Tiffany's and the Lace Room at A. T. Stewart's (From "The Holiday Attractions of the Metropolis—Incidents of Mr. and Mrs. Brown's Christmas Peregrinations," (*Frank Leslie's Illustrated Newspaper*, Jan. 4, 1879: 300–301; courtesy of the New-York Historical Society, New York City)

Fig. 126. Singer patented sewing machine, 1890s. (Courtesy of the New-York Historical Society, New York City)

Fig. 127. The Wheeler and Wilson New York sewing machine and carpet to catch oil spills, ca. 1879. (Courtesy of Avery Library, Columbia University, New York City)

duced a water pitcher that became extremely popular.[148] Other silversmiths joined in Tiffany's success: by 1900 a total of nine different silversmiths stood along the Mile.

In the 1880s Ladies Mile was unquestionably the most luxurious retail district in the city. The success of Sixth Avenue had also become apparent although it never matched the fashionableness of Broadway. Luxury retail continued to prosper: G. Schirmer (music company), Decker Brothers (pianos), Brentano's (booksellers), Gorham (silversmith), and Magnin and Guedin (clocks) could all be found on Broadway. The statistics, begin, however, to show a shift in retail merchandising. More booksellers, china and glass manufacturers, confectioners and florists, as well as jewelry manufacturers, tailors, painters, architects, and photographers dominated the Mile. But two large retailers had also moved onto Broadway in the 1880s (W. & J. Sloane and Brooks Brothers), and Twenty-third Street was beginning to make its mark.

By the 1890s the shift toward loft manufacturing and offices was apparent. Only a few ladies' dry goods stores remained in the area. The directories of 1900 show a decline in almost every category of retail business while carpet wholesalers, jewelry manufacturers, and architectural services begin to dominate. The early years of 1900 would see the move uptown of Tiffany's (1905), Gorham (1906), W & J. Sloane (1912), Lord and Taylor and Arnold Constable (1914), and Brooks Brothers (1915).[149]

Dry Goods and Sewing Machines

Women's dress styles of the day involved quantities of ribbons, ruffles, buttons, braids, laces, and yards of fabric. A visit to the grand emporiums along Ladies Mile was a necessity for any lady of fashion, who was constantly in search of the newest and the most luxurious fabrics and trimmings to make up an outfit. By 1870 A.T. Stewart's Ninth Street store had expanded to cover the whole block, and buyers traveled all over Europe to bring back the finest goods from Manchester, Glasgow, Paris, and Berlin. Two Stewart warehouses in Lyon stored silk goods purchased by these buyers, and the kid glove factory of Alexander and Courvoisier in Paris worked exclusively for the store.[150] The James McCreery store, across the street from Stewart's, was also noted for its rich and elegant offerings, specializing in the latest novelties in styles and materials, and for its importation and making-up of sumptuous ball gowns and wedding dresses.[151] Although the two dry goods stores of Arnold Constable and Company and Lord and Taylor both were divided into the three main divisions of a department store —that is, into dry goods, carpets and upholstery—they appealed to different customers. The conservative shopper frequented Arnold Constable's, while Lord and Taylor—which advertised its wares with mannequins in its store windows and miles of silk and dress goods, hosiery, linens, small wares, and men's furnishings displayed on the counters of its first floor—appealed to the more adventurous shopper. Two of the most famous items at Lord and Taylor were Ladies Trousseaux A and B: version A contained 51 different articles and cost $230, while version B contained 46 articles and cost only $200.[152]

One of the most important inventions that supported the dry goods trade along Ladies Mile was the newfangled contraption called the sewing machine. Sigfried Giedion noted in *Mechanization Takes Command* that the high point of mechanization was reached with the elimination of complicated handwork and that this transition took place in America during the last half of the nineteenth century.[153] While he explored many effects mechanization had on the housewife and the home, he neglected to study the revolutionary impact of the sewing machine. In 1891 Robert S. Taylor, addressing the Patent Centennial Celebration, commented:

> It is too soon yet to estimate the full effect of the sewing machine upon human life and destiny. . . . It ushered in an epoch of cheap clothes, which means better clothes for the masses, more warmth, more cleanliness, more comfort. . . . The indirect consequences of the invention of the sewing machine reach farthest beyond our ken. Time was when half the human race were occupied chiefly in making clothes. When the machines took that avocation away from them they turned to other employments. The invasion of all occupations by women and the sweeping changes which have taken place in their relation to the law, society and business can be ascribed in large measure to the sewing machine.[154]

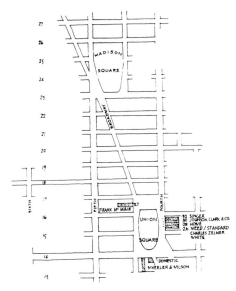

Fig. 128.. Sewing machine companies on Ladies Mile.

Exactly who was the inventor of the first sewing machine is difficult to ascertain, and jealous rivalries, legal battles, and trade monopolies dominate its early history. Nevertheless, the first patents appeared in 1849 and 1850 in England and America respectively. One of these early machines, patented by the Americans Morey and Johnson, was sent to the London Crystal Palace Exhibition of 1851. Few people paid attention to this peculiar machine except to make fun of such American eccentricities. In this vein an Italian reporter joked:

> A little further on you stop before a small brass machine about the size of a quart bottle; you fancy it is a meat roaster; not at all. Ha! Ha! It is a tailor! Yes, a veritable stitcher. Present a piece of cloth to it; suddenly it becomes agitated, it twists about, screams audibly—a pair of scissors are projected forth—the cloth is cut, a needle set to work, and lo and behold, the process of sewing goes on with feverish activity, and before you have taken three steps a pair of inexpressibles are thrown down at your feet, and the impatient machine, all fretting and fuming, seems to expect a second piece of cloth at your hands.[155]

By the 1850s, the name Isaac Merrit Singer had become indelibly associated with the sewing machine. An intrepid inventor, Singer suggested the to and fro shuttle, the up and down needle, a vertical pressure foot to hold the material under tension, as well as a table to hold the cloth, which was fed horizontally instead of vertically (fig. 126). All of these advances helped to produce the modern sewing machine, yet Singer had trouble manufacturing his patents. Proponents of hand-sewing believed that the sewing machine was the great competitor of labor, accomplishing the work of twelve tailors, although the work itself was held to be inferior in quality and durability. Another inventor of the sewing machine, Elias Howe, whose patent began in 1849, demanded that Singer pay him $25,000 for infringing on his territory and give up the business. Most competing developers in the 1850s and 1860s operated under license to Howe, who charged $25 for every machine the competitors sold. Singer, however, was soon joined by Edward Clark, a New York lawyer and financier, and by 1854 they had obtained a license of their own to manufacture Singer's machine.

Another developer was Allen Wilson, who also obtained his sewing ma-

Fig. 129. Madame Demorest's patterns and magazines, 17 East Fourteenth Street, 1874. The pattern industry, prompted by the home sewing machine, brought the world of fashion into every American home. The latest styles from Paris, Vienna, Berlin, London, and New York were quickly translated onto tissue paper, packaged with illustrated instructions, and mailed to subscribers around the world. (Courtesy of the Bella C. Landauer Collection, the New-York Historical Society, New York City)

chine patent in 1849. Within a few years the Wheeler and Wilson Company had become a large manufacturing concern (fig. 127). Those inventors who obtained early patents dominated the industry, taking out more patents as they added new inventions, and all but controlled the industry until 1877 when their patents expired and competition was open to new developers. As new companies entered the field, Union Square became the national headquarters for many of these firms. One centennial guide to New York in 1876 proclaimed that Union Square "sometimes had been called Sewing Machine Square." By 1880, on the east side of Union Square (fig. 128) between Fifteenth and Sixteenth streets, Weed Sewing Machine Company was located at number 26 Union Square East, Howe Sewing Machine at number 30, and on the corner, the Singer Sewing Machine Company at number 34. To the south of Fourteenth Street between University and Broadway, the Domestic Sewing Machine Building stood on the Broadway corner, and nearby the Wheeler and Wilson Sewing Machine Company stood at 44 East Fourteenth Street.[156]

In the Domestic Sewing Machine Building a lady could view the famous Domestic machine as well as fashion shows where models displayed the latest changes in styles imported directly from Europe. These were quickly translated into Domestic paper dress patterns and published in the company's quarterly, the *Fashion Review.*[157] It was, however, Ellen Demorest who first displayed two dozen different paper patterns for women's dresses in her Philadelphia home in the 1850s, marking the beginning of a fantastic empire. Moving to New York City in the 1860s, she began Demorest's Mirror of Fashions, a business selling tissue-paper patterns by mail order across the country.[158] William J. Demorest invested heavily in property along Fourteenth Street andf moved his Demorest Emporium of Fashion to 17 East Fourteenth Street in 1874 (fig. 129). Meanwhile, E. Butterick and Company had already opened a pattern shop on Broadway in 1867 and by the 1880s had become a strong competitor of the Demorests when they too moved to 40 East Fourteenth Street. These companies were joined by James McCall and Company's Bazaar Patterns, which located a few doors away at 48 East Fourteenth Street.[159]

During these years women's fashions, popularized by the paper dress pattern, made use of every stylistic device, changing a silhouette as soon as it had been accepted. In the 1860s, as the crinoline and hooped dresses were beginning to fade in style, a more angular line was created by wide box pleats that radiated from a corseted waist. By the end of the decade, the hoops had disappeared from the front of the skirt where a straight and flat front allowed all of the fabric to be massed at the back. Peripatetic fashion would not stop there and the decade of the 1860s witnessed the era of the preposterous bustle. During this period a stylish dress often combined two or more rather garish colored fabrics, and was ornamented by a multiplicity of trimmings and variously textured materials, all supported by a sturdy understructure, which created the bustle. By the end of the 1870s, however, the bustle was banished, and the silhouette had become ridiculously restricted, with the tightened lines of the bodice falling to the knees, producing a tubular look (fig. 130). Even with this style, the skirt was still the showpiece, with swags of material draped from the waist to the hemline, often in a curved or diagonal manner. By the 1880s the back of the skirt had begun to bulge again, reaching its maximum dimension by the mid-decade and declining in importance toward the 1890s. In the 1890s a simpler, more rational silhouette

Fig. 130. "New Year's Day in New York—Criticism of the First Caller," *Frank Leslie's Illustrated Newspaper,* Jan. 12, 1878. Yards of trimmings, laces, and silk went into the creation of this 1878 receiving dress with its flowing train. Mabel Osgood Wright recalled in *My New York* (p. 229) that in the late 1870s "the time-honored custom of making New Year's calls in flocks was dwindling and becoming confined to the elderly, and in restricted localities, for the growing city was rapidly dividing east and west of the Park, while at the same time the younger people began to rebel at the monotonous rounds of either receiving or making duty calls, and the competitive excitement of having the longest list was dead." (Courtesy of the New-York Historical Society, New York City)

Fig. 131. Men's fall and winter fashions, 1872–73. (Courtesy of the New-York Historical Society, New York City)

began to dominate in opposition to fanciful yet restricted modes of dress. The skirt fabric fell unhampered to the floor from a small, tightly corseted waistline. Skillfully cut over the hips, the skirt slanted outward as it reached the hem. Attention was now shifted to the sleeve, which began to reach outlandish proportions: Most popular was the leg-of-mutton effect, obtained with many layers of fabric. Although this dress appeared more rational, the obsession with ornamentation, in the form of beads, trim, laces, and ruffles, continued.

The manufacture of clothing in the nineteenth century was still largely a handicraft industry yet, as early as 1800 ready-to-wear shops, known as slop-shops, had begun to appear. The transition to factory-made apparel was slow, but was accelerated by the preference among men after the 1860s for machine-made items like the uniforms they had become accustomed to during the Civil War. Nevertheless, custom-made clothing in the 1860s accounted for more than 80 percent of the sales volume, and even in 1890 it retained 50 percent of the trade.[160] The increasing use of machine-made men's clothing was aided by the trend toward a business style of dressing, and already by the 1870s matched suits with coats, vests, and trousers of the same sober material had appeared as had the boxy outlines of the slack suit similar to present-day styles (fig. 131). In general, though, plaid patterns and vibrant stripes in men's costumes would continue to echo the same popular combinations of unrelated textures, colors, and patterns that women's styles displayed. It was not until the 1890s that men's clothing became a staid and conservative prop to be used mainly as a foil for the rich materials and luxurious styles of ladies' costumes.[161]

Whatever the prevailing style was, quantities of materials—cashmere, serge, twill, poplin, satin, velveteen, heavy silks, and scotch plaids—were needed to maintain a fashionable women's silhouette. Braids, fringes, bows, rushings, and elaborate flower constructions were used profusely to decorate the costumes. All these notions could be purchased along Ladies' Mile. Hats were also important and millinery shops abounded. Langdon and Armstrong at 868 Broadway for example, supplied the lace, ribbons, velvet, flowers, feathers, and stuffed birds needed for individual creations. If a lady wished, the shop would construct a hat to her request. High-buttoned shoes and party slippers, kid gloves, and jewelry to complete an outfit could also be purchased along the Mile. Lockwood's *Illustrated Guide to New York City* of 1872 suggested that beautiful boots and shoes for "Ladies, Gents, Boys, and Children, could be found at Miller and Company at #3 Union Square West where white satin gaiters, boots and slippers with bows and rosettes could also be purchased to match ball gowns and costumes for weddings."[162]

Household Furnishings

> The absence of all trifles is as betraying as the presence of inferior articles is, for if there is much free expenditure elsewhere in the room, it is apt to show that articles sought for by the vulgar are in more esteem than those where sometimes one looks for beauty twice before finding it; and yet just as tale-telling is the presence of a multitude of the smaller affairs that have no especial value, for they declare a too eager love of acquisition and a less fastidious task than full purse. The mere shape of a lamp shows whether people buy what their neighbors buy, or have any individual taste of their own to exercise, or give a thought to the matter of educating what we may call aesthetic sense.[163]

Expanding wealth, the increase in mass-produced household items, and a desire among the middle class to emulate the ostentatious display of the truly rich produced a catholic taste and a plurality in styles that prompted Harriet Prescott Spofford, author of *Art Decoration Applied to Furniture* to comment in 1877 that Moorish conservatories, next to Pompeian parlors and Chinese boudoirs, as fancy dictated, often were housed together under the same roof. The shops along Ladies Mile offered the household decorator a wide array of fashionable items, the most celebrated stores being Herter Brothers at 877 Broadway and D. S. Hess at 876 Broadway. The Herter Brothers were famous for their Rennaissance revival furniture and their interior furnishings in the Louis XV mode, as well as being one of the first companies to produce Anglo-Japanese furniture. Both Herter Brothers and D. S. Hess offered decorating services for a room or a complete house, while other less prestigious firms along Ladies Mile offered fashionable furnishings for a more modest clientele (fig. 132).[164] An 1885 edition of

Fig. 132. The Art Gallery, Mrs. William Astor's Residence, Thirty-fourth Street and Fifth Avenue, 1894. Open to the public, the Astors' picture gallery exemplified the highest standards in decorative arts, which many New Yorkers sought to imitate. In front of the ornate fireplace is a French "comfortable," a heavily upholstered chair in plush with fringes and tassels. (Courtesy of the Museum of the City of New York, New York City)

Fig. 133. Advertising poster for Thonet Brothers, furniture manufacturers, ca. 1873. (Courtesy of the New-York Historical Society, New York City)

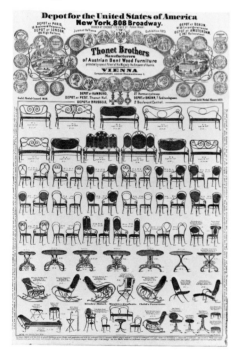

the *Ladies Shopping Guide* listed more than eighteen firms in the area that sold furniture; among the better-known firms today was Thonet (fig. 133), which moved to 860 Broadway (the Lienau building) in 1877. Other household items could be found as well: W. & J. Sloane at 880 Broadway sold carpets and upholstery; Gilman Collamore at 19 Union Square West became the most famous of several shops selling china, glass, and earthenware (fig. 134), and more than fourteen different florists on Broadway alone sold freshly cut as well as artificial flowers and plants to complete a room's decor.[165]

A kind of novelty-seeking craze underscored the popularity of Ladies Mile. In 1872 Charles Eastlake's *Hints on Household Taste* first reached American audiences. Preaching the ideals of simplicity in design and sincerity in construction, it

Fig. 134. Decorated faience and porcelain. (From Constance C. Harrison, *Woman's Handiwork in Modern Homes*, New York, Charles Scribner and Sons, 1881: 98.) Early examples of the Aesthetic movement advocated by Louis C. Tiffany and Candace Wheeler in the 1880s, these objects reflect a luxurious concept of interior decoration that combined a free use of color with rich materials, adapting native American forms of flowers and plants to ornaments and conventional objects such as vases, lamps, textiles, and wallpapers. (Courtesy of Avery Library, Columbia University, New York City)

VOLKMAR JAR   PORCELAIN TILE   BENNETT LAMP   IVORY WARE   BENNETT JAR

Fig. 135. Design for a library. (From H. Hudson Holly, *Modern Dwellings in Town and Country*, New York: Harper Brothers, 1878.) Holly offered designs depicting tastefully decorated interiors, which could be created in the typical New York town house. The library, which was located on the second floor of his plan, adjacent to a billiard room, contained a bay window and alcove for books, separated from the main room by a transom from which curtains could be hung. An open timber ceiling, parquet floor, paneled walls to the height of the doorways, and a mantel and fireplace made of Sienna marble completed the design. (Courtesy of Avery Library, Columbia University, New York City)

tried to turn the Victorian notion of luxury and taste upside down.[166] H. Hudson Holly was also one of the early advocates of the uplifting and education of American taste, for bad taste, he railed, was commonly evidenced in more than nine-tenths of all private dwellings in New York City (figs. 135, 136). This, he insisted, was the fault of the ladies, who simply believed that good taste could be learned intuitively. The home decorator would begin by purchasing a showy house, such as those built by dozens of speculators, and then commence his campaign for fashionable furnishings with carpets — mixing Persians and Axminsters with those from Brussels—in a kaleidoscope of dazzling hues and overblown patterns. Next came the wall hangings and furniture, which promiscuously mingled imitative styles from various countries and ages without regard for what might have been more suitable for a particular home.[167]

Instead, Holly taught, use and durability must mark the material and form of furniture. Veneering, graining, and marbleizing were shams that never should be allowed. For windows, the fashion to dress them elaborately in silk, damask and lace, festooned and looped up like a lady's dress, seemed cumbersome and totally inappropriate. This age of perverted bad taste, Holly cried, simply perpetuated horrors done in the name of good taste. But the return to simplicity, which Holly and other writers advocated, was liberally interpreted by avid decorators and exploited by manufacturers. Their advice produced just the opposite: the multiplication and rapid manufacturing of complex and overelaborated means for making houses more beautiful (fig. 137). "In an age when manufacturers believe that they have touched the utmost limits of improvement, and still more, at a time when capitalists think that nothing is denied to well-directed combinations," a commentator on New York's household taste added, ". . . the notion of simplicity and inexpensiveness possess no charm whatever to the modern everyday mind."[168]

The home furnisher, the upholsterer, and the advising "artist" were guaranteed to break up every blank space into sections and fill every void with ornaments and curios. Giedion traces the triumph of this decorator in the nineteenth century:

> He was the man to gather superficially loose ends. He provided oil paintings and their gold frames for a middle class unable to afford the originals. He arranged still lifes from the bric-a-brac of a mechanized past. *Décorations mobiles,* the French of 1880 called these strange compositions that were set up with an air of casualness on tables or chairs. Cushions and heavy draperies completed the effect.[169]

In the last half of the nineteenth century, a theatrical type of decoration, which grouped helmets, vases, and drapery in random disarray, increasingly invaded American interiors, parlors, and boudoirs. The unity of interior space dissolved into a series of isolated forms and objects that overran everything. Furniture began this disintegration of space, but it was soon followed by drapery and volumes of bric-a-brac and stamped, pressed, and silver-plated objects (figs. 138–140). Bloated cushions, nooks and alcoves, and the three-cushioned Turkish divan conjuring up the mystery and romance of the Orient, appeared everywhere. Harriet Prescott Spofford complained in 1877:

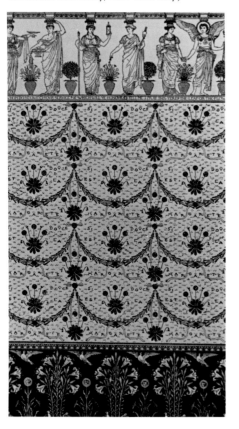

Fig. 136. Wall decorations. (From H. Hudson Holly, *Modern Dwellings in Town and Country*.) Holly believed that the architect was seldom consulted in the matter of wallpaper or wall hangings, home owners usually preferring the decorator's advice and following "stylish" trends. Holly set forth some basic principles for wallpaper: "For a room in which convivial conversation, wines and viands are enjoyed, the colors should never be bright, but of a mutual or complementary tint. In reception rooms or parlors the eye should be gratified, the sense of palate not being brought into competition, and hence floral designs and gay colors . . . would be appropriate." (Courtesy of Avery Library, Columbia University, New York City)

The dissemination of money among the many . . . has put it within the power of the millions to make the home attractive, and fill it, with furniture, with objects that it gives pleasure to look at . . . He wants beauty and he wants cheapness, but solidarity and durability do not enter into the bargain . . . nor does he care for purity of style.[170]

Americans, E. L. Godkin said in 1868, "are less provincial than their fathers, they have seen more, they have read more, they have mixed with more people of other nationalities, they have thought more and had to think more, they have spent more for ideas and given more away." But this culture, he continued, "lacked depth, it was a 'chromo-civilization' without established canons of taste."[171] Thus Americans mixed John Rogers's statues with outrageously gilded wallpapers, florid carpeting, and overblown furniture and then considered this the height of decoration. Americans, another commentator of the late 1880s complained, have a tendency for flashy appearances: too much gold and "figure subjects [on wallpapers] fare favorably with the chromo-lithographic work on the bills heralding the approach of traveling shows" but hardly reflected notions of good household taste.[172]

Most of the shoppers along Ladies Mile who bought at Tiffany's, Herter Brothers, or Arnold Constable incurred enormous expenses. Clarence Cook discussed this American tendency to decorate with money but seldom with taste in a series of *Scribner's* essays entitled "The House Beautiful." Cook felt that:

A person with no need to think about the cost of anything may go into Cottier's [a decorating house on nearby Fifth Avenue] and buy and order right and left, and give the house commission to decorate and furnish, and upholster, and fill big cabinets with "old blue," and never spare for cost, and when it is all done, nobody who comes to visit him shall say, "How beautiful this is! How interesting! What taste you have! but only, "Oh, then, I see Cottier has been with you." There has simply been a transfer of goods from one showroom to another.[173]

Here in New-York, people go to the houses which supply the needs and cater to the whims of the rich—houses where you are told plainly that they cannot afford, and do not propose, to sell cheap things. Then there is complaint and disgust, and those who have proferred their advice on the subject are taxed with ministering to luxury and expense. But it may safely be said that many more people might becomes the owners of the things they admire, and justly too, at Herter's or Cottier's, if they would be content with one thing or two; but they want all, or want everything 'in keeping', as the phrase is—a thing not necessary at all.[174]

In sharp contrast to this furniture of the ruling taste, Giedion notes the development from the 1850s onward of American patented furniture. "The unexplored complex of patent furniture stands apart from the ruling taste. It called forth nearly all the constituent powers of the century. It revealed the century as it liked to relax when wearing none of its masks. This patent furniture tackled problems in a manner completely new to the century."[175] American ingenuity was put to its test: how to create a chair that moved both forward and backward as well as up and down, that was portable, that could be transformed into a

Fig. 137. Washstand in ladies' boudoir, draped and festooned like an extravagant woman's dress. (From Williams and Jones, *Beautiful Homes*, H. I. Williams, 1878.) The boudoir of a Fifth Avenue belle, George Ellington (pseudonym) wrote in 1870 in *The Women of New York: Or Social Life in the Great City*, was richly carpeted and ornamented. On the mantel stood a vase of flowers, and in the center of the room was a marble-topped table with a large silver-plated cooler filled with ice to cool the room. Long mirrors lined the walls and all the furniture, walls, and picture frames were covered in chintz in large, gaudy patterns. (Courtesy of Avery Library, Columbia University, New York City)

Fig. 138. Ottoman. (From Williams and Jones, *Beautiful Homes*.) A low cushion on casters enabled the ottoman to be propelled from one spot to another. It was advised that every room should have one or more of these since it was the little adjuncts rather than the matching suites of furniture that gave a room a tasteful appearance. (Courtesy of Avery Library, Columbia University, New York City)

Fig. 139. Side chairs. (From Williams and Jones, *Beautiful Homes*.) The straight-back chair, with its wooden frame, was derived from the American farmhouse chair and might have pleased Eastlake followers, but most household improvers felt that its frame had to be padded and upholstered. (Courtesy of Avery Library, Columbia University, New York City)

lounge or a table? This furniture responded to specialized needs, resulting in railway seats, typewriter chairs, and sewing machine tables. It also tried to answer both the leading ideas of comfort and the need in cramped apartment interiors to utilize objects and furniture for more than one purpose. Some of this patented furniture could be found along Ladies Mile. One of the earliest manufacturers, the New York Folding Table Company, was headquartered in the Domestic Building in 1870. Another company, the Marks Adjustable Folding Chair Company, located at 930 Broadway, advertised their chair as "combining a parlor, library, smoking and reclining chair, a lounge, full-length bed and child's crib; having over fifty changes of positions." This strange combination won the company a gold medal at the Paris Exposition of 1889 and again in 1891. Marks boasted that over 45,000 of their adjustable chairs had been manufactured and sold.[176] Even so, patent furniture, as an ingenious response to functional needs hardly responded to the notions of fashion and luxury that controlled the ruling taste.

To promote a decorative item as "new" or in the "height of fashion," as described by a nineteenth-century collection of home decoration notes, guaranteed the salesman an eager buyer.

> Fashion is a common bait thrown by the tradesman to allure the wary dollars from our pockets. What could be expected from such a motive? A high standard of merit endeavoring to elevate and purify the public taste? No. The fisher with such a bait would go hungry for dollars. He must throw something more palatable to the multitude. So he fits up something nice, new and bright, calls it the latest style and fills his basket with dollars. This latest style is a very popular bait. The later it is the better.[177]

Even the *Real Estate Record* plunged into this promotion of the ruling taste in the mid-1880s, dictating to its readers through a series of "Home Decorative Notes" the use of faddish novelties and popular items, all of which could be purchased along Ladies Mile (figs. 141, 142). For example, in 1883 it declared that old Venetian red would be the prevailing color for the autumn, and that while woolen fabrics were still popular, wall hangings of silk were being preferred by those who could afford them.[178] But by 1885, grape, a soft purplish-red, was to be accepted as de rigueur.[179] Decorative art, the *Real Estate Record* explained, was no child's play; Eastlake and early English had each had their day, while now Americans were embarrassing the Renaissance for fresh inspiration. But one might prefer not to furnish in any particular style or period and being gifted with taste and experience choose correctly to furnish with pieces from various periods.

No style, the *Real Estate Record* believed, ever offered a more common-sense solution to the problems of how to unite elegance with comfort in furniture than the Louis XV style. Sofas, fauteuils, armchairs, along with woodwork and paneling, could all be seen and purchased at Herter Brothers.[180] And the treasures of Japanese decorative art, the *Real Estate Record* noted in 1885, were now in fashionable demand.[181] Greater attention was given to table appointments, another lesson drawn from Japanese designers. A special design, described by the *Real Estate Record,* called for the placement of two strips of brightly colored Korah silk, crossing each other at right angles on a white damask covering; six Japanese fans of varied shapes placed on and off these strips were then strewn with flowers and foliage. A few rare Japanese vases filled with single blossoms and copper trays of fruits completed the design.[182]

The *Real Estate Record* kept its eye on furniture too, noting that rattan furniture decorated with ribbons displayed in oddly shaped tables, bookshelves, and baby carriages had gained many admirers. A choice assortment of such items could be purchased at F. W. Richardson and Company at 28 West Fourteenth Street.[183] The taste of the day in 1885 ran to very low bookcases, the tops of which could be used for displaying bric-a-brac at eye level, and a folding bed that doubled as an ornamental fireplace and mantelpiece.[184] Mirrors, too, had taken on every conceivable shape: one appeared as a mandolin, another as a lyre, and still a third as a palette.[185] Needlework, the *Real Estate Record* noted, had become newly fashionable in 1884. A unique piece could be found at Haas and Wirland on Broadway: a piano stool shaped like a mushroom with a white velvet seat and the stem in olive green plush resting on an olive plush base.[186]

Chinaware and silverware also received full attention. A "new" idea in 1884 seemed to be the etching of silver flatware, and handsome specimens of this art in pitchers, punch bowls, and spoons, and entire tea and coffee sets could be seen at the Gorham Manufacturing Company on Ladies Mile.[187] Shallow ember bowls set in a base of silver leaves with twisted silver handles to be used for fruit or sauces and many other novelties in silver and glassware were displayed at the Reed and Barton store on Union Square and Sixteenth Street.[188] A very effective cordial set, the *Real Estate Record* found, was a duck-shaped decanter surrounded by a "brood" of glasses, found at Wilhelm and Graef on Twenty-sixth Street and Broadway.[189]

As the popularity of Ladies Mile began to ebb, however, the *Real Estate Record* stopped its column on home decoration. Changes occurred very rapidly along the Mile and by the turn of the century, almost all of this retail activity was gone. Shopping directories began to list a large number of shirtwaist, knit goods,

Fig. 140. Decorative mantelpiece. In one of many attempts "to bring the beautiful in form and color home to the household, to mingle its subtle influences and the whole framework of social and family life," Williams and Jones set down simple rules each decorator should follow for tasteful interiors: to select beauty of form, to follow a harmonious combination of colors, and to secure the fitness of each article for its special function. Even though their rules appeared disciplined, they failed to eliminate the ornateness, drapery, and upholstery that governed the predominant styles. (Courtesy of Avery Library, Columbia University, New York City)

Fig. 141. Mrs. Leoni's Residence, 1894. A simple New York interior, carpeted, and filled with bric-a-brac, drapery, wicker chairs, and an upholstered sofa. (Courtesy of the Museum of the City of New York, New York City)

Fig. 142. Entrance to the studio of the Tiffany house, Seventy-second Street and Madison Avenue, ca. 1880s. Louis C. Tiffany, who stressed the sumptuousness of materials and appropriateness of styles, nevertheless filled the interior of his studio with cluttered objects, plants, and fabrics. (Courtesy of Avery Library, Columbia University, New York City)

and ladies' and children's garment manufacturers in the new lofty structures on Union Square West. Although tailors and seamstresses had always been present along Ladies Mile, these new manufacturers of ready-to-wear garments were sweatshop employers, relying on cheap and exploitable unskilled labor. In 1905, for example, seventeen shirt and shirtwaist makers, six knit goods and undergarment companies, and nine ladies and children's undergarment makers were located in the Lincoln Building alone at 1 Union Square West. The era of Ladies Mile had drawn to an end.[190]

THE WANING OF LADIES MILE

In the late 1890s the introduction of tall manufacturing buildings and office towers along Ladies Mile signaled its demise as a center for luxury trade and amusement. The presence of so many sweatshop workers crowding the streets at noontime tarnished the district's luster, causing fashionable retail businesses to relocate farther north. In addition, office buildings were attracted to Ladies Mile. Since an intensive competition for land at the tip of Manhattan made commercial development near Wall Street an expensive venture, the cheaper land around Union and Madison squares appealed to developers. But as the office worker moved onto Ladies Mile, retail establishments fled even faster.

When Ladies Mile began in 1865, New York was a city of four- and five-story structures; but with the rapid expansion of American business after the Civil War and with its relentless drive toward centralization and diversification, strictly commercial buildings arose for the sole purpose of renting floor space. This business architecture was conceived as a source of revenue, rather than a work of art. It was intended to produce the maximum amount of office floor space within the confines of its building line and thus expanded vertically as high as available funds would permit. Banks, newspaper offices, and insurance companies were pioneers in these new tall structures.

Sometime in the mid-1870s New York real estate capitalists discovered that there was plenty of room in the air and "that by doubling the height of its buildings, the same result could be reached as if the island had been stretched to twice its present width. And so they began to run the buildings upward."[191] This upward development was aided by technical innovations such as the elevator. Arthur Gilman and Edward Kendall, with the aid of a young engineer, George Post, were the first first to introduce the elevator ito New York's commercial buildings in the five-story Equitable Life Insurance Company (130 feet high) in 1869–70. The elevator immediately enabled the fifth floor to be as commercially successful as the second floor.[192] This development hastened the building of other structures, including Griffith Thomas's Domestic Sewing Machine Building, a monument towering over Ladies Mile (110 feet high). The first tall elevator buildings, however, appeared in 1873. These were George Post's Western Union Telegraph Building, reaching ten-and-a-half stories, or 230 feet, and Richard Morris Hunt's Tribune Building, nine stories high, or 260 feet. The tallest structure in New York at this time, Trinity Church, was only slightly taller, with a 286-foot spire.[193]

The tall office building, "a nouveau riche if ever there was one . . . rose from obscure beginnings and surprised the city without other authority than its own acquisitive skill."[194] Yet there was considerable debate on how to organize these very tall buildings structurally. Two schools of thought on the subject existed side by side in the late nineteenth century. One school proposed the stacking style. These architects were timid about expressing the height of the building and therefore emphasized its horizontality by stacking individual two-or three-story structures, one layer on another, adding elaborate cornices, projecting balconies, and squat towers to relieve the monotony of a plane wall. The other school took up the challenge of the towering structures and tried to emphasize verticality by taking the traditional parts of the Renaissance-revival commercial boxlike building and stretching them over the length of the entire wall. This stretching phase became standardized by the 1880s in the tripartite system of composition. "A work of art," Montgomery Schuyler wrote, "must have a beginning, middle and end, which could best be observed by dividing the skyscraper into base, shaft and capital . . . and by leaving the shaft unadorned, and undivided except by the necessary division of the stories."[195]

The debate between monumentality and organizational unity continued to confront the New York tall building throughout the rest of the nineteenth century. If monumentality was desired and verticality stressed, the significance of the building's parts was necessarily reduced and the exterior facade became monotonous and dull. On the other hand, if organizational unity was desired, achieved through an attractive subdivision of the parts and an enlivened ornamentation, the effect of grandeur was always jeopardized. Had the elevator remained the only technical innovation affecting tall buildings in the nineteenth century, their height would have remained at a practical limit of ten stories or less and the debate might have continued back and forth over the correct compositional treatment. But with the invention of the steel frame, or skeleton construction, the era of true "sky-building" arrived. Before this, masonry buildings of ten stories required extremely thick walls at their base, necessitating costly excavations and consuming valuable rental area on the first floor. By introducing a skeleton frame of iron or steel, the load of the walls and floors could be carried down to the ground foundations. Although New York building laws still required in the 1880s that nonbearing walls be nearly as thick as bearing ones, the time was approaching when a relatively thin masonry facade would be "hung" from a skeleton frame reaching twenty or more stories into the sky.[196] Design, simply, practically, and efficiently would allow undecorated office buildings to express themselves through their mass: the less ornament, the less their fronts were broken up; conversely, the more magnificent they became, the more stunning their individual effect. Gone were the days of the commercial palace, the ornamental porticoes, the enriched roof systems, and the elaborate base structure. In their place stood a featureless skyscraper.[197]

The early skyscrapers, Montgomery Schuyler noted, were based on faith in the dollar and were replaced again and again by even taller structures to ensure their commercial success. "Commodity in the crowded centers of great cities, is as strictly subserved by those towering structures as community is defied."[198] Skyscrapers to Schuyler were "un-neighborly objects": there seemed no way for them to be designed as an ensemble yielding a common impression. The architectural excellence of the new urban skyline had to be sought in its parts, not in the unattainable whole.

Driven by high land prices on Wall Street and the difficulty of finding sites large enough for these tall structures, the skyscraper began to push farther north into the retailing district of Ladies Mile, extending the New York panorama as "a chain of peaks rising above the horizon, itself a five or six story horizon, and struggling or shooting towards the sky. For another mile, for two miles more, the peaks continued to emerge, but they no longer form a chain."[199] For a brief moment, Ladies Mile would be the northern frontier of this staccato skyline (fig. 143).

Although Madison Square and the east side of Union Square in the early 1880s were still unadorned by tall office and manufacturing buildings, the stretch of Ladies Mile along Broadway had changed (figs 144, 145). The *Real Estate Record* drew attention to the northeast corner of Seventeenth Street and Broadway (860 Broadway) where a building stood of such poor architectural composition that it gave the appearance of two buildings, one set on top of the other (see fig. 145). As the building was conspicuously located, the *Real Estate Record* found its commonplace design by Detlef Lienau regrettable. On the other hand,

Fig. 143. Tall structures near Ladies Mile.

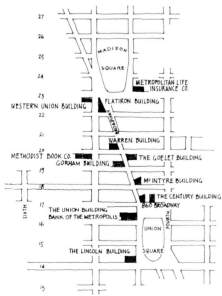

Fig. 144. Ladies Mile, west side, Broadway from Fourteenth to Twenty-third Street, ca. 1898. The appearance of relatively tall structures along Ladies Mile, shown above and on the following page, although they were not much higher than the five-story warehouses or department stores, marked a new departure for commercial architecture in which, for the first time, the problem of height versus monumentality began to find a solution. (Courtesy of the Museum of the City of New York, New York City)

Number	Name	Number of Floors (without mansards)	Architect	Date	Status
1	Lincoln Building	9	R.H. Robertson	1885	extant
2	Spingler Building	8	William H. Hume and Sons	1896	extant
3	Tiffany Building	5	John Kellum	1869	altered
4	Union Building	11	Alfred Zucker	1892	extant
5	Hoyt Building and Arnold Constable Store	5	Griffith Thomas	1868	extant
6	Gorham Building	8	Edward Kendall	1883	extant
7	Lord and Taylor Store	4	James H. Giles	1869	extant
8	Warren Building	7	McKim, Mead and White	1890	extant
9	Mortimer Building	5	unknown	ca. 1864	extant
10	St. Germain Hotel	9	unknown	1850s	demolished 1901

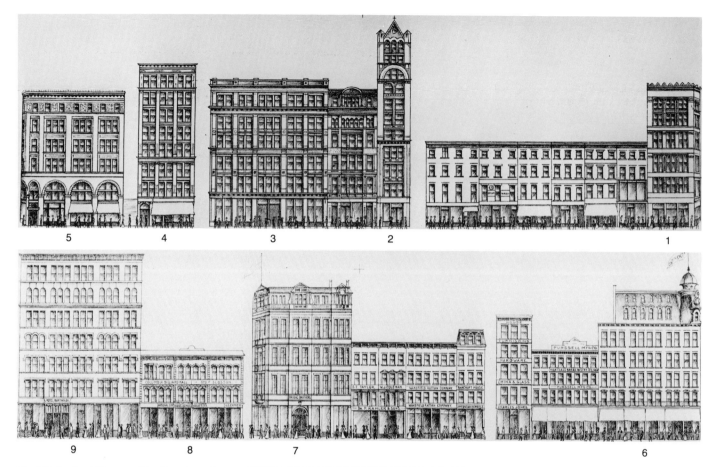

Fig. 145. Ladies Mile, east side, Broadway from Seventeenth to Twenty-third Street, ca. 1898. (Courtesy of the Museum of the City of New York, New York City)

Number	Name	Number of Floors	Architect	Date	Status
1	Lienau Building	6	Detlef Lienau	1883	extant
2	McIntyre Building	10	R.H. Robertson	1890	extant
3	W. and J. Sloane Store	6	W. Wheeler Smith	1881	extant
4	Office building	8	John B. Snook and Sons	1897	extant
5	Shoninger (Goelet) Building	6	McKim, Mead and White	1886	extant
6	DePeyster House	4	unknown	1845	extant
7	Brooks Brothers Store	4	Charles Haight	1884	demolished 1937
8	American Art Association	3	unknown	1880s	demolished 1966
9	Bartholdi Hotel	7	unknown	1870s	demolished 1983

the Gorham building by Edward Kendall, nearing completion at the northwest corner of Nineteenth Street and Broadway, was designed to be noticed (see fig. 144). Occupying a plot about 60 feet along Broadway by 100 feet on Nineteenth Street, and standing eight stories high, the structure was composed of brick, brownstone, and iron.[200] Another tall building that garnered the *Real Estate Record*'s approval was the new seven-story Western Union Building, designed by

Henry J. Hardenbergh at the northwest corner of Twenty-third Street and Fifth Avenue in 1884 (fig. 146). Montgomery Schuyler commented that it was "...in its kind, one of the most successful commercial buildings we have...and its quaint picturesqueness is the more valuable for seeming to have come unsought from the most straightforward treatment of the problem."[201]

A few years later, the Shoninger Building, later known as the Goelet Building, designed by McKim, Mead and White, was erected at the southeast corner of Twentieth Street and Broadway (see fig. 145). This early prototype of the columnar skyscraper, broken into base, column, and shaft, prompted Russell Sturgis to note that "especially successful is the arrangement of the three stories of windows above the arches. Always in these big buildings, with so many stories all alike, is the designer trying to bring two or three stories into one. Almost always does he fail...[but in this building] there is no pretense at the three windows being one...it does seem a masterly solution of a very troublesome problem.[202]

While the columnar building was being developed, Robert H. Robertson was experimenting with a tall structure on the northeast corner of Fourteenth Street and Union Square West. Approaching the problem tentatively, Robertson preferred to layer his structure. Montgomery Schuyler criticized Robertson for not taking his tall buildings seriously enough and ignoring the maxim that buildings must have a beginning, middle, and end. Robertson did experiment structurally, however, and the Lincoln Building, a nine-story granite structure suspended from a steel-skeleton frame, erected in 1885, remains one of the earliest examples of this type of construction (fig. 147).[203]

A building for the Methodist Book Company—another "stretched" Renaissance structure—opened in 1889 on the southwest corner of Fifth Avenue and Twentieth Street. The chief success of this building, the *Real Estate Record* claimed, lay in the manner in which the designer, Edward Kendall, framed the composition: by repressing the detail and ornamentation of the corners, he set them apart from the middle section, with a resulting scholarly treatment.[204] The

Fig. 146. Western Union Building, ca. 1884. (From the *Architectural Record* 6, Jan.–March 1897: 340.) The seven-story office structure was divided horizontally by architect Henry J. Hardenbergh into a red brick pattern ornamented with stone arches, lintels, stringcourses, and cornices and with a terra-cotta frieze under its main cornice and terra-cotta decorative panels. The six bay arcaded windows on the Twenty-third Street side terminate in a recessed tower containing the entrance to the stories above. A steep roof is relieved at its base by six gabled dormers receding from the plane of the main wall. The building is extant. (Courtesy of Avery Library, Columbia University, New York City)

Fig. 147. A 1902 view of the still existing but altered Lincoln Building, northwest corner of Fourteenth Street and Union Square West, designed by Robert H. Robertson, in 1885. By stacking the nine stories of this office building, the architect focused all attention on six different horizontal divisions. Large arcaded windows on the lower part of the building that diminished in size as they moved toward the top pushed the structure skyward. The Spingler and Tiffany buildings stand to its right. (Courtesy of the New-York Historical Society, New York City)

Fig. 148. The McIntyre Building, northeast corner of Eighteenth Street and Broadway, 1985. This marvelous experiment with a tall structure (ten stories) designed by Robertson in 1890, is divided into five horizontal layers stacked one upon the other. The Broadway facade, only one bay wide, and the long Eighteenth Street facade, are organized with rectangular triple windows on the second through fifth stories, followed by four stories of double windows. The ninth story contains large arched windows, the tenth a row of small arched windows, and the Broadway corner is crowned with a tower.

next year, another structure by McKim, Mead and White appeared on the Mile, the Warren Building, a seven-story commercial building on the northwest corner of Twentieth Street (see fig. 144). Russell Sturgis complained that it was not as successful as the firm's Goelet Building, that its organization was too confused, its parts too large for a small structure, its facade too busy with projecting balconies whose shadows cut the building in two, and that the building was so covered with signs and advertisements that it looked deranged.[205] Finally, the tallest structure, the ten-story McIntyre Building on the northeast corner of Eighteenth Street and Broadway, designed by Robertson in 1890, was built (see fig. 145). Still designing stacked structures, Robertson divided this building into five elaborately ornamented horizontal parts and then crowned the whole with a squat tower on the Broadway corner (fig. 148). Clearly, this was an example of what Montgomery Schuyler called "wild work" gone astray.[206] In this composition, as in his Lincoln Building, Robertson grouped the largest windows at the base, reducing their size in subsequent layers in order to stress the building's verticality. The organizational massing of each horizontal layer, however, remains the dominant effect.

Madison Square, the *Real Estate Record* announced in 1890, was at last succumbing to commerce. Like Union Square, it too would be covered with skyscrapers. Madison Square Garden, the most magnificent entertainment palace in the world, already commanded the block to the northeast of the square (fig. 149). A 400- by 200-foot site alloted to a freestanding building was a rarity in New York and the *Real Estate Record* noted that it offered the architects McKim, Mead and White the opportunity to make the building's horizontal lines impressive (see fig. 58). But Stanford White, who provided the original scheme, decided to divide the long sides into bays of four openings each, which effaced the grandeur of the horizontal lines. Thus the main architectural feature was a tower reminiscent of the Giralda in Spain.[207] Madison Square Garden was the swan song of Ladies Mile, retrograde in its location, at a time when the Broadway theater district was moving uptown to Forty-second Street, and progressive in reflecting both the concentration of wealth and the organization of entertainment required for the production of twentieth-century amusement.

J. P. Morgan and Andrew Carnegie, among others, had formed the Madison Square Garden Company with Stanford White in 1889 in order to purchase the old Gilmore Garden from the Vanderbilts and to plan the development of an amusement complex combining a huge amphitheater, a concert hall, a roof garden, a restaurant, and a series of shops. Madison Square Garden would open in June 1890, although it would never be a financial success, mounting a deficit almost every year of its existence until it was demolished in 1925.[208]

As if a harbinger of things to come, opening night began with trouble. Edward Strauss's Orchestra from Vienna was supposed to celebrate the event, but the Musical Protection Society threatened the Garden with legal action on the grounds that these musicians were not artists but common laborers, and indeed some music lovers agreed. Nevertheless, the argument was eventually settled in favor of Strauss. Then, theatrical managers from Broadway and Fourteenth Street banded together, probably because they feared competition from so huge an amusement center, and petitioned the mayor to refuse the Garden an operating license on the grounds that the building was unsafe. The license, somehow, was granted. Even light entertainment had trouble when the theatrical costumes of forty-eight "ballet girls" were seized by the Treasury Department from the docks of the Cunard Line after a rival costuming company complained that the girls had not paid enough duty. But the show would go on, and the amphitheater, a simple unadorned structure with its exposed columns and roof girders painted plainly in buff, became the arena for horse shows, dog shows, circuses, and orchestras. Without a stage, this arena with 110 boxes could seat 5,000, and when a stage was temporarily erected on its eastern end, more than 9,000 patrons could attend a show. The Garden was clearly an obsession of White's, and he spent endless hours designing new schemes to make it successful. Long before Walt Disney thought of simulated worlds, White reproduced the Globe Theatre of London, recreated Dickens's Curiosity Shop, produced a toy town for Christmas, and tried to lure Buffalo Bill and his Wild West Show away from Staten Island. In spite of these attempts, Forty-second Street's lights would prove more alluring to New Yorkers.[209]

No longer an entertainment center, Madison Square was quickly becoming an office center for twentieth-century business. Southeast of the square, the Metropolitan Life Insurance Company was preparing to build an immense structure (fig.150). The company had slowly acquired all of the private residences in the area adjoining the Madison Square Presbyterian Church, and along Twenty-third Street, and would not stop until it had purchased the Academy of

Fig. 149. Panorama north from Twenty-third Street, showing the tower of Madison Square Garden, 1893. Although the central tower, rising 300 feet above the sidewalk was part of the original scheme provided by Stanford White for the team of McKim, Mead and White, it was abandoned as the Garden's construction costs continued to escalate. White protested vehemently until the contractor himself agreed to put up half the cost if the Garden committee paid for the rest. The tower was capped by an 18-foot statue of Diana by the sculptor Saint-Gaudens, a brazen display of nudity so shocking to New Yorkers that the statue was removed and sold to the city of Chicago in 1893. The Garden was demolished in 1925. (Courtesy of the New York Public Library, New York City)

Fig. 150. The Metropolitan Life Building, 1904. The eight-story office building, designed by Napoleon LeBrun and Sons in 1890, stood only 125 feet high above Madison Square. It was not until 1909 that a tower rose next door to this base, a replica of the Campanile of the Piazza San Marco in Venice, running 700 feet straight up from the street to its pyramidal crown. The buildings are extant. (Courtesy of the Museum of the City of New York, New York City)

Design on the corner of Fourth Avenue. By 1880 workmen were busy tearing down the residential structures ten years before the plans of the architects Napoleon LeBrun and Sons for the Metropolitan Life Building were known.[210]

The era of the true skyscraper was rapidly descending on New York. In 1890 the *Real Estate Record* reviewed the New World Building by architect George Post, a thirteen-story structure on Park Row and Frankfort Street. The anomaly that drew the *Real Estate Record*'s attention was that the architect had made no effort at all to limit the building's height and had even increased it by superimposing a two-story dome, which itself was crowned by a cupola. Nowhere, the *Real Estate Record* complained, had the architect emphasized the horizontality of the structure, instead stressing verticality alone.[211] A few years later, the *Real Estate Record* had changed its tone and was, like most of New York, becoming adjusted to these new tower structures. In fact, the major characteristic of a sixteen- to twenty-story building was that it had to be seen; no matter how he organized the elements, an architect could not make the structure modest. The sixteen-story buildings being constructed in New York were meant to be obvious and aggressive. Whether for advertising purposes or from an interest in form, corporations were turning to the best architects to design skyscrapers. These architects, the *Real Estate Record* advised, must know that they were making history and that designers of crude, ugly, senseless buildings were now public enemies.[212]

Having experimented with tall office structures in the late nineteenth century, Ladies Mile was ready to embrace the twentieth century's skyscrapers. The first slablike tower on Union Square was Bruce Price's Bank of the Metropolis, built in 1902 (see fig. 281). But it is not surprising that the ultimate achievement in commercial architecture came from the Chicago firm of Daniel H. Burnham who constructed the Fuller (or Flatiron) Building in 1901 as an isolated block-long, wedge-shaped tower, a spectacular urbanistic solution to a problematic site. On one of the few conspicuous sites in Manhattan, this bold twenty-story building stretched to the limits of its triangular lot lines and was twice as high as its neighbors (see fig. 22). Its great prow, like an ocean liner, sailed up Fifth Avenue unashamedly.[213]

Daniel H. Burnham alone seemed to understand the language of urbanism, the effect of juxtaposing site and structure, and it was he who advised a young architect on his first trip to Europe to go to the top of the Eiffel Tower to read the juxtaposition of the images of Paris, to spend time with map in hand trying to remember Paris as a whole: "After thus studying Paris, you will not be able at first to recall it except as a confused mass. But later on, when the problems great and small come up in your work, details will suddenly jump up in memory and be a great help to you."[214] So fortified, Burnham's young architect would know how to design his buildings, not as isolated monuments, but in relation to a city's urban form and in memory of its history.

Most contemporary critics, however, thought these tall buildings were elitist statements neither serving the public nor enhancing the city's image. As Henry James wrote upon revisiting New York in 1904:

> They are crowned not only with no history, but with no credible possibility of time for history, and consecrated by no uses save the commercial at any cost, they are simply the most piercing notes in that concert of the expen-

sively provisional into which your supreme sense of New York resolves itself.[215]

New York, James continued, is the

expression of unattempted, impossible maturity . . . I build you up to tear you down, for if I were to let sentiment and sincerity once take root, were to let any tenderness of association once accumulate or any "love of the old" once pass unsnubbed, what would become of us . . . ? Fortunately, we have learned the secret of keeping associations at bay. We've learned that the great thing is not suffer it so much as begin. . . . It's the reason if you must know why you shall "run," all, without exception, to the fifty floors. We defy you even to aspire to venerate shapes so grossly constructed as the arrangement in fifty floors.[216]

With the arrival of tall commercial buildings Ladies Mile as an amusement center disappeared. By the late 1890s and early 1900s the theaters, the great department stores, the jewelry shops, and the luxury hotels, had moved uptown, following the retreating footsteps of the luxury residences and pushed out by the invading tall structures. Forty-second Street to Fifty-ninth Street, from Broadway to Fifth Avenue, would become the twentieth-century entertainment district, with Ladies Mile no longer even a memory to make New Yorkers pause with regret (fig. 151).

Fig. 151. Union Square, looking north along Fourth Avenue, ca. 1915. By the early twentieth century, dramatic changes had occurred in the area of Ladies Mile. In this photograph the old Union Square Hotel still stands underneath the Uneeda Biscuit advertisement, the statue of Washington is being prepared to be moved, and the subway station entrances can be seen in the left foreground. The Everett Hotel, which once stood on the northwest corner of Seventeenth Street and Fourth Avenue, has been replaced by the Everett Building, a sixteen-story loft erected in 1908 (located in the left background). Across from its stands the Germania Life Insurance Company building, constructed in 1910. South of the square along Fourteenth Street (not in photograph), the old Domestic Building, a Union Square landmark, would soon be replaced by a tall loft building; the Morton House, another landmark, would be demolished in the 1920s, while S. Klein's, the first low-cost heavy-volume clothing store to move to the square, would take over all the small buildings on Union Square East between Fourteenth and Fifteenth streets in the 1920s until it would be demolished in 1984. (Courtesy of the Museum of the City of New York, New York City)

CHAPTER FOUR

FASHIONABLE ARCHITECTURE: THE LIMITS OF GOOD TASTE

Harmony, taste, style, are a part of architecture, and a great point has been gained when one can correctly decide what is good taste and what is not, entirely independent of fashion. For although fashion exercises despotic sway in the matters of dress, ready made furniture, etc., that extends even to architecture . . . still, no person of refinement will allow himself to be influenced by fashion beyond the limits of good taste.—William Le Baron Jenney "Lecture on Architecture (1883–1884)":18

A fashionable residential address was a shifting quantity in nineteenth-century New York, moving in a continuous sequence from Bowling Green along Broadway through Murray and Chambers streets, with a slight diversion westward to Saint John's Park and then north to Washington and Union squares. In the 1830s Bleecker and Fourth streets, Astor Place and Lafayette Street, and Washington Square and Waverly Place were redolent of wealth and society. Lower Second Avenue and Stuyvesant Square tried to capture their share of fashion without success but were too close to nonresidential and commercial property to survive for long. The distinction of fashion eventually was conferred on Fifth Avenue and its adjacent streets within very narrow dimensions. Unlike other neighborhoods, the march of improvement followed the so-called backbone of the island along Fifth Avenue.[1]

By 1868, the elite of New York had settled on Fifth Avenue between Twenty-third and Thirty-fourth streets, and were already beginning to move beyond Forty-second Street where a few asylums, churches, and isolated rows of brownstones had already located (fig. 152). Construction of Saint Patrick's Cathedral had begun in 1858 at Fiftieth Street and Fifth Avenue, although it would not be completed until 1879 (fig. 153); and a conspicuous synagogue, the Temple Emanu-El, designed by Leopold Eidlitz in 1868 in an attempt to combine a Gothic structure with Saracenic decoration, was being erected on the east side of Fifth Avenue and Forty-third Street[2] (see fig. 157). Saint Luke's Hospital (fig. 154) was established as early as 1858 (and demolished in 1895) on the west side of Fifth Avenue, facing Fifty-fourth Street. A cluster of hospitals and asylums could be found near Fiftieth Street; and Columbia College, too, had moved nearby between Madison and Fourth avenues where eventually it would develop the entire block between Forty-ninth and Fiftieth streets[3] (fig. 155).

Into this new luxury quarter moved the millionaires, those new American heroes whose ranks swelled after the Civil War and whom Herbert Croly called the great social experiment of the late nineteenth century. Because, according to Croly, these men devoted their entire energy to their business enterprises, they lived "by tradition alone in intellectual, moral and aesthetic affairs." The American millionaire was to blame for the historicist mark of much fashionable architecture, for he wanted things "rich in historical association," and since he

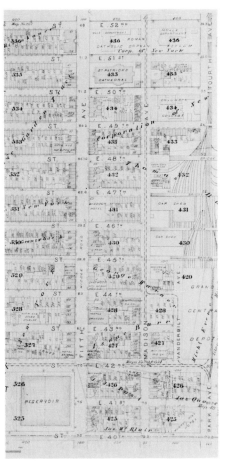

Fig. 152. Robinson Insurance Map of 1885. The fashionable residential quarter, Forty-second to Fifty-second Street, along the spine of Fifth Avenue. (Courtesy of the New York Public Library, New York City)

Fig. 153. Saint Patrick's Cathedral under construction, Fifth Avenue and Fiftieth to Fifty-first Street. Looking east along Fifty-first Street, ca. 1878. (Courtesy of the Museum of the City of New York, New York City)

Fig. 154. Saint Luke's Hospital, Fifth Avenue, between Fifty-fourth and Fifty-fifth streets, ca. 1866. Designed by W. P. Esterbrook in 1858. (Courtesy of the New-York Historical Society, New York City)

Fig. 155. Columbia College, north side of Forty-ninth Street. Looking east from Madison to Fourth (Park) Avenue, ca. 1867. (Courtesy of the New-York Historical Society, New York City)

Fig. 156. Fifth Avenue, looking south from Forty-second Street, ca. 1879. In the 1870s both sides of Fifth Avenue were lined with rows of identical high-stooped brownstone town houses, with the dramatic exception of the Croton Reservoir on the west side between Forty-second and Forty-first streets and the brick Methodist Church on the northwest side of Thirty-seventh Street. (Courtesy of the New-York Historical Society, New York City)

Fig. 157. Fifth Avenue, view north from Forty-second Street, ca. 1879 showing the Temple Emanu-el on the northeast corner of Forty-third Street, designed by Leopold Eidlitz in 1868 and demolished between 1927 and 1929. (Courtesy of the New-York Historical Society, New York City)

Fig. 158. Fifth Avenue, east corner of Sixty-third Street, ca. 1869. Runyon W. Martin's house, designed by Jacob Wrey Mould, was the first to be built above Fifty-ninth Street. In 1869 five adjacent lots were being offered for sale at public auction, the terms of the sale being 10 per cent of the closing price on the day of the sale, with two-thirds of the remaining purchase money to be put up in the form of bonds and mortgages. The lots were to be sold with restrictions against any undesirable uses, such as for stables, saloons, or manufacturing. (Courtesy of the New-York Historical Society, New York City)

Fig. 159. Manhattan neighborhoods, 1870–75.

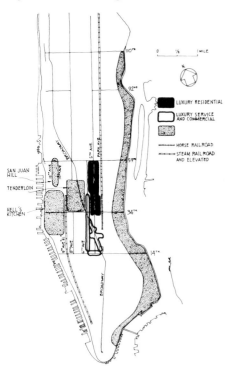

was not a connoisseur of fine objects for their beauty, he hired those with expert taste to design and decorate his extraordinarily complete and beautiful home.[4]

By the 1870s the most desirable residential district lay between Thirty-second Street and the entrance to Central Park at Fifty-ninth Street, on the narrow strip of land between Fourth and Sixth avenues (figs. 156, 157). Above Fifty-ninth Street, parallel to Central Park, Fifth Avenue seemed marred by a topographical blunder. The *Real Estate Record* editorialized that the park never should have been allowed to extend its boundary to the avenue, as it had deterred rather than attracted stylish residences. The wealthy and the fashionable, in the late 1870s resisted crossing above Fifty-ninth Street. Most remained unwilling to live opposite a dreary and vast open space, and the few who had erected stately homes in this area had quickly learned, the *Real Estate Record* claimed, "that it takes more than one swallow to make a summer, and one residence, however costly and elaborate, does not constitute a palatial neighborhood"[5] (fig. 158).

To the east and west of the fashionable quarter, industry and tenement districts limited luxury development (figs. 159, 160). The shoreline had been reserved for industries engaged in noxious enterprises such as fat rendering, bone boiling and the production of fertilizers. To the west, Sixth Avenue had been appropriated for business purposes. In 1851 the Hudson Railroad broke through the rural estates of the West Side, followed in 1867 by the first elevated railway on Greenwich Street. The railway extended in 1870 as far as Twenty-ninth Street and the Hudson River Station on Ninth Avenue; by 1875 it reached Forty-second Street and continued up the West Side of Manhattan. The popularity of elevated railroad travel brought competition, and by the late 1870s a similar elevated structure was erected along Sixth Avenue reaching as far north as Fifty-eighth

Street. Here soot and noise from the El created a boundary line beyond which luxury development would not penetrate.

To the east of the luxury quarter, Fourth (Park) Avenue presented a series of anomalous land uses, some opposing and some promoting luxury. The major intrusion was the uninterrupted series of railroad vents from the coal-fired New York and Harlem trains that cut through Murray Hill between Thirty-second and Forty-second streets. Luxury development had been constrained since 1832 because of this intrusion. Tenements and stores had located along Fourth Avenue parallel to the established luxury quarter between Twenty-third and Fifty-ninth streets. Corner lots held structures that presented their gable ends to the avenue and their facades to the cross streets in order to escape the sights and sounds of the railroad. In 1852 the Common Council forbade steam travel below Forty-second Street; consequently, the terminal on Twenty-sixth Street near Madison Square became a horsecar depot, attracting inferior hotels, cheap restaurants, and low drinking saloons—catering to delivery men and truckers—stigmatizing the surrounding neighborhood.[6]

Periodic attempts had been made to improve Fourth Avenue as a more appropriate boundary for the luxury quarter. By the 1870s the corner of Twenty-sixth Street had been developed into model apartments, and A. T. Stewart's mammoth Park Avenue Hotel stood as far north as Thirty-second Street (fig. 161). The great railroad tunnel that pierced through the high bluff at Thirty-fourth Street in the early 1850s and buried the train tracks for a few short blocks eventually would bring the resplendent homes of commercial magnates to the avenue. A series of enclosed parks was designed in the late 1850s above the tunnel between Thirty-fourth and Thirty-ninth streets, and the section was renamed Park Avenue in the hopes that this would attract a few rows of costly homes. But even this improvement was seen as both a delayed and chance event; the *Real Estate Record* believed that millionaires were hesitant to leave their former mansions near Union Square until the pressure of commerce had become unbearable in the late 1860s. At that time they found most of the choice Murray Hill lots (Fifth Avenue and its side streets in the thirties) to have been developed already. Consequently, they were forced to build their homes on the improved portions of Park Avenue whether or not they liked its location: Jonathan Sturges and Commodore Garrison constructed new town houses near Thirty-sixth Street; James Brown and William Libby's new houses stood at Thirty-seventh Street; and A. W. Barney and C. P. Huntington's were built at Thirty-eighth Street.[7]

It was only in 1869 that Vanderbilt consolidated the New York Central Railroad with the Hudson River Railroad and proposed that a new terminal, to be shared by the New York, New Haven, and Hartford Railroad, be built on a site between Forty-second and Forty-fifth streets and Fourth Avenue (fig. 162).[8] Although called the Grand Central Depot, as it neared completion in 1871 *The New York Times* declared that it was neither "grand" nor "central" (fig. 163). This terminal, located in the midst of what developers believed would be the last luxury quarter ever to be built in Manhattan, was seen as the most notorious invasion of private property, spewing over the district repulsive and discordant sights and sounds and closing off from residential development no fewer than ten streets and thoroughfares. Thus the practical limits of Park Avenue for residential purposes was Fortieth Street. By Forty-second Street, all traces of the avenue had dissolved into a gridiron of railroad tracks, and the sidewalks did not loom into

Fig. 160. Shantytown located near Central Park. (From *Valentine's Manual*, 1926: 27)

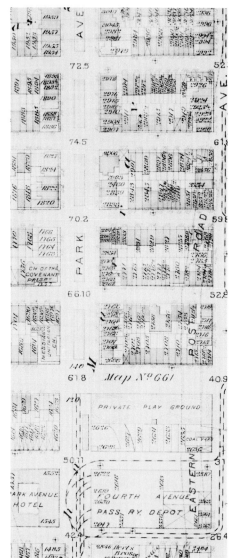

Fig. 161. *Above left.* Detail from the Robinson Insurance Map of 1885, showing Fourth Avenue and the Park Avenue Hotel (west side between Thirty-second and Thirty-third streets) and the improvements that turned Fourth Avenue into Park Avenue above Thirty-fifth Street. (Courtesy of the New York Public Library, New York City)

Fig. 162. *Above right.* Grand Central Depot at Forty-second Street, ca. 1872. Authorized by the government to take the necessary land at fair market value for a new terminal, Cornelius Vanderbilt erected an L-shaped depot designed by John B. Snook having a 240-foot facade along Forty-second Street and 696 feet on Vanderbilt Avenue. The tracks, hidden behind the Second Empire-style depot, were covered with large cylindrical vaults constructed of steel and glass. (Courtesy of the New-York Historical Society, New York City)

Fig. 163. *Opposite, below left.* Detail from Jalt and Hoy Map of New York, 1879, showing fashionable Fifth Avenue and the Grand Central Depot and railway tracks. Park Avenue South has recently been improved, while the open railway tracks above Forty-ninth Street will still retard its northern development. (Courtesy of the New-York Public Library, New York City)

Fig. 164. *Left.* Park Avenue, looking north from Forty-sixth Street, ca. 1913. By the early twentieth century, the railroad tracks were covered over and this section of the avenue was ready for future development. (Courtesy of the New York Public Library, New York City)

sight again until Forty-ninth Street (fig. 164). The freight yards, the tracks running down the middle of Fourth Avenue, and warehouses, breweries, and manufacturers continued to exert a negative influence as far north as Fifty-sixth Street. Only occasionally from that point to Ninety-sixth Street did Fourth Avenue take on the appearance of a grand boulevard (figs. 165–167), after which point it once again was lost in a maze of viaducts and inferior housing.[9]

In the vicinity closest to the depot, on Forty-fifth Street and Fifth Avenue, the cheapest and most common class of retail stores had existed for years. It was feared that the depot would do nothing to upgrade these nuisances. On the same block, between Fifth and Sixth avenues, the erection of a livery stable and several private stables had long ago obstructed improvement of that area. If the fashionable quarter moved again, the *Real Estate Record* warned, it would be because of the "scarcity of suitable and restricted lots, free from objectionable surroundings."[10]

The fashionable quarter of New York was by the late 1870s

. . . the very acme of the metropolitan system. Here the highest prices are paid for vacant lots, the most sumptuous edifices are erected and the greatest variety of the institutions of modern civilization abound. It is no wonder that all eyes are turned to operations in this quarter as furnishing the concert pitch for the entire real estate symphony. The influence here exerted sends its vibrations for good or for ill to the very extremities of our city's real estate system. It is folly to attempt to place any real estate outside of this quarter upon a level with that within it, or to suppose that equal eclat can be conferred upon other real estate at a moment's notice. The distinctive dignity and value of property within the fashionable quarter are the result of many years of slow development, patient self-assertion and gigantic investment of capital. In this quarter real estate may be compared

Fig. 165. Ninety-third Street, between Park and Fifth avenues, looking west, ca. 1900. The foreground shows an old colonial house at Park (Fourth) Avenue. Behind it stands a five-story tenement building; the Jacob Ruppert mansion stands at Fifth Avenue, behind which can be seen the Central Park Reservoir. (Courtesy of the New-York Historical Society, New York City)

to old books and old wines, which ripen and mature and appreciate in value with the lapse of time.[11]

The *Real Estate Record* observed that despite economically hard times during the 1870s, houses in this area were readily sold at prices that might have been considered extravagant in the 1850s. In 1876 the *Real Estate Record* was of the opinion that fashionable New Yorkers would remain fixed below Fifty-ninth Street, where there was plenty of undeveloped land for the next ten or twenty years. To the east and west of Central Park, where the city was already laid out and ready for development, the *Real Estate Record* foresaw the spread of plain and inexpensive buildings, perhaps leaving some isolated parts of the great avenues and boulevards for costly houses. In general, it was convinced that the greater parts of the upper east and west sides of the park would be improved in a manner that would be far from fashionable.

> In other words, the bon ton of our city will no longer be at liberty to choose sections of vacant territory, to the extent of a mile in length whereon their costly edifices may be uniformly erected, but will find a style of buildings adapted to the great middle-classes, continue to spread and extend their growth until the greater part of the vacant territory between 59th Street and Harlem River is covered and appropriated. . . . In a word fashion has asserted her sway for the last time in the real estate market of New York and the present fashionable quarter is probably the last extensive and distinctive one that New York will ever know.[12]

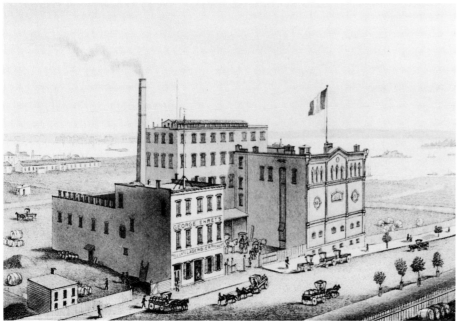

Fig. 166. *Above.* George Ehret residence and garden, at the southeast corner of Ninety-fourth Street and Fourth Avenue. At several points along Fourth Avenue above Forty-second Street, a medium class of apartments developed by the late 1870s. Ehret, a lager beer brewer, erected his costly city chateau in 1877 at the point where the avenue descended toward the Harlem Flats (Ninety-sixth Street). It was demolished in 1928. (Courtesy of the New York Public Library, New York City)

Fig. 167. *Left.* George Ehret's Hellgate Lager-bier Brewery, view from Ninety-second and Ninety-third streets, between Second and Third avenues, 1875–86. Much of the East River waterfront in this area was occupied by industries: stone, coal, and lumber yards stretched from Eighty-ninth to 102d Street: the Consolidated Gas Tanks stood near Ninety-eighth Street, and the Second Avenue Railroad Depot was located at Ninety-sixth Street. (Courtesy of the Museum of the City of New York, New York City)

BOURGEOIS TOWN HOUSES AND CITY CHATEAUX

Within the firmly established luxury quarter centered on Fifth Avenue between Thirty-fourth and Fifty-ninth streets in the last decades of the nineteenth century, the Victorian bourgeoisie treated the private home as a compensatory realm, isolated from the public sphere and marking the city's urban form with its separateness and exclusivity. The bourgeois family town house of the 1860s to the 1890s, along with the more elegant princely mansion of the wealthy elite, was a display case for consumption and possession. A rich man seldom had been content to be unobtrusively rich, and the richer he was, the more he was likely to spend his money in the manner in which the general public expected him to spend it. "His expenditure was, therefore, in a certain sense, the product of popular manners," and unfortunately for America, there was no well-founded tradition to tell the rich just how to spend their money.[13] Thus before the question arose in the 1890s as to the social obligations of wealth, before the apprehension that ostentatious display unnecessarily excited envy, hatred, or malice, New York's upper and middle classes built and decorated without restraint.

The architects of these fashionable houses, however, rarely generated an architectural form suitable to the urban setting, although there were a few early attempts to give a common public order to the facade of terraced rows: the House of Mansions (fig. 168), the Marble Row (see fig. 19), and the Colford Jones Row (see fig. 20) were three examples that lent prestige to Fifth Avenue in the 1860s.[14] As the wealthy grew in numbers following the Civil War, it was hoped that they would be attracted to the large lots near Central Park, which would afford them space for ceremonial gateways, carriage drives, and lawns and thus hasten the demise of the rectilinear brownstone town house that had reigned in the years before the Civil War and had lined the streets of Murray Hill in monotonous rows.[15] Instead, in the new luxury quarter above Thirty-fourth Street, or so it was firmly believed, the wealthy who already had shown their taste for fashionable display

Fig. 168. The House of Mansions, ca. 1875. Designed by Alexander Jackson Davis in 1856, this row of eleven buildings on the east side of Fifth Avenue between Forty-first and Forty-second streets, was one of the early examples of terraced housing in New York and offered a coherent and impressive arrangement in a castellated Gothic mode. (Courtesy of the New-York Historical Society, New York City)

through promenading or in carriage drives, at the theater or in sumptuous hotels, would finally come to demonstrate their status in the arrangements and proportions of their elegant new houses. Consequently, architects in the late 1860s began to pay attention to architectural styles effecting the illusions of wealth and to the creation of scenographic arrangements of luxury, although these designs in the end produced neither great architecture nor created a new urban order.

In this vein, the architect John Kellum once again designed a mammoth overdecorated structure for the department store magnate A. T. Stewart. Stewart purchased Samuel B. Townsend's brownstone mansion around 1864 on the northeast corner of Fifth Avenue and Thirty-fourth Street. Proceeding at first to gut the mansion, Kellum then demolished it and between the years 1864 and 1869 constructed a huge three-story marble mansion crowned with a slate roof, measuring 150 feet along its main facade on Thirty-fourth Street and approximately 112 feet along Fifth Avenue (see fig. 26). A profusion of ornamentation, porticoes, projected domes, and columns adorned this great marble box that towered over its neighboring brownstones and even dwarfed the freestanding Astor mansions on the opposite side of Thirty-fourth Street.[16] Architectural critics were hardly delighted with this monstrous structure. P. B. Wight noted:

> It has caused more surmise and gossip than any other house ever erected in America. . . . Various are the surmises, but no one knows what it cost. Few persons have ever seen the interior, which is said, however, to be plain, cold, and severe, by reason of the large quantity of Italian marble used in it, though it is rich in frescoes by Gribaldi. Nothing concerns us except the bad influence which its exterior design is calculated to obtain with those who might otherwise have been elevated and educated through the benign influence which the expenditure of so much money might have exerted, had it been invested in a well-designed and artistic structure. It is hard to conceive that any one surrounded by works of art, as was Mr. Stewart, could have had so little understanding of what constituted a work of architecture. Yet he went on steadily, piling up bricks and marble and iron, until it was completed. . .[17]

In spite of the high hopes of architects and critics that wealthy New Yorkers would demand an architecture of elegance, it appeared instead that many residents after the Civil War still preferred to reside in unimaginative houses. The brownstone front remained à symbol of equality, housing both the millionaire and the middle-class owner. Without drawing class distinctions, it enabled the truly rich to satisfy their need for displaying their wealth through interior decorations, pictures, statuary, and bric-a-brac and provided ample opportunity for the not-so-rich to lavishly decorate the brownstone facade with carvings and moldings effecting the airs of a wealthy man's abode. The first ostentatious exception to this type of private dwelling was Stewart's marble mansion, but this example was not followed until the early 1880s when the Vanderbilt mansions ushered in a new era in luxury housing.[18] Instead, as Montgomery Schuyler noted "' . . . this nefarious structure [the brownstone house] . . . became epidemic . . . between 1850–1880 . . . from Fourteenth Street to Fifty-ninth it raged and prevailed."[19] He believed, "untold architectural harm was done by the malefactor who discovered that a house of brick and brownstone could be constructed, by using the stone not legitimately to bind the brickwork and span its openings, but to conceal the brickwork altogether by plastering a veneer of brownstone four inches deep upon a brick wall, leaving the actual material to expose itself at the rear.''[20]

In the most extreme cases, brownstones displayed a Corinthian ornamentation; the fragility of its leafage as well as the ideal perches it made for birds led to the common enclosure of these capitals in wire cages. Lintels and windowsills were molded and projected to an exaggerated degree, and the use of huge stone blocks and joints as narrow as possible produced the effect of a single sheet of brownstone veneer.[21] Brownstone was neither an expensive material—its abundance made it cheap to acquire—nor a durable one, as it had a tendency to scale. If the wall were faced with the largest brownstone slabs obtainable, it gave the illusion that the veneer was a continuous sheet of stone, like a marble front. Being a soft stone it could be easily carved into fanciful shapes and thus lent itself to the addition of unnecessary ornamentation. The brownstone facade, Montgomery Schuyler pronounced, was far from an honest expression of construction. ''To live in and among them, to become inured to them, was to suffer a depravation of taste and the more pitiable for being unconscious.''[22]

Nevertheless, between 1868 and 1872, the most active era for private house construction, a steady stream of buyers was willing to purchase every brownstone town house produced, even before its completion. Manhattan's speculative builders who responded to this market thus controlled the development of New York's domestic architecture.[23] During this period, Fifth Avenue and its adjacent side streets from Thirty-fourth Street to Fifty-ninth Street were filled with construction debris and building materials, boxes, barrels, and carts blocking the thoroughfare but marking the extent of building improvements. Frequent explosions racked the neighborhood as the outcroppings of rock were blasted away from construction sites and from the streets that were leveled and graded.[24]

Fig. 169. Queen Anne houses at 127–129 East Eightieth Street, west of Lexington Avenue, ca. 1911. The addition of houses such as these in the 1880s helped to vary the New York streetscape. (Courtesy of the New York Public Library, New York City)

Fig. 170. Fifth Avenue, view north from Forty-fifth Street, showing the Windsor Residential Hotel on Fifth Avenue between Forty-sixth and Forty-seventh streets (far right), ca. 1885. Through its size and proportions, the Windsor Hotel broke up the monotony of continuous rows of high-stooped, porticoed brownstone houses. It was opened in 1880 and destroyed by fire in 1901. (Courtesy of the Museum of the City of New York, New York City)

By the mid-1880s the uniform linear brownstone streetscape would be broken up by the introduction of mammoth apartment houses and the appearance of picturesque Queen Anne houses (fig. 170). Before the introduction of the apartment house, which first began to appear in numbers in 1875, Manhattan's residential streets suffered from a lack of monumental effects typically created by deep shadows, fine entrances, and other architectural features, which an ordinary city town house could not provide. Only in the 1880s did the stately height and ornamental features of the apartment house facade lend beauty and variety to the city's streets.

The Queen Anne city dwellings were also welcome additions (fig. 169), although the *Real Estate Record* warned:

> in the so-called revival of the Queen Anne style, especially in this country, almost anything that is antique, picturesque and odd may be introduced into the architect's design with a good prospect that it will please the popular taste, and its correctness will never be questioned. For this reason, the merit of the style . . . depends mainly on the taste and judgment of the architect, who modifies or makes it to suit his own views or those of his patron. Modern and antique features often appear together, as when the lower sash of a window has a single sheet of glass, while the upper is broken up into small squares like those of two or three hundred years ago.[25]

Fig. 171. William Rockefeller house, Fifth Avenue and Fifty-fourth Street. Designed by Stephen Hatch and erected in 1876. (Courtesy of the New-York Historical Society, New York City)

Despite much that was false in the Queen Anne style, which the eye might soon tire of, its asymmetrical massing of architectural elements and commodious arrangement of groups of houses offered considerable variation to the rectilinear pattern of streets.

After a period of speculative growth, the economic crisis of 1873 gripped New York City, negatively affecting domestic construction until 1879. In spite of economically difficult times, the building of lavish, expensive houses in the fashionable district was still important for the nouveau riche. The *Real Estate Record* remained critical of most of these buildings:

> To say that the culture and taste of our people have demanded a higher order of domestic building, fails to account for the lavishness which characterizes these structures. Instead of homes, we have palaces, instead of stables, we have mansions of rosewood and plate glass for the noble brute. The palace of Mr. Stewart, the Gothic mansion of Mr. Stevens, the elaborate house of Mr. Fiske, are [early] examples of this princely munificence. . . . From the florid though unique efforts of the enterprising and talented firm of builders who lead this branch of business, who have left their indelible imprint on our leading avenues and its adjacent by-ways, down through all the grades of house building to the humble three-story dwelling, the one feature of lavish expense characterizes all.[26]

The *Real Estate Record* was, however, quick to praise William Rockefeller's mansion, designed by Stephen Hatch, at the corner of Fifth Avenue and Fifty-fourth Street in 1876 (fig. 171). Remarkably, it was the only mansion in the city besides the Stewart residence constructed entirely of fire-proof materials (especially important as this structure would house works of art and other costly items). But the *Real Estate Record* also noted that this structure was beautifully

Fig. 172. J. A. Bostwick mansion, Fifth Avenue and Sixty-first Street, before 1895. A bay window running up to a mansard roof ornamented the Sixty-first Street side of the Renaissance-style house designed by D. and J. Jardine in 1878. A conservatory was located in the rear. The first floor consisted of a vestibule, hall, and reception, drawing, and dining rooms, as well as a butler's pantry. The second and third floors each contained sitting rooms and libraries in front with bedrooms in the rear, while the fourth story was allocated to servant's quarters and a huge children's playroom that extended across the length of the house. For his own amusement and experimentation, Bostwick located a shop with steam-powered machinery on the third story, complete with every kind of mechanical tool. In addition, the entire house was electrically powered. Gaslights could be ignited by electricity, at least sixty speaking tubes ranged through the house, and all the kitchen and laundry doors were self-closing and could be shut without the aid of the servants. (Courtesy of the Museum of the City of New York, New York City)

designed in its outlines and in its general arrangement.[27] Yet it would surprise many a New Yorker of that era to know that, of all the compact and imposing blocks of expensive first-class private residences that lined the streets of the fashionable district, only a quarter of the houses had been constructed by private owners and architects; the remaining houses had been erected by speculative builders and then sold. With surprise the *Real Estate Record* noted that with the exception of William Rockefeller, only J. A. Bostwick, another "petroleum king," had decided to build his own mansion, albeit of modest scale, with the aid of architects D. and J. Jardine, just north of the fashionable district on Fifth Avenue and the northeast corner of Sixty-first Street[28] (fig. 172).

Even though practice proved otherwise, the *Real Estate Record* still hoped that wealthy homeowners would soon tire of the common brownstones standing shoulder to shoulder in the fashionable quarter and come to prefer city chateaux or urban villas: roomy elegant edifices, like Mr. Bostwick's, which commanded unobstructed views and were surrounded by their own landscaped gardens. In other words, the *Real Estate Record* supposed that "these favorites of fortune were already feeling cramped and oppressed in their brownstone town houses and would grow into more suitable abodes more symbolic of their wealth and their status."[29] Nevertheless, the economic depression and the uniform division of blocks and lots afforded few people opportunities to exploit this ideal. Instead, it fell to builders such as Duggin and Crossman, (architect-builders, as they preferred to be called), to realize in the late 1870s that the wealthy still wanted to buy already constructed fashionable residences with frontages that might exceed the 25-foot standard lot but that would be much smaller than villa dimensions (see fig. 30). In 1876 Duggin and Crossman constructed a 42-foot town house on Fifth Avenue and Fifty-seventh Street, a 35-foot house along Fifty-seventh Street, and an assortment of others in the following years ranging from 25 to 30 feet in width on Fifty-seventh and Fifty-sixth streets near Madison Avenue[30] (fig. 173).

Wealthy Manhattanites wanted to live in the fashionable quarter, not in order to make sound real estate investments but because they wanted to live both elegantly and luxuriously. Consequently, the market for expensive houses in the fashionable quarter resisted the depression, and other builders soon learned that the more artistically and expensively their town houses were embellished, the more readily they found eager buyers. Thus the streets between Fifty-fourth and Fifty-eighth streets, Sixth to Madison avenues, were solidly built up in the 1870s so that the 405 vacant lots of 1878 were reduced to 272 the following year[31] (fig. 174).

Giving still further credibility to the hold of the super-rich below Fifty-ninth Street in the early days of 1879, it became known that William H. Vanderbilt had

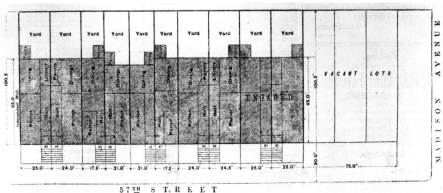

Fig. 173. Fifty-seventh Street, south side, between Fourth and Madison avenues (ca. 1877). Although not attributed to the builders Duggin and Crossman, this row of town houses is located in the area that they were developing in the 1870s. The rise of a fashionable elite in New York led to experimenting with the floor plan of town houses. Previously, in high-stooped or English basement houses, the kitchen and dining rooms were buried in the basement. "Under the influence of highly cultivated habits of life," the *Real Estate Record* commented in 1877, "it is no longer considered the elegant thing for families to use the basement for dining-room purposes." Suggestions of health as well as of fashion, tended to recommend the use of more elevated and commodious dining rooms. In many houses of the 1870s, the introduction of back extensions, such as those shown in the plan, provided space on the parlor floor for the dining room and pantry, while the basement was used for a playroom, a billiard room, or a servant's parlor. (Courtesy of the Museum of the City of New York, New York City)

Fig. 174. Fifty-third to Fifty-ninth Street, west of Fifth Avenue. Detail of Jalt and Hoy Map of 1879. Rows of two, three, or four costly brownstone houses between Fifty-fourth and Fifty-eighth streets, off Fifth Avenue, were erected by speculative developers such as R. B. Lynd, Cornelius O'Reilly, and Bryan McKenna, and ranged in price from $40,000 to $65,000 in 1878. (Courtesy of the New York Public Library, New York City)

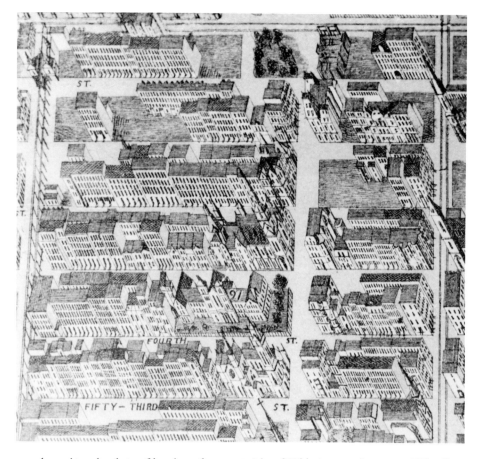

purchased twelve lots of land on the west side of Fifth Avenue between Fifty-first and Fifty-second streets, running a depth of 150 feet, and that his son, William K. Vanderbilt, had purchased a plot running 100 feet on the avenue and 125 feet in depth on the northeast corner of Fifty-second Street and Fifth Avenue. Another son, Cornelius Vanderbilt, had purchased the northwest corner of Fifty-seventh Street and Fifth Avenue, a plot with a frontage of 48 feet on the avenue and 100 feet in depth and that already contained two first-class dwellings and a stable to the rear of the property. In addition, Cornelius Vanderbilt planned to incorporate his two houses under a new facade composed by George B. Post; William K. Vanderbilt immediately intended to improve his plot with a new mansion designed by Richard Morris Hunt; and William H. Vanderbilt expected to erect family residences on his new property with the aid of architect John B. Snook.[32]

By mid-1881 the Vanderbilt mansions were beginning to attract attention. Montgomery Schuyler found their architectural merit questionable, pronouncing Hunt's building "a building in design. . .the others are only so mechanically."[33] Nevertheless, the *Real Estate Record* was pleased; finally rich men were willing to decorate the city in a suitable urban mode. They prophesied that a new era of city chateau would now beautify Riverside Drive, the Boulevard (renamed Broadway after the 1890s), Morningside Park, and Washington Heights with magnificent structures; places in the city where nothing intruded on the privacy of the extremely well-to-do.[34]

Hunt's Vanderbilt mansion was perhaps the most successful and Snook's the most questionable. Snook, aided by the Herter Brothers (fig. 175), designed brownstone houses for himself and his two daughters, causing Montgomery Schuyler to ask:

> . . . . what leading motive, or indeed, what subordinate motive, of an architectural kind, can be found here? There is no development of lines or of masses, and no organized relation of parts is aimed at. The openings are not grouped or spaced so as to tell the story of the interior, nor so as to bear any reference to each other, nor are the structural features which every building must possess brought out by modelling, nor is the ornament applied to accentuate the structural features, nor is it designed with reference either to its place or to its function as an ornament. . . . Much of the detail is carefully designed, but the absence of a general design makes it ineffective. Except for the refinement of some of this detail, the building would be as vacant of architectural interest as any work of our architectural period of darkness. The Stewart mansion does not interest students of architecture; but the Stewart mansion itself exhibits a nearer approach than these houses to an architectural design, and certainly a coherent design with coarse detail is less depressing, even if it be more irritating, than an entire absence of architectural meaning, with here and there a pretty architectural phrase which in some other context may have meant something. These houses have another misfortune in their very lugubrious color.[35]

Richard Morris Hunt's French Renaissance chateau for William K. Vanderbilt received the most popular acclaim as well as contemporary architectural praise

Fig. 175. William H. Vanderbilt houses, looking north along Fifth Avenue from below Fifty-first Street, 1888. Twin brownstone mansions were designed by John B. Snook and the Herter Brothers for Vanderbilt and his two daughters. The northern house was demolished in 1927, the southern house in 1947. (Courtesy of the New York Public Library, New York City)

Fig. 176. William K. Vanderbilt house, looking north along Fifth Avenue from below Fifty-second Street, ca. 1890. On the northwest corner of Fifty-second Street, just across from William H. Vanderbilt's massive brownstone mansion, stood William K. Vanderbilt's chateau, designed by Richard Morris Hunt in 1881 (demolished 1926). Occupying almost its entire site, the main entrance of the mansion faced Fifth Avenue and was reached by a short flight of stairs. The entry pavilion contained a deeply recessed balcony above the door with dormer windows above, flying buttresses, and other ornaments. To the left of the pavilion was a corbeled tourette capped with a conical roof. (Courtesy of the New York Public Library, New York City)

(fig. 176). Schuyler, however, did not think highly of its soft gray limestone nor of its tormented skyline. But he did feel the composition arrived at a powerful and massive statement.

> This is secured mainly by the unbroken breadth of the flank of wall between the porch and the angle on the Fifth Avenue front of the building—unbroken except by the simple and square-headed openings with which it is pierced, and the crisp and emphatic though not excessive string courses which traverse it and mark the division of the stories. It is questionable whether this massiveness is not carried too far, but everybody will admit that an excessive weight of wall is a "good fault" in the street architecture of New York, and that of the two, a dwelling is more dignified which approaches the solidity proper to a prison than one that emulates the precarious lightness proper to a greenhouse. The depth of the porch and of the recessed balcony over it in the central division of the avenue front assists this expression of solidity, and helps the building to wear its burden of decoration "lightly, like a flower."[36]

The leading motif of the composition, Schuyler pointed out, was the "pyramidization" of the whole construction toward the apex of the steeped hipped roof where massive chimney stacks and dormers wantonly assaulted the skyline. Schuyler continued, however:

> It cannot be said that the sky-line is so effective as might have been expected from what is beneath it. There is an undeniable piquancy about the statued gable which terminates the roof of the principal mass, and the rela-

tion between this roof and the steep hood of the turret is picturesque, taken alone. Unfortunately, it cannot be taken alone, and the effect of the whole series of roofs is not a harmonious grouping, but—there is no other word for it—a "huddle." It is in the roof, too, that the shortcomings of the architect in the solution of what may be called his academic problem are most apparent. The style of this work is the transitional style of France, the modification of medieval architecture under the influence of the Italian Renaissance, until what was all Gothic at the beginning of the transition had become all classic at its close. This is, in fact, an attempt to summarize in one building the history of a most active and fruitful century in the history of architecture. . . . Mr. Hunt's skill has not sufficed to introduce together these features, the outcomes of different modes of thought as well as of different systems of construction, without a visible incongruity; nor are they in all cases successful, taken singly.[37]

Schuyler finally concluded that of the three Vanderbilt architects, George B. Post achieved the more successful design. His too was a French chateau, but from a later, more classical period (fig. 177). Instead of the monotonous limestone used by Hunt, Post had substituted red brick with a red slate roof and limestone trim. Unfortunately, the Fifth Avenue side was marred by too much stonework, with only patches of brick, but the floor lines were clearly marked, the corners of the third story enhanced with corbeled turrets, and the whole parallelogram drawn together under a great four-hipped roof.

Perhaps it is because Mr. Post, the architect of the house of Mr. Cornelius Vanderbilt, has not attempted so much as Mr. Hunt that his work be called at

Fig. 177. Cornelius Vanderbilt II house, Fifty-seventh Street at Fifth Avenue, ca. 1891. Designed by George B. Post, in 1880, this chateau was characterized by a more scholarly treatment of detailing than appeared in the other Vanderbilt houses. It was enlarged to include all of the block on Fifty-eighth Street in 1894 (demolished 1927). (Courtesy of the Museum of the City of New York, New York City)

Fig. 178. Panorama of New York, looking north along Fifth Avenue from the tower of Saint Patrick's Cathedral, 1888. Notable are Hunt's Vanderbilt chateau (left) on Fifty-second Street, and the already dramatically changing streetscape of Manhattan, which includes the Langham Hotel (right) and the outcroppings of a new apartment district on Fifty-ninth Street south of Central Park, the tallest structure being the eleven-story Central Park Apartment House. (Courtesy of the New York Public Library, New York City)

Fig. 179. Henry Villard houses, east side of Madison Avenue between Fifty-third and Fifty-fourth streets ca. 1910. The six town houses, grouped around an open square, were a disciplined and restrained imitation of a High Renaissance Italian palazzo. For some architectural critics the Villard houses represent a clear reaction against the picturesque French chateau built for the Vanderbilts along Fifth Avenue and a call for a more rational urban order. (Courtesy of the New-York Historical Society, New York City)

once more successful and less interesting. In color it has more and in design less of variety. . . . It is much more simple and compact in composition than the other . . . much more within conventional decorum of a town mansion in its scheme, while it is equally far from having the appearance of having been designed by contract, and is studied with equal thoroughness, although with a very different motive.[38]

While picturesque French chateaux (fig. 178) were beginning to dominate the streetscape of upper Fifth Avenue, a more refined urban order was arising on Madison Avenue. Instead of free-licensed copying from the memory book of historical styles, a U-shaped courtyard mansion seriously tried to imitate the urbanity of an Italian High Renaissance palazzo (fig. 179). Henry-Russell Hitchcock has claimed that after the appearance of these houses, built for Henry Villard, and designed by McKim, Mead and White in 1884, the pathway opened toward a more abstract order and disciplined sobriety called the "academic reaction."[39] But in comparison to the picturesque Vanderbilt mansions, the new Villard Houses received little praise from the *Real Estate Record*. Giving up a whole block on Madison Avenue and Fifty-fourth Street in the fashionable district for the erection of six houses seemed an outrageous expense, but then to offer the city such a monotonous and simple composition simply added further injury. Taking its cue from the Roman palazzo, the overall treatment lacked the massiveness and compositional relationship between stories that had made its prototypes so effective. Instead, the six houses were unified by a low sloping roof, but the simplicity of the whole was so pervasive and the detailing so inadequately elaborated that the *Real Estate Record* complained the "whole pile was dumpish and monotonous."[40]

REAL ESTATE PROJECTIONS

During the late 1870s greater investment opportunities in genteel row houses and mammoth apartment houses were anticipating new residential districts near Ladies Mile and on the upper east and west sides of Central Park above Fifty-ninth Street (fig. 180). In 1877 the *Real Estate Record* first drew attention to the sprouting of a residential quarter above East Fifty-ninth Street.[41] As the number of available building lots diminished in the old fashionable quarter and as the wealthy began to erect extravagant mansions on their unimproved lots, the master builder, intent on speculation, was driven out of this market. Tentatively but unmistakably, as the economy began to improve, the most adventurous builders in 1877 began to build a class of "genteel houses" on the east side of the park between Seventy-second and Eighty-Sixth streets (fig. 181). The leap over vacant land to Seventy-second Street was in part explained by the opening of the new Harlem railroad depots at Seventy-third and Eighty-sixth streets as well as the reasonable prices of lots that afforded a builders a clear margin of profit. Lots between Fifty-ninth and Seventy-second streets were held at inflated prices, in expectation of luxury improvement.[42]

In the new residential quarter, the *Real Estate Record* projected, buildings of every character, style, and cost would be constructed. Four grades of housing were expected to be built simultaneously but without intermixing or overlapping and without monopoly of any one type. Along Fifth Avenue and the short block toward Madison Avenue, city chateaux and the villas of the wealthy would .

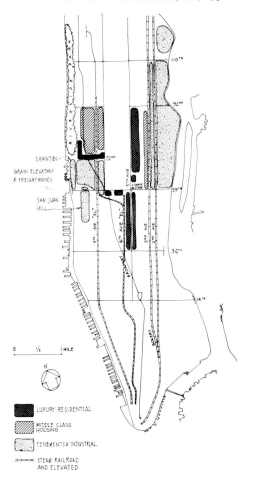

Fig. 180. Residential districts projected for the east and west sides of Central Park, 1875–93.

Fig. 181. *Above left.* Detail from Jalt and Hoy Map of New York of 1879, showing the new residential development on the east side of Central Park, Fifty-ninth to Ninety-first Street. (Courtesy of the New York Public Library, New York City)

Fig. 182. *Above right.* Detail from Jalt and Hoy Map of New York of 1879, showing the sparse development of the Upper West Side, Fifty-ninth to Ninety-sixth Street. By this time the American Museum of Natural History's first building had located on Manhattan Square, and clusters of random buildings had been constructed. These small structures would all be swept away when the West Side finally began to develop in the late 1880s. (Courtesy of the New York Public Library, New York City)

be erected; on the land between Madison and Fourth (present-day Park) avenues it was thought, genteel town houses would be built. On the the other side of the boundary of Fourth Avenue and as far east as Second Avenue, smaller three-story dwellings would predominate. Tenements and flats would fill in the region remaining alongside the waterfront.[43]

The West Side, on the other hand, presented developers with a problem: although it was the most picturesque portion of Manhattan, in many parts until the 1890s it was bleak, barren, and undeveloped (fig. 182). City officials had tried as early as 1860 to attract improvements to this area by providing the West Side with a wider and more alluring park drive than the East Side had, by improving the Eighth Avenue circle (Columbus Circle) in a manner more magnificent than the Fifth Avenue Plaza, and by designing the Grand Boulevard to surpass its European models. Building improvements remained, nevertheless, for many years too few and insignificant to recount.[44] Those who had acquired land on the West Side in the 1850s and 1860s were baffled by the one-sided development of Manhattan. As late as the 1880s parts of the West Side were still used as goat pastures and market gardens while corresponding East Side property had been occupied for some time with miles of elegant town houses and populous tenements. Not surprisingly, in 1866 a group of property owners had formed the West Side Association with the explicit intent of hastening improvements. As a result of their promotional efforts, Riverside Drive was paved in 1866, Morningside Park was opened, and the Boulevard north of Fifty-ninth Street was widened and landscaped. The West Side, however, continued to lag behind what would become the more fashionable Upper East Side.

One other building improvement would make a significant impact on both the development of these new residential districts and the district near Ladies Mile: the large-scale construction in 1875 of the apartment house, or, as it was sometimes called, the French flat. New York's first apartment house has often been attributed to Richard Morris Hunt who designed the Stuyvesant Apartments in 1869 on the south side of East Eighteenth Street west of Third Avenue (fig. 183). Since large costly buildings gave a better return than any other real estate in New York, these new structures were believed to be good investments; it was predicted in the mid-1870s that whole blocks east and west of the park would be developed with apartments. "Palatial in size, imposing in style, and occupying the very choicest locality of the city, [apartments] will yet furnish . . . an ample, complete and perfect home to the man of the most refined taste and yet of the most moderate means.[45] New York's streets began to welcome the apartment

Fig. 183. Stuyvesant Apartments at 142 East Eighteenth Street, 1925. Claimed to be the first New York apartment house, the five-story Stuyvesant was designed or remodeled by Richard Morris Hunt in 1869. Crowned with a steep mansard roof, the apartment house was divided into two identical sections, each served by their own entry and stairways. Four seven-room suites of apartments were planned for each of the individual four floors and for the four studios of six rooms in the attic (demolished 1956). (Courtesy of the New York Public Library, New York City)

house: a second apartment was built in 1872; in 1875, 112 apartments were built, 115 were built the following year, and so on until by 1900 thousands of these structures had filled out the city.[46]

THE MAMMOTH APARTMENT HOUSE

The first important apartment house, as far as the *Real Estate Record* was concerned, was the Haight House on Fifth Avenue and Fifteenth Street, which David H. Haight remodeled from an old mansion in 1871. It was acclaimed for returning a profit of 30 percent on its investment after only three or four years of operation.[47] By 1877 the *Real Estate Record* predicted that this recent experiment in housing for the middle and well-to-do classes would soon rival the private row house as an investment and would begin as well to attract the luxury class. Yet problems needed to be worked out, as many apartments in the early years contained vacancies. Developers did not always realize that elevators were essential. In addition, an ideal building type has not been developed, as most architects had not been given a second chance to plan an apartment. There were problems of management as well; the concierge was an unwelcome element to American residents, yet an apartment house needed a chief of staff to manage its twenty or forty families and to maintain suitable discipline so that thefts from the supply rooms were infrequent and linen baskets arrived unsoiled.[48]

Hoping to introduce Americans to the European model of apartment living, Sarah G. Young, in her book describing French flats in 1881, quoted extensively from, César Daly's *L'Architecture privée.* Daly had been a believer in and popularizer of both the power of architecture to affect social life and the need to develop new building types to reflect modern nineteenth-century life. Although Daly considered the apartment house a banality, as a dwelling for the masses it was the practical reality of everyday life, and its plan could at least be perfected to secure a good rental income, and he offered several suggestions to architects.

> A good apartment house ought not to be remarkable by any feature too exceptional. It ought to conform to all tastes, without bending to anyone in particular . . . the architect has a number of interesting problems to resolve; the best possible division of space, light, air and heating; the most healthy manner of conducting off rain and slop-water, a convenient distribution of drinking water, and perhaps of gas, and a good ventilation; the arrangement of each room in such a way as to preserve the liberty and privacy of the different members of the family . . . facilities of overlooking domestic service; and to render the most easy access to the rooms destined to receive visitors, family, the most complete possible separation of different apartments, so that noisy habits, perhaps of one tenant, do not trouble the repose and tranquility of his neighbors.[49]

In a city racked by economic stress and lacking an effective rapid transit system, the elevator enabled the New York architect and developer to build story upon story on a small plot of land, stretching the newfangled apartment system to its highest investment potential. Scarcely aware of its impact on the physical form of Manhattan, and not particularly concerned with the development of its architectural style, New York architects and developers were aware of the relationship between the apartment's floor plan and the attainment of good rental income. Thus with painstaking plans and sometimes at lavish expense, with elaborate facades and luxurious appointments, the apartment house was perfected, concentrating in the late 1870s and 1880s in two different districts: one in close juxtaposition to the clubs, theaters, and department stores along Ladies Mile; and the other in the new apartment district, near Central Park, west of the luxury quarter (figs. 184, 185).

Because the desire to abandon row house living may not have been caused by economics alone, but rather by a desire to avoid housekeeping problems, the hybrid apartment hotel also arose. This building combined the best features of the apartment house with those managerial and gastronomic advantages of the best hotels. Suites of rooms often included a parlor, a library, a dining room, bedrooms, and a bathroom, but excluded a kitchen. Meals were provided in the suite or in a common dining room, in addition rooms were cleaned and beds were prepared by the house maid service. Hunt's second apartment house, the Stevens Flat House on Broadway and Twenty-seventh Street, designed for Paran Stevens, the successful manager of the Fifth Avenue Hotel, was an early example in 1872 of such an arrangement. Never successful as an apartment house, it was soon remodeled into an apartment hotel, the Victoria.[50]

Promising to be the finest apartment house in the city, the Osborne, situated on the east side of Fifth Avenue between Fifty-second and Fifty-third streets, was just being completed in 1876 by the firm of Duggin and Crossman (figs. 186, 187). The *Real Estate Record* noted that while taste and elegance were displayed everywhere in this magnificent apartment house, nowhere was there any demonstration of "bawdiness or gaudiness," and to the contrary, everything was of solid comfort and convenience.[51]

The most expensive scheme, the *Real Estate Record* claimed, was the Bradley Apartment House, designed by John G. Prague, on Fifty-ninth Street between Fifth and Sixth avenues in 1877 (fig. 188). In it a prototype for the luxury apart-

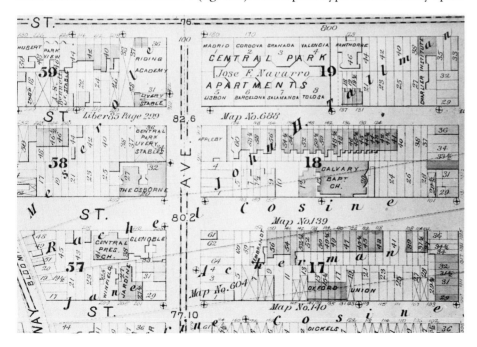

Fig. 184. Robinson Insurance Map of 1885. The new apartment house district south of Central Park and west of the fashionable quarter. (Courtesy of the New York Public Library, New York City)

Fig. 185. *Above right.* View south from the roof of the Dakota Apartment House, Central Park West and Seventy-second Street, 1887. Across the shacks and undeveloped blocks of the Upper West Side, tall apartment houses dominate the horizon. On the left stand the massive Spanish Flats, on Fifty-ninth Street and Seventh Avenue; to the right can be seen the back of the ten-story second Osborne Apartment House on Fifty-seventh Street and Seventh Avenue. Several other apartment houses rise farther west of these structures. (Courtesy of the New-York Historical Society, New York City)

Fig. 186. *Right.* Fifth Avenue, east side from Fifty-second to Fifty-third Street, ca. 1879. The six-story apartment house in the middle of the block is the first Osborne, erected by the builders Duggin and Crossman in 1876. The corner four-story building is the Langham Hotel. A row of coach houses and stables can be seen on the north side of Fifty-second Street. (Courtesy of the New York Public Library, New York City)

ment house had been fully developed, a specialty type that was to be limited in number, located near the fashionable quarter, and of the highest order of excellence in workmanship and design. Unlike the smaller squares of lower Manhattan that lent themselves to town house development, the oppressive expanse of Central Park with its distant margins and vistas would hardly appeal to the bourgeois residence. But no grander field could be imagined for the luxury apartment house, where it could expand in height and magnificence, overcoming every vestige of loneliness by congregating its convivial residents under one mammoth roof.[52]

In 1878 the *Real Estate Record* brought attention to a new red brick apartment house, the Bella, being erected by Oswald Ottendorfer, a German newspaper publisher, on the corner of Twenty-sixth Street and Fourth Avenue close to the terminus of the Harlem railroad.[53] Designed by William Schickel, its plan was divided into two five-story sections, one on Twenty-sixth Street and the other on Fourth Avenue, each containing two sets of apartments per floor and each served by separate staircases. The same year, a more imposing structure, the Florence, was built by a Mr. Matthews on a lot 200 feet by 53 feet at the northeast corner of Eighteenth Street and Fourth Avenue. This seven-story Florentine Renaissance apartment house had a center pavilion standing well forward from its flanking side wings and the entire composition was crowned by a massive dome (see fig. 52). Three different classes of residents were expected to occupy its forty-two suites of rooms: families who adhered to the old style of housekeeping and wanted a separate kitchen; young married couples who wished to escape the burdens of cooking; and the old bachelor class who never kept house. Four passenger elevators, a freight elevator, and even a package lift supplemented the main staircase and the ordinary servants' stairs.[54] The architect Stephen Hatch was at the same time designing a new "family hotel," the Burlington, on the south side of Thirtieth Street between Broadway and Sixth Avenue.[55]

Finally in the late 1870s, the promise of Central Park took hold and its margin along Fifty-ninth Street began to be developed with small apartment houses. In 1878 two lots were acquired by the wholesale cutlery merchant C. Robert Peters between Fifth and Sixth avenues. With the aid of his architect, William Huhles, he erected a six-story house with two apartment suites on each floor. The ornamental facade was arranged so that its lower two stories were of Nova Scotia and Ohio stone, the upper stories completed in brick with stone window arches, stone balconies, and a stone cornice. Polished granite columns with Ionic capitals graced the entranceway, while sgraffita or terra-cotta medallions imported from Germany relieved the monotony of the facade. Other experimental devices entered the design: enameled brick was tentatively used; and for the first time in Manhattan the master mason had used black cement mortar in an attempt to find an adhesive that would not wash out or discolor.[56]

Nearby, Mr. Canvet designed the Elise apartment house for Mr. Betz on Eighth Avenue a few doors south of Fifty-seventh Street, but still in close proximity to Central Park. Each of the twelve suites, two on every floor, contained seven rooms: a parlor, sitting room, dining room, kitchen, and three bedrooms. One of the finest panoramas of the metropolis was offered to the residents of the upper floors whose windows looked out on a landscape that included a unobstructed view of Staten Island, the New Jersey shoreline, and Central Park. All the paraphernalia of modern housekeeping conveniences could be found in these suites

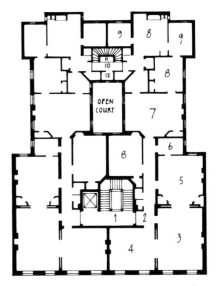

1. MAIN HALL	5. BEDROOM	9. SERVANT'S BDRM.
2. VESTIBULE	6. BATHROOM	10. BACK HALL
3. PARLOR	7. DINING ROOM	11. BAGGAGE ELVTR.
4. LIBRARY	8. KITCHEN	12. SERVANT W.C.

Fig. 187. Plan of the first Osborne Apartment House, built by Duggin and Crossman. (Redrawn from the *Carpenter and Builder*, Jan. 1880.) The kitchen and cooking odors were completely separated from the rest of the apartment. Novel devices for washing and ironing clothes were located in the laundry at the top of the building. A separate elevator enabled household goods and provisions to be brought in by the rear entrance so as not to interfere with the "style" that necessarily accompanied fashionable residences. (Courtesy of Avery Library, Columbia University, New York City)

Fig. 188. Bradley Apartment House, designed by John S. Prague in 1877, located on Fifty-ninth Street between Fifth and Sixth avenues. A red brick structure with Nova Scotia stone trimming, the Bradley had a low, stooped entryway. Two projecting wings surrounded an interior courtyard, which provided air and light for every suite. Each apartment comprised a parlor, library, principal bedroom, two minor bedrooms, drawing room, bathroom, butler's pantry, kitchen, and servant's bedroom. The interiors of suites were finished in pine, and marble mantels with grates and mantel mirrors decorated the principal rooms. Laundry tubs were located in each kitchen, and drying facilities were at the top of the house. A hydraulic elevator, furniture elevator, provision elevator, ash chute, and refrigerators were additional conveniences. (Courtesy of the Museum of the City of New York, New York City)

— electric bells, ash chutes, laundries, speaking trumpets, and elaborate bathrooms. On the adjoining site, Betz's brother would soon erect a similar apartment house.[57]

After five long years of experimentation, the *Real Estate Record* proclaimed in 1879, the city would achieve an apartment building, a monument that would keep alive the great building tradition of the Dutch of New Amsterdam and one that would be, simultaneously, a courtyard building such as the Parisians understood it to be. For Edward Clark, president of the Singer Sewing Machine Company, Henry Janeway Hardenbergh had designed the first mammoth apartment building, a six-story brick building, the Vancorlear fronting the entire block of Seventh Avenue from Fifty-fifth to Fifty-sixth Street (see fig. 184). Hardenbergh referred to this structure as "pure Renaissance with considerable of the Queen Anne features about it." Its major innovation was the impressive courtyard that extended over 3,500 square feet and was entered by carriage from the west over a paved passageway. The two main entrances to the apartment house were located on the side streets, leaving the entire avenue facade as 200 feet of unbroken barrack like lines. Each floor contained six suites of rooms, and each suite had at least nine rooms; yet because of the large courtyard, not one dark room could be found since a window in each looked out either on the street or onto the courtyard. Each suite, in addition, was provided with a lobby opening off of the main hallway, and an antechamber as well. No stores were designed in this thoroughly private dwelling house, and so eagerly did New York society desire fashionable suites that its rooms were all rented by well-to-do tenants long before the structure had been formally opened. Taking off from the success of the Vancorlear, which had begun to draw fashionable residents to the west side of Manhattan, Clark announced in 1879 that he intended to erect another mammoth apartment on the northwest corner of Eighth Avenue (Central Park West) and Seventy-second Street in the near future. Although the designs by Hardenbergh were yet unknown, the *Real Estate Record* believed that opposite an entrance to Central Park, this site would soon be developed with a structure as colossal and magnificent as the grand hotels of Paris.[58]

James H. Giles, the architect of the Lord and Taylor building on Ladies Mile, was experimenting with the apartment type in 1879, constructing the Windsor Apartment House on the southeast corner of Broadway and Fifty-fourth Street. Built of brick with stone trim, the remarkable aspect of this six-story structure was its bay window on the corner simulating a tower: the first story was triangular, the second round, and the third through the fifth stories were octagonal. Another courtyard structure, the building was designed around a 23- by 40-foot opening in the center of its lot.[39]

Each year the new apartment house district gained in popularity. In 1881 the Windermere Apartment House was constructed on the southwest corner of Fifty-seventh Street and Ninth Avenue. Designed by William F. Burroughs, it was seven stories high, built of Ohio stone and Philadelphia brick in red, black, and buff colors. Thirty-eight suites of apartments containing seven to nine rooms each were arranged around a 30-foot square central courtyard. And not very far away, on Sixty-second Street and Broadway a new family hotel, the Inca, was built, also in 1881, by the architect J. C. Martin. This hotel, seven stories high, covered five city lots.[60] Another elegant set of apartment houses arose on Fifty-ninth Street a few feet west of Eighth Avenue where a Mr. Heerlein constructed four five-story brownstone apartment houses with ornamental fronts of carved stone with specially designed iron guards protecting their windows.[61] And fronting Central Park, between Sixth and Seventh avenues, running through from Fifty-eighth to Fifty-ninth Street, Hubert and Pirsson designed the most elegant series of apartment houses the city had yet seen in 1881. On property owned by Jose F. de Navarro, eight distinct apartments were planned to be connected together only on their first floor (fig. 189). These buildings, the Spanish Flats, constituted the largest apartment complex yet designed; some of the suites would cover an entire floor while others would be constructed after the firm's patented duplex plan.[62]

Throughout the early years of the New York apartment house, architects continued to experiment with its floor plan, hoping to arrive at the ideal solution that would assure a high rental value. Privacy was essential, and the duplex apartment house, where communal space was minimized as much as possible, was assumed successfully by the Hubert-Home Cooperative Association, which built several cooperative apartments in the early 1880s.[63] Light and air were also important as well as the complete segregation of procedural entryways from service facilities, and consequently the Parisian courtyard apartment house became in-

Fig. 189. Central Park Apartments, or Spanish Flats, Fifty-ninth Street and Seventh Avenue, ca. 1889. Looking east along Central Park South. Designed in a "Moorish" style, by Hubert, Pirsson and Company for the builder Jose F. de Navarro in 1883, these houses were composed of granite, brownstone, Ohio stone, and Milwaukee and Philadelphia brick. Two double structures connected only at the first floor were separated by a longitudinal courtyard and crossed by three transverse courts, which then expanded into octagonal shapes containing fountains and flower beds. Each structure contained four separate apartment houses; the first four were named the Lisbon, the Barcelona, the Salmanca, and the Tolosa. Each house was 85 feet square, eight stories high, and contained twelve apartment suites (demolished 1927). (Courtesy of the New-York Historical Society, New York City)

creasingly popular. At first the competition was seen as a battle between two styles of living; the private row house versus the communal apartment house, and architects tried to reproduce horizontally, on separate floors, the typical town house while retaining its appearance in the facades and the high-stooped entryway. But soon, the popular apartment dwelling began to simulate luxury hotels, and developed elaborate entryways, services, appointments, and facades that no bourgeois family could afford in a private town house. All over Manhattan vast new apartment houses offered novel features, elaborating the basic building type.

James E. Ware designed a massive apartment house in 1884, a second Osborne on the northwest corner of Fifty-seventh Street and Seventh Avenue (fig. 190). A new feature in this apartment house was the provision of a croquet ground and garden on the roof for the use of its guests and their friends which could be shaded by drawn blinds in the summer and heated by steam in the winter. A private billiard room, a florist, a doctor, and pharmacist were also located within the structure.[64] Other apartment houses contained Turkish or Russian baths for the use of their residents; and a magnificent scheme thought up by W. H. Post for an apartment building designed to cover an entire block west of Central Park proposed cooperative features such as the daily provision of foods, coal, and so on in bulk and at wholesale prices, with the intention of eliminating the need for the corner grocery man and hence save its residents the extra cost they normally paid to the shopkeeper.[65]

The more luxurious the appointments, the more successful the developers expected the apartment to be. Such an example was the Saint Catherine at Madison Avenue and Fifty-third Street, designed by Hugo Kafka in 1884, an eight-story building containing one suite of twenty-one rooms on each floor. In this luxury building, the Fifty-third Street rooms commanded a splendid view of the park while the southern view opened on the Villard Houses and the Fifth Avenue Cathedral. The main entrance hall was approached through massive sliding doors, with inner doors made of amaranth, one of the richest woods in the world. Windows were decorated with elaborate opaline-jeweled cathedral glasswork, and the walls had carved cabinetwork of quarter-sawn oak. Bronze lamps of cut and beveled glass, two side lights of bronze representing beautiful female figures, and stained glass windows containing peacocks with outstretched feathers completed the entryway. In addition, the first floor contained a superbly outfitted drugstore in finely carved hardwood, with a frescoed ceiling and marble floor. Access to each suite was from an elevator or the main staircase, and each room in the suite was entered from a 6-foot wide by 80-foot long hallway that ran through the center of its plan.[66]

The most successful design of all the mammoth apartment houses constructed in New York, the *Real Estate Record* announced in 1884, was the Dakota, designed by Henry J. Hardenbergh, on Seventy-second Street and Eighth Avenue (present-day Central Park West), a ten-story structure that could be seen from most of Central Park (fig. 191). ''The building,'' it was said, ''actually helps the Park. Its picturesqueness of outline and effect is attained without any sacrifice of unity, or even of formal symmetry, for each front is laterally, as well as vertically a triple composition. . .carefully studied in mass and detail.'' The Dakota, large enough to house 3,000 guests, was in addition the first apartment house to use electricity extensively for domestic purposes.[67]

Fig. 190. Second Osborne Apartment House. Looking west at Fifty-seventh Street and Seventh Avenue, ca. 1885. The still existing ten-story structure, designed by James Ware in 1884, originally contained forty suites, some of which were duplex apartments with twelve rooms each. (Courtesy of the New-York Historical Society, New York City)

Fig. 191. Dakota Apartment House, Central Park West (Eighth Avenue) and Seventy-second Street, ca. 1890. Designed by Henry Janeway Hardenbergh in 1882, the extant apartment house was constructed of Nova Scotia buff-colored stone and fine-pressed brick, extending 200 feet down Seventy-second Street and 204 feet along the avenue. Each of the four corners of the courtyard contained an entrance and stairway that led to fifty-six suites of apartments, ranging in number of rooms from two to twenty. (Courtesy of the Museum of the City of New York, New York City)

Fig. 192. Chelsea Cooperative Apartment Hotel, 220 West Twenty-third Street, ca. 1905. Hubert, Pirsson and Company designed the Chelsea in 1884 among many experiments with cooperatively owned apartments. The firm also patented duplex plans in early New York apartment houses. (Courtesy of the New-York Historical Society, New York City)

The Real Estate Record estimated that between 1880 and 1885 over ninety apartment houses had been erected. Nevertheless, the building of these structures still was considered experimental, and it was not known whether New Yorkers would demand additional apartments in the future. As a rule those apartments that had been most expensively finished, and where the responsibilities of housekeeping had been reduced to a minimum, rented successfully. But as a real estate investment they had realized a much smaller profit than had been expected. In the case of the Spanish Flats, for example, built in two separate groups of four apartment houses each, only the westernmost four had been completed by 1885. Of the 128 apartments, one half had been sold cooperatively, but the other half remained to be rented. Few of these rental units had been successful in finding clients, and it appeared that the buildings would operate at a substantial deficit. An attractive U-shaped apartment building, the Berkshire Association, designed by the architect Carl Pfeiffer and located on the northwest corner off Madison Avenue and Fifty-second Street, had not been a profitable investment. The Dalhousie, another duplex and cooperative apartment on Fifty-ninth Street near Sixth Avenue, consisted of two adjoining nine-story structures following the designs of J. Correja, the first of which was nearing completion in 1885. This building, however, had been generally unsuccessful in securing tenants, and rents had to be reduced considerably. Even the Dakota was only half rented by 1885 and never was expected to yield an investment return greater than 4 percent, even if fully tenanted. The Chelsea Cooperative Apartment Hotel by Hubert, Pirsson and Company, on the south side of Twenty-third Street between Seventh and Eighth avenues, standing eleven stories high and containing 100 suites of rooms, also was not a profitable investment[68] (fig. 192).

In the meantime a few modest French flats had begun to be built on the Upper East Side. None had surpassed the Seward apartment houses, a series of seven buildings designed by W. Scott West in 1882 and located on the north side of Ninety-second Street between Third and Lexington avenues.[69] Another handsome East Side apartment house, the Lenox Hill, opened in 1886 on the southeast corner of Madison Avenue and Seventy-seventh Street. Designed by W. B. Franke, the six-story building contained two suites of rooms on each floor[70] (fig. 193).

The mammoth New York apartment house began to reach gigantic proportions—often ten stories high and covering half a city block—and it is not surprising to find that a bill before the state legislature in 1884 prohibited tall residential structures even though the elevator and New Yorkers' taste for apartment life had made such apartment buildings possible and sometimes profitable. The new building law of 1885 stated that no residential building could be higher than 70 feet on a side street or 80 feet on an avenue. Why, the *Real Estate Record* asked, should this law be imposed opposite a park? There were in Manhattan some 1,000 lots that faced a square, a park, or the river and there seemed to be no need in these locations to impose a limit on building height. In addition, where it was proposed to erect a tall residential building on the site of a whole block, could not the building be as tall as the developer desired as long as there was a plan for sidewalks and setbacks that would provide sufficient air and light to its opposite neighbors?[71] The fear among property owners that a nine- or ten-story apartment house locating opposite a three- or four-story town house would shut off both its light and air, reducing its property values, had pushed the new law into effect. None of the town house owners close to the Windsor and Buckingham hotels and the Osborne Apartment House, all on Fifth Avenue in the midst of the luxury quarter, had approved of the development plans of these buildings, and they now complained that the taller structures were a detriment to the real estate value of their luxury housing. Many plans had been put into motion for erecting tall apartment structures along Fifth Avenue. On the site of Madison Square Garden, Hubert, Pirsson and Hoddick, for example, had proposed a thirteen-story courtyard building, the first story to contain stores, to be followed by six "layers" of duplex houses connected by aerial sidewalks and serviced by elevators at each corner. The new building law stopped all these projected developments.[72]

Fig. 193. Lenox Hill Apartment House, elevation and plan, southeast corner of Madison Avenue and Seventy-seventh Street. Designed by W. B. Franke in 1886, this apartment building was based on a peculiar American plan. The three main sitting rooms of each apartment could be connected with each other through wide double doors that slid into recesses in the wall, making a suite. Privacy was assured by a butler's pantry separating the kitchen and servant's room from the rest of the apartment, and bedrooms that were entered from a private hall or a small receiving lobby. (Elevation courtesy of Avery Library, Columbia University, New York City; plan redrawn from the *Real Estate Record*, 37, March 6, 1886: 283, courtesy of Avery Library)

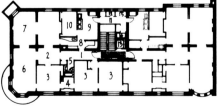

I. PRIVATE HALL	6. PARLOR	II. SERVANT'S HALL
2. RECEPTION ROOM	7. DINING ROOM	12. SERVANT'S W.C.
3. BEDROOM	8. BUTLER'S PANTRY	13. PASSENGER ELEVATOR
4. DRESSING ROOM	9. KITCHEN	14. SERVANT'S ELEVATOR
5. WATER CLOSET	10. SERVANTS' ROOM	15. WOOD AND COAL

Fig. 194. The first Plaza Hotel, Fifth Avenue and Fifty-ninth Street, ca. 1905. As early as 1883 promoter Ernest Flagg, with architect William A. Potter, developed plans to erect an apartment house on this site that would have combined cooperatively owned apartments with rental units, duplexes, and single-floor suites, and would have contained a restaurant and a men's dining room. These proposals were soon abandoned as too extravagant. Intead, the first Plaza Apartment House, following plans developed by the architect Carl Pfeiffer in 1890, opened in 1891 and was believed to be the largest and most costly apartment house that would be erected in the United States. It was demolished in 1905. (Courtesy of the New-York Historical Society, New York City)

When questioned by the *Real Estate Record*, the architect Ernest Flagg, who had designed several duplex apartments in the early 1880s, thought the height limit on apartment houses was completely unnecessary. Of course, he argued, tall structures injured town houses, but where one or two people may be hurt, a hundred were benefited. New York must be a city developed by tall apartment houses: those who resided on the upper floors had the pleasantest and healthiest locations for homes in the entire city, and these tall structures also enabled those of moderate means to remain within the desirable neighborhoods in the middle of the city rather than fleeing to Brooklyn or New Jersey. The city benefited as well from apartment buildings, he noted, for the land itself became more valuable by accommodating a greater number of people per square foot, and thus property tax revenues were increased substantially.[73]

Fig. 195. View across Central Park, showing the Majestic Hotel and Dakota Apartment House, 1894. The erection of mammoth apartment buildings was restricted by an 1885 law, which was not repealed until 1901. Hotels, not covered by the law, were constructed instead. The *American Architect and Building News* of 1885 observed of the new, tamer apartments, "As now constructed they admit of few pleasing architectural effects, while they efface, so to speak, the buildings of ordinary size. . . . We are becoming so accustomed to vast open spaces in our cities that anything which casts a shadow across the street seems a grievance." (Courtesy of the Museum of the City of New York, New York City)

Fig. 196. Majestic Hotel, view from Seventy-first Street, along Central Park West, ca. 1890. (Courtesy of the New-York Historical Society, New York City)

With the law banning large apartment structures, an outbreak of new hotel construction suddenly occurred. The Hotel Beresford, built on the corner of Eighth Avenue (Central Park West) and Eighty-first Street in 1889, was one of the first apartment hotels to be built on the West Side, a building type that had already begun to appear in lower Manhattan. A number of suites for families and bachelors were provided in the Beresford, with no cooking facilities. It soon became known, however, that the plans for the Beresford were really the result of the new building law, for another owner, a Mr. Brennan, had also filed plans for a double seven-story apartment house (on Eighth Avenue between Seventy-fourth and Seventy-fifth streets) to be completely fireproof and not to exceed the height allowed by the building law. His final calculations, however, revealed that he would not be able to compete with rental levels in older nonfireproof flats, and he decided instead to add two more stories in order to obtain a larger rental return. The Health Department objected and refused him a building permit. Consequently, Brennan was forced to change his plans and build an apartment hotel, a building type that fell outside the stringent controls limiting the height of tall residential structures.[74] In the early 1890s new apartment hotels became the current lucrative investment: the Plaza Hotel was erected in 1891, followed soon after by the Imperial Hotel, the Holland House, the Hotel Savoy, two new Astor hotels, and many others (fig. 194). In addition, a number of new West Side hotels such as the San Remo, the Endicott, and the Majestic Hotel were important additions (figs. 195, 196). But the development of these impressive new hotels and the problems of the new building law (its restrictions were not removed until 1901), jumps ahead of the story of development in nineteenth-century Manhattan, for the new luxury quarters expected to grow east and west of Central Park were improved in the 1870s and 1880s with picturesque row houses and commodious French flats.

CHAPTER FIVE

THE FABRICATION OF STYLE ON THE UPPER EAST SIDE

There is a prevailing impression that an architectural style consists of a set of forms—a sort of architectural clothing—to be used as fancy dictates. But the forms of a style, apart from its principles, which are its soul and life, are no more a style than the wooden image in front of a cigar store is a man. Taste, climate, materials, social conditions, wealth, and various other circumstances, have given rise, in different countries and at different periods of time, to certain methods and principles of design, the application of which, in the erection of monuments and buildings of those countries and periods have created certain architectural forms which have been systemized and called styles. The frequency we see buildings dressed in these various styles without any regard to applicability, scattered along our thoroughfares like a great international masquerade . . . [is due to the fact that we have] no education with respect to the fitness of things.—*Home Decoration*, 1886–1889, Collected Papers: 5

Constantly seeking the new and the innovative, American architects and builders of the late nineteenth century, according to one foreign critic, were "freed of all preconception, both audacious and rich enough to allow themselves the experiments whose results moreover have very often been favorable."[1] Not everyone agreed. As the building line for domestic architecture moved north above Fifty-ninth Street in the 1870s and 1880s, Montgomery Schuyler, for example, felt that a new departure in architecture had occurred—a general "breaking up" in the composition of a building, a sort of explosion that had produced nothing grand in the way of architecture. Others believed that the decades of slow improvement, out of which a mature American architectural style might arise, had been passed over in this quest for originality, and the concomitant eclectic mixture of styles, materials, and techniques, in favor of an architecture determined to resolve material needs. Because this current work defied classification, the broad description Queen Anne was most often applied to it. Perhaps American architects and builders had borrowed liberally from their English predecessor, Norman Shaw, who, with his taste for piquant and picturesque groupings, had been the chief author of this new movement, but Americans decorated their Queen Anne buildings far more lavishly in ways that only money could buy. ''They have built,'' observed Schuyler, commenting on the blossoming of Queen Anne styles on the Upper East Side in the 1870s and 1880s, ''so much and so expensively that they have produced in minds. . . like some of their own. . . which do not reflect much upon these things, the impressions that if luxury and art are not synonymous, they are at least inseparably connected.''[2]

''Architectural taste,'' H. J. Dyos has written of Victorian London, ''like manners, travels downward.''[3] Following the example already established by the city chateaux of Fifth Avenue, the more modest bourgeoisie on the Upper East Side symbolized in its domestic architecture its style of life. But the bourgeoisie was also intent on maintaining a strict separation from the more populous classes, cultivated through a distinct set of social manners, aesthetic tastes, and family moralities. Thus the architectural facade of the bourgeois town house, both in its respectable individuality and its public decorum, symbolized the bourgeois world to itself. It strenuously guarded the social status and standards already achieved, a fragile mask that for a time still concealed the eroding line between a social order of rank and propriety and an overwhelmingly relativizing and painfully private modern life.

Architectural criticism abetted this distinction. With abrupt changes in direction, from Gothic Revival to Queen Anne to Richardsonian Romanesque to Renaissance Classicism, American domestic architecture in the late nineteenth century offered no continuity of stylistic expression but reflected instead idiosyncratic individualism. The streetscapes of New York's fashionable quarter, however, were expected to teach moral respectability and taste. Architectural critics believed that overelaborated structures and eclectic pastiches were showy and vulgar as well as historically incorrect. In contrast, a certain truth in construction, genuineness in form, or scholarly reference to historical styles were characteristically underscored in the very best buildings. This belief in the ''heightened'' art of exemplary forms already reveals a nostalgia for moral and social art being destroyed by the tremors of fashion. Montgomery Schuyler's commentary on New York clearly reveals this tendency within nineteenth-century architectural criticism. The pursuit of novelty, or a profuse array of ornamentation, or a too vivid use of color, were cases, he said, of disorderly conduct that an architectural police might control.

> In doing Queen Anne [Schuyler asked], have they done anything but follow a fashion set, as fashions in millinery and tailoring are set, by mere caprice? A professional journal has indeed declared that ''architecture is very much a fashion,'' and architects who take this view of their calling will of course build in the fashion, as they dress in the fashion, in spite of their own knowledge that the fashion is absurd. But it is impossible to regard an architect who takes this view as other than a tradesman, or to discuss his works except by telling what are the latest modes, in the manner of the fashion magazines.[4]

Bounded by the constraints of real estate development and entrepreneurial capitalism, architectural critics of New York's domestic architecture were intent on separating and classifying the diversity of architectural expression by distinguishing historical styles from one another, beauty from popular taste, and the professional architect from the speculative builder. Setting norms and conferring distinctions was essential as the gap between rich and poor widened toward the end of the century. In consequence, the well-to-do increasingly secluded themselves within privileged domains or retreated to homogeneous suburbs. Within limited regions, the bourgeoisie would conspicuously display the correct clothes, manners, attitudes, and tastes. This dichotomy between bourgeois and working class neighborhoods was reinforced on the Upper East Side by the open railroad culvert that ran down the middle of Fourth Avenue. An architecture of fashion, one based on constantly renewable bourgeois tastes, and an architecture of necessity, one that responded to demographic pressures and need, developed on either side of the gap. Fourth Avenue was not to be renamed Park Avenue until 1888, after all the railroad tracks had finally been lowered: ventilation holes still allowed smoke and steam to escape making the avenue a barrier for fashionable residents until the early 1900s. To the west of Park Avenue, New York row house development continued to reflect and reinforce bourgeois values and preferences.

Peter Gay explains in *The Bourgeois Experience* that no other class was more devoted to appearances, to privacy, and to the family than the middle class, and no other class ever surrounded itself with higher psychological and physical boundaries making the gulf between the public and private spheres as wide as it could possibly be. There appeared, in Gay's words, an incredible "lust to conceal," to retreat into the sanctity of the family, to stand behind or underneath the authority of the church and the father, to have a private room of one's own. And yet the very democratization of comfort, the vast array of sensuous household items and elaborately decorated interiors, overupholstered furniture, and sentimental statuary, meant that these "comfortable surroundings could become insinuating aphrodisiacs for the most respectable."[5] Thus the bourgeois home, located in its secluded neighborhoods and suburbs became the incubator for ambivalent feelings. It was also, as Henry James observed of wealthy New Yorkers on his return home in 1904 after a lapse of twenty years,

> a society trying to build itself, with every elaboration, into some coherent sense of itself, and literally putting forth interrogative feelers, as it goes, into the ambient air; literally reaching out . . . for some measure or some test of its success. This effect of certain of the manifestation of wealth in New York is, so far as I know, unique; nowhere else does pecuniary power so beat its wings in the void and so look round it for the charity of some hint as to the possible awkwardness or possible grace of its motion, some sign of whether it be flying, for good taste, too high or too low . . . The whole costly uptown demonstration was a record, in the last analysis, of individual loneliness; whence came, precisely, its insistent testimony to waste—waste of the still wider sort than the mere game of rebuilding.[6]

As wealth and leisure increased, no one stopped to ask how the architect might have arranged the streetscapes to be more beautiful. People only asked how they might be comfortable, how they could move from one part of the city to another as rapidly as possible, how electric lighting might be produced on a grander scale, how new materials could be adapted and used. So eager were Americans to become wealthy, to enjoy their comforts and luxuries, that beauty was most often overlooked. No true architectural style, *The Builder* lamented in 1888, can arise until a development and a consensus of taste occurs as well as a directing of that taste.[7] Instead, Americans were restless: the brutal force of money and a vagueness of purpose prevailed over architectural taste. Novelty was the stimulus for a new residential address, for a grander facade, for the use of new materials. Henry James noted how impermanent and gauchely assertive of raw newness was New York's temporizing architecture. Novelty, for its own sake, clearly repressed the concept of duration.

> Is not criticism wasted [he asked], in other words, just by the reason of the constant remembrance, on New York soil, that one is almost impudently cheated by any part of the show that pretends to prolong its actuality or to rest on its present basis? Since every part, however blazingly new, fails to affect us as doing more than hold the ground for something else, some conceit of the bigger dividend, that is still to come, so we may bind up the aesthetic wound, I think, quite as promptly as we feel it open . . . The whole thing is the vividest of lectures on the subject of individualism, and on the strange truth, no doubt, that this principle may in the field of art—at least if the art be architecture—often conjure away just that mystery of distinction which it sometimes so markedly promotes in the field of life. . . . A manner so right in one relation may be so wrong in another, and a housefront so "amusing" for its personal note, or its perversity, in a short perspective, may amid larger elements merely dishonour the harmony. And yet why *should* the charm ever fall out of the personal, which is so often the very condition of the exquisite? Why should conformity and subordination, that acceptance of control and assent to collectivism in the name of which our age has seen such dreary things done, become on a given occasion the one *not* vulgar way of meeting a problem?[8]

Instead, a rigid classification of status and rampant individualism were the characteristics the bourgeoisie desired in their private sphere, and these were the ones they underscored with their choice of residential location and architectural forms. James hoped that the art of alignment and uniformity, a subordination of architectural parts in order to heighten the ensemble, would accompany the advent of modernism in the twentieth century. But it remained for the architects and builders preoccupied with the bourgeois representation of propriety and status to embellish the upper east and west sides of Manhattan during the late 1870s to 1890s with rows of town houses. Decorating their facades with square and polygonal bows and bays, oriels of every shape, irregular skylines, and strange juxtapositions of building materials and colors, they allowed the visual effect of this picturesque architecture to demarcate the symbolic boundaries of exclusion. This individualizing effect could have been enhanced if a clearer picture of city-making had controlled the development of upper Manhattan. Agreeing with Henry James, the *Real Estate Record* noted: "An American city was instead. . .a most perfect illustration of how mathematically minded a creature man is. A city is 'all made up' of straight lines and corners. Simplicity of arrangement is necessary; but to the untutored simplicity always becomes uniformity."[9] A deadly uniformity affected the development of all of Manhattan above Fourteenth Street, producing a city where there was no beginning, no middle, and no end. No opportunity was offered for architectural display because no one location was superior to another. Instead of the monotonous grid, the *Real Estate Record* ar-

Fig. 197. *Above.* Lenox farmhouse and outbuildings, between Seventy-first and Seventy-second streets, looking west along Seventy-first Street, across Madison Avenue, ca. 1880. The first building of the American Museum of Natural History stands across Central Park. (Courtesy of the Museum of the City of New York, New York City)

Fig. 198. *Right.* Lenox Library, Fifth Avenue between Seventieth and Seventy-first streets, ca. 1909. The classical, stone-faced building was designed by Richard Morris Hunt in 1870–77. It stood for twenty years as the major improvement on Fifth Avenue, its immediate neighbors to the north being a farmhouse, the passenger waiting room for the Fifth Avenue Stage, and unruly vacant lots. It was demolished in 1913. (Courtesy of the New York Public Library, New York City)

gued, upper Manhattan should have been designed with a central square, a point toward which all roads would have led and the site where all public buildings and important private structures could have been located. Leading away from this center should have been broad and imposing boulevards that occasionally swelled into smaller residential squares or parks, from whose center still smaller streets could have radiated.

Yet neither the Upper East Side nor the Upper West Side in the 1870s lacked picturesque advantages. The Upper East Side had always been the site of magnificent farms and country estates (see fig. 181). The 30-acre Lenox Farm lay between Sixty-eighth and Seventy-fourth streets, Fifth to Fourth avenues. Acquired by Robert Lenox in 1818, most of this farm was not lotted or sold until 1864 or developed until the 1880s, while the farmhouse and its grounds would remain at Fifth Avenue and Seventy-first Street for several more decades (fig. 197). Richard Morris Hunt designed monumental public and private structures on portions of the Lenox estate, greatly embellishing the Upper East Side long before it became a fashionable quarter.[10] The Presbyterian Hospital would rise on the north side of Seventieth Street between Madison and Fourth avenues in 1869, while the Lenox Library would grace Fifth Avenue to the south between Seventieth and Seventy-first streets the following year (fig. 198). On the north side of Seventy-third Street, east of Madison Avenue, Lenox donated four lots to the Presbyterian Home for Aged Women in 1869, designed by Joseph Esterbrook. Farther east, Union Theological Seminary stood between Sixty-ninth and Seventieth streets on Fourth Avenue, and to the north the German Hospital occupied the southeast corner of Fourth Avenue and Seventy-seventh Street, with its open grounds reaching to Seventy-sixth Street. Saint Catherine's Convent could be found on the north side of Eighty-first Street east of Madison Avenue; and old Hamilton Square (Sixtieth to Sixty-eighth Street, Fifth to Third Avenue) had long been the location of public institutions such as the Hahnemann Hospital, the Institute of Instruction for the Deaf and Mute, the New York Normal College (Hunter College), and Mount Sinai Hospital.[11] In 1877–79 between Fourth and Lexington avenues, Sixtieth and Sixty-seventh streets, a red brick medieval French fortress with crenellated towers designed by Charles W. Clinton was constructed, housing the Seventh Regiment Armory (fig. 199). Another magnet, the first building of the Metropolitan Museum of Art, designed by Calvert Vaux and Jacob Wrey Mould, neared completion in 1880 on the west side of Fifth Avenue between Eightieth and Eighty-fourth streets[12] (fig. 200). All of these institutions, surrounded with open grounds and parklands, greatly enhanced the natural beauty and architectural development of the Upper East Side.

The large area of unoccupied land above Fifty-ninth Street was thought in the late 1870s to be of sufficient size and appeal to provide the entire building trade of New York with enough work for fifty years to come. The whole of Manhattan was already marked out with street lines, and vast new territory had become accessible by elevated railways. If the city would only move forward with street improvements there was no reason that development of these lands would not rapidly follow.[13] As building activity began to revive after the depression of the 1870s, the 300 or so vacant lots within the established fashionable quarter below Fifty-ninth Street continued to be held off the market by owners who were loath to sell them until prices dramatically improved. Thus real estate investors in fashionable property were forced to move in a northeasterly direction between

Fig. 199. Seventh Regiment Armory, looking across the Fourth Avenue railroad cut. Designers of armories from the 1880s to 1910 used medieval fortifications as their architectural prototypes, military symbols that Montgomery Schuyler claimed suggested warfare of the bow and arrow period, or at most, the ballista and catapult period, thus acknowledging their inability to deal with modern modes of warfare. The Seventh Regiment was a prestige unit; its interiors, designed by Stanford White and Louis C. Tiffany, were more appropriate for the regiment's meetings, annual grand fairs, and fashionable balls than they were for military drilling. (Courtesy of the Museum of the City of New York, New York City)

Fig. 200. Metropolitan Museum of Art, west side of Fifth Avenue between Eightieth and Eighty-fourth streets, 1894. Although Frederick Law Olmsted did not approve of architectural intrusions into Central Park, the Metropolitan, designed by Calvert Vaux and Jacob Wrey Mould in 1879, acted as a magnet, pulling fashionable residences northward. (Courtesy of the Museum of the City of New York, New York City)

Fifth and Fourth avenues above Fifty-ninth Street and as far north as Eighty-sixth Street.[14]

It seemed certain that Fourth Avenue would be the easterly border of fashionable land in this new district. Fifth Avenue, on the other hand, was less defined, and no one could foresee whether it would be developed with mansions, town houses, apartment houses, hotels, public buildings, or a medley of all of these. As a result it would be slow to develop, and building improvements would center instead along Madison Avenue and the short blocks to its east and west. Rather than following a consecutive path, development would be scattered within an extensive area, concentrating on the elevated regions—Lenox Hill in the east sixties and seventies and Prospect Hill in the east nineties.[15] By 1879 it was clear that a new elite district was emerging on the Upper East Side. In this revived market a dozen corner lots along Madison Avenue and innumerable interior lots had changed ownership, and prices had greatly improved. This was a real estate market, it was predicted, that the new millionaires would dominate, as evidenced by the purchasing of empty lots by the estates of Arnold and Constable, H. DeForest, and W. A. Thompson and the private mansions planned in the area by H. Havemeyer, David Dows, and Richard Arnold, among others.[16]

LENOX HILL EMBELLISHMENTS

With the completion of the magnificent Seventh Regiment Armory on Fourth Avenue imminent and with the opening of a steam railroad depot at Seventy-third Street, the Lenox Hill area centering on Sixty-eighth Street west of Fourth Avenue became in the late 1870s and early 1880s the focus of active real estate development.[17] A new generation of builders had emerged out of the economic crisis of the 1870s and now found ready house buyers among such prominent men as Professor Dwight of Columbia College; Mr. Johnson, the well-known dry-goods merchant; and Mr. Shoemaker, the lithographer. In 1878 these men had all purchased four-story basement brownstone houses built by Ira Doying on Sixty-seventh and Sixty-eighth streets between Madison and Fourth avenues[18] (fig. 201). Doying would continue to lead the development on the Upper East Side, erecting in 1879 a cluster of thirty different houses on the block to the south between Sixty-sixth and Sixty-seventh streets, and in 1881 ten more houses on the west side of Madison Avenue between Sixty-second and Sixty-third streets and three others on the south side of Sixty-seventh Street just east of Fifth Avenue.[19]

Many other builders, such as Muldoon and Mowbray, Breen and Nason, and McCafferty and Buckley, were working on the side streets of Lenox Hill (fig. 202).[20] For the most part, the *Real Estate Record* claimed, these builders all conformed to acceptable standards of taste and merit, and what had appeared to be an isolated and lonely settlement soon became the heart of fashion. Nathalie Dana remembers that during her childhood in the 1880s Lenox Hill was in the process of changing from open country to city streets. She was born in 1878 in a house on Seventy-first Street near the corner of Lexington Avenue. The only house west of her family's row was the bright blue Lenox farmhouse near Central Park, and a shanty where an Irish family lived stood behind their house toward Seventy-second Street.[21] After their old house burned down in 1882 the family moved into a new house in 1884, one of a row erected by a builder on the east side of Fourth Avenue, between Sixty-ninth and Seventieth streets.

Fig. 201. Houses on East Sixty-seventh Street, designed by James Ware for the developer Ira E. Doying, 1878–80. These buildings were among the first to be built above the fashionable Fifty-ninth Street line, and the earliest indication that the Upper East Side would become the new stylish quarter in the 1880s. (Courtesy of Avery Library, Columbia University, New York City)

[Fig. 202]

SELECTED DEVELOPERS ACTIVE IN LENOX HILL: 1877–1884

1877   5 houses, south side of 68th Street, near Madison Avenue
(Richard W. Buckley, architect-developer)

4 houses on 63d Street, between Fifth and Madison avenues
(Mr. Wilson, developer)

3 houses on the corner of 75th Street and west side of Madison Avenue
(Edward Kilpatrick, developer)

3 houses on the corner of 75th Street and west side of Madison Avenue
(Mr. Taylor, developer)

2 houses on 62d Street, near Fifth Avenue
(Mr. Bookman, developer)

1878   3 houses, south side of 68th Street, east of Madison Avenue
(McCafferty and Buckley, architect-developers)

5 houses on 68th Street between Madison and Fourth avenues
(William and William, developers)

10 houses, north side of 67th Street and south side of 68th Street between Fifth and Madison avenues
(Muldoon and Mowbray, developers)

6 houses, both sides of 66th Street, between Fifth and Madison avenues
(Breen and Nason, developers)

1881   2 houses, north side of 69th Street, between Fifth and Madison avenues
(William E. Mowbray, developer)

1882   7 houses on 75th Street between Madison and Fourth avenues
(Terence Farley and Sons, developers)

1884   10 houses, east side of Park Avenue between 68th and 69th streets
(developer unknown)

Data compiled from the *Real Estate Record and Builders' Guide* (1877–1884).

Home, Dana recalled, was the most important experience for Victorians. Since visiting at night or going to the theater were rare occasions for her parents, the family was almost always "at home," collecting in the library after dinner where they awaited callers. They decorated their new house with considerable care, requesting the advice of McKim, Mead and White. The home decorator, it was believed in the 1880s, must start with a definite purpose, for different rooms required different treatments. Since the parlor, or library, was devoted to receiving society, it should be brilliant and scintillating in itself, enabling small groups to assemble comfortably. Boxlike emptiness was to be avoided and should be broken up with bays, recesses, and nooks and oversize furniture.[22] Dana recalled that the highest praise one could give furniture and bric-a-brac of the 1880s was "unique" and nearly as high a praise was "chaste."[23] In order not to give off an aura of the nouveau riche, the decorators used color to modify the clutter of the "refined" Victorian interior. Thus the dining room had wallpaper embossed to imitate leather in red and gold tones, and light oriental rugs were used for window curtains suspended from carved Japanese screens. A carved sideboard heavily laden with silver was also draped with an Oriental shawl, while the dining room table was covered with another Oriental rug and held a silver ornamented "fernery" with small plants in its center.

Beyond the dining room, through an archway, could be found a small Oriental "nook," of the kind so popular among Victorians, which ladies used for receiving gentlemen callers and holding private meetings. In this small room muted blue and silver materials pleated against the wall were gathered into a knot at the center of the ceiling. Shelves filled with vases and gold filigree work dimmed the light from the window, while a narrow uncomfortable sofa and a small table holding weapons of war finished off the nook. The other room on the first floor was the library, something between a parlor and a living room. Dana recalled that the library's collection of bric-a-brac was "managed" by the overall color scheme, which had various shades of tan with accents of olive green and black. Burnt-orange window curtains were hung from oak spindle screens while the walls were papered in a tan floral motif. Copies of paintings in the style of Raphael complemented the bric-a-brac strewn around the room. The centerpiece and controlling motif was a Milton shield designed in silver by Tiffany and incorporated into the woodwork above the mantel shelf. Intricately shaped shelves emanated from the shield and were always filled with mementos from Dana's parents' travels or the latest treasures purchased on Ladies Mile.

New York was a walking city at this time, and although Lenox Hill was far above Fourteenth Street, it was not unusual for Dana and her friends to walk down Fifth Avenue in the afternoons to Huyler's for an ice cream soda and then back again, a jaunt of at least five miles. Once a week, her mother and aunt visited Ladies Mile. Since it was nearly an hour's trip by horsecar, they took a whole day to visit the department stores, to be instructed in the latest fashions and novelties, and to lunch at Pursell's before returning home.

No matter how far above town the East Side appeared, it was apparent by the 1880s that Lenox Hill was not to be the area for speculative developers; its lots had quickly passed into the hands of the well-to-do. A mania for special building occurred as these owners turned to architect-builders to design elegant private houses modeled after the Continental Gothic or popular Queen Anne modes (fig. 203). Architectural innovations always captured the eye of the *Real*

[Fig. 203]

FREESTANDING AND ARCHITECT-DESIGNED HOUSES ON THE UPPER EAST SIDE: 1879–1893

1879　Judge Pearson residence, southeast corner of 70th Street and Madison Avenue
3 houses, south side of 71st Street between Park and Lexington avenues
(John Prague, architect)

1880　David Dow residence, north corner of 69th Street and Fifth Avenue
(Herter Brothers, designers)
Herbert Bishop residence, north of 69th Street and Fifth Avenue (C.V. Clinton, architect)
Armour residence, 67th Street and Fifth Avenue (Lamb and Rich, architects)
G. Quintard residence, northeast corner of 73d Street and Fifth Avenue
(A. Gilman, architect)

1881　5 houses, north side of 73d Street, just east of Fifth Avenue
(D. and J. Jardine, architects)
H. G. Marquand residence, northwest corner of 68th Street and Fifth Avenue
(R. M. Hunt, architect)
J. Sloane residence, 997 Fifth Avenue (R. H. Robertson, architect)
Stuart residence, northeast corner of 68th Street and Fifth Avenue
(W. Schickel, architect)

1882　Tiffany residence, northwest corner of 72d Street and Madison Avenue
(McKim, Mead and White, architects)
Double house, 23–25 67th Street (R. H. Robertson, architect)
8 houses, southeast corner of 69th Street and Fourth Avenue
(Lamb and Wheeler, architects)
Residence, 712 Fifth Avenue (R. H. Robertson, architect)

1883　Cook residence, Fifth Avenue and 78th Street (Wheeler Smith, architect)

1885　Ogden Mills residence, southeast corner of 69th Street and Fifth Avenue
(R. M. Hunt, architect)

1886　Ruppert residence, Fifth Avenue and 93d Street
Ehret house, Fourth Avenue and 94th Street
Untermeyer residence, Fifth Avenue and 92d Street (Hugo Kafka, architect)

1887　Brokaw residence, northeast corner of 79th Street and Fifth Avenue
(Rose and Stone, architects)
Livingston residence, 6 East 69th Street (R. M. Hunt, architect)

1889　Collis Huntington residence, southeast corner of 57th Street and Fifth Avenue
(G. B. Post, architect)
Havemeyer residence, northeast corner of 66th Street and Fifth Avenue
(C. C. Haight, architect)

1890　Residence, south corner of 78th Street and Fifth Avenue (R. M. Hunt, architect)
Rhinelander residence, northeast corner of 89th Street and Lexington Avenue

1891　Inman residence, 874 Fifth Avenue (R. H. Robertson, architect)
Burden residence, south corner of 72nd Street and Fifth Avenue (R. H. Robertson, architect)
Eldridge T. Gerry residence, Fifth Avenue and 61st Street (R. M. Hunt, architect)

1892　Bayles residence, southeast corner of 71st Street and Fifth Avenue
(Boring, Tilton and Mellon, architects)
Sherman residence, southeast corner of 65th Street and Fifth Avenue
(W. H. Russell, architect)
Colby residence, 8–10 East Sixty-ninth Street (Peabody and Stearne, architects)

(continued on following page)

Herter residence, 817–819 Madison Avenue (Carrère and Hastings, architects)
Hoe residence, 11 East 71st Street (Carrère and Hastings, architects)

1893   John J. Astor residence, 840 Fifth Avenue and 65th Street (R. M. Hunt, architect)
Brown residence, southwest corner of 72nd Street and Madison Avenue (McKim, Mead and White, architects)
Yerkes residence, southeast corner of 68th Street and Fifth Avenue (R. H. Robertson, architect)
Alexander residence, 6 East 64th Street (R. H. Robertson, architect)
Martin residence, 802 Fifth Avenue (H. F. Kilburn, architect)

Data compiled from the *Real Estate Record and Builders' Guide* and *A History of Real Estate Building and Architecture in New York City.*

Estate Record, for example, the houses designed by John G. Prague for Charles MacDonald on the south side of Seventy-first Street between Fourth and Lexington avenues. By dividing the parlor floor into three separate rooms, this architect turned the front room into a large reception area for expected callers. In the middle room he placed the parlor proper, and beyond lay the dining room which was lighted by a dome and connected to the basement kitchen by a stairway and dumbwaiter.[24] Among the choicest dwellings on Lenox Hill, the *Real Estate Record* noted, was a row of eight four-story houses designed by the architects Hugh Lamb and Lorenzo Wheeler in 1882, on the southwest corner of Sixty-ninth Street and Fourth Avenue. The brownstone structures facing the street had octagonal and square bay windows extending to the second story, while the houses on the avenue were arranged so that their first two stories were of plain brownstone, above which pressed ornamental brick decorated their facades.[25]

Fig. 204. Madison Avenue, looking northwest from Fifty-fifth Street, 1871. To the right stands the Madison Avenue Reformed Church on the corner of Fifty-seventh Street. The white structure to the left is the corner building of Marble Row, located on Fifth Avenue and Fifty-seventh Street. Relatively barren in the early 1870s, within a decade Madison Avenue and its adjacent side streets were desirable addresses. (Courtesy of the Museum of the City of New York, New York City)

RESIDENCES FOR THE RICH

Since the majority of wealthy New Yorkers preferred to live in close proximity to the fashionable district, lots along Madison Avenue above Fifty-ninth Street as far as Sixty-ninth Street ranged in price from $50,000 to $100,000 and could be expected to be graced with extremely expensive town houses (figs. 204, 205). Again it was hoped that New Yorkers would break away from their pattern of high-stooped brownstone houses. But, constrained by its 25-foot width, the bourgeois town house had to be narrow. In addition, the high value of land forced the developer to crowd five houses onto lots where once four had stood. By the mid-1880s, especially in the expensive blocks of the Upper East Side, the town house facade seemed an intractable problem as its dimensions were not wide enough to allow for lateral subdivision, and its stories too similar in height and importance to offer a basis for design. Nevertheless, architects designing these small street facades began to achieve considerable success by converting the whole facade into one dominant feature or emphasizing one element—such as an oriel—and subordinating the others.[26]

The first evidence of grandiose building could be found in a row of five houses, erected by Charles Buek and Company (the successors to the architect-builders Duggin and Crossman) in 1885 on the northeast corner of Sixty-ninth Street and Madison Avenue (fig. 206). These houses were close to a new French town house designed by Richard M. Hunt for Henry Marquand in 1881, on the northwest corner of Sixty-eighth Street and Madison Avenue (fig. 207). The largest residence of all was constructed on Fifth Avenue and the southeast corner of Sixty-ninth Street: the home of Ogden Mills, erected in 1885[27] (fig. 208). Also designed by Hunt, this was a more restrained city chateau than the Marquand

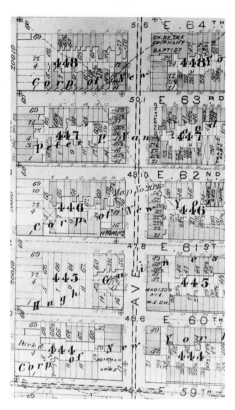

Fig. 205. Detail from the Robinson Insurance Map of 1885, showing development of Fifty-ninth Street to Sixty-fourth Street, east of Fifth Avenue. (Courtesy of the New York Public Library, New York City)

Fig. 206. Madison Avenue, looking south from Seventieth Street, ca. 1885. The three vacant lots on the east side of Madison Avenue and north of Sixty-ninth Street, separated by two town houses, were developed by Charles Buek and Company with a row of five town houses in 1885. Farther south, high-stooped brownstone houses dominate, even in this region of extremely expensive lots. (Courtesy of the Museum of the City of New York, New York City)

Fig. 207. Tiffany and Marquand houses (From *Harper's Weekly* 30, 1880.) Theatrical features such as grandiose entryways, arched openings, picturesque window groupings, and box-stooped side entrances greatly affected the streetscapes of the Upper East Side in what Montgomery Schuyler referred to as a ''bursting'' of architectural discipline. (Courtesy of the New-York Historical Society, New York City)

house, the latter being definitely more remarkable for its eclectic rooms decorated in the style of Pompei, Japan, Spain, or the Orient[28] (fig. 209). Development was sparse again until Seventy-second Street, where the regal Charles L. Tiffany house was a definite landmark (fig. 210). Designed by McKim, Mead and White (actually Stanford White's fantasy aided by Louis C. Tiffany) in 1882 on the northwest corner of Madison Avenue opposite the truck farms of the Lenox estate, it was a structure conspicuous both for its massiveness and choice of materials. The biggest fault of the building, the *Real Estate Record* criticized, was "an attempt not so much to make a picture out of a building, as to make a building out of a picture," for it had a roof so animated with chimneys that one suspected that some of these were dummies used only because they were picturesque. In addition, the street front contained a great mullioned window over what appeared to be a brick balcony, but the balcony was too large to be built of brick unless an iron girder carried its weight and the brick was merely a plastered facade. Such structural solecisms, in an era when criticism in architecture was stressing honesty and decorum, yielded an unreal and fictitious character to the entire building and, in the opinion of the *Real Estate Record*, detracted considerably from its overall architectural value.[29] Excessive detailing and juxtaposition of materials seemed to be the architectural lessons of the Tiffany house, the latest variation of the Queen Anne style, which was running its course on the Upper East Side. Opposite the Tiffany residence, on the northeast corner of Seventy-second Street and Madison Avenue, on the last available lots on the block, the Lynd Brothers had just built two houses in 1885. The *Real Estate Record* reported that they, too, all unfortunately promised to be overelaborate and excessive in scale[30] (fig. 211).

By the mid-1880s the central area for first-class residences on the Upper

Fig. 208. Ogden Mills mansion and adjacent houses, southeast corner of Sixty-ninth Street and Fifth Avenue, 1939. Designed by Richard Morris Hunt and built in 1885, this mansion for the heir of a California gold rush millionaire was located near many other public and private structures that Hunt designed on the Lenox estate during the 1870s and 1880s. The house was demolished in 1939. (Courtesy of the New-York Historical Society, New York City)

Fig. 209. Interior of the Henry Marquand residence, at 11 East Sixty-Eighth Street, 1890. Designed by Richard Morris Hunt in 1881, the house was in its time more celebrated for its eclectic interior decoration than for its architecture. The rooms became the showcase for Marquand's extensive collection of objets d'art. (Courtesy of the New-York Historical Society, New York City)

East Side lay between Seventy-fifth Street and Eightieth Street, west of Fourth Avenue (fig. 212). Homeowners began to pay new attention to interiors, and it seemed that all of a sudden a rebirth in the decorative arts had occurred in New York. Perhaps it began with the Philadelphia Centennial Exposition of 1876, which taught Americans that civilization and refinement lay in linking the mechanical to the decorative arts. The building of the Vanderbilt chateaux on Fifth Avenue was the watermark of a new order; houses, the *Real Estate Record* proudly stated, were built and equipped in a manner that brought out the artistic resources of the country. The decorative work found in the panels of the dining room in Cornelius Vanderbilt's house, the *Real Estate Record* ventured, could be surpassed only by fifteenth-century ornamentation. Such splendor was the result of mechanical as well as artistic talent, as new materials and methods were devel-

Fig. 210. Tiffany house, northwest corner of Seventy-second Street and Madison Avenue, ca. 1885. The stone, brick, and glazed black tile-roofed structure lent prestige to the fashionable quarter rising above Fifty-ninth Street in the 1880s. The 75-foot-wide gable end onto Madison Avenue, another gable on the Seventy-second Street front, and a turret at the Madison Avenue corner gave the whole building a distinctive, if peculiar character. Filling nearly four city lots, this composition of three houses in one rested on a massive stone basement (a story and a half in height), above which rose three full stories, with an additional story on the roof. (Courtesy of the New-York Historical Society, New York City)

Fig. 211. Madison Avenue, view north from Seventieth Street across the truck garden of the Lenox Estate to the Tiffany House (left), ca. 1885. Opposite, facing Seventy-second Street, two town houses erected by the Lynd Brothers are nearing completion. The tower in the background rises from Philipp's Presbyterian Church on the northeast corner of Seventy-third Street. (Courtesy of the Museum of the City of New York, New York City)

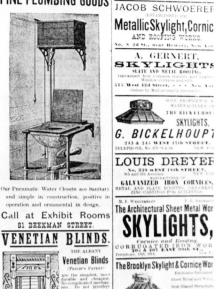

FINE PLUMBING GOODS

Our Pneumatic Water Closets are Sanitary and simple in construction, positive in operation and ornamental in design.

Call at Exhibit Rooms
81 BEEKMAN STREET.

VENETIAN BLINDS.

THE ALBANY
Venetian Blinds

JACOB SCHWOERER

Metallic Skylight, Cornic
AND ROOFING WORKS

A. GERNERT,
SKYLIGHTS

G. BICKELHOUPT

LOUIS DREYER

GALVANIZED IRON CORNICES

The Architectural Sheet Metal Wor
SKYLIGHTS,

The Brooklyn Skylight & Cornice Wor

John Seton & C

HAYES SKYLIGHTS

Fig. 213. *Above.* Trade advertisement, *Real Estate Record and Builders' Guide*, May 2, 1890. Besides offering a description of real estate activity in New York, the *Real Estate Record* was continuously aware of advances in the mechanical arts and became a trade catalog advertising the latest equipment in stoves, plumbing, skylighting, ironwork, and refrigeration. (Courtesy of Avery Library, Columbia University, New York City)

Fig. 214. *Below.* Cabinet designed by Cicero Hine (From the *Architectural Record*, 1880.) Cabinetwork was increasingly important in the luxury apartment houses and town houses of the 1880s, showcasing exotic woods and inlaid materials as well as family silver and china. (Courtesy of Avery Library, Columbia University, New York City)

[Fig. 212]

SELECTED DEVELOPERS FROM SEVENTY-SECOND TO EIGHTY-SIXTH STREET ON THE UPPER EAST SIDE: 1885–1890

5 houses, southwest corner of 72d Street and Lexington Avenue (Breen and Nason, developers)

10 houses, south side of 73d Street, east of Madison Avenue (R. W. Buckley, developer)

5 houses, north side of 73d Street, connected to an apartment house on the northwest corner of Fourth (Park) Avenue (J.G. Prague, architect)

7 houses, southeast corner of Madison Avenue and 76th Street (Charles Graham and Sons)

6 houses, northwest corner of 76th Street and Madison Avenue (Charles L. Guilleaume, developer)

5 houses, northwest corner of 76th Street and Madison Avenue (Frederick Pietz, developer)

1 apartment house, southeast corner of 77th Street and Madison Avenue

3 houses, west side of Fourth Avenue between 78th and 79th streets

5 houses, northwest corner of 79th Street and Fourth (Park) Avenue

oped in order to obtain the appropriate hues. For the Tiffany houses the Perth Amboy Tile Company set about specially to create the blue-hued brick the architect desired. These alliances between the mechanical and decorative arts encouraged designers to experiment with metallic tints, enamel paints, and unusual tiles and materials—nowhere more effective than in the individual town houses on the Upper East Side[31] (figs. 213, 214).

One of the most beautiful private interiors of this new era, according to the *Real Estate Record*, was the home of A. J. White. Its vestibule offered the visitor merely a foretaste of the ostentatious display to come. This ample room was wainscoted in large panels of English oak that spanned the depth of the enclosure up to the walls where they joined a seamless frieze of dark Numidian marble and a ceiling composed of a single slab of Sienna marble. Double doors of predominantly blue Tiffany glass led into the second entrance hall, which had arched vaulted ceilings of oak. Another set of massive doors led into the drawing room. Here the spirit of the Italian Renaissance took over, with paneled dados in white enamel and gold, walls covered with rosy tinted brocade, and a cornice of gold with an ivory stenciled design surrounding the ceiling—all accented by the deep red and yellow splashes in the Numidian marble fireplace and mantel.[32]

PROSPECT HILL DEVELOPMENT

Other parts of the East Side, however, suffered from lack of improvement until the 1890s. One such area, called Prospect Hill, lay north of Eighty-sixth Street as far as 110th Street where the side streets and avenues were poorly paved and the Madison Avenue streetcar tracks wandered randomly down its roadbed and sidewalks (fig. 215). Easily accessible by the Central and Harlem railroads, with stations at Eighty-sixth and 110th streets, as well as the elevated stops, and adequately serviced by the Madison Avenue horsecars and crosstown cars, developers would be quick to see the advantages of this favored locality when it finally began to improve.[33] In addition, the new Eighth Regiment Armory at Ninety-fourth Street would also spur neighborhood development (fig. 216). Ninetieth Street, however, seemed to be a cutoff point for luxury development, beyond

which lay a mass of tenements and flats (fig. 217). The cause seemed to be both the lack and undesirability of rapid transit in the area. The Third Avenue El was a good ten- or fifteen-minute walk from the fashionable areas along Fifth and Madison avenues and travel on the El was uncomfortable and crowded with the laboring classes who lived and worked along the East River. In consequence, most of the residents in the new luxury district preferred to take horsecars down Madison Avenue to Fifty-eighth Street and Sixth Avenue ''where a seat is surely attainable and your neighbor does not smell of tenement houses.''[34]

The highest regions of Prospect Hill, between Ninety-first and Ninety-fourth streets, however, were beginning in the 1890s to be improved with elegant new residences. As early as the 1880s the Ruppert residence stood on Fifth Avenue and Ninety-third Street, the Ehret house adorned the southeast corner of Fourth Avenue and Ninety-fourth Street, and the Untermeyer house could be

Fig. 215. Prospect Hill, looking west from Park Avenue and Ninety-fifth Street, ca. 1880. On the left stands the isolated Jacob Ruppert Mansion on Fifth Avenue and Ninety-third Street, erected in 1886. Madison Avenue and Ninety-fourth Street were unpaved, and had yet to be filled and graded for development. Across the reservoir of Central Park lies the Upper West Side. (Courtesy of the New-York Historical Society, New York City)

Fig. 216. Eighth Regiment Armory, west side of Park Avenue between Ninety-fourth and Ninety-fifth streets, ca. 1890. The home of the prestigious First New York Hussars, the armory was the site for polo games, horse shows, and mounted military tournaments. Completed in 1894, it was one of the attractions that began to draw stylish New Yorkers north in the 1890s. It was demolished in 1964, except for sections of its Madison Avenue facade and turrets. (Courtesy of the New-York Historical Society, New York City)

Fig. 217. *Above.* View north (with Park Avenue on the right) from a rooftop on Ninety-third Street, 1886. The *Real Estate Record and Builders' Guide* claimed that Ninetieth Street was the northern limit of fashionable development, beyond which lay tenements, flats, and cheap speculative developments. The working classes followed the elevated railroads and spread north and east into the inexpensive lands of northern Manhattan long before the most costly lots on the Upper East Side were fully developed. (Courtesy of the New-York Historical Society, New York City)

Fig. 218. *Below.* Samuel Untermeyer house, Fifth Avenue and Ninety-second Street, 1890. The most expensive residence on Prospect Hill in the late 1880s, the Untermeyer house, designed by Hugo Kafka, was projected at a cost of $100,000, excluding the cost of land. (Courtesy of Avery Library, Columbia University, New York City)

seen on Ninety-second Street and Fifth Avenue (fig. 218).[35] Once elegance had taken hold of an address, other fashionable buildings usually followed, and in 1890 it was not surprising to find another new chateau, the Rhinelander estate, on the northwest corner of Eighty-ninth Street and Lexington Avenue.

On the crest of Prospect Hill, at the southwest corner of Eighty-ninth Street and Madison Avenue, appeared the first apartment hotel on the East Side—the Graham, designed by Thomas Graham in 1890.[36] This massive seven-story structure of Indiana limestone contained nearly 400 windows, making it one of the most well-lighted apartment houses to be erected in New York (fig. 220). Nearby, on the south side of Ninety-second Street between Fifth and Madison avenues, Graham was completing a row of four-story high-stooped brownstone houses (see fig. 219). In addition, the Prospect Hill Apartment House, a six-story structure, was built by John Livingston on the southeast corner of Ninety-first Street and Madison Avenue. Heretofore it had been the practice to erect a French flat on a typical 20- by 100-foot corner lot, but Livingston's larger structure of 80- by 100 feet, enabled him to experiment with the plan of each suite. Three main rooms, the parlor, and the music and dining rooms were all capable in his scheme of being joined together by sliding doors that opened and closed so that a family need not feel "cabined, cribbed, or confined" in a small, stuffy apartment.[37] Throughout the 1890s the hammer and chisel could not be stilled, and row after row of town houses and flats began to fill in the vacant fields surrounding Prospect Hill.

FIFTH AVENUE DEVELOPMENT

In the early years of the 1890s, although money was becoming scarce and overall building expectations were lowered, upper Fifth Avenue began to enjoy one magnificent improvement after another. The exceptionally rich New Yorker apparently did not care to build anywhere else. The Metropolitan Club (McKim, Mead and White, architects) secured the northeast corner of Sixtieth Street in 1891, and no doubt helped to keep the loyalties of millionaires from wavering from the avenue (fig. 221). Now it seemed obvious that below Eighty-fifth Street

on the blocks just east of Fifth Avenue, and all along the avenue fronting Central Park, the homes of New York's wealthiest millionaires would be built for years to come.[38] Thus upper Fifth Avenue achieved its status as the premier avenue of the fashionable East Side and on it one would find the best works of New York architects (see fig. 203). Nearly all the elaborate houses, the "city chateaux," stood on the avenue corners, the better-designed buildings having their entrances and main facade on the street, while the windows of their principal rooms opened on the park (fig. 222). This plan allowed the architect breadth for his design and offered proportions that could be arranged artistically. Those houses confined to the interior of Fifth Avenue lots had another distinct advantage, as archi-

Fig. 219. *Above left.* Row of town houses, designed by Thomas Graham on the south side of Ninety-second Street between Fifth and Madison avenues, 1890. Charles Graham and Sons were one of the largest developers operating on the Upper East Side in the 1880s, erecting more than twenty-three houses near Prospect Hill alone. By 1891, however, the company was in financial trouble, eventually going bankrupt in 1898. Part of their trouble, it was explained by the *Real Estate Record*, was that New Yorkers with taste and money were not quite ready to move so far beyond the established Fifty-ninth Street mark. (Courtesy of Avery Library, Columbia University, New York City)

Fig. 220. *Above right.* The Graham Apartment Hotel, southeast corner of Eighty-ninth Street and Madison Avenue, 1890. Planned in an L shape, the apartment hotel, designed by Thomas Graham, contained eleven studios, ranging in size from the smallest unit with only a sitting room and a bedroom to the largest suites with a sitting room, library or music room, bedrooms, and dining room. Each suite had its own bathroom, a luxury in the nineteenth century, and was serviced daily by chambermaids. Meals were provided in the Graham's main dining room or served in one's suite. (Courtesy of Avery Library, Columbia University, New York City)

Fig. 221. *Left.* Metropolitan Club, designed by McKim, Mead and White, northeast corner of Sixtieth Street and Fifth Avenue, ca. 1894. Following luxury residences, the elite clubs moved north above Forty-second Street in the 1890s. The club exemplified the monumental, academic style of architecture intended to educate and uplift the public. (Courtesy of the New York Public Library, New York City)

Fig. 222. *Right.* Eldridge T. Gerry mansion, southeast corner of Sixty-first Street and Fifth Avenue, 1899. Designed by Richard Morris Hunt in 1891, this house, like the William K. Vanderbilt House, took as its leading structural motive the ''pyramidization'' of architectural elements, a convergence toward the apex of the corner tower. Taking advantage of an unbroken Fifth Avenue facade, Hunt located the entrance, with a port cochere, on Sixty-first Street. The house was demolished in the late 1920s. (Courtesy of the Museum of the City of New York, New York City)

Fig. 223. *Below left.* Collis P. Huntington mansion, southeast corner of Fifty-seventh Street and Fifth Avenue, 1926. Designed by George B. Post in 1889–94, and demolished in 1926. (Courtesy of the New York Public Library, New York City)

Fig. 224. *Below right.* W. C. Whitney mansion, southwest corner of Fifty-seventh Street and Fifth Avenue, ca. 1894. The house was designed by William Schickel in the early 1880s for the sugar magnate Robert L. Stuart, and sold to financier and politician William Collins Whitney in 1896. It was demolished in 1942. (Courtesy of the New York Public Library, New York City)

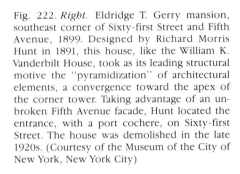

tects could place their entrances to the side and bow out the remainder of their avenue facades.[39]

Just below the park, it was announced in 1889, five lots on the southeast corner of Fifty-seventh Street had been sold to Collis P. Huntington, who would build a handsome new mansion (to be designed by George B. Post; fig. 223). This exceptionally fine location already had on its opposite corners elegant city chateaux such as the Marble Row of Mary Colford Jones to the north, and the mansions of W. C. Whitney and Cornelius W. Vanderbilt across the avenue on the west side (figs. 224, 225). Unfortunately, the two blocks to the north on the east side of the avenue seemed to be losing their residential character: between Fifty-ninth and Sixtieth streets a row of shanties stood housing a liquor saloon, a stable office, and a dairy kitchen next door to the large structure containing the Park and Tilford grocery store with six rental flats. In 1891, however, one of the most expensive buildings planned for the Upper East Side, the seventeen-story New Netherland Hotel, to be financed by W. W. Astor, would locate on the northeast corner of Fifty-ninth Street and Fifth Avenue, firmly securing this entrance to Millionaire's Row[40] (fig. 226).

Fig. 225. Cornelius Vanderbilt house, southwest corner of Fifty-eighth Street and Fifth Avenue. View south along Fifth Avenue from Fifty-ninth Street, ca. 1894. Vanderbilt enlarged his house on Fifty-seventh Street in 1894, until the mansion reached as far as Fifty-eighth Street. It was demolished in 1927. To the south can be seen the corner of the Whitney Mansion. (Courtesy of the New York Public Library, New York City)

Fig. 226. The New Netherland Hotel, northeast corner of Fifty-ninth Street and Fifth Avenue, 1913. This seventeen-story hotel, which marked the new entrance to the Millionaire's Row of the twentieth century, replaced a group of one-story shacks in 1891. The Park and Tilford Grocery Store, with six stories of flats above, is located in the middle of the block. Next door is the Union Trust Company on the southeast corner of Sixtieth Street. (Courtesy of the New-York Historical Society, New York City)

Fig. 227. The Henry O. Havemeyer mansion, north corner of Sixty-sixth Street and Fifth Avenue, 1925. Designed by C. C. Haight in 1889 for a sugar refinery king, the three-story mansion borrowed heavily from ponderous Tuscan architectural forms, such as the moat. (Courtesy of the New York Public Library, New York City)

Fig. 228. Isaac Vail Brokaw mansion, north corner of Seventy-ninth Street and Fifth Avenue, 1916. Designed by Rose and Stone in 1887 for a clothing manufacturer, the three-story granite house achieved massive proportions. The street front featured many different elements, with the gable end of the Fifth Avenue facade occupying the avenue corner and a turret marking its eastern end. It was demolished in 1965. By the second decade of the twentieth century, high-rise apartments, seen in the background, were becoming a common feature along Fifth Avenue. (Courtesy of the New-York Historical Society, New York City)

If one walked north on Fifth Avenue in 1889, the first noteworthy house could be found between Sixtieth and Sixty-first streets—the old Bostwick mansion standing next door to vacant lots (see fig. 172). More modest residences, new clubhouses, shanties, saloons, and vacant lots shared the next several blocks, until the excavations for what would be the Havemeyer mansion (designed by C. C. Haight) could be seen on the northeast corner of Sixty-sixth Street (fig. 227). Americans, the *Real Estate Record* noted, had always been somewhat flamboyant, desiring things that were strikingly peculiar, and it was not surprising that Fifth Avenue should boast novel exteriors and original designs.[41] Just south of the Lenox Library, the Ogden Mills mansion stood on Sixty-ninth Street, while to its north the Lenox farm still claimed the entire block between Seventy-first and Seventy-second streets. Toward Seventy-third Street the passenger waiting room of the Fifth Avenue Stage could be found standing amid vacant, untended lots. North of Seventy-third Street the old Pickhardt and Quintard residences still fronted the avenue.

On the northeast corner of Seventy-eighth Street stood one of the largest residences on the avenue, yet it was scarcely notable for its architectural beauty. Fronting half the avenue block, Mr. Cook's mansion, designed by Wheeler Smith, had been an eyesore since the early 1880s. Its massive proportions were greatly marred by a heavily balustraded, deep dry moat guarding the house on the street side. A simple, rectangular granite structure, the house rose to a pyramidal slate roof of unusually steep pitch, a monotonous scheme for so large and bulky a structure. The architect had attempted to enliven its appearance by monumental chimneys of apparently no utility, or queer projections in the main wall, using three different granites of white, bluish-gray, and red, but without success.[42]

Nearly opposite an entrance to Central Park, on the north side of Seventy-ninth Street, however, a truly grand building appeared, the Brokaw mansion[43] (Rose and Stone, architects) erected in 1887 (fig. 228). But having to fit a city chateau to the requirements of Manhattan's rectangular grid pattern gave it a rather prim and stiff appearance that could have been offset only in a park of fine natural approaches. As one moved north, development grew sparser (fig. 229). Be-

Fig. 229. Private town house at 5 East Eightieth Street aspiring to Fifth Avenue style, 1890. Designed by F. A. Minuth, 1890. (Courtesy of Avery Library, Columbia University, New York City)

Fig. 230. Charles T. Yerkes house, south corner of Sixty-eighth Street and Fifth Avenue, 1898. Robert H. Robertson was the architect for many upper Fifth Avenue houses in the early 1890s, such as this one, designed in 1893 for the Chicago street railway czar. (Courtesy of the Museum of the City of New York, New York City)

Fig. 231. Fifth Avenue and Seventy-fifth Street, looking north, 1892. The vacant lots adjacent to the newly erected Temple Beth-El, designed by Brunner and Tryon in 1891 and demolished in 1947, would soon be filled with millionaires' mansions. Courtesy of the New-York Historical Society, New York City

tween Eightieth and Eighty-first streets, the Stern house stood in the middle of a vacant block, followed by more vacant blocks.[44] The Arnold residence could be seen on the northeast corner of Eighty-third Street, followed by a series of vacant lots, town houses, and flats, until one reached the Collis house at Eighty-sixth Street, the Ruppert residence on the southeast corner of Ninety-third Street, and then saloons, vacant lots, and shanties took hold of the avenue all the way to 110th Street.[45] The days were soon coming, however, when the millionaires, through clever combinations and astute business acumen, would become the billionaires of the turn of the century, and the vacant lots on upper Fifth Avenue would be filled with their mansions (figs. 230, 231).

DEVELOPMENT STATISTICS

Although the east and west sides of Manhattan above Fifty-ninth Street were rivals for development in the 1880s and early 1890s, they took on decidedly different appearances. As a whole, the West Side, where a Renaissance town was taking form, might have seemed architecturally more interesting, but single examples of solid, costly, and elaborate residences would remain the distinct advantage of an East Side location. North of Ninety-second Street, and east of Park Avenue, however, the Upper East Side was dominated by row upon row of tenements, flats, and machine-made dwellings with scarcely a trace of beauty or charm. In addition, the number of churches, hotels, and stores erected on the East Side lagged far behind its western competitor while intruding stables, factories, and objectionable structures were common in the midst of East Side elegance.

The high watermark for building on the Upper East Side occurred in 1887. The following year, many of the most successful developers, finding themselves outpriced by the rising cost of land, shifted their focus to the Upper West Side. By 1890 it seemed obvious that the best and most costly improvements on the East Side in the years to come, with the exception of a few elegant mansions, would be six- or seven-story flats (fig. 232). After thirteen years of improvement, during which over $125 million had been spent, a disproportionate amount on the East Side had been expended on flats and tenements. When compared to the Upper West Side, a figure somewhere between $1 million and $2 million on the East Side had been allocated annually for private town houses, while $8 to $9 million was spent on these residences on the precocious West Side. New developments in rapid transit and new building laws would bring unforeseen developments to both sides of the park in the twentieth century, but real estate investors could foresee that the era of the bourgeois town house was beginning to draw to a close.

In 1890 at least 40 per cent of the land above Fifty-ninth Street on the East Side still remained unimproved (fig. 233). The fewest vacant lots could be found in the heart of the new luxury district on the blocks between Fifth and Park avenues, from Fifty-ninth to Eighty-sixth Street. Side streets from Madison to Third Avenue, especially between Fifty-ninth and Seventy-second streets, were mostly built upon, but as one moved northward development grew thinner. Fifth Avenue in places resembled a country road; shacks and vacant lots stood next to elegant mansions. The avenue and its adjacent side streets had developed slowly, as had been predicted, controlled by the dictates of fashions and the high price of its lots. Nevertheless, New Yorkers were proud of the beginnings of this million-

Fig. 232. Fifth Avenue Apartment House, southeast corner of Eighty-fifth Street and Fifth Avenue, 1890. The first apartment house on upper Fifth Avenue, the building was designed by McKim, Mead and White. It was the leader of a new development trend that would see six- and seven-story flats rapidly erected on the upper east and upper west sides of Manhattan. Herbert Croly claimed that so many of these flats were built in the last years of the 1890s, that land values became inflated beyond the level at which town houses could be produced at profitable returns. The turn of the century marked a threshold in the history of the New York row house; few would be constructed in the twentieth century and many would be demolished. (Courtesy of Avery Library, Columbia University, New York City)

[Fig. 233]

VACANT AND UNIMPROVED LOTS ON THE UPPER EAST SIDE: 1890

	Total Lots	Vacant Lots
59th–72d Street	4,199	1,415
72d–86th Street	4,648	1,399
86th–96th Street	3,092	1,491
96th–110th Street	4,194	2,157
Total	16,133	6,462

AVENUES				
	Fifth	Madison	Park	Lexington
59th–72d Street	49	26	29	10
72d–86th Street	81	61	73	38
86th–96th Street	71	119	50	62
96th–110th Street	112	170	116	58
Total	313	376	268	168

SIDE STREETS				
	Fifth to Madison	Madison to Park	Park to Lexington	Lexington to Third
59th–72d Street	68	10	15	19
72d–86th Street	107	56	40	31
86th–96th Street	130	77	48	50
96th–110th Street	217	168	99	67
Total	522	311	202	167

Data compiled from the *Real Estate Record and Builders' Guide* (May 3, 1890):8–9.

aires' row where the parsimony that forced an architect to design merchandise rather than houses was particularly absent. As one traveled eastward, however, prices of lots fell considerably, so that cheaper houses were erected near Madison Avenue, still cheaper ones near Park Avenue, continuing until tenements and flats claimed a monopoly over all the land east of Lexington Avenue.[46]

CHAPTER SIX

THE AWAKENING OF THE UPPER WEST SIDE

New York has come at last, far up on the West Side, into possession of her birthright, into the roused consciousness that some possibility of a river-front may still remain to her; though, obviously, a justified pride in this property has yet to await the birth of a more responsible style in her dealings with it, the dawn of some adequate plan or controlling idea. Splendid the elements of position, on the part of the new Riverside Drive (over the small suburbanizing name of which, as at the effect of a second-rate shop-worn article, we sigh as we pass); yet not less irresistable the pang of our seeing it settle itself on meagre, bourgeois, happy-go-lucky lines. The pity of this is sharp in proportion as the ''chance'' has been magnificent, and the soreness of perception of what merely might have been is as constant as the flippancy of the little vulgar ''private houses'' or the big vulgar ''apartment hotels'' that are having their own way, so unchallenged, with the whole question of composition and picture. The fatal ''tall'' pecuniary enterprise rises where it will, in the candid glee of new worlds to conquer; the intervals between take whatever foolish little form they like. . .—Henry James, *The American Scene* (Bloomington: Indiana Press, 1964):140

T he development of the Upper West Side had always been fraught with controversy: conservative developers tried to understand the strange hold of depressed land values that kept the entire West Side plateau from being developed until the mid-1880s and thus proposed modest improvements; more optimistic land owners believed the picturesqueness of the plateau destined it to become the most magnificent residential quarter Manhattan had yet known (see fig. 182). In reality, the Upper West Side in the late 1870s was a rural backwater; the only way to reach it was by omnibus along the Grand Boulevard (Broadway) until 1876 when a street railway ran up Eighth Avenue (Central Park West) as far north as 125th Street.[1] This was joined in 1879 by the opening of the Ninth Avenue (Columbus Avenue) elevated railway, with stops at Seventy-second, Eighty-first, Ninety-third, and 104th streets. For a mere ten cents fare every New Yorker could enjoy the beauty of the West Side's panorama, at the same time noting that a considerable number of cross streets, even as low as Seventy-second Street, had yet to be opened.[2]

Fig. 234. Intersection of Broadway and Eighth Avenue (Central Park West), 1861. In 1867 the Central Park Commission acquired control over the planned Circle (not named Columbus Circle until 1892) at Fifty-ninth Street and Eighth Avenue, intending to improve it, lay a curbed circle fifty feet in diameter, and erect a monument at its center. The commission delayed for years, and the Circle eventually became the meeting point of eight different surface lines and elevated railways. It took more than two years for the city to grade Eighth Avenue from Fifty-ninth to Seventy-seventh Street, and another three years to grade the section beyond. (Courtesy of the Museum of the City of New York, New York City)

THE BUCOLIC UPPER WEST SIDE

In colonial times, many farms had settled along the Great Kill, which flowed north of West Fortieth Street. The Bloomingdale Road (Broadway), with its origin at Union Square, extended north to 102nd Street, meandering obliquely along the West Side plateau as it followed the path of an old Indian trail (fig. 234). Harsenville, a small hamlet, was located near the Hudson River between Sixty-ninth and Seventy-fourth streets, with Harsen's Road cutting across the island at Seventy-first Street (fig. 235). Bloomingdale Village (fig. 236), originally Bloemendael ("vale of flowers"), was a residential village centered around a Reformed Dutch church built in 1816 at West Sixty-Eighth Street. Another such village was Manhattanville, located on a bluff above the Hudson River at West 120th Street. Most

Fig. 235. Apthorp mansion, West Ninety-first Street and Ninth (Columbus) Avenue. The unimproved Upper West Side of the late nineteenth century was marked occasionally by squatter settlements, vegetable gardens, small eighteenth-century farmhouses, and old colonial mansions. The Apthorp estate lay between Ninetieth and Ninety-sixth streets, where the mansion, erected in 1764, remained a landmark until it was demolished in 1892. (Courtesy of the Museum of the City of New York, New York City)

Fig. 236. Bloomingdale Village, 1867, showing the Bloomingdale Reformed Dutch Church at Broadway and Sixty-eighth Street. (Courtesy of the Museum of the City of New York, New York City)

of these West Side villages were autonomous rural developments in the nineteenth century, supporting small-scale agricultural enterprises called market farms.[3]

By the late 1870s, however, many of the farmhouses and colonial mansions that dotted the West Side had been turned into boardinghouses and taverns (fig. 237). In addition, a shantytown had cropped up along Seventieth Street from Eighth to Ninth Avenue; another shanty province controlled Seventy-ninth Street near the Boulevard, and the entire region between Fifty-ninth and Seventy-second streets, west of Eighth Avenue, was affected by the intolerable nuisance of shanties, for who was going to build on a lot where next door lived miserable squatters or where life was unsafe at certain hours of the night? J. J. Astor predicted that building would commence around Seventy-second Street and move southward, crowding out these shacks. Others believed that the growth of the city would remain along Fifth Avenue, continuing across the far edge of Central Park before descending southward from Morningside Park. As early as 1879 clusters of buildings appeared in different sections of the West Side: at Morningside Heights, and at 104th, Ninety-second, and Seventy-second streets. In its lower regions, West Side development, however, was thwarted by huge limestone outcroppings that dominated the blocks between Fifty-ninth and Sixty-seventh streets, from Eighth to Ninth Avenue, obstructing the sale of this land.[4]

Fig. 237. Luke Welsh House, Eighty-seventh Street near the Hudson River, 1884. A Tammany politician and judge, Luke Welsh held renowned chowder and clambake parties on the lawn of this old house in the 1880s. If he was detained on the bench and could not attend one of his parties, a quart of chowder was sent to him by one of the boys of the house. Leopold Eidlitz's house was located only a block to the south (West Eighty-seventh to Eighty-sixth Street) and Egbert Viele, an enthusiastic supporter of West Side improvements, lived a block north on Eighty-eighth Street. (Courtesy of the Museum of the City of New York, New York City)

Fig. 238. Detail of Jalt and Hoy Map of 1879, showing the Children's Asylum at West Seventy-third Street and Riverside Drive. (Courtesy of the New York Public Library, New York City)

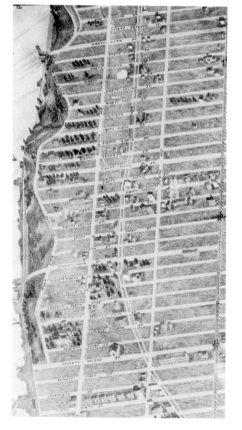

By the mid-1880s the bucolic Upper West Side had become the home for an assortment of asylums and breweries, as well as recreational facilities (fig. 238). The New York Orphan Asylum took up three-quarters of the block fronting Riverside Drive between Seventy-third and Seventy-fourth streets; the Home for the Aged run by the Methodist Episcopal Church could be found on Tenth Avenue between Ninety-second and Ninety-third streets; and the Home for Respectable Indigent Females, designed by Richard Morris Hunt in 1881, stood between 103d and 104th streets on the east side of Tenth Avenue, on the same block as the Bloomingdale Green Houses. The New York Cancer Hospital, designed by C. C. Haight (1885–87), was located on the southwest corner of Eighth Avenue and 106th Street. Farther north, Leake and Watt's Orphan Asylum took up considerable acreage from Morningside Park to Tenth Avenue, from 110th to 113th Street, and the Bloomingdale Asylum occupied 113th to 120th Street, Tenth Avenue to the Boulevard. In addition, the Manhattan Athletic Club grounds had settled on three city blocks between Eighth and Tenth avenues, Eighty-sixth to Eighty-Seventh Street; Elm Park occupied another two blocks between Ninetieth and Ninety-second streets, Ninth to Tenth Avenue; and the large Lion Brewery near Ninth Avenue, from 107th to 109th Street, closed several blocks to development.

Besides the character of its early development, the West Side confronted other barriers to the establishment of luxury housing. Although the region promised unparalleled scenery, such housing developments also required proximity to other luxury dwellings, central promenades, and secluded quarters where the elite could avoid all contact with undesirable people and land uses. Many critics also believed that the wealthy would not invest on the West Side because of the limited amount of space (lots could not extend beyond the usual 25-foot width, and the whole West Side was only 3,200 feet wide from park to river, compared to 5,000 feet on the East Side), precluding boundary areas sufficiently wide to keep away polluting intruders.[5]

In addition, the riverfront below Seventy-second Street had already become the central location for grain elevators, slaughterhouses, gasoline tanks, planing mills, and railroad elevators and freight houses. Because of this stigma it was expected that the nearby side streets would house local employees, creating a stretch of simple dwellings and tenements from the river to the Boulevard. The Grand Boulevard, conservative developers believed, would remain a standing menace and a rebuke to the corrupt Tweed officials who speculated in West Side lots in 1868 and laid it out with pretentious improvements. Appropriations had been set aside for improving the Boulevard with asphalt as far north as Eightieth Street, but the work had yet to begin. A park had been planned for the middle of the Boulevard, but this strip of land still resembled an untended barnyard. Since horsecars ran close to its curbing, passengers were forced to crush whatever little greenery still remained while entering and descending from the cars (fig. 239). The Boulevard's future lay in commercial development rather than luxury residences. The other avenues also could be expected to house unremarkable stores and plain tenements; by 1878 the tenement already had advanced along Tenth Avenue as far as Sixty-ninth Street and could be expected to push farther north.

The only regal avenue on the Upper West Side appeared to be Riverside Drive, and yet even the prediction that this would be the future home for city chateaux appeared dubious if compared to the experience on the Upper East Side. Tenements and common flats overlooked the splendid panorama all along the East River. Only the West Side plateau, the side streets between Seventy-second and Ninety-sixth streets, remained as a possible source for luxury development. Although it contained many unmanageable promontories of rock and swampy depressions, it also held the most picturesque vista and would surely be exploited by select improvements. Here would lie, or so it was hoped, the prospective fashionable quarter of the Upper West Side.[6]

Fig. 239. Broadway, view north from Eightieth Street, ca. 1894. Although a few churches, an armory, some residences, and flats dotted the Grand Boulevard, as upper Broadway was called until 1899, for the most part until the late 1890s, its blocks were vacant and unpaved. At its junction with Seventy-second Street and Amsterdam Avenue, driving was said to be perilous. (Courtesy of the New-York Historical Society, New York City)

West Side development lagged far behind that of the East Side and of even the Harlem flats, for several additional reasons. Apparently, wide tracts of land were held by estate owners such as the Astors, Higginses, and Marches, who were not interested in stimulating development. Instead they seemed content to bide time by supporting the creation of descriptive diagrams and development plans and by waiting for the day when their lots would bring the highest prices.[7] Another complication occurred during the widening of Bloomingdale Road into the Boulevard in the 1860s: by reducing the depth of many lots it produced parcels of land too small for subsequent development. The unsightly presence of the Croton Aqueduct, which ran through the blocks to the west of Ninth Avenue, was believed to have yet another deleterious effect on real estate values.[8]

On the other hand, there were many dreamers who believed in the West Side's potential. One of the earliest was Egbert Viele, whose villa graced Riverside Park at Eighty-eighth Street (see fig. 237). He had been the engineer of Central Park and an unsuccessful competitor against Frederick Law Olmsted in plans for its improvement. Believing that "westward the empire runs," in 1879 he published a map of the West Side plateau; Viele claimed that the fashionable growth of all great cities such as London and Paris had always been toward the west, for the great elements responsible for topography—ice and water—had always operated from the northwest to the southeast, the result being alluvial deposits to the east and rounded hills to the west. In addition, the prevailing summer winds came from the southwest so that the east side of a crowded city always received the city's polluted air. The West Side, Viele believed, should be held intact until the time was ripe for the development of the finest domestic architecture.[9] Like Viele, most of the members of the West Side Association, which had been formed in 1866 to promote the rapid development of the city above Fifty-ninth Street, believed in the advantageous siting of the West Side plateau. One of their members, Dwight H. Olmstead, approached the association in 1879 with an original plan for the region developed by the Central Park Commissioners, which had been long forgotten. According to this plan, two separate parks were intended for the side hills of the plateau, which had deep depressions at Seventy-ninth and Ninety-sixth streets; a network of terraced roads or boulevards had been designed to accommodate this topography, in contrast to the monotonous gridiron pattern imposed on lower Manhattan.[10] Nothing became of this idea, and property owners struggled independently without an overall city plan, at random and as development seemed "ripe," to create the Upper West Side.

It was left to the West Side Association to regulate building on the plateau. One of the members, a Mr. Cammann, exhibited plans in 1879 for a group of first-class tenements he was erecting on Tenth Avenue. During the discussion that followed his presentation, he recommended that only private first-class residences be allowed on the side streets of the West Side, and that the tenements which would naturally congregate along the avenues also be of a better-than-ordinary type. An agreement, he felt, must be reached among all property owners to preserve the beauties of the region. There was, of course, far from complete agreement, and John D. Crimmins, another developer, claimed that there was plenty of room for modest cottages as well. If only the wealthy were lured to the Upper West Side, it would be a long time before the plateau were properly developed.[11]

Edward Clark, president of the Singer Sewing Machine Company, and an early promoter of the advantages of a West Side luxury quarter, stated in 1879 that

the mushroom style of building characterizing lower Manhattan, in which the tearing-down and building-up process had often been done as many as three times, had passed out of fashion. It was fortunate that so little building west of Central Park had occurred, for there was little to tear down except shanties. It could be expected that improvements in this area would be built to last more than one hundred years. It was hoped, Clark continued, that the era when individual owners developed their land as they wished was over and that a new era was beginning—one which would produce novel and splendid ideas. It was conceivable that a block of West Side property owners could combine their lots and by pooling their resources employ a single architect to develop an entire block as one unified ensemble. Clark favored magnificent apartment houses for the plateau such as the Vancorlear and the Saint Catherine in lower Manhattan, reasoning that many New Yorkers were eager to occupy part of an elegant, palatial apartment building.[12]

Yet little splendor existed on the Upper West Side. A single structure for the American Museum of Natural History stood on Manhattan Square (fig. 240). As early as the 1840s the Common Council had ordered the square to be opened, but only after it was annexed to the Central Park Commission in 1864 was it finally improved. Even so, deep holes, stagnant pools of water, protruding fragments

Fig. 240. American Museum of Natural History, Central Park West at Seventy-seventh Street, ca. 1877. At this time, the blocks around Manhattan Square, where the first museum building (designed by Calvert Vaux and Jacob Wrey Mould between 1872 and 1877) stood among rocks and ponds, were completely undeveloped. It was hoped that the opening of the museum in 1877 would encourage the city to move forward with improvements, grading the streets and laying the sewers so that development could follow. (Courtesy of the Museum of the City of New York, New York City)

of rock, masses of loose stone, and debris cluttered the park for fourteen years. In 1879 some money was appropriated for the draining of the square and for the filling in of some of the low spots.[13] Riverside Drive was another problem: in 1871 the city had passed an act to create Riverside Park and its drive but the Frederick Law Olmsted plan was not fully implemented until 1885. This delay, the West Side Association believed, was the cause of the West Side's desperate condition. By purchasing such a large tract of land for Riverside and Morningside parks, and then allowing them to sit fallow, the Tweed Ring had robbed the West Side of its natural inheritance. In addition, a special tax levied on West Side property owners to pay the cost of park acquisition without return of any benefit was a further injustice to private property. Not only did the unsightly conditions of these parks retard improvements, they were objectionable for sanitary reasons as well.[14]

Continuing to press forward with the creation of an elite fashionable neighborhood, Egbert Viele suggested to the West Side Association in 1880 that the name of Eleventh Avenue be changed to West End Avenue; this beautiful avenue was one of the original nineteen broad longitudinal avenues laid down by the commissioners in 1811 and one of the longest in the city. Although its lower portion was a thriving commercial area above Seventy-second Street, he argued, it was isolated from commerce by Riverside Park and too close to Broadway, which merged with it at 106th Street, ever to become a business street. Since the development of its upper portion had been delayed so long, its originally planned width of 100 feet could now be reduced to 30 feet. Thirty-five feet on either side of the drive could be laid out with strips of sod ("parking") and footpaths, with room for four rows of shade trees. Surely, Viele argued, the West End would soon be filled with commodious homes.[15]

Perhaps what was needed to spur development, the West Side Association considered, was a link that would unite the fashionable East Side with the rural West Side. One contractor suggested that Seventy-ninth Street be laid out across Central Park as a great transverse road for the easy transfer of filling and other building materials from the East Side lumberyards. Because there was no direct access to the West Side, most of the building material was diverted to Harlem where transportation costs were not as great. Almost all the available dumping grounds, however, lay on the West Side, and if a transverse road could be built, the low-lying land adjacent to Seventy-ninth Street would be filled quickly with debris from the East Side, spurring on the West Side's development. Adding to the argument for a transverse road was the fact that only one wharf lay along the West Side at Seventy-ninth Street, but at such a steep grade to the West Side plateau that it cost a developer 15 percent more if he transported materials by barge. The Seventy-ninth Street wharf was so crowded during the business season that vessels were required to remain there for several days, only adding to the cost of construction. By 1881 the Vanderbilt Docks could be seen under construction from Sixty-fifth Street to Seventy-second Street, an event that fueled the fire of anticipated growth. It seemed imperative that a way be found to unite the east side with the west side of the park, and many special meetings were called in the hopes of finding a solution by which materials and population would flow to the Upper West Side. All its dedicated promoters never lost faith; they remained convinced that the pressure for housing eventually would be felt in this section of town and that its days of retarded development soon would be a thing of the past.[16]

Fig. 241. View west from the top of the Dakota Apartment House, along the row of town houses on West Seventy-third Street, ca. 1886. Designed by Henry J. Hardenbergh in 1882, the row covered a street frontage of 550 feet, each house having a 20-foot facade. The Columbus Avenue corner was occupied by an apartment house, one story higher than the row but architecturally united with it by means of a high stone basement running the entire frontage of the row and by a molded stone cornice. The effect was of a continuous line interrupted only by gable fronts. The side streets in the vicinity of the Seventy-second Street El station were rapidly developed with town houses in the mid-1880s. Portions of the row on the north side, east of Amsterdam Avenue, were developed by George W. Hamilton; other parts have been attributed to Hardenbergh. Sections of the southern row were erected by Terence Farley and Sons in 1885. (Courtesy of the New York Public Library, New York City)

THE STRUGGLE FOR DEVELOPMENT

Under the leadership of Edward Clark and the West Side Association, the Upper West Side began in the 1880s slowly to show signs of improvement.[17] In 1880 the foundations were erected for a fantastic new apartment hotel, the Dakota, designed by Henry Janeway Hardenbergh on Seventy-second Street and Eighth Avenue (see fig. 191). It was Clark's idea to build this elegant and lavish apartment house to resemble a castle, in order to give impetus to West Side improvement, to define the character of the buildings that would grace the West Side plateau, and to offer the city a fine hotel with all the comforts and luxuries of first-class town houses.[18] In addition, Hardenbergh designed for Clark a row of twenty-seven town houses on the north side of Seventy-third Street between Eighth and Ninth avenues (figs. 241, 242). Yet at least a dozen shanties stood on the south side of Seventy-third Street, a few feet away from Clark's new development, and only 150 feet west from the corner of Ninth Avenue, a hog-slaughtering establishment could be found. But as the Clark buildings were erected, the shanties east of

Fig. 242. *Above.* Hardenbergh row, West Seventy-third Street, north side, ca. 1883. Originally a unified row of twenty-seven town houses, together with the apartment house at the corner of Columbus Avenue, the Hardenbergh row is now broken mid-block by an apartment house. Like the Dakota, also designed by Hardenbergh, this work was intended to set a precedent for subsequent West Side development but few repeated the example. (Courtesy of Avery Library, Columbia University, New York City)

Fig. 243. *Below.* Detail from the Robinson Insurance Map of 1885. West Eighty-first Street to West Eighty-fifth Street (reading up), Central Park West to Columbus Avenue. (Courtesy of the New York Public Library, New York City)

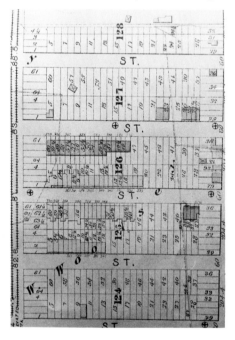

Ninth Avenue between Seventieth and Seventy-third streets were cleared away and these lots were readily sold.[19]

In spite of the exemplary addition of the Dakota, West Side property owners continued to complain that elsewhere no pressure was exerted to hasten additional luxury improvements. The impact of tenements along the avenues and cheaper housing on some of the side streets seemed to threaten the West Side's future development. Just above Sixty-fifth Street, for example, between Eighth and Ninth avenues, a row of inexpensive, poorly built houses had been erected. Ninth Avenue had been taken over by stores and tenements, while the side streets off Tenth Avenue were filling up with smaller buildings. Between Fifty-ninth and 125th streets, west of Eighth Avenue, a total of 106 buildings existed in 1881; this number increased to 127 by 1882.[20] Most of this activity, however, was far from luxury development. The popular builder George W. Hamilton, taking notice of the increasing demand for modest houses, completed in 1882 six four-story brownstones on the north side of Seventy-third Street just east of Tenth Avenue. In close proximity to Clark's lavish improvements, Hamilton's row of buildings in contrast, consisted of extremely narrow houses: three were 16 feet wide, two were 18 feet, and one was 17 feet wide.[21] This was the core of the problem in terms of luxury settlement on the Upper West Side: small sections of fashionable housing were scattered far apart, only a row here or there. Since the pace of development was slow, spaces in between these luxury clusters were randomly filled in with lower-grade homes, tenements, and French flats. As a result the overall West Side development pattern was inconsistent and its architecture too varied for the fashionable elite to gain control over the entire terrain. As Montgomery Schuyler noted, the advantages of restrictive agreements and conformity of design

> by no means impressed themselves upon [all] the pioneers in the building of the belated West Side. Here for the first time in nearly half a century there seemed to be offered an opportunity for a quarter of small houses. So much land was at once thrown open to settlement by the completion of the elevated railroad that its price was low enough to encourage speculative builders to provide for the wants of people of moderate means. . . . For these people no provision at all had been made during the brownstone period.
>
> Being left to supply and demand, [the seeker of a modest home] fell among the speculative builder, who, not being trained to take thought, but only to do what he was used to doing, and not choosing to go the expense of a trained architect, undertook to supply the demand by imposing his own "ideas" on his own cheap draughtsmen. The front was narrowed from twenty feet to seventeen, or even less, and the depth somewhat increased, the house still consisting of four floors.[22]

The areas that began to develop first were in close proximity to the Ninth Avenue El stations at Seventy-second, Eighty-first, and Ninety-third streets (fig. 243). By 1884 the *Real Estate Record* noted that the blocks near these stations between Seventy-first and Seventy-third streets and Eighty-second and Eighty-third streets were largely built up with rows of town houses, and a number of houses were going up along Ninth Avenue and on the side streets of Ninety-sixth,

Ninety-seventh, and Ninety-eighth streets[23] (fig. 244). Nevertheless, in spite of this spurt of activity on the West Side, little of architectural interest existed above Seventy-second Street. The mammoth Dakota, which rose high above every building in the neighborhood, remained the principal attraction for miles around. Reminiscing to the West Side Association, a Mr. Olcott recalled that in 1884

> looking northward from the rear of [a house on Seventy-third Street] . . . there was nothing in the way of permanent construction until one reached Manhattanville. . . . Most of the property between . . . 73rd Street and 125th Street was kitchen gardens and goats wandered around without any control. . . . There was a green-grocer's garden at Broadway and 74th Street. . . . All Angel's Church at 81st and Eleventh Avenue, was a little bit of a wooden building which had been physically moved from 66th Street and Seventh Avenue when Central Park was built. This little shack was perched upon a little hill and one had to climb a ladder to get to its entrance.[24]

Fig. 244. West Seventy-second Street, looking southwest from the top of the Dakota, ca. 1886. The El station at Columbus Avenue and Seventy-second Street is visible. Toward the south, the roof of the Bloomingdale Reformed Dutch Church can be seen near Sixty-ninth Street, beyond which are the Hudson River grain elevators. The row of ten identical town houses on the south side of Seventy-first Street near Ninth Avenue was erected by the developer George W. Hamilton. The most important development can be seen along Seventy-second Street itself: five brick and brownstone houses directly opposite the fenced vacant lots in back of the Dakota, erected by William Noble. The central three houses are gabled against a mansard roof while the two flanking houses have flat roofs. (Courtesy of the New York Public Library, New York City)

Fig. 245. Bloomingdale Reformed Dutch Church, Broadway and Sixty-eighth Street, ca. 1902. Designed by Samuel B. Reed in 1883 and demolished ca. 1905. (Courtesy of the New-York Historical Society, New York City)

These conditions would soon change. By August 1885, it was proclaimed that the time for West Side development had arrived; soon afterward the architectural character of different sections would be firmly established. To the south, on the west side of Ninth Avenue between Sixty-first and Sixty-second streets, the massive new Twelfth Regiment Armory towered over dwellings and stores. East of Tenth Avenue, between Fifty-ninth and Sixtieth streets, the College of Physicians and Surgeons was erecting a hospital next door to the Sloane Maternity Hospital. Not far away, the Equitable Gas Light Company would occupy the southern side of Fifty-ninth Street between Tenth and Eleventh avenues. Stables, flats, tenements, and stores were rapidly filling in the side streets up to Sixty-seventh Street. From there north to Seventieth Street, in the blocks off of Eighth Avenue, the area remained vacant where immense quantities of rock had yet to be removed. But west of Ninth Avenue many improvements were underway: the Bloomingdale Reformed Dutch Church (fig. 245), rebuilt sometime in the 1870s, already adorned the Broadway frontage between Sixty-eighth and Sixty-ninth streets, and rows of town houses fronted the side streets.[25]

As one neared Seventy-second Street a new city seemed to be taking shape (fig. 246). It had been foreseen as early as 1866 that a new fashionable district would arise on the first broad street above Fifty-ninth Street, opposite an entryway to Central Park. At this time the large Harsen Estate was subdivided into 500 different lots, and each parcel was sold, restricted to residential use. In addition, Seventy-second street came under the jurisdiction of Central Park; its plantings and trees were supervised and tended by park employees, and its length protected from trucks (even delivery wagons were limited to early morning hours). So groomed, it could be expected to become a street of first-class residences.

But was the New York dwelling type changing its form in this new residential district? Everything, the *Real Estate Record* seemed to think, was still in an architectural flux, although the flat brownstone facade that had discredited so much of lower Manhattan seemed to have fallen out of favor on the Upper West Side. This old front had only two or three kinds of ornamentation: its cornice and moldings were often oversized and bloated, and the front door was either a projecting lintel or a pair of columns supporting a pediment. But a favorite scheme of West Side developers seemed to be a row of five 20-foot houses, varied and individualized with respect to their architectural features but treated as an ensemble (fig. 247). There were lessons to be learned from all these novel departures, but, unless a schooled architect was employed, the *Real Estate Record* warned, it was far better to stay with the tried and tested brownstone front than to venture into new territory with potentially disastrous results.[26]

In spite of this warning, Montgomery Schuyler would claim that the tyranny of brownstone was finally struck down on the Upper West Side of New York, and for the first time architects and builders began to express the fact that the row house could be an individual structure, which might be united into a row, but could contain varied features within the row, diversified materials, and reflect a great deal of architectural license. Such diversions were also prevalent on the Upper East Side, although the staid and true brownstone still held sway. On the West Side, however, Schuyler believed that most of the row houses were erected by speculators and consequently designed for profit. These developers replaced the traditional brownstone facade with rock-faced stone. Terra-cotta and brick in different colors were other popular treatments, the high stoop be-

[Fig. 246]

SELECTED DEVELOPERS AND ARCHITECTS
ON THE UPPER WEST SIDE: 1880–1886

1880   The Bedford, northeast corner of 82d Street and Amsterdam Avenue

The Dakota, 72d Street and Central Park West
(Henry J. Hardenbergh, architect)

1882   27 houses, north side of 73d Street, east of Central Park West
(Henry J. Hardenbergh, architect)

8 houses, north side of 82d Street, east of Columbus Avenue
(George S. Miller, developer)

1884   3 houses, north side of 82d Street, near Columbus Avenue
(R. Deeves, developer)

7 houses, 83d Street between Columbus and Amsterdam avenues
(William Noble, developer)

3 houses, 83d Street between Columbus and Amsterdam avenues
(D. and J. Jardine, architects)

2 houses, 83d Street between Columbus and Amsterdam avenues
(T. Cochrane, developer)

3 houses, 83d Street between Columbus and Amsterdam avenues
(G. Da Comba, developer)

7 houses, 83d Street between Columbus and Amsterdam avenues
(R. Deeves, developer)

1885   4 houses and 1 flat, northwest corner 70th Street and Columbus Avenue
(Terence Farley, developer)

7 houses, north side of 71st Street, west of Central Park West
(Owen Conohue, developer)

5 houses, south side of 71st Street, west of Columbus Avenue
(George W. Hamilton, developer)

5 houses, south side of 71st Street, east of Columbus Avenue
(George W. Hamilton, developer)

5 houses, south side of 72d Street, west of Central Park West
(William Noble, developer)

9 houses, southeast corner of 74th Street and West End Avenue
(Lamb and Rich, architects)

1886   20 houses, north side of 63d Street between Columbus and Amsterdam
avenues (Manhattan Development Company)

3 houses, northeast corner of West End Avenue and 70th Street
(E. K. Angell, architect)

5 houses, north side of 72d Street, west of Columbus Avenue
(Thom and Wilson, architects)

10 houses, west side of West End Avenue between 74th and 75th streets
(W. E. B. Stokes, developer)

5 houses, south side of 74th Street, west of Columbus Avenue (W. E. B.
Stokes, developer)

9 houses, northeast corner of West End Avenue and 75th Street

6 houses, north side of 78th Street, west of Columbus Avenue
(R. Guastavino, architect)

9 houses, south side of 78th Street, west of Columbus Avenue
(R. Guastavino, architect)

4 houses, north side of 81st Street, east of Columbus Avenue
(S. Colcord, developer)

Data compiled from the *Real Estate Record and Builders' Guide* (1880–1886).

Fig. 247. *Above.* 312–316 West End Avenue, southeast corner of Seventy-fifth Street, ca. 1912. Claimed to be one of the oldest row of town houses erected on the West Side in the early 1880s (demolished ca. 1912), the original set of six houses was attributed by the *Real Estate Record* to Lamb and Rich. The row is representative of the license many builders took with their town house facades by combining different materials and architectural elements. (Courtesy of the New York Public Library, New York City)

Fig. 248. *Below.* 157 West Eighty-eighth Street. Montgomery Schuyler asserted that architectural "wild work" proliferated on the Upper West Side, creating vulgar facades. (Courtesy of the New York Public Library, New York City)

Fig. 249. West Seventy-second Street, north side, west of Columbus Avenue, 1985. Originally a row of five houses, developed by Thom and Wilson in 1885 (of which two are extant), the buildings were constructed of stone, rock-faced up to the second story, featuring prominent tower bay and oriel windows with considerable ornamental carving.

came a basement or box-stooped entrance, and a complete abandonment of all architectural standards and restraint eventually resulted (fig. 248). Such violent indecorum reflected an extreme vulgarization of the public taste.[27] Seldom in domestic architecture did purity of style prevail, but on the Upper West Side, Schuyler noted, no restraint guided the architects and builders, and in consequence the whole picturesque region was thrown open to the wiles of speculative developers who erected block upon block of small houses for the modest or petite bourgeoisie. By narrowing the fronts from 20 feet to 17 feet or less, and by increasing the depths of the structures with back buildings and extensions, these speculators turned the streets of the West Side into an architectural nightmare.[28]

While many of the blocks below Seventy-second Street or above Eighty-sixth Street were becoming the province of the small three-story house, or the French flat, a few large-scale, flamboyant houses were being erected along Seventy-second Street and in the vicinity of Manhattan Square. The designers Thom and Wilson blended different architectural styles together, producing a novel effect in their row of five houses on the north side of Seventy-second Street, just west of Ninth Avenue[29] (fig. 249). Six new houses on the north side of Seventy-eighth Street, a few feet west of the Museum of Natural History, were also excellent examples of the new West Side architecture. Built by the Spanish architect,

Rafael Guastavino for B. S. Levy, these three- and four-story houses were executed in a decorative Moorish style (fig. 250). Opposite these houses, Levy and Guastavino experimented with another block of nine four-story brownstone houses the following year. The major feature of these houses was a system of fireproof tiled arches supporting the floors and thus leaving the basements entirely unobstructed by either iron or brick support pillars.[30] On the north side of Eighty-first Street, just west of Central Park, four houses developed by Samuel Colcord drew the attention of the *Real Estate Record*. Three of these houses were handsome examples of the fashionable Renaissance style, while the fourth was in English Gothic[31] (fig. 251).

By 1886 considerable development had begun on the West Side although it was concentrated in specific locations (fig. 252). East Side developers were beginning to shift their attention to the Upper West Side; indeed it appeared that a new city was taking form. Perhaps the most important factor in the development of the West Side lay in the exceptionally high prices vacant East Side lots commanded. It was not unusual to pay $50,000 for a lot plus an additional $50,000 for a house on the East Side, compared to $20,000 to $25,000, which would secure both a lot and a house on the Upper West Side.[32]

Fig. 250. West Seventy-eighth Street, north side, west of Columbus Avenue, 1985. Designed by Rafael Guastavino in 1885 and still standing, this row of six houses made use of a rock-faced brownstone for the basements and brick and terra-cotta for the upper stories. Heavy courses of Nova Scotia stone encased the windows, including the decorative bay windows on the second story. Each house had an inlaid tile vestibule floor. Expensive woods were used throughout: black walnut on the parlor floors, mahogany on the second floor, and poplar on the third and fourth floors. Experimenting with a Moorish style that previously had been more popular for interior design, this row and its opposite row, developed by Levy and Guastavino, represented the kind of West Side architecture that the *Real Estate Record* called homelike as well as artistic and which was beginning to win the approval of even the most old-fashioned and conservative tastes.

Fig. 251. West Eighty-first Street, north side west of Central Park, from within the grounds of Manhattan Square, 1905. To the right of the twelve-story Colonial Hotel stands a row of three Gothic houses developed by Samuel Colcord in 1886. To their right, with projecting conical towers, stand the Peerless houses, erected by Richard Deeves in 1891. At first it was feared that Deeves's expensive French Renaissance chateau design was too elegant for the Upper West Side, but the houses all found ready buyers. (Courtesy of the New York Public Library, New York City)

[Fig. 252]

VACANT AND UNIMPROVED LOTS ON THE UPPER WEST SIDE (WEST OF EIGHTH AVENUE: 1886)			
	Total Lots	Vacant Lots	Developed Lots
59th–72d Street	3,298	2,412	886
72nd–86th Street	2,708	2,232	476
86th–96th Street	2,238	1,993	245
96th–110th Street	2,980	2,590	390
110th–116th Street	1,087	1,056	31

Data compiled from "Vacant Lots on Manhattan Island," the *Real Estate Record and Builders' Guide* (May 15, 1886):636.

Fig. 253. Frontispiece of the "West Side Number," the *Real Estate Record and Builders' Guide* Supplement, 1893. By keeping an attentive eye on who was building what kind of house and where, and by advertising new architectural achievements and interior conveniences, the *Real Estate Record* during the 1880s and 1890s "sold" the Upper West Side to the middle classes who were increasingly outpriced on the East Side and in lower Manhattan. (Courtesy of Avery Library, Columbia University, New York City)

PROMOTING THE WEST SIDE

When the West Side finally awoke, it rushed into development at an unparalleled rate, full of what appeared to be illimitable expectations. All the developers, fearing overbuilding, were wary of the frenzied buying and selling and building activity between 1886 and 1888. Their fears were justified; by 1888 there were hundreds of houses left vacant and many construction shells abandoned in unfinished states. But overbuilding was neither widespread nor prolonged; land values had appreciated considerably since the beginning off the West Side's development and some builders were able to raise money to cover their costs of construction, so building continued. By this time the solid middle class, for the first time being accommodated with houses in Manhattan, eagerly sought to purchase or rent many of the new modern structures with their novel fancy fronts and decorative interiors (fig. 253).

In spite of hopes and predictions, a luxury residential area comparable to the fashionable Upper East Side did not materialize on the West Side. The housing market in the late 1880s, nevertheless, took on specific characteristics in spite of its random appearance: tenements and flats seemed to control the blocks from Fifty-ninth to Seventy-second Street, while three-story modest homes sold best above Seventy-second to Eighty-first Street and more expensive four-story houses dominated the market from Eighty-first to Ninety-third Street. North of Ninety-third Street, development was still sparse; between Ninety-third and 116th streets, where building was just beginning, a few tenements could be found interspersed with three-story structures, while beyond 116th Street building was represented by only a few flats and tenements.[33]

The faults of the Upper West Side became increasingly apparent. More attention had gone into promotional acitivity of the area than into the actual improvement of its sidewalks and streets (fig. 254). The Boulevard, the finest and widest avenue of the West Side remained a disgrace. At its entrance near Fifty-ninth Street and for several subsequent blocks two riding academies and stables were located. From there until Sixty-ninth Street, where Bloomingdale Church stood, both sides of the Boulevard contained a ragged assortment of structures, ranging from shanties to liquor saloons, blacksmith shops, coal yards, and a few flats with stores (see fig. 239). The same was true of the northern blocks until Christ Church (designed by C. C. Haight) appeared at Seventy-first Street, followed by more shanties and liquor and grocery stores until the Dakota's livery and boarding stables between Seventy-fourth and Seventy-fifth streets were reached. A few five-story flats were located above Seventy-sixth Street; Clark's greenhouse lay between Seventy-eighth and Seventy-ninth streets and then once again, until Eighty-sixth Street, the Boulevard became a mixture of shanties, vacant lots, saloons, and gardens with tenements or flats scattered throughout. Near 110th Street a village of shacks emerged, and just to its north where the Boulevard crossed West End Avenue, a pond of water collected every time that it rained. Since it was still in vogue to lease lots for cultivation, more than twenty picturesque and profuse gardens could be counted in this area.[34]

Although the landscaping of Riverside Drive was nearing completion in the late 1880s, those who pioneered its development were looked on with some curiosity, for the drive remained basically a barren and isolated part of Manhattan (see fig. 238). It should have been a quarter for magnificent villas, but the entire

Fig. 254. View along Ninety-fourth Street, across West End Avenue toward Riverside Drive, ca. 1889. In spite of the promotional activity of the *Real Estate Record*, most of the West Side, except for the areas near the El stations, remained undeveloped. (Courtesy of the Museum of the City of New York, New York City)

Fig. 255. Cyrus Clark residence, Riverside Drive and Ninetieth Street, south corner. One of the earliest villas on Riverside Drive, built long before all of its side streets had been graded and connected with the drive, the house was designed in the late 1880s by H. F. Kilburn for Cyrus Clark, known as a "father of the West Side." Occupying two city lots, its three stories of light gray Indiana limestone topped with a red tile roof were separated by heavy molded stringcourses. (Courtesy of the Museum of the City of New York, New York City)

West Side, it was argued, lay too far from the center of amusement, the district of Ladies Mile, which had attracted and held most of the leading theaters, the finest clubs, the major department stores, and the fashionable hotels. In consequence, the West Side's service functions could be expected only to be of local neighborhood interest, and its residents far from the fashionable elite.[35] There were a dozen or so detached houses on Riverside Drive that aspired more to the status of suburban villas than of urban chateaux, and most of questionable architectural merit. The first of these houses erected in the 1880s was situated on the south corner of Ninetieth Street and was designed for one of the "fathers" of the Upper West Side, Cyrus Clark (fig. 255). A few years later in 1891, architects Lamb and Rich would erect the John Matthews residence for the soda-water merchant on the opposite corner of Ninetieth Street (fig. 256). At 100th Street a large red brick house was built, and while it was not offensive, the *Real Estate Record* found it was far from an embellishment to the drive; and at 102d Street, a vulgar outmoded construction of cast iron, erected for the glove-hook heiress Bertha Foster, resembled an advertisement for an ironmonger. Nearby stood another curiosity, a fortified castle with battlemented parapet. Samuel G. Bayne's Romanesque mansion, designed by Frank Freeman in 1891, a learned disciple of Henry Hobson Richardson, was the most artful of the Riverside suburban villas and stood on the south side of 108th Street[36] (fig. 257).

Central Park West, as Eighth Avenue had been renamed in 1883, was another magnificent street that languished while waiting for its possibilities to be realized. The avenue, it was believed, was destined to become the site for grand apartment houses and hotels following the pattern established by the Dakota. As one developer wrote in 1890, "It [was] too public a thoroughfare to become a private residential street, too much traffic and second-rate Eighth Avenue cars are a detriment. Central Park West should have been restricted but it's too late. It should be asphalted; would greatly benefit the property fronting on the Avenue

Fig. 256. John H. Matthews residence, Riverside Drive and Ninetieth Street, north corner. Architects Lamb and Rich combined turrets, open porches, massive tile roofing, stone, brick, and terra-cotta walls to create a rambling picturesque ensemble in 1891, resembling a suburban villa more than a city house. (Courtesy of the Museum of the City of New York, New York City)

The Upper West Side • 211

Fig. 257. Samuel G. Bayne residence, Riverside Drive and 108th Street, south corner, ca. 1921. One of two suburban villas erected by Frank Freeman on opposite corners of 108th Street and Riverside Drive. Freeman, an expert interpreter of the American Romanesque style, which had become so popular on the Upper West Side in the late 1880s, utilized in this house deep Sullivanesque archways, floral ornamentation, and a square corner tower with turret and chimney as the main features of the Riverside facade. The house itself was composed of yellow brick, relieved by moldings and encasements of rich red sandstone, and crowned with a black varnished tile roof. (Courtesy of the New York Public Library, New York City)

Fig. 258. Three private residences, Central Park West, south corner of Eighty-fifth Street, 1985. The original row consisted of nine houses, designed by Edward K. Angell in 1888. The northern half of the block was a mirror image of the southern half, and each used a variety of materials including red brick, buff-colored brick, brownstone, and limestone. Only the northern three houses remain today. (The southern six were demolished in 1930.)

and would start a building movement.''[37] Even after the initial surge of West Side development, approximately two-thirds of the entire frontage of Eighth Avenue remained vacant and unimproved. In addition, at least thirty-two lots had been devoted to the Museum of Natural History, ten more to Durland's Riding Academy between Sixtieth and Sixty-first streets, and eight lots to the Dakota between Seventy-second and Seventy-third streets. In 1890, from Sixty-first to Seventy-second Street, Central Park West contained only saloons, shanties, and vacant lots. Between Seventy-third and Seventy-seventh streets, the blocks were vacant except for a saloon and a new ten-story apartment house on the southwest corner of Seventy-fifth Street, the San Remo, erected in 1890 by Michael Brennan. North of Manhattan Square, the Beresford Hotel (1889), on the northwest corner of Eighty-first Street, could be seen, and between Eighty-second and Eighty-fourth streets a row of flats was built, developed by William Hall and Sons, next to another flat by Edward Purcell, followed by four five-story brick houses built by Charles H. Lindsley on the south corner of Eighty-fourth Street. William Noble had built in 1888 nine exceptionally handsome residences designed by Edward K. Angell between Eighty-fourth and Eighty-fifth streets (fig. 258), with the northern half of the block being a mirror image of the southern

Fig. 259. West End Avenue, looking south from Ninety-eighth Street, 1889. In 1880 Egbert Viele successfully initiated a movement to rename Eleventh Avenue above Seventy-second Street West End Avenue, and to plant thirty-five foot parkings on either side of its length, beginning its improvement. Nine years later urban development had not yet moved farther north than Ninety-first Street. (Courtesy of the Museum of the City of New York, New York City)

Fig. 260. Residences on the south side of West Seventy-second Street, between Broadway and West End Avenue, 1893. Exemplary of the fads and fashions of West Seventy-second Street architecture, this row of four houses, owned by the famous carriage maker W. H. Gray, sported an eccentric ''look-out'' tower supposedly used to catch Hudson River breezes. The buildings are extant. (Courtesy of Avery Library, Columbia University, New York City)

half. A few hospitals, more flats, and even more shanties and unkept vacant lots occupied the rest of the avenue to the northern edge of Central Park.[38]

If one had examined the side streets in 1889, it would have been apparent that development was still limited to certain blocks. Some streets had been improved with a superior quality of housing and others had neither care nor money expended upon them. Only one or two streets north of Seventy-second Street had both flagging and paving; the only thoroughfares on which asphalt had been laid were West End Avenue from Seventy-second to Seventy-sixth Street and Seventy-third Street from the Boulevard to West End Avenue, and in both these cases the work had been done by property owners rather than by municipal authorities. In the few spots where the Department of Public Works decided to improve a street, a rough granite pavement was used, a far from pleasing sight. Most of the West Side streets remained country lanes, a disgraceful condition for the projected flowering of the Upper West Side[39] (fig. 259).

The character of the most elegant neighborhood on the West Side, the blocks between Eighty-fifth and Eighty-seventh streets just off Central Park, was determined by three men, D. W. James, John G. Prague, and T. E. D. Power. They claimed that Eighty-sixth Street was the handsomest street in Manhattan, having sidewalks twenty-five feet in width and being restricted by covenants to first-class residences. Consequently, these three men had erected no fewer than seventy-six buildings in 1888, all designed by Prague. The interiors were luxuriously appointed: hardwood trim throughout; floors parqueted and ceilings paneled in oak; and a dining room fireplace with two bric-a-brac receptacles enclosed in glass and a central shelf decorated by two small curtains of velour or satin.[40] Few houses on the West Side attained frontages of 25-foot widths, but near the Prague houses two handsome fronts of light stone with high boxed stoops, designed by Charles H. Bliss, stood at 62 and 63 West Ninety-fifth Street,[41] and fronting Manhattan Square, Richard Deeves erected three handsome houses, the Peerless houses, according to the design of a French Renaissance chateau[42] (see fig. 251).

The most ostentatious residential street on the West Side was Seventy-second Street, with its tree-lined frontage and grass plots along its sidewalks (fig. 260). The street was filled with the latest fads in residential architecture that the

Real Estate Record termed "positively vulgar and inartistic."[43] Its avenue corners were improved with apartment houses. The Parkway, a six-story structure developed by Charles Buek and Company in 1889, took up two lots on the south side of Seventy-second Street near Central Park[44] (fig. 261). Another apartment building being developed in 1889, the Adrian by Terence Farley's sons, stood on the southeast corner of Seventy-second Street and Ninth Avenue.[45]

Of all the streets on the West Side, none became as famous and as highly promoted in the nineteenth century as West End Avenue. This area, which had been restricted by covenants to first-class private dwellings, was touted as the ideal domestic environment, with no undesirable neighbors and clean, fresh air and a sublime view. Below Fifty-ninth Street, residential areas were being invaded by trade so that the side streets off Fifth Avenue and even the avenue itself were being transformed for business uses. Consequently, the only private residential section in Manhattan in the 1890s was the section of the West Side between West End Avenue and Riverside Drive.[46] Here architects were experimenting with new town house ensembles and American basement houses. In these constructions, four or five houses were designed as one unit while their individual architectural elements were varied. Bow fronts, bay windows, balconies, balustrades, corner turrets, and ornamented gables were composed into picturesque groupings. In addition, the high stoop was removed and the entry now lay at the basement level. Some of the best work could be seen along West End Avenue near Seventy-fifth and Seventy-sixth streets (figs. 262–265). At Seventy-sixth Street the building line terminated where the Poignant—an old dilapidated frame dwelling still used for business purposes—stood. The next several streets had

Fig. 261. Parkway Apartment House, south side of Seventy-second Street near Central Park, 1889. The salmon-colored Raritan brick apartment house, developed by Charles Buek and Company in 1889, was organized internally into a series of six two-story duplex houses. The first floor of each duplex included a reception room or library, a drawing room that fronted on Seventy-second Street, a dining room with a butler's pantry, a kitchen, and a servant's bedroom. The second floor, accessible from a wide staircase located in the interior of each duplex suite, led to four sleeping chambers and a spacious bathroom. (Courtesy of Avery Library, Columbia University, New York City)

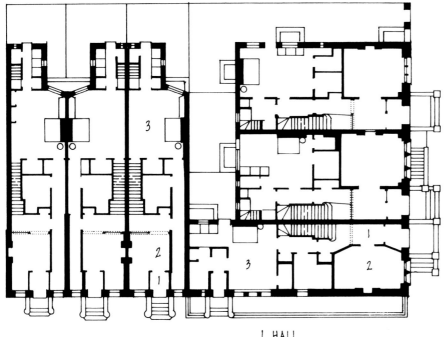

1. HALL
2. RECEPTION ROOM
3. KITCHEN

Fig. 262. American basement house, designed by Clarence True for West Seventy-fifth Street. (Redrawn from the *Real Estate Record*, Sept. 16, 1893: 314.) The plan shows the difference between the high-stooped town house and the American basement scheme. By eliminating the costly and illogical high stoop, the parlor floor gained the full width of the house. In addition, entry into the house was on the ground level where adequate reception and cloak rooms could be provided. Visitors could then be ushered ceremoniously up the main staircase in the middle of the house to the parlor floor above. (Courtesy of Avery Library, Columbia University, New York City)

Fig. 263. Row of five American basement houses, designed by Clarence True, on the north side of Seventy-fifth Street, between West End Avenue and Riverside Drive, 1893. By 1889, True had begun to purchase all the available lots below Eighty-fourth Street along Riverside Drive and its adjacent side streets. During the next decade, he would improve this section of the West Side with town house ensembles. (Courtesy of Avery Library, Columbia University, New York City)

Fig. 264. Northwest corner of Seventy-fifth Street and West End Avenue, 1915. Built in the late 1880s, this row of red-brick houses contained little ornamentation, producing its architectural effect by the massing of its elements. (Courtesy of the Museum of the City of New York, New York City)

Fig. 265. Northeast corner of Seventy-sixth Street and West End Avenue, ca. 1910. Five extremely large houses were designed by Edward Angell for Don Lyons in 1889–90, with popular Romanesque features. (Courtesy of the New-York Public Library, New York City)

Fig. 266. Northwest corner of Seventy-eighth Street and West End Avenue, 1985. Row of eight houses designed by Fred B. White in 1885–86 in the style of the old gabled Dutch houses of lower Manhattan (extant). Many buildings along West End Avenue utilized the Dutch theme, such as Robert W. Gibson's Collegiate Dutch Reformed Church at Seventy-seventh Street, completed in 1892, the Grammar School at Eighty-seventh Street, designed by C. Snyder in 1893, and a row of five houses attributed to McKim, Mead and White on the southwest corner of Eighty-third Street, erected in 1885.

Fig. 267. Row of private residences built by James T. Hall on West Seventy-fifth Street, 1890. Described by the *Real Estate Record* as being "in free Romanesque" style, the varied fronts of these houses (extant but altered) contained rough, smooth, and carved stone with massive stoops, some of which were box stoops. (Courtesy of Avery Library, Columbia University, New York City)

only a scattering of houses built on the blocks toward Riverside Drive. Between Seventy-eighth and Seventy-ninth streets, however, on West End Avenue, a number of small red brick dwellings were clustered (fig. 266); development grew sparse until Eighty-first Street where structures once again were densely situated.[47] Above Eighty-sixth Street, however, one encountered buildings that were borrowed too liberally from pattern books and "the seeker after architectural beauty feels that he is in a land of his enemies, and when he reaches the symphony of ochre, light yellow, green, scarlet and blue between Eighty-ninth and Ninetieth streets, he is delighted to find that beyond stretch rural felicities and kitchen gardens, for there there is peace."[48]

The fashion of the late 1880s and early 1890s on the West Side for Romanesque-style houses caused the *Real Estate Record* to complain that architects were taking their sources too literally, producing "archaeology, not architecture." Montgomery Schuyler noted in 1891 the existence of a

Fig. 268. Residences on the south side of Seventy-fourth Street near Central Park, erected by Cornelius Luyster in 1892. The row of four box-stooped houses contained several novel features, including a combination storm and front door of oak, carved in a pattern of creepers and leaves, with a center, operable door window of beveled glass. Continuing with the popular American trend of throwing rooms together, Luyster planned the parlor and music rooms of these houses as one space, their divisions being marked only by a woodwork screen. In both rooms, mirrors set into the walls ran from floor to ceiling, reflecting the two rooms and making them appear larger. (Courtesy of Avery Library, Columbia University, New York City)

new quarter, amounting to a new and strange city, that has been built up within the past few years upon the "West Side". So strange and exotic of aspect is this new quarter that a New Yorker of 1880 even, who might be suddenly dropped into it, would never recognize it as a part of the downtown brown stone city that he knew. The West Side is not in any strictness a Romanesque town, to be sure, but the prevailing and pervading architectural element which gives it its character is undeniably Romanesque . . . and they are all evidently suggested immediately or remotely by the work of Mr. Richardson.[49]

A block of ten Romanesque houses on the south side of Seventy-fifth Street, between Central Park and Ninth Avenue, was constructed by James T. Hall, for example, in 1890 (fig. 267).[50] In this same area Cornelius W. Luyster was actively developing rows of Romanesque houses in the early 1890s. Having built a row of nine four-story houses on the south side of Seventy-second Street, a site that commanded an excellent view of the Hudson River and Riverside Drive, he then turned to erect four other houses on the south side of Seventy-fourth Street,

200 feet west of Central Park (fig. 268). The last of the Luyster buildings consisted of a row of five houses on West Seventy-sixth Street.[51]

THE RISE OF THE FAMILY APARTMENT HOUSE

During the second half of the nineteenth century town house development had filed up the length of Manhattan, stretching across its side streets above Fourteenth Street, until it reached the outskirts of the Upper West Side. In this area it began to ebb and wane in the 1890s. Between 1880 and 1900 nearly half the West Side building lots above Fifty-ninth Street to 110th Street (fig. 269) had been improved with three- or four-story row houses. Yet one developer, Frank L. Fisher, listed in 1894 no fewer than 572 row houses from Fifty-ninth Street to 104th Street on the Upper West Side that remained unoccupied and without prospective buyers—nearly one fifth of the entire row house construction for the preceding two decades.[52] As a result the number of projected new buildings declined in the early 1890s. Only fifty-six building plans were filed for 1890, and this was reduced to fourteen for 1891. By then it was believed builders were wary of erecting further structures on the Upper West Side until they finally knew whether or not a rapid transit system would be built on the Boulevard, ending its isolation.[53] The future of the Boulevard depended on the kind of system intended, for if the road was to be elevated then it would, like Ninth and Tenth avenues, be lined with tenements and second-class apartments; but if the solution was to be

[Fig. 269]

UNIMPROVED LOTS ON THE UPPER WEST SIDE: 1892

	Total Lots	Vacant Lots
59th–72d Street	3,105	1,612
72d–86th Street	2,755	1,110
86th–96th Street	2,304	1,118
96th–110th Street	2,957	1,924

AVENUES

	Central Park West (8th)	The Boulevard (Broadway)	Columbus (9th)	Amsterdam (10th)	West End End	Riverside Drive
59th–72d Street	86	121	41	40	105	96
72d–81st Street	26	94	25	36	63	64
81st–93d Street	61	153	35	97	91	83
93d–104th Street	70	168	17	44	129	83

SIDE STREETS

	Central Park West– Columbus	Columbus– Amsterdam	Amsterdam– West End	West End– Riverside
59th–72d Street	244	104	308	467
72d–81st Street	87	79	81	77
81st–93d Street	160	197	208	211
93d–104th Street	196	197	179	182

Data compiled from the *Real Estate Record and Builders' Guide* (February 11, 1893):15–16.

Fig. 270. Broadway, looking north from 114th Street, 1900. The buildings of Columbia College stand to the right of Broadway at 116th Street. The arrival of the subway in 1904 would open Morningside Heights to residential development. (Courtesy of the New York Public Library, New York City)

an underground system, then perhaps the avenue would finally become the central spine, lined with the hotels, clubhouses, theaters, churches, and good apartment houses and department stores that the West Side so sorely lacked.[54] Thus speculation remained sluggish during the 1890s and until the Broadway subway neared completion in 1904.

Other events would bring significant changes to the Upper West Side. In 1888 the *Real Estate Record* announced that the Bloomingdale Asylum planned to move to White Plains and that its Morningside Heights estate would be leased and restricted to first-class residences. An authority for the asylum quickly denied these intentions and it became publicly known by 1892 that no less than three important institutions, besides the Cathedral of Saint John the Divine, which was to rise on the site of Leake and Watt's Orphan Asylum, had decided to locate on Morningside Heights. Saint Luke's Hospital would occupy a block on Morningside Drive adjoining the Cathedral; Columbia College would plan a new campus site on four blocks between 116th and 120th streets, Tenth Avenue to the Boulevard; and Teacher's Institution would locate on a small block to the north of 120th Street (fig. 270).[55]

Except for the Clark Estate near Seventy-third Street, where eighteen new town houses were being erected, there were very few plans in the early twentieth century to erect private row houses on the Upper West Side. In the first five years of the new century, only seventy-five new private residences were built per year for the entire island of Manhattan, and this small demand for luxury living was restricted to the elegant Upper East Side. Only one instance of overblown development, the Schwab residence, which took over the old orphan asylum block fronting Riverside Drive between Seventy-third and Seventy-fourth streets in 1903, ever intruded on the West Side (fig. 271). But this development was seen as anachronistic in an area of modest residences—an overindulgence and a quirk of a rich man's fancy in which ordinary economy played no role.

Rather than seen as a positive addition enhancing future luxury development, as earlier promoters of the West Side would have viewed it, this chateau was feared by real estate developers for its potential negative effect on the neighborhood if it should be abandoned and left to deteriorate.[56]

New York's population, nearly a million and a half in 1870, had reached the level of 3,437,202 in 1900. Development interests abandoned their concern with luxury housing and began to address the issues of population needs, the congestion of tenement house districts, and the desires of middle-class clients. With each year of the early 1900s, family apartments, instead of private homes, dominated the streets of the Upper West Side. A brief flurry of small apartment house building took place on almost every street on the vacant lots between Sixtieth and 110th streets, from 1898 until the new Tenement House Act was passed in 1901. For these four years an apartment house under seven stories did not need to be fireproof, a loophole in the housing laws that was quickly closed. In addition, taller eight- to ten-story fireproof structures began to appear on the avenues of the Upper West Side. The electric elevator, an invention of the late 1890s, suddenly made taller apartments extremely profitable investments. One of the tallest of these new family apartment houses was the seventeen-story Ansonia, on the west side of Broadway between Seventy-third and Seventy-fourth streets, containing 350 suites, which was designed in 1901–1904 by Graves and Duboy and owned by W. E. D. Stokes[57] (fig. 272).

Fig. 271. Riverside Drive, north from Seventy-second Street, ca. 1911. An anachronism on the Upper West Side, the Schwab mansion stood near to rows of elegant town houses along Riverside Drive and Seventy-fourth, Seventy-fifth and Seventy-sixth streets, which had been developed in the 1890s by architects Clarence True, Lamb and Rich, and Charles P. H. Gilbert. Tall family apartment structures rose on the horizon along West End Avenue, completely transforming what had been a residential enclave in the first two decades of the twentieth century. (Courtesy of the Museum of the City of New York, New York City)

West Side development began to take on a new life with the opening of the Broadway subway in 1904 and the Eighth Avenue subway the following year (fig. 273). Between 1902 and 1910, 4,425 new apartment houses were erected in Manhattan.[58] The vacant lots along Riverside Drive, Broadway, Central Park West, and even residential West End Avenue were being covered with ten-story apartment houses. The most luxuriously appointed and massive of these family apartments included the Dorilton (1901), the Turrets (1902), the Apthorp (1908), and the Belnord (1909).[59] The Turrets, for example, spreading along Riverside Drive and Eighty-fourth Street, provided family suites ranging from ten rooms and three

Fig. 272. The Ansonia, west side of Broadway and Seventy-third Street, ca. 1902. Owned by W. E. D. Stokes and designed by Graves and Duboy in 1901–1904, the Ansonia brought many middle-class residents to the Upper West Side. (Courtesy of the New-York Historical Society, New York City)

baths to twenty rooms and six baths. In addition, this apartment house offered its tenants a white marble swimming pool, a fully equipped gymnasium, billiard rooms, a ballroom, a banquet hall, bowling alleys, and basketball courts. These exaggerated twentieth-century proportions far outstripped the nineteenth century's concept of luxury and comfort.[60]

The New York family apartment house was a clear response by the real estate community to those members of the middle class who wanted to live on valuable West Side land. This demand alone outpriced the developer of Manhattan row houses. The Upper West Side had never been considered "fashionable," and although many prosperous New Yorkers resided in comfortable town houses above Seventy-second Street and below Eighty-sixth Street, they never could match the stylishness of the Upper East Side. In 1899 E. Idell Zeisloft said that

> the dwellers [on the Upper West Side] are not as a rule of the old and historic New York families, or very wealthy as a class, but all are people exceedingly well-to-do, a fair proportion of them are Hebrews, and many are former residents of other cities who have found here the best value for their money.[61]

Similarly, the *Real Estate Record* proclaimed in 1903 that the Upper West Side was a family neighborhood, expressly suited for the middle class of ample means. Although these families could obtain cheaper apartments in Chelsea or in Greenwich Village, they preferred, in the twentieth century, to pay more for what they believed to be a superior location.[62]

Fig. 273. View north across the roof of the Apthorp Apartment House on Broadway between Seventy-eighth and Seventy-ninth streets, ca. 1901. (Courtesy of the New-York Historical Society, New York City)

CHAPTER SEVEN
THE DREAM OF A RATIONAL CITY

Yet a small white cloud no bigger than a man's hand was soon to appear above the horizon. The name of this cloud was eighteen hundred and ninety-three. Following the little cloud was a dark dim cloud more like a fog. The name of the second cloud was Baring Brothers.—Louis H. Sullivan, *The Autobiography of an Idea* (New York: Dover Publications, 1956):314

The Chicago World's Fair in 1893 popularized classical architecture, yet it was New York architects such as McKim, Mead and White, Carrère and Hastings, and Ernest Flagg who saw in the return to Beaux-Arts classicism the potential for both a national style of architecture and a rational urban order. A new interest in the public realm was awakened in which the promenading, quixotic consumer would become the subdued spectator of composed theatrical stage sets—backdrops of ornamental facades, axial perspectives, and autonomous monuments. Dismayed by the transitory and ephemeral styles of fashion, the proponents of the classical reaction hoped to separate works of art from their contaminated environments of popular taste. But by opting for one uniform architectural style—the classical—and ignoring innovations in engineering, they produced what Montgomery Schuyler referred to as the defect of modern architecture, "the estrangement between architecture and building—between the poetry and prose, so to speak, of the art of building."[1]

Even though the provocative twentieth-century architecture of New York streets would be anything but ordered and monumental in a classical sense, the small body of elite architects leading the classical reaction pursued an illusory synthesis, dreaming that the anarchy of the nineteenth-century streetscapes could be disciplined through the unified aesthetic consciousness of Beaux-Arts architecture. This was a futile attempt to return to solid ground, to find a fitting solution from an unattainable past. In the portals of the city, in its public landscape and civic scenery, rational architectural forms were to expel the spontaneous and experimental, the uneducated and untrained, in order to install their own fictive reality of an upscaled art. Yet this elite art drew upon elements that appealed to mass audiences—calculated architectural ensembles, universal symbolism, and phantasmagorical illusions—producing a play on the surface of the city full of references and quotations from a historical past.

Dressed in the illusionary clothing of imperial empires, American architecture in the late nineteenth and early twentieth centuries retreated backward, utilizing the representational images of sovereign power that it believed could be localized in and deduced from scenographic ensembles inserted into the order of the city. By formulating the logic of city planning, however, this classical reaction was paradoxically reaching toward the modern era, anticipating the day when control over urban form and the city populace would no longer be expressed symbolically and ceremonially (that is, stylistically), but would be embedded within the procedural discourses of the professions of architecture and city planning. In this spirit, the classical reaction joined the modern quest for an architectural and urban form expressive of a modern scientific age. Ernest Flagg was happy to announce in 1900:

> A revolution is in full progress among us and it is beginning just where it ought to begin; that is, with the students. Let no one mistake the introduction of what appears to be modern French architecture as only a passing fancy to go the way of the ''Richardsonian Romanesque,'' ''Queen Anne'' and ''Italian Renaissance.'' It is an entirely different affair. It means much more than appears on the surface. The French resemblance is only an incident: it may, indeed, soon pall and pass away, but the movement means that the principles which the French use are being introduced here, and these will last because they are founded on good taste, guided by common sense. Henceforth American architects are to be properly instructed before they enter upon their duties. American architecture is not to be ''Frenchified,'' unless France can dominate the fashions of the world in building by her taste and skill, as she has dominated them in dress. The movement means that our architects of the future will apply to the art in this country, the same logical reasoning, and that they will have the same careful preparation for the work that helps the Frenchman to lead the world in fine arts. It also means that in the future the whole body of American architects are to work together along the same lines—to think in the same style. Thus we are about to enter upon a course which will make possible the evolution of a national style of our own, or perhaps enable us to set the fashion for the world.[2]

The World's Fair ushered in the era of the City Beautiful, a movement that not only clothed American cities in the artificial grandeur of Beaux-Arts architecture but also stimulated the idea of rationally organizing and planning their development and growth. Manhattan certainly felt the force of this impact: the Municipal Building on Chambers Street, the new Grand Central Station at Forty-

Fig. 274. The New York Public Library, Fifth Avenue and Forty-second Street, 1930. Designed by Carrère and Hastings in 1897–1911. (Courtesy of the New York Public Library, New York City)

second Street, the New York Public Library, the Pennsylvania Station, the entryway to the Manhattan Bridge, and the Washington Arch are all exemplary remnants of this beautification (figs. 274–276). But social transformations were also bringing changes to the gilded era of elegance. From 1890 to 1930 New York was indisputably the financial and commercial capital of America, and although this preeminence stimulated extravagant displays of wealth, it also produced an expanding middle class that increasingly submerged and outnumbered the fashionable elite. The wealthy would withdraw privately into a much remodeled fashionable Upper East Side, while the middle class would congregate gregariously in large family apartments making up the modish Upper West Side.

The era of the private bourgeois row house was coming to an end. From 1889 to 1892, plans were filed each year for close to 700 private dwellings; in 1893 the numbers began to decline until in 1899 only 338 plans were filed, in 1900 only 112 plans, and in 1901 only 99 plans; the downward trend continued (fig. 277). In the meantime, the price of constructing a private town house rose each year as the value of New York's real estate increased. The fashionable multistoried apartment, which began to dominate the real estate market in 1898, pushed up land values even higher. These monumental structures would completely reorder the twentieth-century streetscapes of Park Avenue, Riverside Drive, West End Avenue, Broadway, and Central Park West.

In addition, in the late 1890s and early 1900s American millionaires became billionaires, descending on New York as kings of copper, iron, and steel, and de-

Fig. 275. Grand Central Terminal, looking north from south of Forty-second Street. Designed by Reed and Stern, and Warren and Wetmore, 1903–13. (Courtesy of the New-York Historical Society, New York City)

Fig. 276. Bird's-eye view of Pennsylvania Station, between Thirty-first and Thirty-third streets, Seventh to Eighth Avenue. Designed by McKim, Mead and White in 1904–10, the terminal was demolished in the early 1960s. (Courtesy of the New-York Historical Society, New York City)

Fig. 277. Row of town houses on the southwest corner of Ninety-third Street, between Broadway and West End Avenue, designed by Charles P. H. Gilbert. (From the *Real Estate Record*, May 6, 1893: 696.) Exemplary of the more formal and classical restraint of the Renaissance revival, which dominated architectural tastes in the 1890s and early 1900s, these houses were among the few to be erected on the Upper West Side where family apartment houses had by this time become the more popular and lucrative investment. (Courtesy of Avery Library, Columbia University, New York City)

Fig. 278. Crimmins residence, 40 East Sixty-eighth Street, 1898. A French-looking Beaux-Arts facade, designed by Schickel and Ditmars in 1897–98 replaced two plain brownstone facades originally erected in 1878. (Courtesy of the Museum of the City of New York, New York City)

manding elegant residences, regardless of expense. The fashionable Upper East Side became a new billionaires' district whose simple brownstone fronts were remodeled to suit the more cosmopolitan tastes of their wealthier owners. Under this reign of reconstruction, streets east of Park Avenue, once deemed on the "wrong side of the tracks," suddenly were upgraded, and new city chateaux appeared, marking the beginning of the development of Fifth Avenue opposite Central Park.[3] In this new billionaires' quarter, the loathesome brownstone facade was stripped away and redesigned, the new fronts often based on Georgian revivals reminiscent of colonial New York while others displayed a Parisian look and still others reflected the pale complexion of London's posh Belgravia district (fig. 278).

Still confined to the 25- by 100-foot New York City lot, these elegant new town houses became elongated and attenuated. A 60- to 70-foot depth, extended to 90 feet for corner houses, was commonplace, and with the arrival of the elevator, a height of five, six, or even seven stories was not unusual. Every technical aid encouraged the development of these seven-story structures: an internal telephone service, a dozen bathrooms with running hot water, machinery to run a double set of elevators (one for the family and another for the servants), and, occasionally, provision for a garage to house the family's new "automobile." "The modern expensive residence," Herbert Croly commented in 1902, "tends to become almost as complicated a piece of machinery as a modern hotel."[4]

Andrew Carnegie's new mansion at Fifth Avenue and Ninety-first Street caught the eye of Montgomery Schuyler at the turn of the century. He prophesied that, following this example, the long overdue development of upper Fifth Avenue would surely take hold and Millionaire's Row would finally begin (fig. 279). The spacious ground that surrounded this mansion, Schuyler believed, was especially important, for it set a new standard of "suburbanization" for other wealthy citizens to follow. Not to be mistaken for the look of the increasingly popular American suburb, however, this mansion offered an example of the more refined appearance of the elegant English "house" on the edge of town. The architects Babb, Cook and Willard through their choice of "heavy quoining, the heavy window framing in stone, the heavy cornice, the huge urns, give the whole the air of the 'comfortable bourgeoisie.' "[5]

Ladies Mile would not be excluded from this wave of redevelopment in the late 1890s. When the drygoods wholesale and manufacturing industry invaded its streets, tall commercial structures and loft manufacturers began to dominate the Mile. Theaters, clubhouses, and luxury hotels had already begun to move uptown. The five-million dollar Waldorf Hotel, designed by Henry J. Hardenbergh, which opened its doors at Fifth Avenue and Thirty-third Street in 1893, marked the end of Ladies Mile as the fashionable address for hotels. This picturesque composition soon was joined by the taller Hotel Astoria in 1896, also designed by Hardenbergh, on the Thirty-fourth Street side of the block: the era of the skyscraper hotel had been born (fig. 280). In this enormous caravansary, the Waldorf-Astoria, every personal desire could be fulfilled without ever venturing outside its walls: lectures, receptions in one of forty different rooms, spectacles and vaudeville entertainment on the rooftop were common features of the hotel. In addition, this massive building held 1,500 guests, serviced by almost as great a staff that included 150 hallboys, 400 waiters, and 250 chambermaids. An enor-

Fig. 279. Andrew Carnegie residence, Fifth Avenue and Ninety-first Street, ca. 1903. Designed by Babb, Cook and Willard in 1899–1900. (Courtesy of the Museum of the City of New York, New York City)

Fig. 280. Fifth Avenue, looking south from above Thirty-fifth Street, ca. 1899. The Waldorf-Astoria Hotel, the first skyscraper hotel, dominated Fifth Avenue between Thirty-third and Thirty-fourth streets, dwarfing the once monstrous Stewart mansion to its north across Thirty-fourth Street. The hotel was demolished in 1929 when the Empire State Building was erected. (Courtesy of the New-York Historical Society, New York City)

Fig. 281. Bank of the Metropolis (left), northwest corner of Sixteenth Street and Union Square West, 1905. The sixteen-story skyscraper, designed by Bruce Price in 1901, was symbolic of the tall structures invading Ladies Mile in the early twentieth century and hastening the retreat of the fashionable shopping district up Fifth Avenue above Thirty-fourth Street. The Union Building, a Moorish-Venetian structure designed by Alfred Zucker in 1891, stands next to the bank. (Courtesy of the New-York Historical Society, New York City)

mous electric plant using sixteen tons of coal per day powering sixteen elevators, a plant making fifty tons of ice per day, and a huge set of boilers heating hot water for all of the suites, were additional luxuries.[6]

More than a dozen ladies' tailoring establishments could be found in the 1900 business directories of New York, in close proximity to the new Waldorf-Astoria Hotel. Downtown along Ladies Mile, the Spingler Building (5–9 Union Square West), constructed in 1896, anticipated the coming decades that would turn the area into a wholesale manufacturing district. By 1900, the Spingler Building contained many shirtwaist-makers in its upper stories. The following year, Bruce Price designed the sixteen-story office tower for the Bank of the Metropolis on the northwest corner of Sixteenth Street and Union Square West (fig. 281). Here, too, the upper floors were rented to at least three shirtwaist-makers, three different ladies' and childrens' undergarment manufacturers, in addition to six different architectural offices.[7] The side streets near Ladies Mile were also invaded by lofty buildings used to house the expanding garment industry that now reached as far north as Thirty-sixth Street. Ten- and twelve-story loft buildings, sometimes as narrow as one city lot, were erected by the hundreds, flooding the fashionable shopping district with thousands of sweatshop workers who had little extra money to purchase the goods in the fancy shop windows along Ladies Mile, but lent the area an unsavory quality.[8]

Ladies Mile was growing shabby, a tarnished grande dame; luxury retail shops moved north, relocating along Fifth Avenue above Twenty-third Street and as far north as Forty-seventh Street. A shopper's account in 1901 noted, just as accounts had been noting since 1830, that retail

> invades old houses, dwelling-places of magnates who within a score of years have moved into the Fifties. It transformed these houses into show-rooms for ladies' tailor-made dresses, for bonnets, imported wraps, and costumes, lingerie and fur . . . all specialties at treble the cost of those found on any side street. No department stores exist here and only one or two specially constructed buildings, most of the stores, in fact, occupying only the lower floors. The rooms above are used by artists and photographers, and for bachelor apartments, rents being proportionately as high here as in those streets in the tenement-house district where trade has been driven out-of-doors.[9]

The department and jewelry stores would soon follow the specialty shops. Tiffany led the way, as it had done when it first located on Ladies Mile in 1867, by moving in 1905, followed by Gorham. Both of these stores relocated on opposite corners of Fifth Avenue and Thirty-sixth Street. B. Altman relocated at the same time; Bonwit and Teller soon followed in 1911, and both Lord and Taylor and Arnold Constable moved to Fifth Avenue near Fortieth Street in 1914.[10]

In the early years of the 1900s, lower Park Avenue above Union Square to Thirtieth Street, was completely reconstructed with at least fifteen new loft structures. The largest of them covered an entire city block, the smallest, nearly half a block; the tallest stood twenty stories high, the lowest only twelve. These were strictly commercial buildings, unlike the earlier Tiffany Building or Gorham

Fig. 282. Fourth Avenue (renamed Park Avenue South sometime in the early twentieth century), west side, view from Eighteenth Street toward Twenty-third Street, 1906. A strictly commercial structure, the American Lithograph Company Building, erected in the late 1890s, rose thirteen stories from sidewalk to cornice line, dominating almost a quarter of the block and overshadowing the older Belvedere house standing to its south. (Courtesy of the New-York Historical Society, New York City)

Building along Ladies Mile, which were American modifications of European residential palazzos. These new buildings were dominated by economic principles and practical requirements so that the maximum amount of unrestricted floor space was planned both horizontally and vertically. the ideal structure was square in shape, usually sited on a corner in order to obtain the greatest amount of light for its upper stories (fig. 282). Upon these austere commercial boxes the classical orders were usually hung, sometimes exploding into cupolas and temples at their rooftops, which, however, did not relieve the massiveness that marked the twentieth-century Manhattan streetscape.[11]

Also in 1900, the garishness of Fifth Avenue below Forty-seventh Street—with its intrusive electric lights, advertising signs, stoops and storefronts randomly obstructing its sidewalks, and its side-street sweatshops pouring out workers who clogged the avenue at noontime and destroyed its atmosphere of luxury retailing—led the Fifth Avenue Association to call for rational control of the avenue's physical appearance. A disastrous fire in the Triangle Shirtwaist Company's loft near Washington Square killed 145 employees in 1911 and brought still greater agitation among businessmen for the passage of a comprehensive zoning ordinance controlling building heights, massing, and land uses across the city.

In the years between 1860 and 1900, market values had begun to dominate land development, the consumer arts, styles of architecture and leisure time. Manhattan seemed to be an island in flux—everything appeared to be adrift, to be exchanged and to be consumed; anyone could build what he liked and where he liked, with few regulations. No central image, no dominating view existed to organize this city into a structural whole. The call for a regulatory plan for Fifth Avenue and the creation of a comprehensive zoning ordinance for the city reflect a new way of visualizing urban form, an attempt, for the first time, to abstract, to draw the city's architectural sites and structural forms into a unified order. Urban space in the twentieth century would be not only an exchangeable commodity, and an exhibitionistic realm for the display of consumer items, it would also be arranged so that it enhanced and promoted the circulation of capital. The needs of corporate capitalism in the early twentieth century posed a new type of metropolitan question: how could harbors, highways, public markets, and railroad networks be coordinated into a comprehensive plan; how might housing and health services for the working population be regulated and managed from a central authority; and how would overcrowding and social unrest be controlled and dispelled? Concepts of efficiency, functionality, and utility begin to invade this urban panorama. The urban critic of the twentieth century would reach out to establish an ideal system of balanced surveillance and regulation, believing that the continually expanding metropolis could be reordered and rationally controlled through ever-increasing scientific and technical knowledge.

The "small white cloud," Sullivan admitted, had come from the East for it had been architects such as McKim, Mead and White and Richard Morris Hunt who perfected the monumental architectural designs of the 1893 World's Fair. But the "dark dim cloud" was the new tendency within American capitalism toward organization, centralization, and intense commercialism, and it too in the guise of a rational city plan and regulatory controls held out an architectural and urban significance that in time would reorder the twentieth-century space of Manhattan.

NOTES

INTRODUCTION: CONTROLLING MANHATTAN'S DESIGN

1. E. M. Barry, "Royal Academy Lectures on Architecture," *The Builder* 38 (1880): 59–61.

2. Sigfried Giedion, *Mechanization Takes Command: A Contribution To Anonymous History* (New York: Oxford University Press, 1948): 329–88.

3. "Very Tall Buildings," *The Architect* 30 (September, 1883): 155. Quoted in Dudley Arnold Lewis, "Evaluations of American Architecture by European Critics: 1875–1900" (Ph.D. diss., University of Wisconsin, 1962): 365.

4. A. D. F. Hamlin, "The Battle of Styles," *Architectural Record* 1 (1892): 265–75, 405–13.

5. "Marble, Iron and Zinc Palaces in New York," *The Builder* 36 (1878): 422.

6. Excellent analyses of mass culture and modernism are contained in the following articles: Thomas Crow, "Modernism and Mass Culture in the Visual Arts," in B. H. D. Buchloh, S. Builbaut, and D. Solkin, eds., *Modernism and Modernity* (Halifax: Press of Nova Scotia College of Art and Design, 1983): 215–64; and Andreas Huyssen, "Adorno in Reverse: From Hollywood to Richard Wagner," *New German Critique* 29 (Spring/Summer 1983): 8–38.

7. For a detailed explanation of this discourse, see M. Christine Boyer, *Dreaming the Rational City: The Myth of American City Planning* (Cambridge, Mass.: MIT Press, 1983).

CHAPTER ONE: THE INHERITANCE OF THE GRID

1. Turpin C. Bannister, "Early Town Planning in New York State," *Journal of the Society of Architectural Historians* 3 (Jan.–April 1943): 36–42.

2. From the text on the margin of a map entitled "The City of New York as Laid Out by the Commissioners with the Surrounding Country," by then Secretary and Surveyor, John Randel Jr., 1812 (located in a folder marked "Randel Notes" at the Topographical Bureau, Manhattan Borough President's Office, New York City).

3. Rebecca Shanor, "Manhattan's Paper Streets: Proposals to Relieve the 1811 Gridiron Plan" (Master's thesis, Columbia University, 1982): 20.

4. I. N. Phelps Stokes, "The War of 1812. Period of Inventing, Prosperity, and Progress 1815–1841," *The Iconography of Manhattan,* vol. 3 (New York: Robert H. Dodd, 1918).

5. Text accompanying the Commissioners' Map as adopted by DeWitt Clinton, mayor of the city of New York (March 1811).

6. Ibid.

7. Stokes, *Iconography*, vol. 3: 1705.

8. Edward K. Spann, *The New Metropolis: New York City, 1840–1857* (New York: Columbia University Press, 1981): 161.

9. Stokes, *Iconography*, vol. 3: 1710.

10. "Theodore Roosevelt Park: 1807–1958," *Curator: A Quarterly of the American Museum of Natural History* 3, no. 2 (1960): 62.

11. Stokes, *Iconography*, vol. 3: 885.

12. Scott L. Jones, "Historical Analysis of Saint John's Park (Hudson Square) in the City of New York, c. 1800–1867" (Unpublished manuscript, 1981).

13. John B. Pine, "Gramercy Park," in Henry C. Brown, *Valentine's Manual of Old New York* (New York: Valentine's Manual, Inc., 1920): 193–248; and J. M. Shaffer, "Report on Gramercy Park in New York City" (Unpublished manuscript, 1980).

14. Mary C. Henderson, *The City and the Theatre* (Clifton, New Jersey: James T. White and Co., 1973): 73–74.

15. Ibid., 74

16. Thomas M. Garrett, "A History of Pleasure Gardens in New York City: 1700–1865" (Ph.D. diss., New York University, 1978): 555–61.

17. Ibid., 561–67.

18. Quoted in Leonard J. Simutus, "Frederick Law Olmsted's Later Years: Landscape Architecture and the Spirit of Place" (Ph.D. diss., University of Minnesota, 1971): 87.

19. W. Schermerhorn, "Letter to James W. Beekman" (December 18, 1852), Beekman Papers, New-York Historical Society. Quoted in E. T. McDougall, "The Political Economy of a Public Park" (Unpublished manuscript, 1973).

20. "Sunday in Jone's Wood," *Harper's Weekly* 3 (Nov. 5, 1859): 70.

21. Allan Nevins, *New York Evening Post* (New York: Boni and Liverright, 1922): 197.

22. *New York Daily Times* (June 30, 1853): 3.

23. "The Daily Press and Real Estate," *Real Estate Record and Builders' Guide* (hereafter noted as *Real Estate Record*) (Oct. 14, 1876): 761.

24. "Central Park Lots," *Real Estate Record* 18 (Nov. 18, 1876): 851–52.

25. Ibid., 851.

26. "The Fifth Avenue," *Real Estate Record* 21 (June 15, 1878): 315–16.

27. F. L. Olmsted developed plans in 1873 for Morningside Park to be located on a steep hillside near the Bloomingdale Plateau.

28. Martha J. Lamb, "Riverside Park," *Manhattan Illustrated Magazine* 4 (July 1884): 52.

29. The Limits of Central Park," *Real Estate Record* 21 (June 29, 1878): 556.

30. "Riverside Drive," *Real Estate Record* 35 (April 25, 1885): 461.

31. "Recent and Prospective Park Improvements," *Real Estate Record* 41 (June 16, 1888): 768.

32. *Real Estate Record* 47 (Oct. 8, 1888): 1188.

33. *Real Estate Record* 45 (Feb. 22, 1890): 253.

34. *Real Estate Record* 44 (Oct. 5, 1889): 1323–33.

35. *Real Estate Record* 44 (Oct. 11, 1889): 1364.

36. *Real Estate Record* 44 (Nov. 2, 1889): 1465–66.

37. *Real Estate Record* 44 (Dec. 28, 1889): 1782.

38. Amos W. Wright, "World's Fair of 1889 and 1892," *Harper's Weekly* 33 (August 10, 1889): 652. Quoted in Reid Badger, *The Great American Fair: The World's Columbian Exposition and American Culture* (Chicago: Nelson Hall, 1979).

39. *Real Estate Record* 45 (March 1, 1890): 291; and *Real Estate Record* 45 (March 15, 1890): 363.

40. *Real Estate Record* 45 (April 12, 1890): 511.

41. "Shall The City Hall Be Removed?" *Real Estate Record* 47 (April 11, 1891): 554-56.

42. Ernest Flagg, "The Plan of New York, and How to Improve It," *Scribner's Monthly* 3 (August 1904): 256.

43. F. L. Olmsted, and J. James R. Cross, "Preliminary Report of the Landscape Architect and the Civil and Topographical Engineer, upon the Laying out of the Twenty-third and Twenty-fourth Wards," in Albert Fein, *Landscape into Cityscape* (New York: Van Nostrand Reinhold Co., 1981): 353–54.

44. J. F. Harder, "The City's Plan," *Municipal Affairs* 2 (1898): 25–47.

45. "Urban Housing III," *American Architect and Building News* 3 (May 1878): 173.

46. "Urban Housing I," *American Architect and Building News* 3 (March, 1878): 91.

47. Montgomery Schuyler, "The Small City House in New York," *Architectural Record* 8 (April–June 1899): 360.

48. Richard M. Hunt, "Architecture," *Crayon* 4 (July 1857): 218.

49. "The Size of Building Lots," *Real Estate Record* 24 (Dec. 6, 1879): 979.

50. "The Adornment of Our City," *Real Estate Record* 24 (Nov. 22, 1879): 934.

51. "An Arcade Store," *Real Estate Record* 52 (Dec. 2, 1893): 680.

52. "Opportunities Lost," *Real Estate Record* 34 (Dec. 13, 1894): 1248.

53. Jean Schopfer, ''The Plan of the City,'' *Architectural Record* 12 (Dec. 1902): 692–703.

54. Franz Winkler (Montgomery Schuyler), ''Mitigating the 'Gridiron' Street Plan,'' *Architectural Record* 29 (May 1911): 379–96.

55. ''The Problem of the Street System of New York,'' *Architectural Record* 13 (Feb. 1903): 175–79.

56. Charles R. Lamb, ''Report of Thoroughfares Committee,'' *Municipal Art Society Bulletin No. 5* (1904): 1.

CHAPTER 2: AN ECONOMIC BASE FOR MANHATTAN ARCHITECTURE

1. Montgomery Schuyler, ''Recent Building In New York,'' *Harper's Weekly* 67 (June–November, 1883): 561.

2. ''About Ourselves,'' *Real Estate Record* 36 (March 7, 1885): 227–28.

3. ''American Architecture,'' *Real Estate Record* 47 (Feb. 7, 1891): 191.

4. ''A Bill to License Architects,'' *Real Estate Record* 47 (Feb. 7, 1891): 192–94; and ''The Bill to Regulate the Practice of Architecture,'' *Real Estate Record* 47 (March 28, 1891): 474–75.

5. ''The Crisis of Real Estate,'' *Real Estate Record* 16 (Nov. 27, 1875): 761–62.

6. For a similar treatment of real estate speculation in nineteenth-century Paris, see Marcel Roncayolo, ''La production de la ville,'' in Maurice Agulhon, ed., *La ville de L'Age Industriel* (Paris: Seuil, 1983): 73–155.

7. ''To the Memory of David Goodman Croly,'' *Real Estate Record* 43 (Supplement, May 18, 1889): 720.

8. ''Fashion as an Element of Value,'' *Real Estate Record* 18 (October 21, 1876): 779–80; and ''Vacant Lots in the Fashionable Quarter,'' *Real Estate Record* 23 (April 12, 1879): 287.

9. *A History of Real Estate, Building and Architecture in New York City* (New York: The Record and Guide 1898). Reprint (New York: Arno Press, 1967): 578.

10. ''Big Bonanza Buildings,'' *Real Estate Record* 17 (April 8, 1876): 255–56.

11. ''The Crisis of Real Estate—II,'' *Real Estate Record* 16 (Nov. 27, 1875): 761–62.

12. *A History of Real Estate*: 58–59.

13. *A History of Real Estate*: 64.

14. Ibid.

15. ''The Crisis of Real Estate—III,'' *Real Estate Record* 16 (Dec. 11, 1875): 789–90.

16. ''The Economics of Building,'' *Real Estate Record* 21 (Jan. 19, 1878): 43–45.

17. ''The Crisis of Real Estate—III,'' *Real Estate Record* 16 (Dec. 11, 1875): 789–90.

18. ''The Situation,'' *Real Estate Record* 18 (Dec. 2, 1876): 887–88.

19. ''New Era of Real Estate Speculation,'' *Real Estate Record* 23 (May 24, 1879): 419–20.

20. ''The Crisis of Real Estate—V,'' *Real Estate Record* 17 (Jan. 1, 1876): 1–2.

21. Ibid., 2.

22. ''The Crisis of Real Estate—VIII,'' *Real Estate Record* 17 (Jan. 22, 1876): 53–54.

23. Ibid. Houses sold in the fashionable district in 1876 averaged over $75,000 each. The houses below were offered at the following sale prices:

1 house	254 Madison Avenue (O'Reilly, builder)	$65,000
2 houses	Fortieth Street between Fifth and Sixth avenues (O'Reilly, builder)	$60,000 each
1 house	234 Madison Avenue (Rathbone, builder)	$100,000
1 house	623 Fifth Avenue (Rathbone, builder)	$100,000
1 house	583 Fifth Avenue (Duggin, builder)	$75,000
1 house	614 Fifth Avenue (Duggin, builder)	$50,000

24. *A History of Real Estate*: 70.

25. "Winter Review," *Real Estate Record* 21 (Feb. 16, 1878): 131–33.

26. "Conditions and Prospects of Building," *Real Estate Record* 23 (June 21, 1879): 505–506.

27. "Available Lots in the Fashionable Quarter," *Real Estate Record* 21 (Feb. 23, 1878): 154–55.

28. *A History of Real Estate*: 71.

29. *A History of Real Estate*: 72.

30. "The Situation of the Real Estate Market," *Real Estate Record* 26 (Oct. 9, 1880): 869–70; and "A Much Needed Improvement," *Real Estate Record* 26 (Dec. 18, 1880): 1110.

31. "The Cause of the Trouble," *Real Estate Record* 33 (Aug. 2, 1884): 809; and "The Real Estate Prospect," *Real Estate Record* 37 (Jan. 2, 1886): 1–2.

32. "Real Estate and the Financial Situation," *Real Estate Record* 51 (May 20, 1893): 786–88.

33. *A History of Real Estate*: 78–79.

34. "The March of Improvements," *Real Estate Record* 20 (Sept. 15, 1877): 709–711.

35. "The Centre of Fashionable Gravity," *Real Estate Record* 22 (Dec. 7, 1878): 983–84.

36. *A History of Real Estate*: 90–94.

37. Ibid., 103–194.

38. "The Building Boom: Its Causes and Prospects," *Real Estate Record* 43 (March 30, 1889): 422–23.

39. "Real Estate During 1890," *Real Estate Record* 47 (Jan. 10, 1891): 32–35.

40. "A Review of the Year," *Real Estate Record* 47 (Jan. 23, 1892): 111–122.

41. *A History of Real Estate*: 106–111.

42. "The Real Estate Market Last Year," *Real Estate Record* 51 (Jan. 28, 1893): 115–120.

43. For a full treatment of the role of land in the development of nineteenth-century America see James Willard Hurst, *Law and the Conditions of Freedom in the Nineteenth Century United States.* (Madison: University of Wisconsin Press, 1956).

CHAPTER 3: LADIES MILE: THE RISE OF A VICTORIAN AMUSEMENT DISTRICT

1. Martha Lamb, *History of the City of New York, Its Origins, Rise and Progress*, vol. 3 (New York: A. S. Barnes and Co., 1896): 52.

2. Quoted from the "Recollections of Mary Eno Pinchot," Pinchot Papers in Nancy Jean Carrs, "Madison Square, The Eno Family and the Fifth Avenue Hotel" (Unpublished manuscript, 1891).

3. *History of Architecture and Building Trades of Greater New York*, vol. I (New York: Union History Company, 1899): 169.

4. Allan Nevins, ed., *The Diary of Philip Hone, 1828–1851*, vol. 2 (New York: Dodd, Mead and Co., 1927): 896.

5. "New York Daguerreotyped," *Putnam's Monthly*, vol. 1 (Feb. 1853): 126.

6. A detailed report on the history of Union Square from 1811 to the present, including a survey of the conveyance records of every lot on the square from the New York City Municipal Records, can be found in Elsa Gilbertson and Sophia Schachter, "Union Square" (Unpublished manuscript, 1982). See also William Pelletrau, *Early New York Houses* (New York: Francis P. Harper, 1900): 187; I. N. Phelps Stokes, *The Iconography of Manhattan, 1498–1909*, vol. 3 (New York: Robert H. Dodd, 1918–1928):705; and D. C. Brinton Thompson, *Ruggles of New York* (New York: Columbia University Press, 1946): 64.

7. Pelletrau, *Early New York Houses*: 68.

8. Land uses and building changes for Ladies Mile were traced by Columbia University students from tax records, building permits, city directories, insurance maps, and conveyance records. This information was compiled in "Ladies Mile: The History of the Retail Shopping District of Manhattan in the Nineteenth Century" (Studio Report, Columbia University, 1981).

9. "New York Daguerreotyped," *Putnam's Monthly*, vol. 2 (March 1854): 233.

10. Carl Leone, "Walks Through Fifth Avenue" (New York: published by the author, 1853).

11. It has been noted by architectural historians that the rage for mansard roofs was actually created by tax problems rather than stylistic concerns. New York laws taxed the stories included beneath a mansard as attic, not floor space, and thus reduced overall taxes that otherwise would have been paid for a taller structure. See, for example, Ellen Kramer, "The Domestic Architecture of Detlef Lienau" (Ph.D. diss., New York University, 1957): 103; and Mary Ann Clegg Smith, "The Commercial Architecture of John Butler Snook" (Ph.D. diss., Pennsylvania State University, 1974).

12. Jay E. Cantor, "A Monument of Trade," *Winterthur* 10 (1975): 165–197.

13. "The Fifth Avenue," *Real Estate Record* 21 (June 15, 1878): 516; and "Patch Work," *Real Estate Record* 21 (July 27, 1878): 628.

14. Carrs, "Madison Square," and Marcus Benjamin, *Historical Sketch of Madison Square* (New York: Meriden Monographs #1, 1894): 14–15.

15. Benjamin, *Historical Sketch of Madison Square*: 14.

16. Carrs, "Madison Square."

17. Carrs, "Madison Square," and W. Johnson Quinn Collection of Historical Materials on New York City Hotels (The New-York Historical Society).

18. Winston Weisman, "Commercial Palaces of New York: 1845–1875," *Art Bulletin* 36 (Dec. 1954): 288.

19. Carrs, "Madison Square," and W. Johnson Quinn Collection.

20. John Summerson, "London, the Artifact," in H. J. Dyos and Michael Wolff, eds., *The Victorian City*, vol. 1 (London: Routledge and Kegan Paul, 1973): 324.

21. Joseph Durso, *Madison Square Garden* (New York: Simon and Schuster, 1979).

22. Edward R. Ellis, *The Epic of New York City*, (New York: Coward-McCann, 1966): 358.

23. *The 1866 Visitors Guide to the City of New York* (New York: John F. Trow, Printer, 1866): 68.

24. Lloyd Morris, *Incredible New York* (New York: Random House, 1951): 111.

25. Moses King, ed., *King's Handbook of New York City*, 2d ed. (Boston: Moses King, Publisher, 1893): 226.

26. Mrs. H. M. Plunkett, "Modern Hotels," *Scribner's Monthly* 6 (1873): 488.

27. A. J. Gale, "English Impressions of American Architecture," *The Builder* 49 (Dec. 19, 1885): 853.

28. "Two Popular Architects," *American Architect and Building News* 5 (March 1, 1879): 71.

29. "Mr. Stewart's Hotel for Working People," *Appleton's Journal* 2 (July 3, 1869): 419.

30. Harry E. Resseguie, "The Decline and Fall of the Commercial Empire of A. T. Stewart," *Business History Review* 36 (Autumn 1962): 275.

31. Most of the hotels near Ladies Mile continued to operated until the early 1900s. The closing dates of some of the important ones are the Union Square Hotel ca. 1880, the Hoffman House ca. 1880, the Clarendon Hotel ca. 1900, the Everett Hotel ca. 1907, the Fifth Avenue Hotel ca. 1900, the Saint Denis Hotel ca. 1920, the Park Avenue Hotel ca. 1920, and the Buckingham Hotel ca. 1920.

32. Mary C. Henderson, *The City and the Theatre* (Clifton, New Jersey: James T. White and Co., 1973): 148.

33. "Our Crystal Palace," *Putnam's Monthly* 2 (August 1853): 121.

34. Arthur Hornblow, *A History of the Theatre in America*, vol. 22 (Philadelphia: J. B. Lippincott and Co., 1919): 166.

35. Hornblow, *A History of the Theatre in America*: 173.

36. Simon Tidworth, *Theatres: An Architectural and Cultural History* (New York: Praeger Publishers, 1973): 154.

37. Donald C. Mullin, *The Development of the Playhouse* (Berkeley: University of California Press, 1970).

38. William C. Young, *Documents of American Theatre History, Famous American Playhouses: 1717–1899*, vol. 1 (Chicago: American Library Association, 1973): 64.

39. Hornblow, *A History of the Theatre*: 167–8.

40. Mullin, *The Development of the Playhouse*: 116–131.

41. The Olympia Theatre was the largest and first real theater complex in New York, combining four different theaters in one building, with street-floor cafés, billiard and bowling rooms, Turkish baths, and a roof garden. Young, *Documents of American Theatre History*: 243–46.

42. Jack Poggi, *Theatre in America: The Impact of Economic Forces: 1870–1967* (New York: Cornell University Press, 1966).

43. Glenn Hughes, *A History of the American Theatre, 1770–1950* (London: Samuel French, 1951): 256.

44. Young, *Documents of American Theatre History*: 192.

45. The following table lists some of the dramatic agents and costumers who located on Union Square; the information is compiled from New York city business directories in "Ladies Mile: The History of The Retail Shopping District":

1880 Union Square East	4	Lena Klueber, costumer
		Francis Koehler, costumer
	10	James E. Johnson, dramatic agent
		Morris Simonds, dramatic agent
	12	Charles R. Gardner, dramatic agent
		Samuel B. Duffield, dramatic agent
	14	Wall and Hamly, dramatic agent
		Horace Wallace, dramatic agent
East Fourteenth Street	14	J. Alexander Brown, dramatic agent
1890 Union Square West	3	E. M. Pirsson, general agent
	21	Ludwig M. Rubern, dramatic agent
	25	James H. Phipps, dramatic agent
East Fourteenth Street	64	J. Alexander Brown, dramatic agent

46. Henderson, *The City and the Theatre*: 134.

47. Quoted in Henderson (without attribution), *The City and the Theatre*: 121.

48. Irving Hall was never a successful theater; it was demolished in 1888 and replaced by a new theater, the Amberg, devoted exclusively to German drama. Greatly remodeled, it was the only theater in the vicinity of Union Square that still stood into the late twentieth century until it was demolished in 1984. Thomas Allston Brown, *A History of the New York Stage: From the First Performance in 1732 to 1901*, vol. 2 (New York: Dodd, Mead and Co., 1903): 352.

49. Wallack's Theatre, following the move uptown by fashionable residences, relocated on Thirtieth Street and Broadway in the 1890s. The old theater on Thirteenth Street became a theater for German-language productions; in 1883 it became the popular Star Theatre until it was demolished in 1901 to make way for a tall office structure. Brown, *A History of the New York Stage*, vol. 2: 244–343.

50. P. T. Barnum acquired Nixon's Alhambra Circus in 1872, but it soon burned to the ground. Brown, *A History of the New York Stage*, vol. 2: 352.

51. Henderson, *The City and the Theatre*: 117.

52. By 1874, Tammany Hall's burlesque and vaudeville hall had become a German theater, taking on a new life in 1881 when Tony Pastor's New Fourteenth Street Theatre opened. During the late 1880s and 1890s it was the most popular burlesque and vaudeville house in the city; Brown, *A History of the New York Stage*, vol. 3; 80–84; 619.

53. Young, *Documents of American Theatre History*: 159–99 and Hughes, *A History of the American Theatre*: 203.

54. Young, *Documents of American Theatre History*: 198.

55. Mullin, *The Development of the Playhouse*: 116–131.

56. Brown, *A History of the New York Stage*, vol. 3: 94–145.

57. The Union Square Theatre was destroyed by fire in 1888. A new theater designed by John E. Terhune and Leopold Eldlitz took its place. By the 1920s, it had become a movie theater and was demolished by 1936. Brown, *A History of the New York Stage*, vol. 3: 145–90; and Young, *Documents of American Theatre History*: 202–204.

58. Brown, *A History of the New York Stage*, vol. 3: 190–208; and Young: *Documents of American Theatre History*, 205–208.

59. Brown, *A History of the New York Stage*, vol. 3: 591–92.

60. Mullin, *The Development of the Playhouse*: 116–31.

61. The Lyceum Theatre was demolished in 1902, to make room for yet another extension of the Metropolitan Life Insurance Company. Tidworth, *Theatres*: 177–98.

62. Hughes, *A History of the American Theatre*: 295; and Tidworth, *Theatres*: 177–98.

63. The following table lists the dates when theaters near Ladies Mile were demolished or radically altered:

Academy of Music	Became a vaudeville theater, later a motion picture house, and was razed in 1926 when the headquarters of the Consolidated Edison Company was erected.
Irving Hall	Demolished in 1888, new theatrical structure erected in 1888, extant in remodeled form until demolished in 1984.
Tammany Hall	Burned and rebuilt in 1888, demolished 1928.
Wallack's Theatre	Demolished in 1901.
Booth's Theatre	Converted to McCreery's Dry Goods Store in 1883, demolished 1900s.
Union Square Theatre	Remodeled in 1888, by 1914 it was a theatre for film and burlesque, demolished in 1936.
Park Theatre	Burned 1882. Never rebuilt.
Chickering Hall	Remodeled for business in 1892, demolished 1900s.
Madison Square Theatre	Demolished 1908.
Lyceum Theatre	Demolished for the Metropolitan Life Insurance Company, 1902.

64. Elsa Gilbertson and Sophia Schachter, "Union Square,": 31; and Daniel Spillane, *History of the American Piano Forte*, (New York: Spillane Publishing, 1890): 289–90.

65. Quoted in Russell Lynes, *The Tastemakers: The Shaping of American Popular Taste*, (New York: Dover Publications, Inc., 1980): 42.

66. Bryan's art gallery closed in 1876. Bryan donated his collection to the New-York Historical Society.

67. Lynes, *The Tastemakers*: 42–46.

68. Gilbertson and Schachter, "Union Square": 66–68; and "Sculpture in America," *Harper's Weekly* 58 (April 1879): 670.

69. Peter Pollack, *The Picture History of Photography*, rev. ed. (New York: Harry Abrams, Inc., 1969): 224–26; and Robert Taft, *Photography and the American Scene* (New York: Dover Publications, Inc., 1964): 346.

70. Alan Burnham, "The New York Architecture of Richard Morris Hunt," *The Journal of the Society of Architectural Historians* 11 (May 1952): 9–14.

71. Henderson, *The City and the Theatre*: 132.

72. Junius Browne, *The Great Metropolis: A Mirror of New York* (Hartford: American Publishing Co., 1869): 266.

73. Data summarized from New York city business directories in "Ladies Mile: The History of the Retail Shopping District."

74. Francis Gerry Fairfield, *The Clubs of New York* (New York: Henry L. Hinter, Publisher, 1873): 229.

75. Browne, *The Great Metropolis*: 442.

76. *Club Women of New York* (New York: The Mail and Express Co., 1904): 8.

77. *Forty Years on Fifth Avenue* (New York: The Fifth Avenue Bank, 1915); and Fairfield, *The Clubs*: 10–11.

78. Fairfield, *The Clubs*: 42.

79. The Jerome Mansion, after 1881, became the home of the Turf Club, the Madison Club, the University Club, the Manhattan Club, and various other twentieth-century clubs, until it was demolished circa 1973. *New York City Architecture: Selection from the Historic American Buildings Survey #7* (Washington, D.C., U.S. Department of Interior, National Park Service, July 1969).

80. This section on "Political Protests" draws heavily from Sophia Schachter's "A Public Place of Assembly," in Gilbertson and Schachter, "Union Square": 47–65.

81. Allan Nevins and Milton Thomas, eds., *The Diary of George Templeton Strong*, vol. 2 (New York: MacMillan Co., 1952): 398.

82. Nevins and Thomas, *The Diary of George Templeton Strong*, vol. 2: 422.

83. "The Great Union Meeting," *Harper's Weekly* 4 (Jan 7, 1860): 1.

84. Nevins and Thomas, *The Diary of George Templeton Strong*, vol. 3: 128.

85. Nevins and Thomas, *The Diary of George Templeton Strong*, vol. 3: 427.

86. Nevins and Thomas, *The Diary of George Templeton Strong*, vol. 3: 53.

87. Joseph G. Rayback, *A History of American Labor* (New York, 1968): 170; and Irving Howe, *World of Our Fathers* (New York: Harcourt Brace Jovanovich, 1980): 119.

88. Emma Goldman, *Living My Life* (New York: Alfred A. Knopf, 1934, 1977): 79–80.

89. Quoted by Elsa Gilbertson, in Gilbertson and Schachter, "Union Square," from the Sewing Machine Scrapbook, Bella C. Landauer Collection, New-York Historical Society.

90. Theodore Zeldin, *France 1848–1945*, vol. 1 (Oxford: Clarendon Press, 1973).

91. Jean Baudrillard, "Sign Function and Class Logic" in *For a Critique of the Political Economy of the Sign* (St. Louis: Telos Press, 1981).

92. "The Growth of Clubs in New York City," *Real Estate Record* 45, Club Number Supplement (March 8, 1890): 1.

93. Quoted in "The Growth of Clubs."

94. Ibid.

95. Richard Terdiman, "Structures of Initiation: On Semiotic Education and its Contradictions in Balzac," *The Pedagogical Imperative: Teaching as Literary Genre, The Yale French Studies* 63 (1982): 203.

96. John Crawford Browne, "Early Days of the Department Store," *Valentine's Manual of Old New York*, vol. 5 (1921): 97–148.

97. *New York Herald* (Sept. 18, 1846).

98. P. B. Wight, "A Millionaire's Architectural Investment," *American Architect and Building News* 1 (May 6, 1876): 147–49.

99. *Broadway Journal*, March 22, 1845, quoted in Mary Ann Clegg Smith, "The Commercial Architecture of John Butler Snook": 26.

100. Robert Hendrickson, *The Grand Emporiums: The Illustrated History of America's Great Department Stores* (New York: Stein and Day, 1979).

101. "New York Daguerreotyped," *Putnam's Monthly*, vol. 1 (April 1853) 353–68.

102. Winston Weisman, "Commercial Palaces of New York": 386.

103. Michael B. Miller, *The Bon Marché: Bourgeois Culture and the Department Store: 1869–1920* (Princeton: Princeton University Press, 1981): 5.

104. Walter Benjamin, *Charles Baudelaire: A Lyric Poet in the Era of High Capitalism* (London: New Left Books, 1973): 56.

105. Browne, "Early Days of the Department Store."

106. "Stewart's Store," *Appleton's Journal* (April 9, 1870): 411–13.

107. Matthew Hale Smith, *Sunshine and Shadow in New York* (Hartford: J. B. Burr and Co., 1868): 59.

108. See, for example, Smith "The Commercial Architecture of John Butler Snook," and Weisman, "Commercial Palaces of New York."

109. Johann Friedrich Geist, *Arcades: The History of a Building Type* (Cambridge: MIT Press, 1983).

110. Miller, *The Bon Marché*.

111. P. B. Wight, "A Millionaire's Architectural Investment": 148.

112. Ibid.

113. Henry Van Brunt, "Cast Iron in Decorative Architecture," *Crayon* 6 (Jan. 1859): 18.

114. Leopold Eidlitz, "Cast Iron and Architecture," *Crayon* 6 (Jan. 1859): 21, 23.

115. Arnold Dudley Lewis, "Evaluations of American Architecture by European Critics: 1875–1900" (Ph.D. diss., University of Wisconsin, 1962): 366.

116. "Our Building Material: Stone Versus Iron," *Real Estate Record* 17 (March 4, 1876): 1.

117. "Iron Fronts," *Real Estate Record* 19 (March 24, 1877): 220–21.

118. *Soho—Cast Iron Historic District Designation Report* (New York: New York City Landmarks Preservation Commission, 1973): 10.

119. *Soho*: 11.

120. Montgomery Schuyler, "The Works of the Late Richard M. Hunt," in William H. Jordy and Ralph Coe, eds., *American Architecture and Other Writings: Montgomery Schuyler*, vol. 2 (Cambridge, Mass.: Harvard University Press, 1961): 517.

121. Schuyler, "The Works of the Late Richard M. Hunt": 518–19.

122. "Iron Fronts," *Real Estate Record* 19 (March 24, 1877): 220.

123. Margaret Gayle and Edmund V. Gillon, *Cast Iron Architecture in New York* (New York: Dover Publications, Inc., 1974): 162.

124. Weisman, "Commercial Palaces of New York."

125. Hendrickson, *The Grand Emporiums*.

126. "A Broadway Railroad," *Real Estate Record* 22 (Jan. 4, 1879): 1-2.

127. "A Broadway Railroad": 1.

128. "Broadway," *Real Estate Record* 18 (Nov. 11, 1876): 834.

129. "Choice Locations," *Real Estate Record* 25 (Jan. 17, 1880): 51–52.

130. "A Much Needed Improvement," *Real Estate Record* 26 (Dec. 18, 1880): 1110.

131. "Trade as an Element of Value," *Real Estate Record* 20 (Oct. 20, 1877): 805–806.

132. "Patch Work," *Real Estate Record* 22 (July 1878): 627–28.

133. "The Spingler Building," *Real Estate Record* 21 (March 30, 1878): 266–67.

134. "The Old Delmonico Corner," *Real Estate Record* 24 (Sept. 20, 1879): 740.

135. "Unimproved Real Estate Burdens," *Real Estate Record* 27 (April 9, 1881): 331.

136. "Yellow Houses," *Real Estate Record* 25 (April 3, 1880): 311.

137. "Stern's Great Department Store in Twenty-Third Street," *Real Estate Record* 22 (Nov. 2, 1878): 886.

138. Richard Harding Davis, *The Great Streets of the World* (London: James R. Osgood, McIlvaine and Co., 1892).

139. Sam A. MacKeever, *Glimpses of Gotham and City Characters* (New York: Richard K. Fox, 1881).

140. Helen Stuart Campbell, *Darkness and Daylight, Lights and Shadows of New York Life* (Hartford: A. D. Worthington and Co., 1892): 257.

141. Campbell, *Darkness and Daylight*: 698.

142. Thomas W. Knox, "Cunning Shoplifters, and Skillful Pickpockets," in Campbell, *Darkness and Daylight*: 698.

143. Edward Crapsey, *The Nether Side of New York: Or the Vice, Crime and Poverty of the Great Metropolis* (New York: Sheldon and Co., 1872): 145.

144. *The Gentleman's Directory of New York City, 1870.*

145. Peter Stryker, "The Lowest Depths of the Great American Metropolis," *The Pulpit and Rostrum* No. 38 (June 1866): 7–8.

146. *Lockwood's Illustrated Guide to New York City and its Environs* (New York: Howard Lockwood, 1872): 20.

147. *Lockwood's Illustrated Guide*: 20.

148. Charles H. Carpenter, Jr. and Mary Grace Carpenter, *Tiffany Silver* (New York: Dodd, Mead and Co., 1978): 26; 85–86.

149. Sophia Schachter, "Study of Business Directories," in "Ladies Mile."

150. "Stewart's Store," *Appleton's Journal*.

151. James D. McCabe, Jr., *Lights and Shadows of New York Life*. 1872. Reprint (New York: Farrar, Straus and Giroux, 1970): 385.

152. Lord and Taylor, *The History of Lord and Taylor* (New York: privately printed, 1929): 38–42.

153. Giedion, *Mechanization Takes Command*: v.

154. Frederick L. Lewton, "The Servant in the House: A Brief History of the Sewing Machine," *Annual Report of the Smithsonian Institution* (Washington, D.C.: The U.S. Government Printing Office, 1929): 583.

155. Lewton, "The Servant in the House": 582.

156. Gilbertson and Schachter, "Union Square": 34.

157. *History and Commerce in New York* (New York: American Publishing and Engraving Company, 1891): 6.

158. Isabel Ross, *Crusades and Crinolines* (New York: Harper and Row, 1963).

159. *Schaft's West Side Saturday Night* (1882).

160. Blanche Payne, *History of Costume* (New York: Harper and Row, 1965): 451.

161. James Laver, *Costume and Fashions: A Concise History*. Reprint (New York: Oxford University Press, 1983).

162. *Lockwood's Illustrated Guide:* 21.

163. Harriet Prescott Spofford, *Art Decoration Applied to Furniture* (New York: Harper and Brothers, 1877): 224.

164. Edgar de N. Mayhew and Minor Myers, Jr., *A Documentary History of American Interiors* (New York: Charles Scribner's Sons, 1980): 193–311.

165. *Ladies Shopping Guide and City Directory* (New York: Putnam's Sons, 1885).

166. Russell Lynes, *The Tastemakers* (New York: Dover Publications, Inc., 1980): 102.

167. H. Hudson Holly, "Modern Dwellings: Their Construction, Decoration, and Furniture," *Harper's Weekly* 53 (1876): 217–18.

168. "New York Household Taste," *The Builder* 36 (May 11, 1878): 477.

169. Giedion, *Mechanization Takes Command*: 387.

170. Spofford, *Art Decoration*: 168.

171. E. L. Godkin, *The Nation* 6 (Jan. 30, 1868) quoted in Allan Nevins, *The Emergence of Modern America: 1865–1878* (New York: MacMillan Co., 1957): 226–27.

172. *Home Decoration: Collected Papers (1886–1889)*: 1–2.

173. Clarence Cook, *The House Beautiful: Essays on Beds and Tables, Stools and Candlesticks* (New York: Scribner, Armstrong and Co., 1878): 318–19.

174. Cook, *The House Beautiful*: 286.

175. Giedion, *Mechanization Takes Command*: 390.

176. *History and Commerce of New York*: 107.

177. *Home Decoration*: 7.

178. "Household Decorative Items," *Real Estate Record* 32 (Sept. 22, 1883): 709–710.

179. "Home Decorative Notes," *Real Estate Record* 35 (May 9, 1885): 521.

180. "Home Decorative Notes," *Real Estate Record* (Jan. 24, 1885): 76.

181. "Home Decorative Notes," *Real Estate Record* 35 (March 21, 1885): 293.

182. "Home Decorative Notes," *Real Estate Record* 38 (Sept. 26, 1886): 1199.

183. "Home Decorative Notes," *Real Estate Record* 33 (Jan. 19, 1884): 55.

184. "Home Decorative Notes," *Real Estate Record* 35 (Feb. 14, 1885): 156.

185. "Home Decorative Notes," *Real Estate Record* 35 (April 18, 1885): 422.

186. "Home Decorative Notes," *Real Estate Record* 33 (Jan. 19, 1884): 55.

187. "Home Decorative Notes," *Real Estate Record* 33 (July 12, 1884): 741.

188. "Home Decorative Notes," *Real Estate Record* 34 (Nov. 22, 1884): 1173.

189. "Home Decorative Notes," *Real Estate Record* 32 (Sept. 29, 1883): 734.

190. Gilbertson and Schachter, "Union Square."

191. "Sky-Building in New York," *Building News* 45 (Sept. 7, 1883): 363.

192. Winston Weisman, "New York and the Problem of the First Skyscraper," *Journal of the Society of Architectural Historians* 12 (March 1953): 18.

193. "Sky-Building in New York," *Building News*.

194. Joseph Hudnut, *Architecture and the Spirit of Man* (Cambridge, Mass.: Harvard University Press, 1949): 212.

195. Montgomery Schuyler, "The 'Sky-Scraper' up to Date," *Architectural Record* 8 (Jan. 1899): 236.

196. *A History of Real Estate, Building and Architecture in New York City* (New York: The Record and Guide, 1898). Reprint (New York: Arno Press, 1967): 466.

197. Barr Ferree, "The Art of High Building," *Architectural Record* 15 (May 1904): 445–46.

198. Montgomery Schuyler, "The Evolution of the Skyscraper," *Scribner's Monthly* 46 (Sept. 1909): 259.

199. Montgomery Schuyler, "The Sky-Line of New York, 1881–1897," *Harper's Weekly* 41 (March 20, 1897): 295.

200. "Middle Broadway," *Real Estate Record* 33 (Feb. 2, 1884): 106.

201. Montgomery Schuyler, "Henry Janeway Hardenbergh," *Architectural Record* 6 (Jan.–March 1897): 341.

202. Russell Sturgis, "The Work of McKim, Mead and White," *Architectural Record* 4 (May 1895): 66.

203. Montgomery Schuyler, "The Works of R. H. Robertson," *Architectural Record* 6 (October. 1896): 184–219; and G. Christopher McAninch, "R. H. Robertson: The Development of the Skyscraper" (Unpublished manuscript, 1982).

204. "The Methodist Book Concern," *Real Estate Record* 43 (May 11, 1880): 646–47.

205. Sturgis, "McKim, Mead and White."

206. Schuyler, "Robertson": 216.

207. "The Madison Square Garden," *Real Estate Record* 46 (June 28, 1890): 944–45.

208. "An Important Up-Town Improvement," *Real Estate Record* 45 (May 31, 1890): 809–810.

209. See Charles C. Baldwin, *Stanford White* (New York: Da Capo Press, 1971); and William H. Birkmire, *The Planning and Construction of American Theatres* (New York: John Wiley and Sons, 1906).

210. "An Important Up-Town Improvement," *Real Estate Record*: 809.

211. "The New World Building," *Real Estate Record* (June 14, 1890): 879–80.

212. "Architectural Development," *Real Estate Record* 49 (June 11, 1892): 916.

213. "The 'Flatiron' or Fuller Building," *Architectural Record* 12 (Oct. 1902): 528–36.

214. William E. Parsons, "Burnham as a Pioneer in City Planning," *Architectural Record* 38 (1915): 13–21.

215. Henry James, "New York Revisited," *Harper's Weekly* 62 (Dec. 1905): 402.

216. Henry James, "New York Revisited," *Harper's Weekly* 62 (May 1906): 906.

CHAPTER 4: FASHIONABLE ARCHITECTURE: THE LIMITS OF GOOD TASTE

1. "Fashion as an Element of Value," *Real Estate Record* 18 (Oct. 21, 1876): 779.

2. Montgomery Schuyler, "A Great American Architect, Leopold Eidlitz–I" *Architectural Record* 24 (Sept. 1908): 164–79.

3. John W. Kennion, *The Architects' and Builders' Guide* (New York: Fitzpatrick and Hunter, 1868).

4. Herbert Croly, "Rich Men and Their Homes," *Architectural Record* 12 (May 1902): 27–32.

5. "The Fifth Avenue," *Real Estate Record* 21 (June 15, 1878): 515.

6. "The Centre of Fashionable Gravity," *Real Estate Record* 22 (Dec. 7, 1878): 983.

7. "Fourth Avenue," *Real Estate Record* 20 (Dec. 15, 1877): 965–66.

8. Mary Ann Clegg Smith, "The Commercial Architecture of John Butler Snook," (Ph.D. diss., Pennsylvania State University, 1974).

9. "Fourth Avenue," *Real Estate Record*.

10. "Neighborhoods and Nuisances," *Real Estate Record* 19 (March 24, 1877): 219.

11. "Vacant Lots in the Fashionable Quarter," *Real Estate Record* 33 (April 12, 1879): 287.

12. "Fashion as an Element of Value," *Real Estate Record* 28 (Oct. 21, 1876): 779–80.

13. E. L. Godkin, "The Expenditure of Rich Men," *Scribner's Monthly* 20 (Oct. 1896): 495.

14. Ellen Kramer, "The Domestic Architecture of Detlef Lienau, A Conservative Victorian " (Ph.D. diss., New York University, 1957): 164–66; 177.

15. Kennion, *The Architect's Guide*; "Red-Brick and Brown-Stone Houses in New York," *The Builder* 36 (March 1878): 318; and "Imitative Architecture in New York," *The Builder* 36 (May 18, 1878): 505.

16. Jay E. Cantor, "A Monument of Trade: A. T. Stewart and the Rise of the Millionaire's Mansion in New York," *Winterthur* 10 (1975): 165.

17. P. B. Wight, "A Millionaire's Architectural Investment," *American Architect and Building News* 1 (May 6, 1876): 148–9.

18. "Distinctive Private Homes," *Real Estate Record* 27 (June 18, 1881): 625.

19. Montgomery Schuyler, "The Small House in New York," *Architectural Record* 8 (April–June 1899): 368.

20. Schuyler, "The Small House in New York": 371.

21. Schuyler, "The Small House in New York": 373.

22. Schuyler, "The Small House in New York": 373.

23. "The Economics of Building," *Real Estate Record* 21 (Jan. 19, 1878): 43–45.

24. Charles Lockwood, *Manhattan Moves Uptown* (Boston: Houghton Mifflin, 1976): 240.

25. "The Architectural Fashions Today," *Real Estate Record* 37 (May 1, 1886): 563–64.

26. "The Crisis of Real Estate II," *Real Estate Record* 16 (Dec. 4, 1875): 776.

27. "Model Building," *Real Estate Record* 18 (Sept. 30, 1876): 724.

28. "Expensive Residences," *Real Estate Record* 19 (March 3, 1877): 155–56.

29. "City Chateaux," *Real Estate Record* 28 (Dec. 23, 1876): 942.

30. "A Successful Enterprise," *Real Estate Record* 19 (April 7, 1877): 259–60.

31. On Fifty-fourth Street, one house was sold by Mr. Lynde for $40,000; on Fifty-eighth Street, two houses were sold by Mr. McKenna for $50,000 each; and two houses were sold by Mr. McMann for $43,000 each. Number 656 Fifth Avenue and lot were sold to Mr. Sheffline for $75,000. The house and lot at 15 West Fifty-seventh Street, was sold to Doctor Huyler for $55,000; and on Fifth Avenue between Fifty-seventh and Fifty-eighth streets, Messrs. Lynde sold one house for $90,000. On Fifty-fifth Street between Madison and Fifth avenues, the Lyndes were selling three houses ranging in price from $42,000 to $65,000.

32. "The Vanderbilt Purchases," *Real Estate Record* 23 (Jan. 18, 1879): 43.

33. "The Vanderbilt Houses Criticized," *Real Estate Record* 27 (June 4, 1881): 573–74.

34. "Distinctive Private Houses," *Real Estate Record* 27 (June 18, 1881): 625.

35. Montgomery Schuyler, "The Vanderbilt Houses," in Jordy and Coe, eds., *American Architecture and Other Writings: Montgomery Schuyler*, vol. 2 (Cambridge, Mass.: Harvard University Press, 1961): 500.

36. Schuyler, "Vanderbilt Houses": 489–90.

37. Schuyler, "Vanderbilt Houses": 492.

38. Schuyler, "Vanderbilt Houses": 493–95.

39. Henry-Russell Hitchcock, *Architecture: Nineteenth and Twentieth Centuries*. 2d ed. (Baltimore: Penguin Books, 1967): 221–32.

40. "Some Up-Town Buildings," *Real Estate Record* 33 (Jan. 5, 1884): 2–3.

41. "The New Centre of Building," *Real Estate Record* 19 (March 31, 1877): 239.

42. "The Centre of Fashionable Gravity," *Real Estate Record* 22 (Dec. 7, 1878): 983.

43. East Side and West Side," *Real Estate Record* 20 (Oct. 13, 1877): 785; and "Conditions and Prospects of Building," *Real Estate Record* 23 (June 21, 1879): 505–506.

44. "East Side and West Side": 785.

45. "The Crisis in Real Estate," *Real Estate Record* 16 (Dec. 18, 1875): 805.

46. "A Word to Large Capitalists," *Real Estate Record* 18 (July 8, 1876): 500.

47. "Apartment Houses," *Real Estate Record* 17 (April 1, 1876): 237–38.

48. "Is the Apartment System a Failure?" *Real Estate Record* 19 (April 14, 1877): 281–82.

49. Sarah G. Young, *European Modes of Living or the Question of Apartment Houses (French Flats)* (New York: G. P. Putnam's Sons, 1881): 9–10.

50. Paul Baker, *Richard Morris Hunt* (Cambridge, Mass.: MIT Press, 1980): 204–225; and "Apartment Hotels," *Real Estate Record* 19 (Jan. 20, 1877): 42.

51. "The Osborne," *Real Estate Record* 17 (June 3, 1876): 428; and "The Osborne," *Real Estate Record* 18 (September 23, 1876): 704.

52. "The Bradley Apartment House," *Real Estate Record* 20 (Oct. 6, 1877): 766–77. Other apartments that located near Ladies Mile included McLittle's Apartment House at Seventeenth Street and Union Square erected in 1877; Griswold and Darling's Apartment at Thirtieth Street between Fifth And Sixth avenues (1877); Spinkler's Wellington Apartment House on the south side of West Twenty-third Street near Sixth Avenue, designed by Griffith Thomas in 1879; and a bachelor apartment, the Benedict, located on the east side of Washington Square and attributed to McKim, Meade and White (1879).

53. "The 'Bella' Apartment House," *Real Estate Record* 21 (March 23, 1878): 243–44.

54. "The Florence," *Real Estate Record* 21 (April 6, 1878): 289–90.

55. "The Burlington," *Real Estate Record* 21 (June 15, 1878): 516–17.

56. "Mr. Peter's Apartment House Facing the Park," *Real Estate Record* 21 (June 29, 1878): 557.

57. "The Elise," *Real Estate Record* 21 (Feb. 2, 1878): 91.

58. "The Vancorlear," *Real Estate Record* 24 (Aug. 30, 1879): 688–89.

59. "The Windsor Apartment House," *Real Estate Record* 24 (Nov. 8, 1879): 896.

60. "About Some Large Buildings," *Real Estate Record* 27 (April 30, 1881): 425.

61. "Central Park Apartment Houses," *Real Estate Record* 26 (Oct. 30, 1880): 943.

62. "Mammoth Apartment Houses," *Real Estate Record* 28 (Aug. 6, 1881): 783.

63. *Real Estate Record* 29 (March 11, 1882): 213.

64. "Prominent Buildings Underway," *Real Estate Record* 33 (March 22, 1884): 289.

65. "Vast Apartment Buildings," *Real Estate Record* 29 (June 3, 1882): 550.

66. "One of New York's Palaces Described," *Real Estate Record* 33 (Jan. 26, 1884): 85.

67. "The Dakota," *Real Estate Record* 34 (Sept. 20, 1884): 948; and "The Mammoth Family Hotel," *Real Estate Record* 26 (Oct. 9, 1880): 872–73.

68. "How the Great Apartment Houses Have Paid," *Real Estate Record* 35 (Feb. 7, 1885): 127–28.

69. "The Seward Apartment House," *Real Estate Record* 29 (April 22, 1882): 386.

70. "The Lenox Hill Apartment," *Real Estate Record* 37 (March 6, 1886): 283.

71. "The High Building Question," *Real Estate Record* 33 (April 12, 1884): 370.

72. "Interesting Talks on High Apartment Houses II," *Real Estate Record* 41 (Feb. 18, 1888): 208.

73. "Interesting Talks": 208.

74. "The Hotel Beresford," *Real Estate Record* 44 (Sept. 21, 1889): 1263; and "The Apartment Hotel," *Real Estate Record* 44 (Sept. 28, 1889): 1295.

CHAPTER 5: THE FABRICATION OF STYLE ON THE UPPER EAST SIDE

1. Adolph Bocage, "L'Architecture aux Etats-Unis," *L'Architecture* 7 (Oct. 13, 1894): 338.

2. Montgomery Schuyler, "Recent Building in New York," *Harper's Weekly* 67 (June–Nov. 1883): 563.

3. H. J. Dyos, quoted in Stefan Muthesius, *The English Terraced House* (New Haven: Yale University Press, 1983): 236.

4. Montgomery Schuyler, "Concerning Queen Anne," In Jordy and Coe, eds., *American Architecture and Other Writings: Montgomery Schuyler*, vol. 2 (Cambridge, Mass.: Harvard University Press, 1961): 485.

5. Peter Gay, *The Bourgeois Experience: Victoria to Freud, Education of the Senses*, vol. 1 (New York: Oxford University Press, 1984): 440.

6. Henry James, *The American Scene* (Bloomington: Indiana University Press, 1968): 159.

7. George Aitchison, "The Revival of Architecture," *The Builder* 55 (1888): 2–3.

8. James, *The American Scene*: 141.

9. "East Side Number," *Real Estate Record* 45 (Supplement May 3, 1890): 1–13.

10. Montgomery Schuyler, "The Works of the Late Richard Morris Hunt," in Jordy and Coe, eds., *American Architecture*: 524.

11. John W. Kennion, *The Architects' and Builders' Guide* (New York: Fitzpatrick and Hunter, 1868): 34.

12. Frederick Law Olmsted, "The Spoils of the Park: With a Few Leaves from the Deep-laden Note-books of A Wholly Unpractical Man (1882)," in Albert Fein, *Landscape into Cityscape* (New York: Van Nostrand Reinhold Co., 1981): 395.

13. "The Daily Press and Real Estate," *Real Estate Record* 18 (Oct. 14, 1876): 761–62.

14. "Renewal of Building Activity," *Real Estate Record* 18 (Sept. 23, 1876): 703–704.

15. "The Center of Fashionable Gravity," *Real Estate Record* 22 (Dec. 7, 1878): 983.

16. "Characteristics of the New Speculation," *Real Estate Record* 24 (July 19, 1879): 579–80.

17. "Sixty-Sixth Street and Park Avenue," *Real Estate Record* 22 (Nov. 23, 1878): 947.

18. "New Residences in the Fashionable Quarter," *Real Estate Record* 22 (Nov. 16, 1878): 927.

19. "Doying's New Thirty Houses," *Real Estate Record* 23 (Feb. 15, 1879): 125; and "Madison Avenue Residences," *Real Estate Record* 27 (Jan. 15, 1881): 49–50.

20. "The Center of Fashionable Gravity": 983.

21. Nathalie Dana, *Young in New York: A Memoir of a Victorian Girlhood* (New York: Doubleday and Co., 1963).

22. *Home Decoration: Collected Papers*: 7–8.

23. Dana, *Young in New York*.

24. "Houses of Novel Construction," *Real Estate Record* 24 (Sept. 13, 1879): 721–22.

25. "Choice Dwellings on Lenox Hill," *Real Estate Record* 29 (April 8, 1882): 325.

26. Montgomery Schuyler, "The New York House," *Architectural Record* 19 (Feb. 1906): 83–103.

27. "Handsome East Side Residences Under Way," *Real Estate Record* 36 (Oct. 24, 1885): 1159–60.

28. Baker, *Richard Morris Hunt* (Cambridge, Mass.: MIT Press, 1980).

29. "The Tiffany House," *Real Estate Record* 34 (July 26, 1884): 785–86.

30. "Upper Madison Avenue," *Real Estate Record* 33 (May 24, 1884): 560.

31. "Development of Decorative Art in America," *Real Estate Record* 35 (Nov. 7, 1885): 1216.

32. "The Residence of Mr. A. J. White," *Real Estate Record* 35 (Nov. 21, 1885): 1279–80.

33. "Some Up-Town Flats," *Real Estate Record* 45 (Jan. 18, 1890): 71.

34. "East Side Number," *Real Estate Record*.

35. "A Group of East Side Residences," *Real Estate Record* 37 (Feb. 27, 1886): 255.

36. "East Side Number," *Real Estate Record*.

37. "Some East Side Houses," *Real Estate Record* 45 (Feb. 15, 1890): 220.

38. *Real Estate Record* 51 (Feb. 4, 1893): 164.

39. "East Side Number," *Real Estate Record*.

40. "The Huntington Purchase," *Real Estate Record* 43 (June 8, 1889): 796.

41. "Novelties in City Architecture," *Real Estate Record* 30 (July 8, 1882): 659.

42. "Millionaires' Houses," *Real Estate Record* 32 (July 21, 1883): 521.

43. "A Fifth Avenue House," *Real Estate Record* 41 (April 7, 1888): 420–21.

44. "East Side Architecture—Fifth Avenue," *Real Estate Record* 45 (May 3, 1890): 640–41.

45. "Fifth Avenue, East of Central Park," *Real Estate Record* 43 (June 15, 1889): 836–37.

46. "East Side Number," *Real Estate Record*.

CHAPTER 6: THE AWAKENING OF THE UPPER WEST SIDE

1. Bloomingdale Road above Fifty-ninth Street was renamed the Boulevard, or the Grand Boulevard, in 1862. At this time it was widened and a strip of greenery was planted down its middle in hopes that it would soon emulate the grand Parisian boulevards that Haussmann's engineers were developing during these years. When more prosaic times returned, the Boulevard was renamed Broadway (1899). In 1880, Eleventh Avenue from Seventy-second to 106th Street was called West End Avenue. Eighth Avenue became Central Park West in 1883; and both Ninth and Tenth avenues received their respective designations as Columbus and Amsterdam avenues in 1890.

2. "New Yorkers' Grand West End," *Real Estate Record* 24 (Nov. 1, 1879): 871–72.

3. "A List of Farms on New York Island," *New-York Historical Society Quarterly* (April 11, 1971): 8–11.

4. "The Great Building Movement on the West Side," *Real Estate Record* 36 (Aug. 29, 1885): 951–52; and "The West End Plateau," *Real Estate Record* 24 (Nov. 29, 1879): 958.

5. "Our West Side," *Real Estate Record* 24 (Dec. 27, 1879): 1055.

6. "Capabilities of the West Side," *Real Estate Record* 21 (Jan. 12, 1878): 20–21.

7. "The Chief Secret of Local Improvements," *Real Estate Record* 37 (April 17, 1886): 487.

8. "Development of the West Side: A Review of the Past and Present Trends," *Real Estate Record* 71 (Jan. 7, 1905): 5–6.

9. Egbert Viele, *The West End Plateau of the City of New York* (New York: Johnson and Pratt, 1878).

10. *Real Estate Record* 24 (Nov. 29, 1879): 958

11. "The West Side Association," *Real Estate Record* 24 (Dec. 20, 1879): 1055–1056.

12. "The West Side Association," *Real Estate Record*.

13. "The Condition of Manhattan Square," *Real Estate Record* 25 (Jan. 24, 1880): 80–81.

14. "The West Side Parks," *Real Estate Record* 25 (Jan. 10, 1880): 23–25.

15. "The Eleventh Avenue," *Real Estate Record* 25 (Jan. 17, 1880): 54–55.

16. Another suggestion for linking the two sides of Central Park came from a group of capitalists who were interested in constructing a surface road to be known as the Central and Riverside Parks and Astoria Ferry Railway. This line would have entered the park at East Eighty-third Street and emerged at West Eighty-sixth Street, where it would have turned south at Ninth Avenue. "The East and West Sides," *Real Estate Record* 27 (March 5, 1881): 195.

17. "The Situation of the Real Estate Market," *Real Estate Record* 26 (Oct. 9, 1880): 869–70.

18. "The Clark Houses," *Real Estate Record* 34 (Oct. 11, 1884): 1019–20.

19. "The Raid on Shanties and Its Results," *Real Estate Record* 27 (Feb. 19, 1881): 155–56.

20. "The Situation on the West Side," *Real Estate Record* 27 (June 4, 1881): 571;

and "The Increased Record on the West Side," *Real Estate Record* 32 (Nov. 24, 1893): 924.

21. "Convenient Well Located Houses," *Real Estate Record* 29 (March 18, 1882): 215.

22. Montgomery Schuyler, "The Small City House in New York," *Architectural Record* 8 (April–June 1899): 375.

23. "Some West Side Residences," *Real Estate Record* 34 (Oct. 25, 1884): 1080; "The March of Improvements on the West Side," *Real Estate Record* 33 (June 28, 1884): 698; and "Attractive West Side Dwellings," *Real Estate Record* 35 (March 28, 1885): 228.

24. "Reminiscences of 1884 by Mr. Olcott," *West End Bulletin* 99 (Jan. 1930): 8.

25. "The Great Building Movement on the West Side," *Real Estate Record* 36 (Aug. 29, 1885): 951–52.

26. "West of the Park," *Real Estate Record* 36 (Nov. 7, 1885): 1215–16.

27. Montgomery Schuyler, "Recent Building in New York," *Harper's Weekly* 67 (June–Nov. 1883): 557–78.

28. Schuyler, "The Small City House."

29. "The Improvement of Seventy-second Street," *Real Estate Record* 38 (Dec. 18, 1886): 1554.

30. "Houses of Novel Features," *Real Estate Record* 37 (May 22, 1886): 674.

31. "West Side Illustrated," *Real Estate Record* 38 (Nov. 20, 1886): 1418.

32. "The Improvement of the West Side," *Real Estate Record* 37 (May 8, 1886): 597–98.

33. "Important West Side Statistics," *Real Estate Record* 42 (Nov. 17, 1888): 1356–59.

34. "The Grand Boulevard," *Real Estate Record* 44 (July 13, 1889): 981–82; and "West Side Illustrated," *Real Estate Record* 44 (Supplement, Nov. 16, 1889): 1–9.

35. "The Building Movement," *Real Estate Record* 42 (Sept. 22, 1888): 1130–31.

36. "On Riverside Drive," *Real Estate Record* 42 (Oct. 6, 1888): 1188–89.

37. "West Side Number," *Real Estate Record* 46 (Dec. 20, 1890).

38. "West Side Number," *Real Estate Record* 51 (Supplement, Feb. 11, 1893): 1–41.

39. "West Side Illustrated," *Real Estate Record* (Nov. 16, 1889).

40. "How Neighborhoods are Created," *Real Estate Record* 42 (Sept. 29, 1888): 1163–64.

41. "Two Handsome West Side Residences," *Real Estate Record* 41 (May 12, 1888): 600.

42. "The Deeves' Residences," *Real Estate Record* 47 (Feb. 21, 1891): 272.

43. "West Side Illustrated," *Real Estate Record* (Nov. 16, 1889).

44. "The Parkway," *Real Estate Record* 44 (Dec. 14, 1889): 1668.

45. "The Adrian Apartment House," *Real Estate Record* 43 (April 27, 1889): 1889.

46. "Examples of Modern Town House Architecture," *Real Estate Record* 52 (Supplement, Dec. 16, 1893): 1–2.

47. "West Side Number," *Real Estate Record* (Feb. 11, 1893).

48. "West Side Illustrated," *Real Estate Record* (Nov. 16, 1889).

49. Montgomery Schuyler, "The Romanesque Revival in New York," *Architectural Record* 1 (July–Sept. 1891): 17.

50. "A Handsome West Side Improvement," *Real Estate Record* 45 (April 12, 1890): 517.

51. "The Luyster Residences on 74th Street," *Real Estate Record* 49 (Jan. 23, 1892): 126–27; and "The Work of a Master Builder," *Real Estate Record* 52 (Dec. 9, 1983): 719–720.

52. Frank Fisher, *A Complete List of West Side Dwellings* (New York: 1895).

53. "What Does this Falling Off Mean?" *Real Estate Record* 47 (March 21, 1891): 428.

54. "The Upper West Side," *Real Estate Record* 79 (Jan. 26, 1907): 157–58.

55. "Morningside Heights," *Real Estate Record* 69 (March 12, 1892): 393–94.

56. "General Market on the West Side," *Real Estate Record* 69 (Jan. 11, 1902): 48; and "Riverside Drive," *Real Estate Record* 70 (Oct. 11, 1902): 456.

57. "New York Apartment Houses," *Real Estate Record* 69 (April 5, 1902): 2–13.

58. Gordon D. MacDonald, *Apartment Building Construction—Manhattan: 1902–1953* (New York: Real Estate Board of New York, 1953).

59. "The Upper West Side," *Real Estate Record* 79 (Jan. 26, 1907): 157–58; and "Real Estate Boom on West End Avenue," *Real Estate Record* 89 (June 29, 1912): 1393–94.

60. "New York Apartment Houses," *Real Estate Record*.

61. E. Idell Zeisloft, *The New Metropolis* (New York: D. Appleton and Co., 1899): 620.

62. "Localization of Population and Business," *Real Estate Record* 72 (Sept. 5, 1903): 410.

CHAPTER 7: THE DREAM OF A RATIONAL CITY

1. This remark by Schuyler is attributed to Leopold Eidlitz; see William H. Jordy and Ralph Coe, eds., "Editors' Introduction to Montgomery Schuyler," in *American Architecture and Other Writings: Montgomery Schuyler*, vol. 1 (Cambridge: Harvard University Press, 1961): 1–89.

2. Ernest Flagg, "American Architecture as Opposed to Architecture in America," *Architectural Record* 10 (Oct. 1900): 180.

3. Herbert Croly, "The Contemporary New York Residence," *Architectural Record* 12 (Dec. 1902): 704–722.

4. Croly, "The Contemporary Residence": 718.

5. Franz Winkler (Montgomery Schuyler), "Architecture in the Billionaire District of New York City," *Architectural Record* 11 (1901–1902): 683.

6. William Hutchins, "New York Hotels, II," *Architectural Record* 12 (Nov. 1902): 621–36.

7. Elsa Gilbertson and Sophia Schachter, "Union Square" (Unpublished manuscript, 1982).

8. Aymar Embury, II, "From Twenty-third Street Up: The Architectural Development of Fifth Avenue and Intersection Streets in New York City," *Architectural Forum* 25 (Oct., Nov. 1916): 255–60, 281–86.

9. Lillie H. French, "Shopping in New York," *Century* 61 (March 1901): 647.

10. Embury, "From Twenty-Third Street Up."

11. A. C. David, "The New Architecture: The First American Type of Real Value," *Architectural Record* 28 (Dec. 1910): 389–403.

SELECTED BIBLIOGRAPHY

Alpern, Andrew. *Apartments for the Affluent*. New York: McGraw-Hill, 1975.

Andrews, Wayne. *Architecture, Ambition, and Americans*. Rev. ed. New York: The Free Press, 1978.

Angevin, Susan F. "Study of the Present Site of The American Museum of Natural History." Unpublished manuscript, Columbia University, 1981.

Appleton's Dictionary of New York and its Vicinity. 4 eds. New York: D. Appleton and Co., 1880, 1885, 1889, 1901.

Artistic Houses, 2 vols. 1883. Reprint. New York: Benjamin Blom and Co., 1971.

Artley, Alexander, ed. *The Golden Age of Shop Design: European Shop Interiors, 1800–1939*. London: The Architectural Press, 1975.

Badger, Reid. *The Great American Fair: The World's Columbia Exposition and American Culture*. Chicago: Nelson Hall, 1979.

Baker, Paul. *Richard Morris Hunt*. Cambridge, Mass.: MIT Press, 1980.

Baldwin, Charles C. *Stanford White*. New York: Da Capo Press, 1971.

Bannister, Turpin C. "Bogardus Revisited." *Journal of the Society of Architectural Historians* 15 (Dec. 1956): 12–20.

———. "Early Town Planning in New York State." *Journal of the Society of Architectural Historians* 3 (Jan.–April 1943): 36–42.

Batterberry, Michael and Ariane. *On the Town in New York: From 1776 to the Present*. New York: Charles Scribner's Sons, 1973.

Bella C. Landauer Collection. New-York Historical Society, New York City.

Benjamin Marcus. *Historical Sketch of Madison Square*. New York: Meriden Monographs #1, 1894.

Benjamin, Walter. *Charles Baudelaire: A Lyric Poet in the Era of High Capitalism*. Translated by Harry Zohn. London: The New Left Books, 1973.

Birkmire, William H. *The Planning and Construction of American Theatres*. New York: John Wiley and Sons, 1906.

Black, Mary. *American Advertising Posters of the Nineteenth Century*. New York: Dover Publications, 1973.

———. *Old New York in Early Photographs: 1853–1901*. New York: Dover Publications, 1973.

Bonner, William T. *New York: The World's Metropolis*. New York: R. L. Polk and Co., 1924.

Boyer, M. Christine. *Dreaming the Rational City: The Myth of American City Planning*. Cambridge, Mass.: MIT Press, 1983.

Boyer, M. Christine, and Jessica Scheer. "The Development and Boundaries of Luxury Neighborhoods in New York: 1625–1890." Working Paper #1, Center for Preservation Planning, Columbia University, 1980.

Bradstreet's New York Shopping Guide. New York: 1876–1877.

Brandon, Ruth. *A Capitalist Romance: Singer and The Sewing Machine*. Philadelphia: J. B. Lippincott Co., 1977.

Bromley, George W. and Co., *Atlas of the Entire City of New York*. Philadelphia: G. W. Bromley and Co., 1879.

Brown, Thomas Allston. *A History of the New York Stage: From the First Performance in 1732 to 1901*. 3 vols. New York: Dodd, Mead and Co., 1903.

Browne, John Crawford. "Early Days of the Department Store." *Valentine's Manual of Old New York*. Vol. 5 (1921): 97–148.

Browne, Junius H. *The Great Metropolis: A Mirror of New York*. Hartford: American Publishing Co., 1869.

Brownell, William C. "The Art-Schools of New York." *Scribner's Monthly* 16 (Oct. 1878): 761–81.

Burnham, Alan. "The New York Architecture of Richard Morris Hunt." *Journal of the Society of Architectural Historians* 11 (May 1952): 9–14.

Campbell, Helen Stuart. *Darkness and Daylight, Lights and Shadows of New York Life*. Hartford: A. D. Worthington and Co., 1892.

Cantor, Jay E. "A Monument of Trade: A. T. Stewart and the Rise of the Millionaire's Mansion in New York." *Winterthur* 10 (1975): 165–97.

Carrs, Nancy Jean. "Madison Square, The Eno Family, and the Fifth Avenue Hotel." Unpublished manuscript, Columbia University, 1981.

"Central Park." *Scribner's Monthly* 6 (Sept., Oct. 1873): 523–39; 673–91.

Club Women of New York. New York: The Mail and Express Co., 1904.

Cohen, Stuart. "The Skyscraper as Symbolic Form. Meanings of Modernism: Form, Function and Metaphor." *Design Quarterly* 118, 119 (1982): 12–25.

Collins, F. A. *The Romance of Park Avenue*. New York: Park Avenue Association, 1930.

Conrad, Peter. *The Art of the City: Visions and Versions of New York*. New York: Oxford University Press, 1984.

Cook, Clarence. *The House Beautiful: Essays on Beds and Tables, Stools and Candlesticks*. New York: Scribner, Armstrong and Co., 1878.

———. "New York Daguerreotyped." *Putnam's Monthly* 2, 3 1853, 1854: 121–36; 353–68; 233–48; 141–52.

Crapsey, Edward. *The Nether Side of New York: Or the Vice, Crime and Poverty of the Great Metropolis*. New York: Sheldon and Company, 1872.

Crawford, William. *The Keepers of the Light: A History and Working Guide to Early Photographic Processes*. New York: Dobbs Ferry: Morgan and Morgan, 1979.

Crockett, Albert Stevens. *Peacocks on Parade*. New York: Sears Publishing Co., 1931.

Croly, Herbert. "The Contemporary New York Residence." *Architectural Record* 12 (Dec. 1902): 704–22.

———. "The Renovation of the New York Brownstone District." *Architectural Record* 13 (1903): 555–71.

———. "Rich Men and Their Homes." *Architectural Record* 12 (May 1902): 27–32.

Crow, Thomas. "Modernism and Mass Culture in the Visual Arts." In *Modernism and Modernity*, edited by B. H. D. Buchloh, S. Builbaut, and D. Solkin. Halifax: The Press of Nova Scotia College of Art and Design, 1983: 215–64.

Dana, Nathalie. *Young in New York: A Memoir of a Victorian Girlhood*. New York: Doubleday and Company, 1963.

Davis, Richard Harding. *The Great Streets of the World*. London: James R. Osgood, McIlvaine and Co., 1892.

De Leeuw, Rudolph. *Both Sides of Broadway: From Bowling Green to Central Park*. New York: De Leeuw Riehl Publishing Co, 1910.

Desmond, Harry W., and Herbert Croly. *Stately Homes in America: From Colonial Times to the Present Day*. New York: D. Appleton and Co., 1903.

Dunshee, Kenneth Holcomb. *As You Pass By*. New York: Hastings House, 1952.

Durso, Joseph. *Madison Square Garden*. New York: Simon and Schuster, 1979.

Eastlake, Charles. *Hints on Household Taste in Furniture, Upholstery, and Other Details*, 4th ed. London: Longmans, Green and Company, 1878.

Eidlitz, Leopold. "Cast Iron and Architecture." *Crayon* 6 (Jan. 1859): 20–24.

The 1866 Guide to New York City. Reprint New York: Schocken Books, 1975.

The 1866 Visitors Guide to the City of New York. New York: John F. Trow, Printers, 1866.

Ellington, George [pseud.]. *The Women of New York: or Social Life in the Great City*. New York: The New York Book Co., 1870.

Elliott, Charles W. *The Book of American Interiors*. Boston: James R. Osgood and Company, 1876.

Ellis, Edward R. *The Epic of New York*. New York: Coward-McCann, 1966.

Fairfield, Francis Gerry. *The Clubs of New York: With an Account of the Origin, Progress, Present Conditions and Membership of the Leading Clubs*. New York: Henry L. Hinter, Publisher, 1873.

Fein, Albert. *Landscape into Cityscape*. New York: Van Nostrand Reinhold Co., 1981.

Ferree, Barr. "Economic Conditions of Architecture in America." Proceedings of the twenty-seventh annual convention of the American Institute of Architects in Chicago (Aug. 1893): 228–41.

Ferry, William John. *A History of the Department Store*. New York: MacMillan Publishing Co., 1960.

Fischler, Stan. *Uptown, Downtown*. New York: Hawthorne, 1976.

Flagg, Ernest. "The Plan of New York, and How to Improve it." *Scribner's Monthly* 3 (Aug. 1904): 253–56.

Forty Years on Fifth Avenue. New York: Fifth Avenue Bank, 1915.

Frankenstein, Alfred. *After the Hunt: William Harnett and Other American Still Life Painters, 1870–1900*. Rev. ed. Berkeley: University of California Press, 1969.

French, Lillie H. "Shopping in New York." *Century Magazine* 61 (March 1901): 644–58.

"French Flats and Apartment Houses in New York." *Carpentry and Building* 2, 3 (1880): 1–2; 107–108; 233–34.

Furniss, L. E. "New York Boarding Houses." *Appleton's Journal* 5 (March 4, 1871): 259–61.

Garrett, Thomas M. "A History of Pleasure Gardens in New York City: 1700–1865." Ph.D. diss., New York University, 1978.

Gay, Peter. The Bourgeois Experience: Victoria to Freud, Education of the Senses. Vol. 1. New York: Oxford University Press, 1984.

Gayle, Margaret, and Edmund V. Gillon, Jr. *Cast-Iron Architecture in New York*. New York: Dover Publications, 1974.

Geist, Johann Friedrich. *Arcades: The History of a Building Type*. Translated by Jane Newman and John H. Smith. Cambridge, Mass.: MIT Press, 1983).

The Gentleman's Directory of New York City, 1870.

Giedion, Sigfried. *Mechanization Takes Command: A Contribution to Anonymous History*. New York: Oxford University Press, 1948.

Gilbertson, Elsa, and Sophia Schachter. "Union Square." Unpublished manuscript, Columbia University, 1982.

Gloag, John. *Victorian Taste: Some Social Aspects of Architecture and Industrial Design, from 1820–1900*. New York: MacMillan Publishing Co., 1962.

Godkin, E. L. "The Expenditure of Rich Men." *Scribner's Monthly* 20 (Oct. 1896): 495–501.

Goldberger, Paul. *The City Observed: New York*. New York: Vintage Books, 1979.

Grafton, John. *New York in the Nineteenth Century*. New York: Dover Publications, 1977.

Guide to New York and Vicinity. New York: J. D. Sheldon and Co., 1873.

Gunn, Thomas Butler. *The Physiology of New York Boarding Houses*. New York, 1857.

Hales, Peter B. *Silver Cities: The Photography of American Urbanization 1839–1915*. Philadelphia: Temple University Press, 1984.

Halpern, John M. "The Changing Face of America: New York City." 12 vols. Columbia University: Avery Library Collection.

Hamlin, A. D. F. "The Battle of Styles," *Architectural Record* 1 (1892): 265–75; 405–13.

Hamlin, Talbot. *Greek Revival Architecture in America*. New York: Oxford University Press, 1944.

———, Talbot. "The Rise of Eclecticism in New York." *Journal of the Society of Architectural Historians* 11 (May 1952): 3–8.

Harder, J. F. "The City's Plan." *Municipal Affairs* 2 (1898): 25–47.

Harford, J. *The Merchant's Directory*. New York: American Publishing and Engraving Co., 1891.

Harrison, Constance Cary. *Woman's Handiwork in Modern Homes*. New York: Charles Scribner and Sons: 1881.

Henderson, Mary C. *The City and the Theatre*. Clifton, New Jersey: James T. White and Co., 1973.

Hendrickson, Robert. *The Grand Emporiums: The Illustrated History of America's Great Department Stores*. New York: Stein and Day, 1979.

History and Commerce of New York. New York: American Publishing and Engraving Co., 1891.

History of Architecture and Building Trades of Greater New York. 2 vols. New York: Union History Company, 1899.

A History of Real Estate, Building and Architecture in New York City. New York: The Record and Guide, 1898. Reprint. New York: Arno Press, 1967.

Hitchcock, Henry-Russell. *Architecture: Nineteenth and Twentieth Centuries*. 2d ed. Baltimore: Penguin Books, 1967.

Hoeft, Kathleen. "Storefronts in Manhattan: 1784–1900." Unpublished manuscript, Columbia University, 1975.

Holly, H. Hudson. *Modern Dwellings in Town and Country*. New York: Harper and Brothers, 1878.

———. "Modern Dwellings: Their Construction, Decoration, and Furniture." *Harper's Weekly* 52, 53 (Dec. 1875–May 1876; June–Nov. 1876): 855–67; 49–64; 217–26; 354–64.

Hornblow, Arthur. *A History of the Theatre in America*. 2 vols. Philadelphia: J. B. Lippincott and Co., 1919.

Howe, Irving. *World of Our Fathers*. New York: Harcourt Brace Jovanovich, 1976.

Hudnut, Joseph. *Architecture and the Spirit of Man*. Cambridge, Mass.: Harvard University Press, 1949.

Hughes, Samuel. *A History of the American Theatre*. London: Samuel French, 1951.

Hunt, Richard M. "Architecture." *Crayon* 4 (July 1857): 218.

Hurst, James Willard. *Law and the Conditions of Freedom in the Nineteenth Century United States*. Madison: University of Wisconsin Press, 1956.

Illustrated New York: The Metropolis of Today. New York: International Publishing Co., 1888.

James, Henry. *The American Scene*. Bloomington: Indiana University Press, 1968.

———. "New York Revisited." *Harper's Weekly* 62 (Dec. 1905; May, 1906): 400–406; 603–608; 900–907.

Jackson, Michael B. "The American Shopfront in the Age of Cast Iron: A Descriptive History from 1850 to 1910." Masters thesis, Columbia University, 1980.

Jenkins, Stephen. *The Greatest Street in the World: Broadway*. New York: G. P. Putnam's Sons, 1911.

Johnson, Kyle. "The Architecture of Henry Janeway Hardenbergh." Unpublished manuscript, Columbia University, 1977.

Jones, Owen. *Grammar of Ornament*. Reprint. New York: Van Nostrand Reinhold Co., 1972.

Jones, Scott L. "Historical Analysis of Saint John's Park (Hudson Square) in the City of New York, c. 1800–1867." Unpublished manuscript, Columbia University, 1981.

Jordy, William H., and Ralph Coe, eds. *American Architecture and Other Writings: Montgomery Schuyler*. 2 vols. Cambridge, Mass.: Harvard University Press, 1961.

Kennion, John W. *The Architects' and Builders' Guide*. New York: Fitzpatrick and Hunter, 1868.

Kent, Mrs. James (Louisa Morris Stewart). Scrapbooks, New-York Historical Society, New York City.

Kerfoot, J. B. *Broadway*. Boston: Houghton Mifflin, 1911.

King, Moses, ed. *King's Handbook of New York City*. 2d ed. Boston: Moses King, Publisher, 1893.

Kirkland, Edward Chase. *Dream and Thought in the Business Community, 1860–1900*. Chicago: Quadrangle Paperbacks, 1956.

Kouwenhoven, John A. *The Columbia Historical Portrait of New York*. New York: Harper and Row, 1972.

Kramer, Ellen W. "Contemporary Descriptions of New York City and Its Public Architecture ca. 1850." *Journal of the Society of Architectural Historians* 27 (1968): 264–80.

———. "Detlef Lienau, An Architect of the Brown Decades." *Journal of the Society of Architectural Historians* 14 (March 1955): 18–25.

———. "The Domestic Architecture of Detlef Leinau, A Conservative Victorian." Ph.D. diss., New York University, 1957.

"Ladies Mile: The History of the Retail Shopping District of Manhattan in the Nineteenth Century." Studio report, Columbia University, 1981.

Ladies Shopping Guide and City Directory. New York: G. P. Putnam's Sons, 1885.

Lamb, Martha J. *History of the City of New York, Its Origins, Rise and Progress*. Vol. 3. New York: A. S. Barnes and Co., 1896.

———. "Riverside Park." *Manhattan Illustrated Magazine* 4 (July 1884): 52–60.

Landau, Sarah Bradford. *Edward T. and William A. Potter: American Victorian Architects*. New York: Garland Publishing Co., 1979.

———. *P. B. Wight: Architect, Contractor, and Critic, 1838–1925*. Chicago: Art Institute of Chicago, 1981.

———. "The Row Houses of New York's West Side." *Journal of the Society of Architectural Historians* 34 (March 1975): 19–36.

Laver, James. *Costumes and Fashions: A Concise History*. Reprint. New York: Oxford University Press, 1983.

Leone, Carl. "Walks Through Fifth Avenue." New York: published by the author, 1853.

Lewis, Arnold Dudley. "Evaluations of American Architecture by European Critics: 1875–1900." Ph.D. diss., University of Wisconsin, 1962.

Lewton, Frederick L. "The Servant in the House: A Brief History of the Sewing Machine." *Annual Report of the Smithsonian Institution*. Washington, D.C.: U.S. Government Printing Office, 1929: 583–85.

Lightfoot, Frederick S. *Nineteenth Century New York in Rare Photographic Views*. New York: Dover Publications, 1981.

Lockwood, Charles. *Bricks and Brownstones*. New York: Harper and Row, 1975.

———. *Manhattan Moves Uptown*. Boston: Houghton Mifflin, 1976.

Lockwood's Illustrated Guide to New York City and its Environs. New York: Howard Lockwood, 1872.

Lord and Taylor. *The History of Lord and Taylor*. New York: privately printed, 1929.

Lynes, Russell. *The Art Makers of Nineteenth Century America*. New York: Atheneum, 1970.

———. *The Domesticated Americans*. New York: Harper and Row, 1957.

————. *The Tastemakers: The Shaping of American Popular Taste.* New York: Dover Publications, 1980.

Maass, John. *The Gingerbread Age.* New York: Rinehart and Co., Inc., 1957.

————. *The Victorian Home in America.* New York: Hawthorne Books, Inc., 1972.

McAninch, G. Christopher. "R. H. Robertson: The Development of the Skyscraper." Unpublished manuscript, Columbia University, 1982.

McBirdge, Theresa M. "A Woman's World: Department Stores and the Evolution of Women's Employment, 1920–1970." *French Historical Studies* 10 (Fall, 1978): 664–83.

McCabe, James D., Jr. *Lights and Shadows of New York Life,* 1872. Reprint. New York: Farrar, Strauss and Giroux, 1970.

McDougall, E. T. "The Political Economy of a Public Park." Unpublished manuscript, Harvard University, 1973.

MacKeever, Sam A. *Glimpses of Gotham and City Characters.* New York: Richard K. Fox, 1881.

McKenna, Rosalie Thorne. "James Renwick, Jr. and the Second Empire Style in the United States." *Magazine of Art* 44 (March 1951): 97–101.

Macoy, Robert. *The Centennial Guide to New York City and its Environs.* New York: Howard Lockwood, 1876. Reprint. New York: Nathan Cohen Books, 1975.

Marcuse, Maxwell. F. *This Was New York.* New York: Carlton Press, 1976.

Marder, William and Estelle. Robert G. Duncan, ed. *Anthony: The Man, The Company, The Cameras.* Amesbury, Mass.: Pine Ridge Publishing Co., 1982.

Marks, Harry H. *Small Change; Or, Lights and Shades of New York.* New York: Standard Publishing Co., 1882.

Marrey, Bernard. *Les grands magasins des origines à 1939.* Paris: Libraire Picard, 1979.

Mayhew, Edgar de N., and Minor Myers, Jr. *A Documentary History of American Interiors.* New York: Charles Scribner's Sons, 1980.

Meyer, Grace M. *Once Upon a City.* New York: MacMillan Co., 1958.

Miller, Michael B. *The Bon Marché: Bourgeois Culture and the Department Store 1869–1920.* Princeton: Princeton University Press, 1981.

A Monograph of the Works of McKim, Mead and White, 1879–1915. Reprint. New York: Benjamin Blom, 1973.

Morris, Lloyd. *Incredible New York.* New York: Random House, 1951.

Mott, Hopper Striker. *New York of Yesterday: A Descriptive Narrative of Old Bloomingdale.* New York: G. P. Putnam's Sons, 1908.

Mujica, Francisco. *The History of the Skyscraper.* New York: Da Capo Press, 1977.

Mullin, Donald C. *The Development of the Playhouse.* Berkeley: University of California Press, 1970.

Mumford, Lewis. *The Brown Decades: A Study of the Arts in America, 1865–1895.* Reprint of 1931 ed. New York: Dover Publications, 1971.

Nevins, Allan, ed. *The Diary of Philip Hone, 1828–1851.* 2 vols. New York: Dodd, Mead and Co., 1927.

————. *The Emergence of Modern America, 1865–1878.* New York: MacMillan Co., 1927.

Nevins, Allan, and Milton Thomas, eds. *The Diary of George Templeton Strong.* 4 vols. New York: MacMillan Co., 1952.

New York City Architecture: Selection from the Historic American Buildings Survey #7. Washington, D.C.: The U.S. Department of Interior, National Park Service, July, 1969.

"New York Daguerreotyped." *Putnam's Monthly* 1, 3 (Feb., April, 1853; March 1854): 121–136; 353–368; 233–248.

New York Illustrated. New York: D. Appleton and Co., 1882.

New York Shopping Guide for 1872. New York: 1872.

New York's Great Industries. New York: Historical Publishing Co., 1885.

Olmsted, F. L., and J. James R. Cross, "Preliminary Report of the Landscape Architect and the Civil and Topographical Engineer, upon the Laying Out of the Twenty-third and Twenty-Fourth Wards." In *Landscape Into Cityscape,* edited by Albert Fein. New York: Van Nostrand Reinhold Co., 1967: 350–73.

Olmsted, Frederick Law. "The Spoils of the Park: With a Few Leaves from the Deep-laden Note-books of a Wholly Unpractical Man." In *Landscape into Cityscape,* edited by Albert Fein. New York: Van Nostrand Reinhold Co., 1981: 391–440.

Omoto, Sadayoshi. "The Queen Anne Style and Architectural Criticism." *Journal of the Society of Architectural Historians* (March 1964): 29–37.

Parsons, William E. "Burnham as a Pioneer in City Planning." *Architectural Record* 38 (1915): 13–21.

Payne, Blanche. *History of Costume.* New York: Harper and Row, 1965.

Pelletrau, William. *Early New York Houses.* New York: Francis P. Harper, 1900.

Perris, William. *Maps of the City of New York.* New York: Perris and Browne, 1859.

Pevsner, Nikolaus. *A History of Building Types.* Princeton: Princeton University Press, 1970.

Pine, John B. "Gramercy Park." In Henry C. Brown. *Valentine's Manual of Old New York.* New York: Valentine's Manual, Inc., 1920: 193–248.

Poggi, Jack. *Theatre in America; The Impact of Economic Forces 1870–1967.* New York: Cornell University Press, 1966.

Pollack, Peter. *The Picture History of Photography.* Rev. ed. New York: Harry Abrams, 1969.

Raybeck, Joseph G. *A History of American Labor.* New York: MacMillan, 1959.

"Recollections of Gillian Webster (Barr) Bailey." Private paper presented to The New-York Historical Society, New York City.

"Recollections of Mary Eno Pinchot." Gifford Pinchot Papers, series IV, container 41. Manuscript Division, Library of Congress, Washington, D.C.

Real Estate Record and Builders' Guide, especially: "The Building Boom: Its Causes and Prospects," no. 43 (March 30, 1889): 423–33; "The Crisis of Real Estate, I, II, III, IV, V, VI, VII, VIII," nos. 16, 17 (Nov. 27, Dec. 4, Dec. 11, Dec. 18, 1875; Jan. 1, Jan. 8, Jan. 15, Jan. 22, 1876): 761–62, 775–76, 789–90, 805–806, 1–2, 19–21, 35–36, 53–54. "East Side

Number," no. 45 (Supplement, May 3, 1890): 1–13; "West Side Illustrated," no. 44 (Supplement, Nov. 16, 1889): 1–9; "West Side Number," no. 51 (Supplement, Feb. 11, 1893): 1–41.

Reed, Henry Hope. "The Vision Spurned: Classical New York." *Classical America* 1, 2 (1971, 1972): 31–41; 10–17.

Resseguie, Harry E. "Alexander Turney Stewart and the Develment of the Department Store, 1823–1876." *Business History Review* 39 (Autumn 1965): 301–22.

———. "The Decline and Fall of the Commercial Empire of A. T. Stewart." *Business History Review* 36 (Autumn 1962): 255–86.

Richardson, James. "The New Homes of New York: A Study of Flats." *Scribner's Monthly* 8 (1874): 63–76.

Robinson, E. and Pidgeon R. H. *Robinson's Atlas of the City of New York*. New York: E. Robinson, 1885.

Roncayolo, Marcel. "La production de la ville." In *La ville de l'Age Industriel*, edited by Maurice Agulhon. Paris: Seuil, 1983: 73–155.

Ross, Isabel. *Crusades and Crinolines*. New York: Harper and Row, 1963.

Roth, Leland M. *McKim, Mead and White, Architects*. New York: Harper and Row, 1983.

Roth, Leland M. *The Architecture of McKim, Mead and White: 1870–1920 A Building List*. New York: Garland Publishing Co., 1978.

Schaffer, J. M. "Report on Gramercy Park." Unpublished manuscript, Columbia University, 1980.

Schuyler, Montgomery [Franz Winkler]. "Architecture in the Billionaire District in New York City." *Architectural Record* 11 (1901–1902): 679–99.

———. "The Art of High Building." *Architectural Record* 15 (May 1904): 445–66.

———. "The Evolution of the Skyscraper." *Scribner's Monthly* 46 (Sept. 1909): 257–71.

———. "A Great American Architect: Leopold Eidlitz—I, II." *Architectural Record* 24 (1908): 164–79; 263–77.

———. "Henry Janeway Hardenbergh." *Architectural Record* 6 (Jan.–March, 1897): 335–75.

———. "Italian Gothic in New York." *Architectural Record* 28 (July 1909): 46–54.

———. "Mitigating the 'Gridiron' Street Plan." *Architectural Record* 29 (May 1911): 379–96.

———. "Modern Architecture." *Architectural Record* 4 (July–Sept. 1894): 1–13.

———. "The New New York House." *Architectural Record* 19 (Feb. 1906): 83–103.

———. "Recent Building in New York." *Harper's Weekly* 67 (June–Nov. 1883): 557–78.

———. "The Romanesque Revival in New York." *Architectural Record* 1 (July–Sept. 1891): 7–38.

———. "The Sky-Line of New York, 1881–1897." *Harper's Weekly* 41 (March 20, 1897): 292–95.

———. "The 'Sky-Scraper' Up to Date." *Architectural Record* 8 (Jan. 1899): 231–57.

———. "The Small City House in New York." *Architectural Record* 8 (April–June 1899): 357–88.

Schuyler, Montgomery. "The Works of R. H. Robertson." *Architectural Record* 6 (Oct. 1896): 184–219.

Shanor, Rebecca. "Manhattan's Paper Streets: Proposals to Relieve the 1811 Gridiron Plan." Masters thesis, Columbia University, May 1982.

Shepp, James W. and Daniel E. Shepp *Shepp's New York City Illustrated*. (Chicago: Globe Bible Publishing Co., 1894).

Sherwood, M. E. W. "New York in the Seventies." *Lippincott's* (Sept. 1898): 393–400.

Simonin, Louis. *Le Monde Américain*. Paris: Librairie Hachette, ca. 1877.

Simpson, Sarah H. J. "New York in 1868." Typescript, the New-York Historical Society, New York City.

Simutis, Leonard J. "Frederick Law Olmsted's Later Years: Landscape Architecture and the Spirit of Place." Ph.D. diss., University of Minnesota, 1971.

Smith, Mary Ann Clegg. "The Commercial Architecture of John Butler Snook." Ph.D. diss., Pennsylvania State University, 1974.

———. "John Snook and the Design for A. T. Stewart's Store." *New-York Historical Society Quarterly* 58 (1974): 18–33.

Smith, Matthew Hale. *Sunshine and Shadow in New York*. Hartford: J. B. Burr and Co., 1868.

Soho-Cast Iron Historic District Designation Report. New York: Landmarks Preservation Commission: 1973.

Spann, Edward K. *The New Metropolis: New York City, 1840–1857*. New York: Columbia University Press, 1981.

Spillane, Daniel. *History of the American Piano Forte*. New York: Spillane Publishing, 1890.

Spofford, Harriet Prescott. *Art Decoration Applied to Furniture*. New York: Harper and Brothers, Publisher, 1877.

Stern, Robert A. M., Gregory Gilmartin and John Massengale. *New York 1900: Metropolitan Architecture and Urbanism 1890–1915*. New York: Rizzoli International Publications, 1983.

Still, Byard. *Mirror for Gotham*. New York: New York University Press, 1956.

Stokes, I. N. Phelps. *The Iconography of Manhattan, 1498–1909*. 6 vols. New York: Robert H. Dodd, 1918–1928.

St.-Pierre, Michel. "1811's Map of New York: Proposed Parks." Unpublished manuscript. Columbia University, 1982.

The Stranger's Mercantile Guide to the City of New York. New York: 1890.

Stryker, Peter. "The Lower Depths of the Great American Metropolis." *The Pulpit and Rostrum* 38 (June 1866).

Sturgis, Russell. "The Art Gallery of the New York Streets." *Architectural Record* 10 (1900): 93–112.

———. "Building of the Modern City House." *Harper's Monthly* 98 (April 1899): 810–822.

———. "The City House in the East and South." *Homes in City and Country*. New York: Charles Scribner's Sons, 1893: 1–34.

———. "The Work of McKim, Mead and White." *Architectural Record* 4 (May 1895):

Summerson, John. "London, the Artifact." In H. J. Dyos and Michael Wolff, eds. *The Victorian City*. Vol. 1. London: Routledge and Kegan Paul, 1973: 311–32.

Taft, Robert. *Photography and the American Scene*. New York: Dover Publications, 1964.

Terdiman, Richard. "Structures of Initiation: On Semiotic Education and its Contradictions in Balzac." *The Pedagogical Imperative: Teaching as a Literary Genre, The Yale French Studies* 63 (1982): 198–226.

Thompson, D. G. Brinton. *Ruggles of New York.* New York: Columbia University Press, 1946.

Tidworth, Simon. *Theatres: An Architectural and Cultural History.* New York: Praeger Publishers, 1973.

Towner, Wesley. *The Elegant Auctioneers.* New York: Hill and Wang, 1970.

Trow's Business Directory of New York City, 1899–1900 Edition. New York: Trow Publishing Co., 1900.

Tuthill, W. B. *The City Residence: Its Design and Construction.* New York: William T. Comstock, 1890.

Van Brunt, Henry. "Cast Iron in Decorative Architecture." *Crayon* 6 (Jan. 1859): 15–20.

Van Rensselaer, Martha G. "Recent Architecture in America, I, II, III." *Century Magazine* 28 (1884): 48–67; 323–34; 511–523.

Viele, Egbert. *The West End Plateau of the City of New York.* New York: Johnson and Pratt, 1879.

Wecter, Dixon. *The Saga of American Society: A Record of Social Aspirations, 1607–1937.* New York: Charles Scribner's Sons, 1937.

Weisman, Winston. "Commercial Palaces of New York: 1845–1875." *Art Bulletin* 36 (Dec. 1954): 285–302.

Weisman, Winston. "New York and the Problem of the First Skyscraper." *Journal of the Society of Architectural Historians* 12 (March 1953): 13–20.

Welling, William. *Photography in America: The Formative Years, 1839–1900, A Documentary History.* New York: Thomas Y. Crowell Co., 1973.

Whiffen, Marcus, and Frederick Koeper. *American Architecture: 1607–1976.* Cambridge, Mass.: MIT Press, 1981.

White, Norval, and Willensky, Elliot. *AIA Guide to New York City.* New York: Collier Books, 1978.

White, Richard Grant. "Old New York and Its Houses." *Century* 26 (1883): 845–59.

Whitman, Walt. *New York Dissected.* (New York: Rufus Rockwell Wilson, Inc., 1936).

Williams, Henry T. and C. S. Jones. *Beautiful Homes.* New York: Henry T. Williams, Publisher, 1878.

Wilson, Richard Guy. *McKim, Mead and White, Architects.* New York: Rizzoli International Publications, 1983.

Wilson's Business Directory of New York City. Editions of 1859–1860; 1869–1870; 1879–1880; 1889–1890; and 1900. New York: Wilson's.

W. Johnson Quinn Collection of Historical Materials on New York City Hotels. The New-York Historical Society.

Wright, Mabel Osgood. *My New York.* New York: MacMillan Publishing Co., 1926.

Young, Sarah. *European Modes of Living, or The Question of Apartment Houses (French Flats).* New York: G. P. Putnam's Sons, 1881.

Young, William C. *Documents of American Theatre History: Famous American Playhouses, 1716–1899.* Vol. 1. Chicago: American Library Association, 1973.

Zabar, Lori. "The Influence of W.E.D. Stoke's Real Estate Career on West Side Development." Masters thesis, Columbia University, 1977.

Zeisloft, E. Idell. *The New Metropolis.* New York: D. Appleton and Co., 1899.

Zelden, Theodore. *France, 1848–1945.* 2 vols. Oxford: Clarendon Press, 1973–77.

INDEX